YOUNG KILLERS

The Challenge of Juvenile Homicide

Kathleen M. Heide, Ph.D.

SAGE Publications
International Educational and Professional Publisher
Thousand Oaks   London   New Delhi

For information:

 SAGE Publications, Inc.
2455 Teller Road
Thousand Oaks, California 91320
E-mail: order@sagepub.com

SAGE Publications Ltd.
6 Bonhill Street
London EC2A 4PU
United Kingdom

SAGE Publications India Pvt. Ltd.
M-32 Market
Greater Kailash I
New Delhi 110 048 India

Printed in the United States of America

Library of Congress Cataloging-in-Publication Data

Heide, Kathleen M., 1954-
    Young killers: The challenge of juvenile homicide / by Kathleen M. Heide.
        p.   cm.
    Includes bibliographical references and index.
    ISBN 0-7619-0062-4 (cloth: acid-free paper)
    ISBN 0-7619-0063-2 (pbk.: acid-free paper)
        1. Juvenile homicide.   2. Juvenile homicide—Case studies.
    I. Title.
    HV9067.H6 H44 1998
    364.15'23'083—ddc21   98-25341

This book is printed on acid-free paper.

99   00   01   02   03   10   9   8   7   6   5   4   3   2

Acquiring Editor:	C. Terry Hendrix
Editorial Assistant:	Fiona Lyon
Production Editor:	Astrid Virding
Editorial Assistant:	Denise Santoyo
Typesetter/Designer:	Rebecca Evans
Indexer:	Jean Casalegno
Cover Artist:	Richard A. Scott, Tampa, FL
Cover Designer:	Ravi Balasuriya

Contents

Foreword   vii
   by Ted Palmer, Ph.D.

Acknowledgments   xvii

PART I   Juvenile Homicide Encapsulated   1

   1. The Phenomenon of Juvenile Homicide   5
   2. Ingredients for Juvenile Murder   28
   3. The Legal Response to Juvenile and Adolescent Homicide   52
   4. Understanding the Juvenile Murderer   65

PART II   Clinical Portraits   87

   5. Peter Daniels   91
   6. Jerry Johnson   112
   7. Calvin Thomas   131
   8. David Collins   148
   9. Malcolm Farrell   161
  10. Joel Westerlund   180
  11. Brian Clark   202

PART III   The Challenge of Juvenile Homicide   219

  12. Treating Young Killers   221
     with Eldra P. Solomon, Ph.D.
  13. Reducing Youth Violence in the 21st Century   239

Notes   255

References   267

Index   289

About the Author   299

To Professor P. H. Pearson
Wise mentor
Devoted friend.

Foreword

YOUNG KILLERS, by Kathleen Heide, is a timely and integrative book about an emotionally difficult topic, one on which most people have strong feelings and, often, few useful facts. This book not only supplies many needed facts, it provides a framework for better understanding the youths themselves, for intelligently moving forward with treatment, and—especially critical—for reducing violence in future generations. Although this book is entirely self-contained and self-explanatory, I would like to focus briefly on what I think are certain key emotional issues and related assumptions or beliefs that are involved in many individuals' responses to violent offenders in general and to those who have killed, in particular. Dr. Heide's book speaks to such issues, in some cases directly, in others indirectly. As will be seen, it also goes well beyond them with respect to its scope and overall importance.

Like interpersonal conflict itself, crime began to steadily grow within the United States in the mid-1960s. *Violent* crime, especially, has deeply distressed this nation's general public since the mid-1970s and has continued to arouse fear. Violent offenses by youths, in particular, have captured—often riveted—the public's attention since the early 1980s and have generated widespread, increasing concern. Of all the types of violence, such as rape, assault, and robbery, homicide is undoubtedly the one most feared; and among juveniles, the incidence of this extreme act has greatly increased since the mid-1980s. Whether committed by youths or adults, violent crimes of all types, when added together, have helped make present-day America an anxious place to live for many adults and youths alike, especially, but not only, in inner cities.

When persons are greatly feared because of their violent crimes and because they may repeat them, most individuals want to physically distance themselves and others from those offenders as soon as possible and for as long as they can; at any rate, they want strong physical controls applied. This desire for protection from present and possible future danger is a natural and understandable reaction by individuals and society alike. It is, however, seldom followed by a strong, let alone sustained, interest, by much of the general public, in learning about the actual nature, backgrounds, and circumstances of the persons who directly produced that danger—in Dr. Heide's book, persons who are young killers. Nor is that desire often followed by much motivation to discover approaches that might supplement and/or otherwise improve upon the above responses. That is, little such interest usually exists, particularly if those responses—distancing and direct physical control—have apparently ended the immediate threat. (These views regarding the general public are not experimentally established facts, nor are those that follow. They are my personal conclusions based on four decades of observing and otherwise learning about the feelings and other reactions of adults regarding crime, offenders, and the justice or correctional system.)

Similarly, and equally understandable, a large portion of the general public is seldom seriously interested in learning about *differences* that exist from youth to youth
(e.g., differences in how they usually view themselves, in how they interact with others,
and in their current levels of ability). This relative disinterest exists especially, but not
only, if these youths have killed individuals with whom certain members of the public
can personally identify or with whom they can equate certain friends and loved ones.
In no small part, that lukewarm interest prevails because these numerous members
largely focus their attention on characteristics that make many of these numerous
youths *similar* to one another, particularly in connection with situations that involve
strong anxiety and concern on the part of others. These situations center on injury,
threat, fear, and loss of control, and the youth-characteristics that typically generate
themselves in members of the public, and which are therefore focused on by these persons,
are high levels of aggression, hostility, impulsivity, and unpredictability—sometimes
combined in explosive rage. Individually and especially together, these features, which
many of the present youths do share in common, have greater emotional impact and
seem more important overall than do various differences, themselves separately and
together. Also, operating here is those persons'—the members'—underlying sense that
distancing and physical control, mentioned above, largely focus on those across-youth
similarities and that knowledge of youth-differences is hardly needed for these responses to occur. Operating, too, is their implicit assumption that, given this focus,
these responses can achieve whatever is needed. Finally, and no less important, relative
disinterest in personal or interpersonal differences among youths who have killed, and
in these individuals' backgrounds and circumstances, also exists because the persons in
question take it for granted that the one or two pictures they have formed of these
youths are largely accurate and, in any event, sufficiently complete. (As strongly suggested below, these pictures have many significant gaps, even though they contain
important elements of truth.)

Two crucial views, I believe, commonly accompany these pictures—pictures that
are also held by many policymakers and other people who influence corrections from
within or without: (1) Most such youths have a strong, often deep-seated tendency or
urge to be physically violent toward others or toward particular types of individuals,
and (2) even after several years in lockup, few such youths either can or will funda-
mentally and clearly change—perhaps even substantially change—with regard to this
strong tendency; few will largely eliminate most of the above-mentioned characteristics
as well. The first view is held even more widely than the second. Together they help
make the above responses to these youths—especially that of physical control—seem
all the more appropriate and essential, and perhaps even sufficient by themselves. At
any rate, whether or not the youths will largely change, and given that they well may
not, very long-term imprisonment, in particular, is viewed as the appropriate way to
achieve necessary control and protection and to simultaneously implement a type and
duration of punishment that is, in any event, considered deserved.

Although views (1) and (2) are very commonly held, another portion of the general
public appears to believe that many young killers *can* change or probably change. Numerous practitioners, various policymakers, and others think they can change and/or
be changed as well, often in major ways. They do so even though they, too, believe that
the above tendency and features such as marked hostility and low impulse control are
indeed common among these youths. In these respects (e.g., the capacity to change
and the presence of those features), many such individuals, within and outside correc-

tions, do not, however, view most young killers as largely or almost entirely different from many or most other violent youths—ones who expressed hostility, for example, but not in ways that resulted in death. At any rate, complementing their view that change can take place under given conditions, many practitioners and other professionals believe improvements are needed, and can probably be made, in today's interventions with violent offenders. This position applies (1) regardless of what these youths' specific offenses may have been (murder included), (2) whatever extrinsic and intrinsic similarities and differences may exist between young killers and other offenders, and among the former themselves, and (3) even when they (the practitioners, etc.) believe strong physical controls must be present while intervention (treatment) occurs.

Still other individuals within the professional community and general public are unsure about, or have mixed opinions about, young killers and their prospects. In this regard, some of these individuals' views vary through time and may even be mutually inconsistent; certain feelings that preceded or resulted from those views may themselves shift considerably. Many of these people believe they do not have much information about young killers in the first place and a clear picture of what most such youths are like. Some have received *mixed* information, and, from this, have formed blurred or jumbled images.

As is evident, diverse views exist among the many individuals who comprise any one group, whether this is the general public, policymakers, practitioners, or others. At the same time, views that are similar or identical to each other exist among many individuals regardless of the group to which these persons belong; thus, such views are also found across groups, not just within them. These differences and similarities each involve such subjects and questions as youths' desire and ability to *change* (Do these exist?); extent and nature of *differences* among youths (Are these substantial and meaningful?); and, as can be inferred, *causation* (What significantly contributes to murder?). Such subjects have more than academic interest alone. Answers to their associated questions can make major, even decisive, differences in what will happen to youths in court, during their imprisonment, and upon releases as adults. Beyond that, increased knowledge regarding these subjects—knowledge on the part of practitioners, policymakers, and others (including the public) can have cumulative effects on correctional and judicial policy and practice.

To address these and related subjects, Dr. Heide, an internationally recognized authority on juvenile murderers and family violence, reviews a wide range of quantitative and qualitative information. Included are the published data, observations, findings, and opinions of numerous scholars, practitioners, and researchers. Also contributing are data and conclusions from her own detailed clinical evaluations of over 90 young males and females charged with murder or attempted murder. Heide's review and discussion of the above-mentioned subjects utilizes these youths' own views and behaviors as well. Throughout her book, she focuses on individuals who have killed, or have participated in the violent death of, one or more acquaintances, friends, strangers, or parents.

Based on convergences that appear across those data, experiences, and views—in particular, by using converging evidence that provides or strongly suggests answers to the questions regarding *change*, *difference*, and *causation*—Heide synthesizes her wide range of information and paves the way for a discussion of correctional treatment. In this discussion, she and Dr. Eldra Solomon present strategies and approaches that reflect the above evidence and that are consistent with her overall synthesis. Collectively, they are designed to not only help young killers address their problems and lead constructive lives but to protect society when these individuals are eventually released from prison—including the external controls it provides. Data are presented that make it clear that most convicted killers eventually *are* released.

After the discussion of treatment and rehabilitation, which centers on individual offenders, the book concludes with a detailed, prescriptive look at America's formidable task of greatly reducing interpersonal violence—not just murder—in future generations. As with treatment itself, the strategies and approaches that are proposed draw heavily on the evidence regarding causation and on Dr. Heide's conceptual framework with respect to it. Consistent with this framework, and directly implied in it, these strategies and approaches strongly reflect major *similarities*, not just differences, that exist among youths with regard to their developmental needs from early childhood forward. Involved here are psychosocial factors as well as environmental conditions on which a wide range of adult, community, and social-policy efforts could be regularly focused in order to promote healthy personal and interpersonal growth.

I would like to highlight several specific features of *Young Killers*. First, this book begins with a valuable overview of what Heide calls the "Phenomenon of Juvenile Homicide," that is, its general parameters and areas. Among these are number of such crimes; changes in volume over time; percentage of all homicides that involve juveniles; homicides in urban and school settings; relationship to group or gang membership; homicide and minority membership; females involved in murder; preteens who have murdered; relationship violence; hate-group killings; killings by cultlike groups; attempted murder; and, accidental homicide. Also included is information and discussion concerning the print and electronic media's depiction of juvenile homicide, the public's view of these crimes, and recent societal responses to them. Information and trends regarding some of these areas are presented with respect to other countries as well, mainly Canada.

The book also contains a succinct, informative review of several fundamental legal practices, issues, and trends relating to youths charged with murder. The main topic-areas are transfers to criminal court; the death penalty; mental status defenses (insanity, automatism, diminished capacity, self-defense); and mitigating and aggravating factors. The critical distinctions between first-degree murder, second-degree murder, and manslaughter are also discussed.

Equally informative is the description of clinical evaluations that mental health professionals—here, "forensic examiners"—carry out in connection with youths who have been charged with murder. The contributions of such individualized assessments to vital decisions that must be made at various stages of the legal process—sentencing included—are carefully spelled out. Also, Heide's concrete account of *how* a thorough clinical assessment is done and of exactly *what* goes into it (e.g., the difficult subjects that must be discussed with the youth and others) should be especially useful to and appreciated by a wide range of practitioners. In my view, this account effectively illustrates the types and range of critical information and impressions that can be obtained via skilled, sensitive interviewing and behavioral observations and in this regard, it could well be used as a model by students and many active professionals. In the final analysis, such an assessment or diagnosis is essential if one wishes to derive an accurate and adequate understanding of the youth as an actual person—an understanding that could also help practitioners/decision makers not only avoid, or at least go beyond, stereotypes and simplified labeling but counter or undo sometimes misleading preconceptions. This level and breadth of understanding could help these individuals and other justice system or correctional personnel with whom they interact better address and carry out their responsibilities.

Central to this book, and, I believe, very consistent with Dr. Heide's broad-based literature review, is her view that "many factors often act in concert" when a youth kills someone. These factors are among the 15 she lists and discusses regarding the youths *collectively*, and any one youth is likely to differ from any other in the particular combination of factors that paves the way for his or her violence. Among the 15 are "child abuse—child neglect—absence of positive male role models—crisis in leadership and lack of heroes—witnessing violence—access to guns—involvement in alcohol and drugs—poverty . . . "—and several specified personality features. Heide believes that such factors and others, again acting jointly, also help explain why, in the United States, "youths today are [collectively] more likely to kill than in prior years."

Multiple causation makes complete sense to me. I have long considered it the only realistic way to account for many of the behaviors and adjustment patterns of most violent and even nonviolent repeat offenders. It is fully consistent with my decades of direct experience with, and/or my examining the detailed background material on and professional assessments of, more than 1,500 juveniles and young adults in the California Youth Authority, several hundred of whom had either killed another person and/or had engaged in other major violence. Besides multiple causation per se, the *particular* factors that are focused on in *Young Killers* seem highly relevant, even though other important factors and conditions may sometimes contribute as well.

(In a related, and not simple theoretical, vein, it might be mentioned that the specific number and the essential content of factors that one regards as such can depend on how broadly or narrowly "factor" itself, and any given factor, is defined. The number and content can depend, for example, on whether one views certain aspects of an already established factor's *effects* as *separate* factors. Such effects or products—say, products of child abuse, child neglect, or family dysfunction such as persistent parental conflict—might, for instance, include such responses by a child or adolescent as the following: marked anger and perhaps confusion; and feelings of helplessness, emotional or physical deprivation, or guilt. Some of these relatively immediate responses may continue as is or might, instead, evolve into possible overcompensations or adaptations such as (1) an identification with the "tough guys" and a persistent wish to be considered powerful or fearless, or (2) a self-concept as being unfazed by feelings and being justified in quickly obtaining or taking almost anything one wants. Some of these products or outputs (e.g., anger or self-concept as tough) can then serve as distinct, long-lasting *inputs*—contributors—themselves. As such, they can further prepare the ground for eventual triggering-events and for destructive behavior toward perceived obstacles or threats; this situation applies whether or not the original, established factors have remained active. It is in this respect that such immediate or later-evolved products of already defined inputs might possibly be considered factors—significant determiners—in their own right. At any rate, however one might define, divide up, label, and count various contributors, the thorough clinical assessment described by Dr. Heide would remain an indispensable means of identifying them as such in the case of any specific individual. This type of tool, probably better than any other, could still help practitioners zero in on the particular sequence of inputs and outputs, and even on parallel sequences, that have led to violence and related problem behavior.)

Heide's case studies of seven young males who were convicted of murder and were then sent to prison illustrate key elements of this book. Each case, which comprises an entire chapter, clearly reveals how numerous internal and external factors jointly helped form a particular combination of thoughts, emotions, expectations, attitudes, and behaviors—one that in turn allowed for, and helped produce, the specific act of murder. Also, these studies collectively indicate that many sharp differences and equally striking or strong similarities do exist in the personalities, backgrounds, and past as well as present environments of the differing youths. Further, Dr. Heide's follow-up interviews with these individuals, together with her examination of prison documents concerning their adjustments, strongly suggest that three of the youths wished to, and did, make sizable personal changes and progress during their first several years in lockup, particularly if and as they accepted responsibility for the murder. Two others—also positively motivated—made moderate changes and progress; the remaining two grew worse.

All in all, these detailed case studies describe seven individuals who were real-life, relatively complex persons at the time of the murder. Seen in toto and *as* actual persons, they do not fit common or even less common stereotypes. This, I believe, is the case even though salient aspects of their behavior, of the murder itself, and of their explanation of it at the time do fit often observed patterns. Nor are these individuals essentially vacuous; yet neither are they enigmas whose violence was unfathomably complex or inherently beyond comprehension. In all the above, and in the sections that focus directly on legal issues and on how these eventually played out, these seven studies concretely and sometimes dramatically display the immediate significance and long-range implications of clinical assessments and of related expert advice or testimony that can help decision makers *understand*, not mainly stereotype or oversimplify, a person and his or her actions.

Regarding this understanding, and as one important aspect of it, each assessment and case study shows the utility of determining a youth's level or stage of personal and social development. Heide describes this level in terms of what is called the "I-level"—integration level—system. This is a conceptual framework that first *distinguishes* youths from each other in terms of their general interpersonal perceptiveness—in this respect, their "level of maturity"—and which then matches each youth to one of the various behavioral response-patterns and *similarities* ("subtypes") within each level. In the present case studies, Dr. Heide shows important links between the youths' particular levels of maturity (including their specific subtypes), on the one hand, and their differing types of emotional and behavioral response to given situations and to internal as well as external pressures, on the other. Such links can directly bear on precursors of violence and on legal issues relating to it. (It might be added that the I-level system has been used, since the 1960s, in several North American correctional settings for serious juvenile offenders. It has been closely associated with the concept and practice of "differential treatment": the use of differing interventions with differing types of youth—for example, youths of a higher rather than middle or lower level of maturity—and of one subtype rather than another. It presupposes multiple causation within each youth and differential causation across youths.)

The chapter on treatment contains an excellent synthesis of the book's preceding sections. In it, Heide and Solomon conclude that (1) young killers can change substantially; (2) however, most of them will need considerable assistance and direction—specifically, treatment—in order to do so; and (3) treatment will usually be difficult and long, mainly because the youths' personal and interpersonal problems and deficits are often numerous, marked (even individually), and long-standing. Their sizable number probably stems from the fact that several interacting factors—many of them strong—generated them and that some of these factors still actively maintain them. To adequately target and help the youths overcome their several problems and deficits and to help them substantially increase their coping skills per se, a range of treatment components is needed—12 of these are proposed and discussed. These components are such that, by utilizing them, practitioners can directly and/or indirectly address some of those earlier-mentioned, 15 possible causal factors found across youths. (Some such factors—for example, "low self-esteem" and "inability to deal with strong negative feelings" are among the problems and deficits themselves.) At any rate, no one or two components, by themselves, are enough.

Because young killers are not all alike with respect to their particular combination of problems, deficits, and related needs, a detailed initial evaluation should be made to determine, among other things, which areas and factors to focus on in the case of any given youth. Information concerning that individual's level of personal and social development could, at this point, further help practitioners identify strategies, techniques, and types of learning environments to which he or she might respond positively, or at least better than to others. All in all, this evaluation could help "treatment be tailored to the youth's development and special needs." Finally, the authors of this chapter strongly suggest that without serious treatment, many, possibly most, young killers will not change to the extent that is needed to successfully and constructively cope with their environments when released from prison. In this connection, they believe that more resources, and stronger rehabilitation efforts overall, are needed in many, perhaps most, present-day prisons. Their several conclusions, explanations, recommendations, and overall framework regarding treatment make a great deal of sense to me.

In the closing chapter, Dr. Heide goes beyond the treatment of individual youths who have killed. She expresses her deep concern with preventing homicide by *future* juveniles and, in particular, with reversing the sharp rise in this and other types of youth violence since the mid-1980s. Heide believes, and I agree, that because this trend has several causes, many of which are closely interrelated, "a multi-faceted, coordinated approach" would be needed to reverse it. She is convinced that because these causes, collectively, encompass *situational factors* (family inputs and lacks), *societal influences, personality characteristics,* and so forth—more specifically, because they involve changes within these areas (e.g., they involve increased witnessing of violence, increased child abuse and neglect, more poverty, greater access to guns and involvement with alcohol and drugs, and more by way of boredom and nothing to do)—the following is the case: Any approach designed to reverse the above trend would have to encompass and modify essentially those *same* areas, and to do so effectively, it would have to involve individuals, agencies, and others that could engage those areas—in some cases, could even activate *themselves* differently and more positively than before—and that could mobilize specific resources and efforts in ways that neutralize, undo, or preclude harmful change and promote constructive development.

For instance, a multifaceted approach would have to focus on issues or problems—causal factors—that involve several parts or segments of society: parents, communities, government leaders, the media, and individuals. To do so, it would have to utilize positive potentials that exist within those segments and in those of the educational system as well. To effectively organize these segments of society against those issues or problems (e.g., to mobilize positive potentials against the problems' increased presence of intensity), sustained, carefully focused efforts would be required, as might the augmenting of some already existing efforts. Often involved, at any rate, would be new directions and emphases, establishment of new resources, reorganization or consolidation of present efforts and resources, and, in general, new or modified policies, initiatives, and practices, plus an increased use of scientifically based findings. These changes and activities would also be designed to promote constructive development and conditions for growth, not just to oppose harmful factors. In both respects, they would attempt to address, and to thereby help children and youths meet, major social-psychological needs.

In this context, Heide provides extensive and convincing details regarding (1) what can be done and achieved with respect to various parts of society—for example, done *for* parents and communities—and concerning (2) the roles and potential contributions of individuals, institutions, agencies, and so on—for example, what can be done *by* parents, communities, the educational system, the media, and government leaders, to achieve those needs. In both respects, she presents recent position statements, recommendations, action plans, actual initiatives, and/or potential activities on the part of national professional associations, of federal, state, county, and local agencies and entities, of nongovernmental community groups and organizations, of private citizens, and/or of established social institutions. As an example of *coordination* within and across these differing parts of society—that is, of joint efforts to target various causal factors in crime—she highlights ongoing initiatives and activities in Allegheny County, Pennsylvania.

Dr. Heide indicates that the needed, multifaceted approach would require strong commitment and broad support, almost certainly for a great many years. In effect, her message regarding youth violence in the United States is that, whereas it might indeed "take a village" to raise an individual child, it would take a *society* to raise this country's next generation in ways that could reverse the recent national trend. In particular, high-priority efforts would have to be made by innumerable communities and jurisdictions. Most or all such efforts would be backed by consistent, standing policies at the state and federal levels, and many of these efforts would be supplemented or complemented by vigorous, specific action and other timely involvement at those levels. Although each *segment* of society (e.g., parents, schools, and the media) would make a large and indispensable contribution of its own toward the common goal, this, by itself, would not suffice. The multifaceted efforts would be focused, coordinated, and based on sound research and experience, not mainly scattershot, otherwise diffuse, and unintegrated.

One of the grim alternatives to eventually reducing the recent trend in youth violence might well be the following: a future in which youth institutions, adult prisons, and related facilities increasingly dot the landscape; in which gates and other physical/electronic barriers shut out and shut in more and more people and communities; and in which—*despite* all that and regardless of other, related societal responses—many or most adults and youths still feel fear when walking along the street, many children and youths continue to be frightened and in danger while in school or at play, and physical injury as well as destruction continue on a large scale with no major relief in sight.

Today's types and magnitude of youth violence will not, I believe, automatically regress to some actual or theoretical mean of many years ago and in that way greatly ease off. Even a large drop in the percentage representation of juveniles within the overall population (a reverse baby boom, as it were) would not, by itself, be likely to *undo* this past decade's sharp climb (i.e., in contrast to perhaps decelerating it and helping it plateau). Nor do I think the past decade's trend would be reversed and largely undone mainly via more physical control and similar external force alone—for example, increased incapacitation—or, for that matter, by more or better rehabilitation alone.

(It goes without saying that boot camps and Scared Straight programs with which the public has been familiar would make little dent.)

In these latter respects, it would be critical, I think, for much more of the public and many more of its representatives to soon, and thoroughly, recognize the following: Although law enforcement, corrections, and the overall justice system are indeed indispensable to making everyday life safer, they cannot, by themselves, largely shape the face of the future with regard to youth violence; at least, they cannot largely undo the present trend. Undoing this trend is now beyond them (just as it is beyond any other single segment), even though community policing—a recent development in law enforcement, is making an important inroad.

The general public must somehow be helped to realize and face the fact that *it* together with other segments of society and *backed* by law enforcement and so forth must do the lion's share of whatever is needed to reverse the increasing problem of youth violence and to then prevent a subsequent resurgence. This is a difficult thing to face and to genuinely accept, for several reasons. To mention a few major ones, it is difficult because the public and many of its key decision makers have long accepted the idea—not without good reason—that police, judges, distancing, and physical control will collectively suffice to keep violent offending at a level that is at least bearable, even though it is associated with much fear and is not considered "acceptable" as is. With considerably *less* reason, and increasingly or something wish-driven, a large portion of the public has implicitly accepted the idea that law enforcement and the justice system can markedly reduce high levels of youth violence at any time simply by getting tougher and stronger; on this score, the counterevidence of the past several years has not yet registered. The above is also difficult to face when there is little clarity about how else to proceed. In this respect, Heide's chapter, "Reducing Youth Violence in the 21st Century," provides much-needed direction and specific grounds for hope.

In conclusion, this book assembles and synthesizes some of the latest and best available information, research findings, and informed opinions regarding the parameters of homicide by youths and concerning the nature of young killers themselves. This information and so forth, especially when combined with several dozen vignettes and with detailed case studies of convicted young killers—including their backgrounds, feelings, and interactions with friends, family, and the overall environment—reveals them as human beings, not as "monsters" or as "a breed apart." It shows them to be young persons, who, for reasons that are not unfathomable, made some drastic mistakes that had tragic consequences for many people. Heide's book also shows that not all these youths are alike, despite their several common needs and problems. It strongly suggests that (1) with treatment (recommended components of which are discussed) many or most of these individuals can make major changes for the better, and (2) to facilitate treatment, it would often be important or even essential to work with youth "A" in certain ways that are substantially different than with youth "B," if these two individuals are, among other things, at differing stages of psychosocial development.

In any event, many youths who have killed can be "turned around"—rehabilitated, and in some respects habilitated—even though the reasons for their having killed are probably multiple, often powerful, and cumulative, and although some of these factors and forces remain active. The treatment of these individuals is neither inexpensive, quick, nor easy. However, its cost and effort can be justified in terms—for one thing—of the problems, pain, and violence that may be avoided in the long run, especially in connection with the many youths who will eventually return to free society. Inde-

pendent of treatment, the book reviews several basic and crucial legal issues relating
to all young killers. Further, it demonstrates how a clear, detailed understanding of the
individual and of the motivational dynamics of his or her offense can influence major
decisions that are made at various points in the legal process, some of which do have
implications for treatment.

Regarding youth violence in general, homicide included, *Young Killers* presents a
clear conceptual framework for mobilizing society's resources in ways that could eventually reverse the past decade's upward trend. Here, too, the book comes at a critical
time—one in which there is a need for broad perspective on the issues and challenges
that are involved, for sharpened concepts by which to describe those issues, for often-
different emphases with respect to *doing* something about them, and for new directions
overall. Heide's recommended approach has much to offer on all scores and could help
many decision makers as well as others immediately begin to develop, reshape, and
otherwise actively support given policies and initiatives. If implemented in a great many
communities and jurisdictions across the United States, these policies and efforts could
have a large, cumulative impact on youth violence in upcoming years, especially if they
are strongly and consistently supported at state and federal levels.

Despite its grim, emotionally, difficult, and often complex subject matter, *Young
Killers* maintains a consistently positive tone and is vigorous, clear, and direct. Dr. Heide
is both objective and empathic in her presentation of youths who have committed
murder and in the discussion of how to help them change. She is *emphatic* in her view
that society must now—without delay—seriously confront the factors that help pave
the way for this extreme act on the part of given individuals and that have predisposed
an increasing number of youths to other forms of violence as well. The goal of this
confrontation, that is, of the multifaceted efforts mentioned above, would not only be
to drastically reduce today's level of homicide, of physical injury, and of everyday
fear—absolutely fundamental though this objective would be. Instead, the goal would
also be to help raise children and youths in ways and under conditions that will greatly
increase the chances of their developing and eventually realizing their positive potentials as human beings. There can be little doubt that these individuals would be more
likely to develop those potentials—certainly, that they would have more realistic opportunities to do so—if they did not grow up and enter adolescence with minds that
are laden with, and energies that are often absorbed or diverted by, fear and images of
violence.

Heide's emphasis on child development is, thus, integral to what she views as a
moral challenge that society has—or, at least, one that it should recognize as such and
should then accept: the generating and implementing of policies and programs that can
help create "a healthy next generation" and, with that, "a more peaceful society." She
believes—and here, too, I think she is right—that scientifically based findings can play
a major role in this regard. They can help guide, can refine, and can even suggest policies
and practices that bear on both aspects of the above goal. Science, in short, can assist
even though both facets of that goal rest on and express something that is not itself
scientific: human concern for the betterment and well-being of adults, youths, and
children alike—those who have seriously offended and others who, hopefully, never
will.

Ted Palmer, Ph.D.
Senior Researcher (retired)
California Youth Authority

Acknowledgments

I WISH TO express my appreciation to colleagues, professional associates, family, and friends whose help, support, and encouragement inspired and guided me while I was writing this book. I am especially grateful to my editor, Charles ("Terry") Hendrix of Sage Publications, for his excellent editorial suggestions and his enthusiasm for this project from its conception to its completion. It has been a pleasure for me to work with Terry and the Sage production team again. Special thanks to Lenny Friedman and his marketing staff for their consistently fine work, great attitude, and good humor over the years.

I am indebted to Eldra Solomon, Ph.D., a master clinician and renowned biologist, for her assistance in co-authoring the treatment chapter (Chapter 12), in reviewing the biological discussion in the book, and in reacting to the content of the entire book. I acknowledge with love and gratitude my mentor, Marguerite Q. Warren, Ph.D., professor at the State University of New York at Albany, who gave me the knowledge and training to understand another's worldview.

I also am very grateful to my office manager and dear friend, Frances Knowles, who read every chapter at least once. Fran's keen eyes, literary acumen, and constructive feedback were very helpful to me in fine-tuning the book. Special thanks also are due to Francis Ranzoni, Ph.D., professor emeritus at Vassar College, for his astute comments on selected portions of the book.

Several students at the University of South Florida (USF) kindly read several chapters to ensure that the material was understandable and likely to hold the interest of students. Special thanks are due to Joyce Hulslander, Lisa Landis, and Tiffany Lawrence for their efforts. I wish to extend my gratitude to three other USF students who served as research assistants to me: Alicia Fieri, Jessica Kessler, and Mark Moffitt. Space does not allow me to acknowledge by name the hundreds of students who, over the years, have expressed interest in my work and in some way contributed to this book. I want them to know that I do remember them and that I am grateful for those lively discussions, challenging questions, case studies, and transcribed tapes.

I extend my gratitude to my chairperson, William R. Blount, Ph.D., and all of my colleagues in the Department of Criminology at USF for their support as I worked on this project. Several faculty members were especially helpful to me. I am grateful to Leonard Territo, Ed.D., for sharing tips he has learned as a very successful author, to James B. Halsted, J. D., Ph.D., for reviewing selected legal sections, to Richard Dembo, Ph.D., for believing in the importance of my clinical work with juveniles, and to Ira Silverman, Ph.D., for encouraging me to write a book on juvenile homicide. I also am thankful to the department's office manager, Shirley Latt, who always lent a hand to help in whatever way she could.

I was fortunate to have received the support of many others at my university. USF President Betty Castor and College of Arts and Sciences Dean David Stamps and Associate Dean Marilyn Myerson were among those who expressed genuine interest in my work over the years. Their enthusiasm for my research and clinical activities has meant a great deal to me. I appreciate the outstanding work done by staff members at the Office of Media Relations and Publications, particularly the broadcasting and marketing coordinator, Ron Faig, with whom I have enjoyed working for many years. The library staff members were very helpful to me in locating sources. Special thanks are due to Karen Roth, who graciously provided assistance with speed and care. I also appreciate the help of Marianne Bell, supervisor of the Information Processing Center, who typed beautiful tables in record time.

The list of people to whom I am grateful extends far beyond the USF campus in Tampa. The Florida Department of Corrections was again invaluable to me in completing this research. Special thanks are due to Bill Bales, director of the Bureau of Planning, Research, and Statistics, and to Research Associate Paula Bryant for helping me to conduct follow-up interviews with those cases I profiled and for providing follow-up data on my original sample of 60 cases.

I also had invaluable input from several academic reviewers: Charles P. Ewing, Ph.D., School of Law, State University of New York at Buffalo; Eric W. Hickey, Ph.D., Department of Criminology, California State University, Fresno; and Robert A. Silverman, Ph.D., dean, Faculty of Arts and Science, Queen's University, Canada. Their suggestions were excellent. The book is a better one because of the care with which they read the first draft and the astute comments that they made. I also wish to thank Norman G. Poythress, Ph.D., Department of Law and Mental Health, USF Florida Mental Health Institute, and Kenneth Gewerth, Ph.D., Department of Criminal Justice, Saginaw University, for examining closely the sections on mental health law.

I also benefited from participating in the Homicide Research Working Group, an international group of scholars and practitioners involved in the study of lethal and nonlethal violence. I particularly wish to express my appreciation to the members who attended annual meetings in Atlanta, Georgia; Ottawa, Ontario; Santa Monica, California; and Shepherdstown, West Virginia.

Over the years, I have had the opportunity to work with many fine attorneys. I want to thank several whose skills, convictions, and ethics were truly exemplary. They have extended themselves to help me in a variety of ways in which I always will remember: Craig Alldredge, chief of the Federal Public Defender's Office, Tampa; Patrick Doherty, Clearwater, Florida; Barbara Fleischer, circuit court judge, Tampa; Claire K. Luten, Luten Law Group, Clearwater; Benjamin Wesley Pardue, hearing officer, Tampa; and William E. Sizemore, Thompson, Sizemore & Gonzalez, PA, Tampa.

I remain indebted to my family for their love and presence in my life. I have been truly blessed to have been raised in a family where people love, value, respect, and enjoy one another. Special thanks to my mother, Eleanor Heide-Halligan, and my step-father, the late James Halligan, for their encouragement and support while I was working on this research. I also am deeply grateful to my brother, Tom, for keeping all of us close over the years and to my sister-in-law, Jennifer, for making sure that we do not take ourselves too seriously.

I appreciate my many friends whose faith in me and loving support over the years has been constant: Eldra Solomon, Rosalind Cummings Murray, M.D., Freda Brod, and Craig Darlak. I am grateful to my colleagues at the Center for Mental Health Education,

Assessment, and Therapy, especially Lois Schifino and Joan Chase, Ph.D., for their friendship and support over the years. I thank Edna McKnight for her good cheer and willingness to use her talents to assist me in myriad research-related activities over the years. Special thanks are due to my Mastermind partners: Marsha Vanderford, Ph.D., Frances Knowles, Lisa Day, Bernard Downs, Ph.D., Carolyn Gross, and Jack and Gina Boland. I extend my deep gratitude to the late Reverend Rosalie O'Connell and to Rabbi Theodore Brod for their spiritual guidance over the years.

I extend my gratitude to the internationally renowned researcher, Dr. Ted Palmer, whose work I have long admired, for writing a magnificent Foreword to *Young Killers* that synthesized my work and alerted readers to issues of fundamental importance in understanding juvenile murderers. Last, but not least, I thank the young men who trusted me to tell their stories in this book, as well as their mothers, for sharing their thoughts with me. Their voices and reflections have the power to change the lives of many young people growing up today.

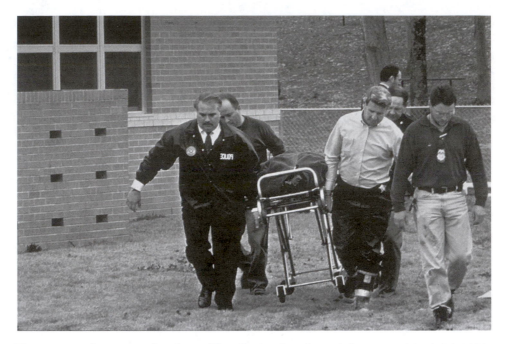

The massacre that occurred at the middle school in Jonesboro, Arkansas, on March 24, 1998, did more than take the lives of five people. It changed the worldview of millions of school children in the United States who now worry that they will be shot or killed by their fellow classmates when they go to school every morning. As we approach the millennium, we must ask ourselves whether "the three Rs" will come to mean "reading, writing, and run for cover" or whether we as a nation will respond to the challenge of juvenile homicide.

SOURCE: Leigh Daughtridge—Memphis Commercial Appeal/SIPA Press. Used by permission.

Part One

Juvenile Homicide Encapsulated

I WAS ABSORBED in my research on adolescent homicide offenders late on a Friday afternoon when my secretary, Peggy, interrupted me with the following message:

> You just had a call from a legal assistant about a case on death row. She said that the inmate was 17 years old at the time of the murder. The governor just signed the second death warrant. The inmate's lawyers want you to take a look at the case. I told them that you had taken the summer off to work on your research and that you would call them back in September. The legal assistant said, "He'll be dead by then."

In less than 48 hours, I was on my way to death row to evaluate Mark, whose case is among those profiled in this book. Professors sometimes are accused of conducting obscure studies and living in ivory towers. As someone who has viewed bodies in the morgue, toured homicide crime scenes, evaluated more than 100 homicide offenders, and spoken to the survivors of homicide victims, I can tell you that the image of academicians as people with their heads in the clouds frequently is mistaken. Our research often has real-world consequences. For Mark and some other young killers, my work and the investigations of other scholar-practitioners have literally meant the difference between life and death, between freedom and a life behind bars, or between parole eligibility and natural life in prison.

This book is about youths who kill. Chapter 1 puts the phenomenon of juvenile homicide in perspective. The chapter concentrates on adolescent murder in the United States, where it is considered an epidemic by health professionals as well as by practitioners in the juvenile justice and criminal justice systems. Killings by youths in Canada and other countries also are addressed. Chapter 1 surveys killings by youths and focuses on important parameters such as the involvement of gangs, girls, "little kids," and minority group members in murderous activities. Juvenile participation in multiple

1

homicides, relationship violence, and killings at school also is examined. The media portrayal and public perception of young killers, and the societal response to them, are highlighted.

Chapter 2 surveys the professional literature regarding why juveniles kill. It then seeks to answer the even tougher question: Why are more adolescents killing today than ever before in U.S. history? This chapter presents more than a dozen factors that are contributing to the dramatic escalation in juvenile homicides as we approach the 21st century.

Chapter 3 examines the legal response to juvenile homicide in the United States. The types of murder with which juveniles may be charged and convicted are highlighted. Discussion focuses on juveniles processed in the adult criminal justice system, where in many states they can legally be executed if convicted of murder. The laws and policies of the states regarding the execution of juveniles are highlighted. In addition to providing data with respect to juveniles sentenced to capital punishment, this chapter looks closely at the circumstances surrounding Mark's being sentenced to death. Mental status defenses are examined because of their importance in understanding why judges and jurors hold some youths fully accountable, others only partly responsible, and still others not accountable for their murderous behavior.

Chapter 4 delves into the mind of the juvenile murderer. The chapter examines the factors that are of critical importance in understanding the motivational dynamics behind the homicide. The role of the mental health expert and the implications of a comprehensive assessment of a homicide offender are addressed. The nature and scope of forensic evaluation is thoroughly discussed, and case illustrations are provided.

Taken collectively, these chapters prepare the reader for the in-depth case studies of adolescent murderers profiled in Part II. In addition, they provide the foundation for understanding the treatment recommendations and prevention strategies discussed in Part III.

I have made five decision rules in writing this book. These center around qualifying statements, reporting race, revealing the identities of the young murderers, capturing the phenomenon of youth violence, and using the word *kids*.

In highlighting cases in the chapters that follow, I have intentionally used the words *allegedly* and *reportedly* when relying on newspaper accounts and even on some of the statements made to me directly by the adolescent murderers themselves. I have adopted this convention because, on occasion, some reported accounts tend to be inaccurate, subject to interpretation, or dependent on an individual's perceptions. In addition, caution seems advisable because facts sometimes are disputed by the parties involved or cannot be proven in a court of law. Accordingly, as a scientist practitioner, I exercise care in qualifying statements and in documenting sources, the absolute accuracy or "truth" of which I cannot ascertain.

When presenting case vignettes, I have not pointed out the race of the juvenile murderer unless it is an important dynamic in the crime. The case excerpts presented typically were chosen to illustrate concepts relevant to the phenomenon of juvenile homicide. The youths whose cases are briefly highlighted are not random cases. Therefore, the racial makeup of these youths might not be representative of young killers in general. Identifying the race might lead the reader to draw conclusions about the racial involvement of youths in murder that would not be consistent with the data. In contrast to the brief vignettes, I have identified the race of these seven youths in the in-depth cases presented in Part II because it usually is helpful in understanding their backgrounds and life experiences.

I have chosen not to reveal the names of juveniles in the brief vignettes because this book is intended to be a serious study of juvenile homicide. I was concerned that the young killers might be vilified, and their lives or criminal deeds might appear "glamorized," if their names were sprinkled throughout the text. Although I have permission to tell the stories of the seven cases in Part II, I have declined to disclose their real identities even when they authorized me to do so. I made this decision because I feared that they might be pursued by media personnel focusing on adolescent murderers. I told them that they, of course, were free to contact the media if they wanted to identify themselves. I assured them that, ethically as a mental health professional, I would not reveal their identities.

Although this book is predominantly about youths who murdered at age 17 years or under, I have included some limited data and a few stories with respect to 18- and 19-year-old adolescents. These older adolescents are considered part of the youth violence problem. Moreover, the lines sometimes are blurred because the professional literature on adolescent homicide has not consistently indicated whether all of the youths in the study were under 18 years old or whether some were 18 or 19. In addition, although the term *juvenile status* typically is interpreted to be children under 18, this designation is not uniform. Although the majority of states in the United States today designate 17 years as the upper age of juvenile court jurisdiction, 11 states designate the oldest age for *original* jurisdiction as 15 or 16, and all 50 states have provisions to try juveniles in adult court under certain circumstances.[1] To further complicate matters, some states have legislative provisions that allow the juvenile court to retain jurisdiction over youths adjudicated as juveniles through their late adolescence or early adulthood, that is, until these youths reach their 19th or 21st birthdays.

On occasion, I use the word *kids* in place of more formal terms such as children, youths, juveniles, or adolescents. I do this with some concern because this term sometimes is seen as a pejorative one. I do not want the reader to marginalize today's youths and relegate them to a lower status. When I use the word *kids*, I am hoping to counteract notions of "young superpredators." The word *kids* frequently evokes a feeling of tenderness in many of us. The showing of more tenderness and concern for today's youths will go a long way in stemming the tide of juvenile homicide.

Chapter One

The Phenomenon of Juvenile Homicide

TWO BRITISH vacationers were on their way from New Orleans, Louisiana, to St. Petersburg, Florida. Tired, the man and woman pulled into a rest stop about 35 miles east of Tallahassee, Florida, shortly after midnight. The couple was startled by a metallic tapping on one of the windows of their rental car. The woman recalled seeing two young men waving guns and yelling, but she did not know what they were saying. When her male companion put the car into reverse in an attempt to flee, he was shot fatally in the neck. The woman, who was shot in the arm and breast, recovered.

Four youths, who ranged in age from 13 to 16 years, initially were arrested in connection with the murder of the Briton and the attempted murder of his companion of nearly 15 years. This homicide, the ninth involving a foreigner in Florida in 1 year, seriously threatened the state's $30 billion tourism industry.[1]

This incident, literally one of thousands that could be profiled in the 1990s, is indicative of a grim reality in the United States. In the words of U.S. Attorney General Janet Reno, youth violence is "the greatest single crime problem in America today."[2] Reports of a declining trend in violent crime arrests in the early 1990s obscured the fact that at a time when the violent crime rate had been decreasing among adults, it had been significantly rising among the nation's young people.[3]

Reno's assessment is particularly evident when youth involvement in murder is examined over time. Dramatic increases in youths being arrested for homicide are apparent whether the frame of reference is youths under 18 years of age or those in their middle to late teenage years.

The term *youth* is a broad one that encompasses both juveniles and adolescents. Although these terms often are used interchangeably in the media and in professional literature, they can be distinguished from each other. Juvenile or minority status is determined on the basis of age and is a legislative decision.[4] The federal government and the majority of the states, for example, designate youths under 18 years of age as juveniles.[5] The Federal Bureau of Investigation (FBI) classifies arrests of "children 17 and under" as juvenile arrests.[6]

Adolescence, in contrast to juvenile status, is based on human development and varies across individuals. It is a stormy period characterized by hormonal changes, growth spurts, psychological changes, and enhancement of intellectual abilities and motor skills. According to child development experts, adolescence begins with puberty, which typically commences by age 12 or 13 years but may start earlier.[7] Adolescence

TABLE 1.1   Numbers and Percentages of Homicide Arrests Under 18 Years of Age: United States, 1984-1996

Year or Period	Total	Number Under 18 Years of Age	Percentage Under 18 Years of Age
1984	13,676	1,004	7.3
1985	15,777	1,311	8.3
1986	16,066	1,396	8.7
1987	16,714	1,592	9.5
1988	16,326	1,765	10.8
1989	17,975	2,208	12.3
1990	18,298	2,555	14.1
1991	18,654	2,626	14.1
1992	19,491	2,829	14.5
1993	20,285	3,284	16.2
1994	18,497	3,102	16.7
1995	16,701	2,560	15.3
1996	14,447	2,172	15.0
1984-1993 (means)	17,326	2,057	11.6
1984-1996 (means)	17,147	2,185	12.5
1987-1996 (means)	17,739	2,469	13.8

SOURCE: Table constructed from data provided in *Crime in the United States* for each of 13 years (Federal Bureau of Investigation 1985-1997).

extends through the teen years to age 19 or 20.[8] The term *children* is commonly used to refer to prepubescent youths.

Analysis of crime patterns clearly indicates that youths are killing in record numbers in the United States as we approach the 21st century.[9] As illustrated in Table 1.1, homicide arrests of juveniles rose every year from 1984 through 1993. None of the 50 states appeared immune to the increase in killings by young people during these 10 years.[10] The dramatic escalation in murders by juveniles during this time frame put the United States in the grip of fear. In 1993, the number of juveniles arrested for murder—3,284—was three times higher than the number arrested in 1984 and had reached an all-time high.[11]

Although the numbers of minors arrested for murder decreased in 1994, 1995, and 1996, it would be wrong to conclude that the crisis in lethal violence by youths is over. The percentage of all homicide arrests involving juveniles more than doubled, from 7.3% in 1984 to 15.0% in 1996.

The dramatic increase in murders committed by those under 18 years of age since the mid-1980s cannot be attributed to an increase in the juvenile population during the past decade. Until recently, the percentage of young Americans generally had been declining.[12] Experts have noted with alarm that murders by juveniles might continue to increase at an unprecedented rate as we enter the 21st century because the teen population currently is growing at a much higher rate than is the total population.[13]

Northeastern University criminologist James A. Fox has successfully forecasted the U.S. homicide rate for almost 20 years. Fox predicted in 1995 that the number of juvenile killers could rise to 5,000 in 2005 if the murder rate stays the same. If the murder rate increases, then the number could easily rise to 6,000 or higher.[14] Other

TABLE 1.2 Percentages of Homicide Arrests Under 18 Years of Age by Location: United States, 1984-1996

Year or Period	City	Suburban	Rural
1984	8.3	5.1	5.4
1985	9.1	5.9	6.5
1986	9.7	6.0	6.1
1987	10.5	7.3	4.9
1988	12.0	7.0	6.2
1989	13.6	8.2	5.6
1990	15.5	10.3	6.0
1991	15.6	9.6	5.8
1992	15.6	12.6	7.0
1993	17.6	12.8	8.4
1994	18.1	12.4	11.0
1995	16.1	14.0	9.8
1996	16.4	10.4	12.6
1984-1993 (means)	12.8	8.5	6.2
1984-1996 (means)	13.7	9.4	7.3
1987-1996 (means)	15.1	10.5	7.7

SOURCE: Table constructed from data provided in *Crime in the United States* for each of 13 years (Federal Bureau of Investigation 1985-1997).

experts have projected that if murders by youths continue to grow at the same pace, juvenile arrests for homicide will number 8,100 by the year 2010, an increase of 145% in less than 20 years.[15]

Although the increasing participation of juveniles in murder has been felt in urban, suburban, and rural areas across America, killings by juveniles have been especially troubling in U.S. cities. The percentages of homicide arrests involving juveniles in the nation's cities, as depicted in Table 1.2, rose steadily from a low of 8.3% in 1984 to a high of 18.1% in 1994. In 1996, about 1 out of 6 homicide arrests in cities involved juveniles. The comparable figures in suburban and rural areas were 1 out of 10 and 1 out of 8, respectively.

The seriousness of the youth homicide problem is underscored when the unit of analysis is 15- to 19-year-olds. Smith and Feiler computed the *absolute* and *relative* levels of youth involvement in arrests for murder during the period 1958 to 1993. Examination of trends in arrest rates revealed a very striking escalation in homicides by youths in their late teens beginning in the mid-1980s. The arrest rates for 15- to 19-year-olds recorded in 1992 (42.4 per 100,000) and 1993 (42.2 per 100,000) were the highest recorded for *any* age group during the 36 years covered by the data.[16] Similarly, the researchers concluded that "the ratio for 15- to 19-year-olds in 1993 marks the greatest relative involvement in murder arrests for any age group during the period under study."[17]

Today's young killers are truly a mixed breed. They come in different shapes, sizes, and colors. Although most live in cities, increasing numbers reside in suburban and rural areas. They come from various backgrounds, ranging from enormous wealth to abject poverty. Some are in school and work at after-school jobs, whereas others are dropouts who make a living in illegal activities. Although some youths kill alone, young killers are more likely than adult murderers to kill in groups.[18] Their victims range in age from children to the elderly. Those whose lives they take include strangers, people they know, and people they love.

Following is a sampling of stories about juveniles recently arrested or convicted of murder across the United States. These vignettes suggest a variety of motives underlying the involvement of these youths in various types of homicide ranging from first-degree murder to manslaughter. These factors include intoxication, peer pressure, revenge, displaced rage, profit, hatred, and possibly even mental illness.

Close reading of these excerpted cases also reveals that young killers employ a variety of weapons of destruction. Juvenile murderers, even more than their adult counterparts, are most likely to select a firearm.[19] In addition to handguns, shotguns, and rifles, youths have used knives, fire, personal weapons such as hands and fists, and bows and arrows to kill.

Minneapolis, Minnesota—A 14-year-old boy stated that he drank about a dozen beers, in addition to some hard liquor, while hanging out with some other kids at the home of his 23-year-old paramour. The youth persuaded his lover to drive him to a hardware store to buy ammunition for his pistol. On the way back from the store, the boy allegedly loaded the gun and the woman reportedly fired the gun at a motorist with whom they had a traffic dispute. When they got back to the woman's house, the 14-year-old supposedly fired six or more shots at the vacant house across the street. He then reportedly walked down the street to a group home where mentally retarded adults lived. Court documents indicated that the youth stood outside a window and trained his .38-caliber handgun at a female employee's head for about 5 seconds before firing the shot that killed her. Police maintained that the boy, who did not know the victim, just wanted to see whether he could really shoot someone.[20]

Passaic County, New Jersey—A 15-year-old boy was accused of killing a man by slitting his throat and stabbing him four times in his back. The boy, along with a female juvenile and a 22-year-old man, allegedly lured the victim to his death on the pretense of a sexual encounter. Authorities believe that the adult male put the victim in a headlock and instructed the boy to kill the man because the boy was a juvenile. This youth had been released from a secure training school to an intensive community supervision program 4 months earlier, despite the protests of the prosecutors and judge who had dealt with his case.[21]

Elyria, Ohio—Two 15-year-old boys were sentenced to life in prison for killing an 8-year-old girl. The two boys were convicted of setting fire to the house occupied by the girl, two of her siblings, and her mother. The boys allegedly poured gasoline inside and outside the house and ignited it. Although one of the killers testified that he only meant to set the family's front porch on fire as a joke, investigators found evidence that the staircase, the only escape route, also had been soaked with gasoline. This same youth reportedly had a number of run-ins with the victim's mother, who had ordered him off her property on prior occasions.[22]

Port Lucie, Florida—A 16-year-old boy allegedly beat a 78-year-old woman to death and returned to the crime scene to cover up the killing. Failing in his attempts to set the elderly woman's body on fire, the youth reportedly covered her body with red spray paint. The youth, a former altar boy from an affluent family, told police that he had been out walking and trying to cool off from an argument he had earlier that evening with his parents when he encountered the victim. The boy allegedly hit the woman in the face with his cassette recorder and then beat and choked her after she criticized him for singing the lyrics of a rap song.[23]

Madison, Wisconsin—A 16-year-old boy was the last of three youths to be convicted in a murder-for-hire plot. This youth, alleged to be the triggerman by his two 17-year-old co-defendants, shot the victim as he was getting ready to go to church services on Easter Sunday. The youths reportedly were hired by the victim's estranged wife.[24]

Ford Heights, Illinois—Five Black youths, ranging in age from 13 to 17 years, were arrested in connection with the death of a 32-year-old White man. The victim, who had been traveling with a friend, was stopped earlier in a high-crime drug area by police who reportedly thought the two men were acting suspiciously. Police arrested the victim's friend on an outstanding warrant and towed the pair's car. The victim who remained behind was attacked within 15 minutes of the departure of the police and his comrade. Two of the five youths allegedly told police that the victim was beaten, doused with lighter fluid, and set on fire because he was White.[25]

Steubenville, Ohio—A 16-year-old boy was convicted of killing his mother with a bow and arrow. The youth allegedly shot her five times in her head and neck as she rested on the sofa in their living room. The boy claimed that he did not remember anything after he fired the first arrow at his mother, whom defense counsel depicted as an abusive and alcoholic woman.[26]

▪ THE PARAMETERS OF JUVENILE HOMICIDE

The cases highlighted in the preceding paragraphs all involved male teenagers acting alone or with others to kill their victims. These cases are typical scenarios and represent the majority of murders perpetrated by juveniles. However, their depiction leaves many questions unanswered. How often do youths kill two or more victims in a single event? Is gang membership associated with this type of violence? What percentage of youths arrested for homicide are members of minority groups? In a culture of rising feminism, where are girls in the ranks of young killers? Are boys and girls prey to the relationship violence that kills many women and men in our society? How many of these young killers are preteens? Are schools really becoming dangerous places for kids? What should we make of attempted murders and accidental shootings?

Juvenile Involvement in Double Homicides and Mass Murders

Juvenile homicide offenders, like their adult counterparts, are far more likely to kill one victim in an incident than several at a time.[27] Available data suggest that when two or more juveniles kill a victim, the victim is more likely to be a stranger than a family member or an acquaintance.[28]

Exact figures of juvenile participation in homicides claiming the lives of two or more victims are not available. The FBI, which collects nationwide data on homicides, does not include information on double homicides or mass murders (i.e., three or more victims slain in one incident) in its annual publication of crime statistics in the United States.[29] Although the FBI collects additional information on murders in its supplementary homicide report database, the database as currently organized does not permit extensive and precise analysis of murders when more than one victim or offender is involved.[30] Research compiled by James Alan Fox and Jack Levin of Northeastern University, leading experts on mass murder, does suggest, however, that mass murder, although a growing phenomenon in the United States,[31] rarely is perpetrated by juveniles.

Media coverage suggests that when multiple victims are slain in one incident by young killers, they are apt to be family members. Several cases of American youths wiping out their families made headline news in the span of a few weeks in March 1995. In late February, two boys ages 16 and 17 years, both Skinhead members, were arrested in connection with the stabbing and bludgeoning to death of their parents and 11-year-old brother in the outskirts of Allentown, Pennsylvania. A few days later and a few miles away, a 16-year-old boy was charged with killing his parents. The boy, allegedly influenced by the film *Natural Born Killers*, aspired to lead a life sparked by the adventure of the adolescent killers, Mickey and Mallory. A few days later, a 15-year-old boy was taken into custody for shooting his parents in Newnan, Georgia. Police alleged that the youth was angry with his mother and father for giving him a curfew.[32]

Cases of multiple killings by juveniles involving family members other than parents as well as complete strangers do exist. Motives range from expressive reasons, including hatred and possible mental illness, to instrumental factors such as the elimination of witnesses and financial gain.

Lincoln, Illinois—A 14-year-old boy was taken into custody in connection with the slaying of his grandmother and the serious wounding of his grandfather. The victims, both shot with a .22-caliber semiautomatic weapon, were found in the yard and inside the house, respectively. Neighbors characterized the teen, who had lived with his grandparents for several years, as a troubled youth. He reportedly was known to dress in camouflage clothing and hide in a tree with his BB gun.[33]

Opelika, Alabama—A 15-year-old boy was charged with the murders of three women killed in broad daylight during a bungled robbery at a shopping center. The youth allegedly packed a pistol, entered a flea market, directed customers to give him their wallets, and then opened fire. Two of the victims, both in their 70s, were hunting for bargains at the flea market when they were gunned down. The third woman was one of the flea market owners.[34]

Young Killers and Group Membership

Some young killers are members of gangs. The number of gangs and gang memberships has increased significantly during the past decade in the United States. Although most noticeable in large urban areas, gangs also have started to appear in suburban areas and smaller towns across America.[35] Racial and ethnic composition of the gangs often varies and in many cities appears to be related to immigration patterns.[36] Substantial evidence exists that gangs have become increasingly responsible for a disproportionate amount of violence,[37] which appears to be largely due to the ready availability of firearms and more sophisticated weaponry.[38]

The escalation of murders in the late 1980s and 1990s in large cities, such as Chicago and Los Angeles, has been associated with gang involvement. Male teenagers and young adults are at much greater risk than other age groups of being both victims and offenders of gang-related violence.[39] Street gang-related homicides are among the "homicide syndromes" identified by Richard and Carolyn Block, internationally recognized leaders in homicide research. In this paradigm, the homicide is associated with a function of the street gang "such as representing, recruitment, defense of turf, or promotion of an enterprise," for example, selling narcotics.[40] Experts disagree whether the gang-related escalation in homicides beginning in the mid-1980s has been due to increased youth involvement in the "crack cocaine wars."[41] Consensus does exist that gang-related deaths such as the following are becoming more common across the United States.

Chicago, Illinois—Two 17-year-old boys were charged with killing a 24-year-old man. The two adolescents were walking down the street when they saw the victim sitting on his front porch. One of the youths allegedly shot the victim after he flashed the wrong gang signs.[42]

Seattle, Washington—Seven juveniles were among the nine people initially arrested in connection with the shooting death of a 16-year-old girl at a local high school. The suspected gunman, still at large, is 16. According to authorities, gang members were riding around in two cars when they spotted other Asian youths standing around. Observing police officers nearby, they left the area. When they returned about 90 minutes later, a gang member in one of the cars started shooting into a crowd of students. The victim apparently got caught in the crossfire of two rival Asian gangs.[43]

Other youths arrested for murder occasionally are identified as members of hate groups. In contrast to street gangs that typically form because of a shared culture and experience of oppression, White supremacy groups are intentionally organized around racism. Members resort to violence to further political change by instilling terror in innocent people.[44] The Ku Klux Klan, Skinheads, Identity Church, and other neo-Nazi groups are among the more well-known hate groups. More than 70 hate groups are estimated to be active in the United States.[45] These groups are believed to be responsible for numerous violent acts, including homicides, committed against victims who they hate for characteristics such as racial or ethnic background, religious belief, or sexual preference.[46]

In June 1995, the Anti-Defamation League (ADL) released the results of the first global study of neo-Nazi Skinheads. Approximately 70,000 youths in 33 countries across six continents identify themselves with the movement. The United States, with about 3,500 members, has one of the largest concentrations of hard-core Skinheads.[47] According to the ADL, "The relative availability of guns in the United States has made American Skin[head]s among the most dangerous and violent in the world."[48] The number of murders attributed to Skinheads in the 1990s has risen noticeably as membership has increased.[49] Whereas juveniles are among the participants in some of these murders, in some cases they are the only perpetrators.

Fort Worth, Texas—Three 16-year-old White boys were charged in connection with a drive-by shooting that resulted in the death of a 32-year-old African American man. The youths, known to have racist affiliations, allegedly shot the man while he sat drinking beer with his friends.[50]

TABLE 1.3 Juvenile Homicide Arrests by Percentages White, Black, and Other: United States, 1984-1996

Year or Period	Total	Percentage White	Percentage Black	Percentage Other[a]
1984	1,004	53.7	45.2	1.1
1985	1,305	48.2	50.7	1.1
1986	1,395	49.4	48.1	2.5
1987	1,591	42.2	55.3	2.5
1988	1,747	41.2	57.1	1.7
1989	2,202	37.0	61.2	1.8
1990	2,550	39.1	59.4	1.5
1991	2,536	40.9	57.3	1.9
1992	2,829	41.1	57.4	1.5
1993	3,281	36.0	62.3	1.7
1994	3,100	38.5	59.4	2.1
1995	2,558	39.4	57.7	2.8[b]
1996	2,171	39.1	57.5	3.4[b]
1984-1993 (means)	2,044	42.9	55.4	1.7
1984-1996 (means)	2,175	42.0	56.0	2.0
1987-1996 (means)	2,456	39.4	58.5	2.1

SOURCE: Table constructed from data provided in *Crime in the United States* for each of 13 years (Federal Bureau of Investigation 1985-1997).

a. Other includes American Indian, Alaskan Native, Asian, or Pacific Islander.

b. Increases in percentage other in 1995 and 1996 are largely due to increases in arrests of Asians or Pacific Islanders.

In addition to gangs and hate groups, some young killers band together in cult-like groups. These groups may be organized around some fantasy or ideology that takes on an increasingly destructive tone.

Washington, North Carolina—A 19-year-old college student reportedly was the mastermind behind a plot to kill his mother and stepfather, who had a substantial estate. The student allegedly assisted one of his friends in gaining access to his parents' home in the middle of the night. The intruder savagely beat and stabbed both parents, killing the youth's stepfather and apparently leaving the mother for dead. Subsequent investigation revealed that the victims' son had a history of extensive drug use and spent an inordinate amount of time playing the game *Dungeons and Dragons.* Evidence suggested that this adolescent increasingly had difficulty distinguishing reality from the game's bizarre rituals. The crime appeared to be a real-life enactment of a *Dungeons and Dragons* adventure.[51]

West Memphis, Arkansas—Three adolescents, ages 16, 17, and 18 years, were arrested in connection with the murder of three 8-year-old boys who were found naked, beaten, and hogtied. Evidence indicated that the victims had been sexually assaulted. Prosecutors dubbed the case the "devil cult killing" and argued that the crime was the result of the youths' involvement in Satanic activities. The oldest youth arrested was believed to have been the group's leader. He reportedly told a psychologist that he saw himself as another notorious killer, such as Charles Manson or Ted Bundy, and that people always would remember him.[52]

Pearl, Mississippi—A 16-year-old male youth took a hunting rifle to the high school he attended and opened fire. He reportedly killed two students and wounded seven others before he was arrested. This teen is believed to have stabbed his mother to death earlier that morning. Early reports suggested that this adolescent was an angry youth who might have been confused by the violent writings of Nietzsche. Within a week, the picture of a disturbed youth operating alone was blown wide apart. Police arrested six other youths; two were 16, two were 17, and the remainder were 18. Authorities related that these seven adolescents fashioned themselves as an elite body of intellectuals known as "The Group" and had been talking about a rampage since the beginning of the school year. Subsequent investigation implied that this group wanted power and money and that its leader was fascinated by Adolph Hitler. Rumors of a Satanic cult abounded in the small town. Sources maintained that the rampage had been planned for Halloween in honor of Satan but that the alleged killer had become upset and literally "jumped the gun."[53]

Race and Juvenile Homicide

Race and juvenile homicide was among the controversial issues debated at the National Conference on Violence Prevention cosponsored by the Centers for Disease Control and Prevention and the University of Iowa in October 1995. African Americans rightly objected to the media's consistent depiction of young killers as Black males. No race has a monopoly on murder in the United States. Juvenile homicide offenders, as well as adult killers, come from all racial groups.

However, examination of national data on homicide offenders and victims reveals that homicide in general, and juvenile homicide in particular, is an especially serious problem in the Black community. From 1985 to 1994, the homicide offending rates for White youths ages 14 to 17 years doubled from 7.0 to 15.6 per 100,000. The rates for their Black counterparts tripled from 44.3 to 139.6 per 100,000 during the same period.[54]

As indicated in Table 1.3, African Americans comprised almost 58% of juveniles arrested for homicide in 1996. During the period 1987 to 1996, Black youths comprised between 55% and 61% of all juveniles arrested for murder.[55] These statistics are quite troubling when one considers that African Americans comprised approximately 14% of the juvenile population in the United States during this decade.[56] The proportion of juvenile murder victims who are African American, as discussed in Box 1.1, is equally distressing.

Girls Who Kill

Juvenile homicide is overwhelmingly a male phenomenon. Although more girls have been arrested for homicide almost each year since 1984, they are hardly responsible for the dramatic escalation in juvenile murder in the United States. Inspection of Table 1.4 suggests that as homicide arrests of juveniles have increased, girls' overall participation has shown a decreasing trend. As depicted in Table 1.4, approximately 6% of juveniles arrested for homicide in 1996 were girls.[57] Research suggests that when girls kill, they are more likely than their male counterparts to murder people they know, either family members or acquaintances.[58]

BOX 1.1   Who Is Dying Anyway? Youths as Murder Victims

In November 1993, U.S. Surgeon General M. Jocelyn Elders presented alarming statistics in support of her position that violence was a public health issue that demanded immediate attention:

> Violence in America is an epidemic. It is one of the leading causes of death and injury for our young people. Gunshot wounds, including homicides, suicides, and unintentional shootings, are the leading cause of death for both African American and White teenage males, and they kill more teenage boys than all natural diseases combined. And for young African American men and women [ages] 15 to 24, homicide is the number one cause of death.
>
> From a public health perspective, the number of deaths caused by violence, which kills over 50,000 persons yearly, is greater than the number caused by AIDS, which kills over 30,000 per year, and greater than the number of deaths caused by drunk driving, which kills nearly 18,000 persons per year.
>
> In 1991, for the first time in our nation's history, the number of homicides exceeded 25,000. And the homicide rate for young males ages 15-34 in the U.S. is the highest of any industrialized country, roughly 20 times higher than rates in most other nations.[a]

In a 1996 book titled *The Color of Justice: Race, Ethnicity, and Crime in America,* University of Nebraska professors Walker, Spohn, and DeLone synthesized available research on homicide victimization in the United States. After a comprehensive analysis of numerous sources of data, they concluded that African Americans, particularly young males, are far more likely to be murdered than are their White counterparts.

> The largest and most striking racial differences in victimization are for the crime of homicide. In fact, all the data on homicide point to the same conclusion: African Americans, and particularly African American males, face much greater risk of death by homicide than do Whites.
>
> . . . In fact, in 1992, the homicide rate for African American males age 12 to 24 was an astounding 114.9 per 100,000. The rate for White males in this age group was 11.7. Among young males, in other words, the homicide rate for African Americans was 10 times the rate for Whites.[b]

In a report released in 1995, Howard Snyder and Melissa Sickmund of the National Center for Juvenile Justice analyzed homicide victimization rates specifically among juveniles over the period 1976 to 1991. Among their findings were the following:

• Homicide victimization rates have increased for both males and females under the age of 18 years since the mid-1980s.
• The male proportion of juvenile homicide victims increased from 64% in 1985 to 72% in 1991.
• African American juveniles were four times more likely than White juveniles to be murder victims.

- Among juveniles ages 14 to 17 years, African Americans were five times more likely than their White counterparts to be murdered.
- Race and gender differences in homicide victimization rates increased in recent years, particularly among juveniles ages 14 to 17 years. The rate of older Black male juveniles becoming murder victims increased from 1984 to 1991 when compared to the rates of Black females (from 3 to 1 to 7 to 1), White males (from 5 to 1 to 8 to 1), and White females (from 9 to 1 to 29 to 1).[c]

Jiafang Chen of the University of Georgia, Athens, analyzed firearm-related deaths in the United States from 1920 to 1990. His observations with respect to juveniles ages 15 to 19 years killed by guns are unsettling. He reported that firearm-related homicides per 100,000 were highest in 1990. In contrast to the gun-related homicide rate for older Americans that peaked in the 1970s, more and more juveniles were being killed by firearms in 1990 than in any other time frame. The rate in 1990 was twice the rate in the 1920s and three times the rate in the 1950s. This pattern was observed for White males and females and for Black males.[d]

a. Excerpts from M. Jocelyn Elders, former U.S. surgeon general, *Violence as a Public Health Issue,* Hearing of the Human Resources and Intergovernmental Relations Subcommittee of the House Government OPS Committee, November 1, 1993. Reprinted courtesy of *Federal News Service.*

b. Walker, Spohn, and DeLone (1996, pp. 34-35).

c. Snyder and Sickmund (1995, p. 19).

d. Chen (1996, pp. 52-53).

TABLE 1.4 Numbers and Percentages of Female Homicide Arrests Under 18 Years of Age: United States, 1984-1996

Year or Period	Total Homicides Under 18 Years of Age	Total Female Homicides Under 18 Years of Age	Percentage of Female Homicides of Total Under 18 Years of Age
1984	1,004	102	10.2
1985	1,311	122	9.3
1986	1,396	93	6.7
1987	1,592	138	8.7
1988	1,765	119	6.7
1989	2,208	139	6.3
1990	2,555	132	5.2
1991	2,626	122	4.6
1992	2,829	159	5.6
1993	3,284	191	5.8
1994	3,102	185	6.0
1995	2,560	158	6.2
1996	2,172	142	6.5
1984-1993 (means)	2,057	132	6.9
1984-1996 (means)	2,185	139	6.8
1987-1996 (means)	2,469	148	6.2

SOURCE: Table constructed from data provided in *Crime in the United States* for each of 13 years (Federal Bureau of Investigation 1985-1997).

West Palm Beach, Florida—Three girls, ages 13, 15, and 17 years, were leaving a shopping mall. Although they had no money, they figured that they would take a cab and avoid the $6 fare by jumping out of the vehicle as soon as they reached their location. Plans apparently went awry. The incident ended with one of the girls shooting the cab driver in the back of his head. Initially, all three girls maintained that the 13-year-old killed the man, believing that the law would treat her leniently because she was so young. Eventually, the 17-year-old admitted that she fired the .25-caliber automatic pistol.[59]

Ontario, Oregon—A 16-year-old girl was charged with the death of her newborn. The girl reportedly told authorities that she hid her pregnancy from her parents and her boyfriend and bore the 6-pound baby girl by herself. She then allegedly placed the infant in a cardboard box littered with some rags and left the baby girl outside a vacant house on a night when the temperature dropped to 11°F.[60]

Land O'Lakes, Florida—A 17-year-old girl fired a bullet from a .22-caliber handgun into her mother's head while she slept. Intending to create an alibi, she then went to a nearby video store, where she browsed through the available selections and pretended to call her mother. The store owner would recall her becoming visibly upset during the faked phone call. She told him that she heard a gunshot as she spoke to her mother. The girl confessed shortly thereafter, claiming that she killed her mother to end her abusive behavior.[61]

When Dating Violence Turns Deadly

The trial of O. J. Simpson focused national attention on domestic violence. Relationship violence clearly is not restricted to adults. Research, although sparse, suggests that many youths currently are involved in abusive relationships with their boyfriends or girlfriends.[62] For example, approximately 25% of the girls and 10% of the boys attending three midwestern high schools, which included inner-city, suburban, and rural schools, reported experiencing severe dating violence (a combined category of physical and sexual violence). The percentage increased to 32% of the girls and 24% of the boys when the category of violence was broadened to include physical, sexual, and verbal violence.[63] Violence among youths in same-sex relationships also exists and often goes undetected because of the typically closeted nature of these relationships and the resulting social isolation of gay and lesbian youths.[64]

Although few violent relationships improve, some do end peacefully with both parties going their separate ways. Others, however, end tragically.

Santa Ana, California—A 16-year-old boy killed himself after fatally shooting his 14-year-old girlfriend and mother of his unborn child. The girl's family described the boy as very controlling of her and her activities. Shortly before killing his girlfriend, the boy told her that he wanted to break up. To his apparent dismay, the girl agreed, the two argued, and the boy ended the altercation with a round of bullets.[65]

Denver, Colorado—Three 17-year-olds, two boys and one girl, and a 20-year-old male were arrested for killing an 18-year-old male and his 17-year-old girlfriend. The 17-year-old girl allegedly persuaded her three male friends to kill the male victim, a former boyfriend, for breaking up with her the previous summer. She reportedly had threatened her former boyfriend and his new girlfriend on previous occasions.[66]

TABLE 1.5 Numbers and Percentages of Homicide Arrests by Age: United States, 1987-1996

Age	1996			1987-1996		
	Number	Percentage of Total Arrests	Percentage of Juvenile Arrests	Mean Number	Mean Percentage of Total Arrests	Mean Percentage of Juvenile Arrests
Under 10 years	17	0.1	0.8	13	0.07	0.5
10-12 years	16	0.1	0.7	26	0.15	1.1
13-14 years	224	1.6	10.3	256	1.4	10.4
15 years	359	2.5	16.5	418	2.4	16.9
16 years	651	4.5	30.0	728	4.1	29.5
17 years	905	6.3	41.7	1,028	5.8	41.6
Total 17 years or under	2,172	15.0	100.0	2,469	13.9	100.0

SOURCE: Table constructed from data provided in *Crime in the United States* for each of 10 years (Federal Bureau of Investigation 1988-1997).
NOTE: Total arrests for 1996 = 14,447. Mean number of total arrests for 1987-1996 = 17,739.

Little Kids Who Kill

More than 98% of juvenile homicide offenders are teenagers. Arrest statistics consistently indicate that youth involvement in homicide increases directly with age. As indicated in Table 1.5, 88% of juveniles arrested for homicide in 1996 were ages 15 (16%), 16 (30%), or 17 years (42%).

Although most young killers are in their mid- to late teens, some are really "little kids." In 1996, 33 children under 13 years of age were arrested for murder. As reflected in Table 1.5, over the period 1987 to 1996, youths 12 or under comprised 1.6% of juvenile homicide arrests and far less than 1.0% of all homicide arrests (0.22%).

Chicago, Illinois—Two boys, ages 10 and 11 years, were arrested for killing a 5-year-old boy who lived in their public housing development. The two young killers lured the victim and his 8-year-old brother into a vacant apartment located on the 14th floor of one of the buildings in their project. After a vigorous struggle, the two older boys hung the 5-year-old out a window. While the child was frantically gripping the fingers of his brother, the older boys were biting the fingers of his would-be rescuer. Eventually, the 8-year-old was forced to relinquish his grip, sending his little brother to his death. The two killers allegedly were attempting to get even with the brothers for getting them into trouble. The brothers recently had told their mother that the older boys had been coercing them to engage in illegal activities.[67]

San Antonio, Texas—A 12-year-old girl was charged with killing a 4-month-old boy and his 2-year-old sister. The two small children and their parents had been staying in the apartment where the girl lived with her relatives. The preteen allegedly suffocated the children when their parents went out for a short time to pay the rent on their new apartment. The parents were planning to move out with their two babies that night.[68]

Killings at School

It is apparent from reading the preceding cases that the killing grounds selected by young killers include homes, storefronts, streets, alleys, vacant lots, and wooded areas. Increasingly, it appears that school buildings and even playgrounds have become zones of death.

Jonesboro, Arkansas—On March 24, 1998, two boys, ages 11 and 13, reportedly stole guns and ammunition, went to their school, and pulled a fire alarm. As their schoolmates and staff evacuated the building, the boys opened fire, killing four girls and one female teacher, and wounding 10 more.

Violence and the fear of violence have become rampant in public schools across the United States.[69] The problem seems to have become worse in schools in urban, suburban, and rural areas in the past 5 years, according to a 1994 survey conducted by the National School Board Association.[70] Startling facts to emerge from recent studies addressing school violence include the following:

- About 430,000 students are victims of violent crime every year in school, according to projections made from a U.S. Department of Justice study released in 1991.
- Approximately 160,000 students stay home from school daily because they fear violence in school or on their way to school, according to the National Education Association.
- More than 270,000 youths bring guns to school, according to estimates provided by University of Michigan researchers.
- Shootings or knife attacks occurred in almost 40% of urban districts in 1993, according to participants in the NSBA survey.
- A total of 35 deaths and 92 injuries in schools were attributed to guns in 1994, according to the National School Safety Center.[71]

In a chilling 1992 article titled "Deadly Lessons," *Newsweek* correspondent Rod Nordand asked the pivotal question: "Kids with guns are setting off an arms race of their own across the country—as a double murder in a New York high school showed. Are schools doomed to become free-fire zones?"[72] The three killings in the following vignettes occurred between September 28 and October 12, 1995.

Tavares, Florida—A 14-year-old boy was arrested for killing a 13-year-old boy at a middle school that both boys attended. Witnesses stated that seconds before the shooting, the two boys passed one another in the hallway and said something to each other. The older boy allegedly fired his semiautomatic gun into the younger boy's chest. While the wounded victim lay bleeding on the ground, the 14-year-old reportedly fired another five shots into him. According to authorities, the older boy pointed the firearm at other students before running away from the school.[73]

St. Louis, Missouri—A 9-year-old boy allegedly punched a substitute teacher numerous times in the chest because he did not like an assignment that the teacher had given to his

4th-grade class. The elementary school teacher died shortly after the attack. The police classified the case as a homicide after reviewing the autopsy reports.[74]

Blacksville, South Carolina—A 16-year-old boy who was on out-of-school suspension reportedly entered his high school, walked past two classrooms, entered a third classroom, and shot and wounded a math teacher with a .32-caliber handgun. After leaving this classroom, the youth walked down the hall, where he shot another math teacher, who subsequently died. The youth then killed himself.[75]

Attempted Murders, Accidental Shootings, and Other Awful Events

The discussion so far has focused on murderous activity in which victims have died. For every homicidal episode in which a juvenile kills one or more victims, there are countless others in which the victims survive. Two factors frequently determine whether a robbery or an assault turns into a murder. As noted by Loyola University sociologist Richard Block, these are the marksmanship of the offender and the speed of the ambulance in getting the victim to a hospital.[76] In my experience, some victims who have been shot, stabbed, severely beaten, or savagely victimized by juvenile offenders also live because they are mentally strong, have healthy bodies, receive good medical care quickly, and are unusually lucky.

Denver, Colorado—Three boys allegedly doused a 12-year-old boy with lighter fluid and set him ablaze. The trio reportedly offered the victim a soda and 25 cents if he went along with their plan. The victim sustained second-degree burns over 20% of his body.[77]

Fort Lauderdale, Florida—A 9-year-old girl was charged with the attempted murder of her 3-year-old brother after investigators concluded that the shooting was deliberate rather than accidental. The girl was baby-sitting for her two brothers, ages 3 and 8, and her 8-year-old cousin. All four children reportedly were playing a video game in the girl's father's bedroom when they found a .357-caliber handgun. After telling the two 8-year-olds to take a bath, the girl continued to play the video game with her little brother. According to statements the girl made to police, she got into an argument with the 3-year-old during the game and shot him in his head. The girl allegedly resented the toddler and believed him to be the favorite in the family.[78]

Although this shooting was found to be intentional, occasionally accounts of shootings by juveniles appear truly to be accidental. In cases such as these, murder charges rarely are brought against the youths involved, although other charges may be filed. In some states, the weapon owners, often the parents, may be charged with a misdemeanor if they failed to take reasonable precautions to secure the firearms in a locked container or other safe location.[79]

Chicago, Illinois—A 15-year-old boy was charged with reckless conduct in connection with the accidental death of a 13-year-old girl. The boy allegedly was showing off the gun that he had just found to four other children when it accidentally discharged and hit the victim in her face.[80]

Tarpon Springs, Florida—A 10-year-old boy apparently shot an 11-year-old girl in the abdomen by accident at a birthday party for another child. The children had gathered in the garage of the boy celebrating his birthday to examine a .22-caliber pistol that he had found that day. The kids reportedly had passed the gun around and tried to fire it twice with no results. The third time the trigger was pulled, the gun fired. The police referred the case to prosecutors to decide whether the parents should be charged.[81]

The discussion of accidental deaths would not be complete without reference to traffic fatalities. Due to increased public concern in the United States, drunk drivers who kill others in traffic accidents typically are charged with driving under the influence (DUI) or driving while intoxicated (DWI) manslaughter. Many youths in the United States drive; some drive drunk, and a few inadvertently kill under these conditions. Do adolescents such as these belong in a book titled *Young Killers*? Before answering, the reader should consider the following recent case that made headline news and provoked vigorous national debate on issues of juvenile and parental responsibility.

Miami, Florida—A 15-year-old boy was charged with three counts of manslaughter and one count of using a phony driver's license after a night of club-hopping turned into a horrific car accident. Charges of manslaughter under the influence of alcohol and marijuana subsequently were dropped because the youth did not meet the legal threshold for intoxication. The youth allegedly was drag racing his brand new Corvette against a high-performance Mustang in the early morning hours. Witnesses estimated that the 15-year-old was traveling in excess of 100 miles per hour when his Corvette slammed into a Chevette that turned into his path. The three young men in the Chevette were killed instantly and their car was cut in half. One of the passengers riding in the Corvette was thrown from the car and is now a quadriplegic.

The youth lived with his biological parents and older siblings in a home valued at $1.5 million and attended a private school. He reportedly was given a second Corvette to use by his father after he totaled his first one the previous summer. His father allegedly helped his son obtain a fraudulent driver's license because the boy was not old enough to drive legally. His father is said to have told reporters at the hospital later that morning that his son was not to blame for the accident because, after all, the other car turned in front of him.[82]

MEDIA DEPICTION, PUBLIC PERCEPTION, AND SOCIETAL RESPONSE

The print and electronic media have given extensive coverage to the rise in killings by juveniles in the United States during the past decade. Recent reports have an ominous ring and echo those made for the past 20 years that youths are increasingly becoming more predatory.[83] The August 2, 1993, cover story of *Newsweek* titled "Teen Violence—Wild in the Streets," for example, was captioned as follows: "Murder and mayhem, guns and gangs: A teenage generation grows up dangerous—and scared."[84] The headlines of the feature story about violent juveniles in the May 22, 1994, edition of the *News Tribune* in Tacoma, Washington, warned, "The most dangerous criminals in America are also its youngest; violent young people are turning on themselves and adults in a cold-blooded trend that has experts searching for solutions."[85] In the January 30, 1994, article in the *Arizona Republic*, "Armed, Young and Dangerous," journalist Victoria Harker crystallized the attitudes of many criminal justice personnel and mental health professionals: "Coming hand-in-hand with the increase in juvenile crime is an escalation in viciousness. Experts say such violence speaks volumes about the kind of youths coming of age in America in the 1990s, a lost generation of neglected teens who have many weapons but no remorse."[86] In a 6-month period in 1997, the cover stories of three *People Weekly* magazines, which typically feature celebrities such as Princess Diana, John Denver, Rosie O'Donnell, and George Clooney, spotlighted a variety of young killers. These crimes seemed cold, callous, senseless, and even gruesome;[87] others were tragic and downright terrifying.[88]

The escalation in violent crime by juveniles is being met with widespread fear among the American public.[89] Although some critics maintain that the media have distorted the juvenile crime problem,[90] apprehension does appear warranted. Forecasts made several years ago by Charles Patrick Ewing, a professor of law and psychology at the State University of New York at Buffalo, that the 1990s would see an epidemic in juvenile homicide have proven accurate.[91] James Q. Wilson, a criminologist at the University of California, Los Angeles, poignantly recapped the current situation:

> The public perception that today's crime problem is different from and more serious than that of earlier decades is thus quite correct. Youngsters are shooting at people at a far higher rate than at any time in recent history. Since young people are more likely than adults to kill strangers (as opposed to lovers or spouses), the risk to innocent bystanders has gone up. There may be some comfort to be had in the fact that youthful homicides are only a small fraction of all killings, but given their randomness, it is not much solace.[92]

Not surprisingly, dissatisfaction with the juvenile justice system is sweeping across the United States. Professionals and the public alike are questioning the purpose of the juvenile justice system and the need for its continued existence. The system is increasingly being viewed as a failure by practitioners such as law enforcement officers, juvenile court judges, prosecutors, probation officers, and corrections staff as well as by the public and the politicians who represent the public.[93] Task forces and committees have been formed and statewide forums have been held to study the problem of juvenile crime and to recommend solutions.[94] In the 1990s, politicians are quick to pit the philosophy behind the development of juvenile court—the "best interests of the child"—against considerations of public safety.[95]

While experts argue whether violent juveniles should be treated or punished,[96] the federal government and legislators in numerous states have either introduced or passed various bills to "get tough" with juvenile offenders.[97] During the period 1992 to 1995, 47 of the 50 state legislatures and the District of Columbia made significant changes to their laws targeting juveniles who commit serious or violent crimes.[98] In many jurisdictions, these measures include lowering the age of majority for all juveniles or for those who commit certain crimes and making it easier to transfer juveniles to adult courts by changing or adding procedures to effect this process.[99] In some states today, for example, youths as young as 13 years old can be tried in adult court for any crime.[100] Youths adjudicated guilty in adult court face potentially longer periods of incarceration, life without parole, or (in some cases) the death penalty.

Some bills and proposals include allowing the press to publish the names of youths arrested for committing a certain type or number of crimes,[101] opening the juvenile court records of serious offenders to pertinent parties, and allowing news reporters to attend juvenile court hearings if they do not publish the children's names.[102] Others as drafted authorize law enforcement officers to disseminate names, addresses, photographs, and descriptions of youths being sought for certain criminal offenses.[103] Other legislation is aimed at prohibiting juveniles from possessing guns,[104] expelling students who bring guns to school,[105] notifying schools when youths get into serious trouble,[106] and setting up alternative schools for youths who have been expelled from regular schools for disruptive or criminal behavior.[107]

"Get tough" legislation also has been introduced or passed in various jurisdictions to detain violent juveniles who will be tried as adults in adult jails[108] and to provide more sentencing alternatives for hard-core delinquents.[109] Provisions also have been drafted to provide for longer and harsher sanctions for young offenders, including boot camps in the juvenile and adult correctional systems.[110] New laws also have imposed curfews[111] and broadened the power of juvenile court judges to hold children and their parents in contempt of court under varying circumstances.[112]

JUVENILE HOMICIDE IN OTHER COUNTRIES

Anxious Americans often ask whether the escalation in murders committed by juveniles in recent years also is occurring in other developed countries outside the United States. Prior to answering this question, it is important to point out that the United States leads the industrialized world in criminal homicide rates. The murder rate in the United States is even higher than the rates reported for Russia and former Eastern Bloc countries during recent periods of social upheaval.[113] During the period 1984 to 1996, 9 people were murdered each year for every 100,000 people living in the United States.[114] The U.S. murder rate has been estimated to be five times higher than Canada's rate and nine times higher than the rates in Great Britain, Germany, Norway, and the Netherlands.[115] The easy availability of firearms in the United States, relative to that in other countries, is believed to account at least in part for the dramatic differences in homicide rates between the United States and other industrialized nations.[116]

Young Killers in Canada

Canada is ideally suited to compare trends in juvenile homicide between that country and the United States. Canada's southern border extends across almost all of the northern part of the United States from east to west. Canadians have become increasingly alarmed in the 1990s about young killers in their country.[117] Highly publicized accounts of murders committed by youths in various provinces now include family massacres[118] and drive-by shootings as well as robbery murders, sexual homicides, and some seemingly senseless homicides. These killings are perpetrated by girls or boys, acting alone or as members of groups or gangs.[119] Media coverage of such events has led many to conclude erroneously that adolescent murder is increasing in proportions seen in the United States.[120]

However, well-respected criminologists, including Neil Boyd of Simon Fraser University, Marc Le Blanc of the University of Montreal, Robert Silverman of Queens University and his colleagues at the University of Alberta, and Irwin Waller of the University of Ottawa, maintain that little evidence exists of any significant change in juvenile homicide. Statisticians employed by the Centre for Justice Statistics, the Canadian government agency responsible for analyzing crime data, also contend that juvenile homicide has remained fairly stable since the 1970s.[121] The number of murders committed by youths in Canada has risen in the 1990s, at least partly due to changes in the law regarding juveniles. These changes made the chronological definition of *youth* consistent across the country and extended the youth category from age 16 to 17 years.[122]

Available data clearly indicate that the homicide rate by juveniles in Canada is substantially lower than the rate in the United States.[123] In 1993, for example, Canadian juveniles ages 12 to 17 years accounted for 7% of homicide arrestees in their country;[124] their American counterparts comprised 17% of total homicide arrests in the United States.

Violence in the schools and gang violence, however, might be becoming more common in Canada, according to Thomas Gabor, University of Ottawa sociologist, and Marc Ouimet, University of Montreal criminologist. It appears that more Canadian youths today are carrying weapons into school for offensive and defensive purposes. The weapons selected typically are knives and other cutting instruments. In Canada, guns are not easily available, unlike the situation in the United States.[125] A few of the juvenile murder cases making headlines in the 1990s in Canada are profiled in the following.

Whitehead, Nova Scotia—A 13-year-old boy was convicted of killing a man who opened the door of his home to him. The boy, armed with a pump-action shotgun, allegedly picked the man's house randomly, rang the doorbell, waited for a response, and opened fire. The youth related later that he was disturbed because his father earlier had refused to give him a cigarette.[126]

Montreal, Quebec—Three young teenagers, ages 13, 14, and 15 years, were accused of breaking into the home of a retired minister and his wife in Beaconsfield, a suburb on the western tip of Montreal Island. The trio allegedly beat the 75-year-old man and his 70-year-old wife to death in their bed, took a few items, and left in the couple's car. The youths reportedly bragged to other kids that they wanted to kill somebody. Police ruled out robbery as a motive for the double homicide and concluded that the teens killed the elderly couple for fun.[127] The youths reportedly were overheard talking about murdering somebody prior to the killings.[128]

Toronto, Ontario—Two 14-year-old girls were charged with robbing and killing a 34-year-old janitor. A third girl, age 15, also was charged with robbery in connection with the incident. The three schoolgirls, all from middle-class families, flagged down the male victim, who was on his way to rent a video. After the man stopped, the trio tried to steal his car. When he resisted, they stabbed him repeatedly. Police reported that this incident marked the first time in the city of Calgary, population 730,000, that girls this young had been charged with homicide.[129]

Valleyview, Alberta—A 15-year-old boy was charged with killing his mother, stepfather, and two younger sisters. He reportedly fired 10 shots into their heads, cut off his mother's breasts, and removed clothing to expose her genitals after the massacre. He then allegedly dragged the four bodies into the bush, took his parents' money, and practiced forging his mother's name. He was apprehended while driving the family van after a high-speed chase by police a few days later.[130]

Montreal, Quebec—A 15-year-old boy was charged with attempted murder after he allegedly fired a 12-gauge sawed-off shotgun into a crowd assembled to watch a parade celebrating Caribbean culture. The incident reportedly led to the hospitalization of four people with gunshot wounds and triggered a riot as police moved in to disperse the crowds. Before order was restored, rocks and bottles were hurled at police, several stores were looted, and two police officers were hospitalized for shock.[131]

Montreal, Quebec—A 16-year-old boy was convicted of killing a convenience store owner in what appeared to be a gang-related crime. The boy was one of seven youths, ranging in age from 12 to 16, and one adult who allegedly attempted to rob the store owner. This boy was identified as the masked and hooded figure, seen on television by thousands of viewers in Montreal, who fired a bullet from a sawed-off .303-caliber rifle at close range into the victim's head.[132]

Victoria, British Columbia—A 17-year-old boy was convicted of killing a 6-year-old neighborhood girl who knew and trusted him. The youth was 16 at the time of the homicide and was on probation for having sexually assaulted two children previously. The adolescent reenacted the crime for police on a videotape shown at his trial. He put the girl on his shoulders, carried her into the bushes, took off her clothes, and raped her. When she screamed for her mother, the boy killed her by choking her and stomping on her face and chest. While the girl's parents were called to the police station later to learn what had happened to their daughter, the youth baby-sat for their two other children.[133]

Canadians have expressed outrage over these homicidal incidents and other juvenile murders making headline news in Canada.[134] Similar to Americans, many Canadians have maintained that their juvenile justice system no longer is equipped to deal with today's youths.[135] National debate has focused on whether the goals of individual treatment should give way to a society's perceived need for punishment and protection.[136] In this climate of fear, groups of Canadians have lobbied unsuccessfully to bring back the death penalty.[137]

Canadians have placed increasing pressure on politicians during the 1990s to enact a variety of crime control measures including amending the Young Offenders Act and tightening Canada's gun law.[138] By early August 1995, more than 120,000 Canadians had signed a petition to change the law to allow juveniles accused of murder to be publicly identified and be tried and sentenced as adults. Since that period, thousands more reportedly have signed the petition, initiated by the family and friends of a man murdered by juveniles.[139] In January 1997, 92% of Canadians polled indicated that youth crime remained a serious or very serious problem and that punishment harsher than that available under the Young Offenders Act was needed.[140]

The federal government began conducting a comprehensive review of the Young Offenders Act and holding hearings across the country during the fall of 1995.[141] Legislation suggested to toughen the law has included lowering the age of juvenile accountability from 12 to 10 years,[142] automatically transferring 16- and 17-year-old violent offenders to adult court,[143] and increasing the maximum sentences given to juveniles convicted of first- and second-degree murder to 10 and 7 years, respectively.[144] Other proposed changes to the act have consisted of permitting the release of juvenile offenders' names to school authorities and other pertinent parties, ordering juvenile delinquents to participate in treatment programs,[145] and making the parents responsible for their children's legal representation in court.[146]

Young Killers in Other Countries

Isolated reports of murders committed by juveniles in countries other than the United States and Canada occasionally are featured in North American newspapers. Accurate statistics are not readily available from many countries abroad, in some cases due to lack of technology and in other cases due to government censorship. In addition, homicide statistics from other countries might not be comparable to U.S. data due to differences in how homicides are defined, investigated, and legally processed.[147] Therefore, it is exceedingly difficult to determine whether these countries are seeing a rise in murders committed by juveniles. It might be that these murders attract notoriety because they are so unusual rather than because they are indicative of a trend.

Available coverage of cases of young murderers in foreign countries often is brief and lacking in precise details such as gender and age.[148] For example, the ages of the four German youths arrested in connection with the home firebombing that resulted in the deaths of five Turks were not specified.[149] This account, as well as similar ones,[150] makes it difficult to discern whether the youthful or teenage perpetrators are juveniles under 18 years of age.

When the media focus on youths involved in murders in countries outside North America, their cases often are extreme or even bizarre. The cases presented in the following are newsworthy precisely because they are so unusual. They involve a half dozen "little kids" who killed in India, France, and England, two teenage boys responsible for several senseless killings in Scotland, and an adolescent mass murderer in France.

Some juvenile killers in other foreign countries that made headline news are so young that they cannot be charged with murder under the existing laws. Two cases that occurred in 1993 are illustrative in this regard.

Purenderpr, India—A 5-year-old reportedly bludgeoned three children to death. Under the law in India, children under age 6 cannot be held responsible for any crime.[151]

Vitry-Sur-Seine, France—Three children ranging in age from 8 to 10 years beat a homeless man to death after he tried to stay in their playhouse located in a poor suburb of Paris. The children could not be charged with murder under French law. They were convicted of inflicting injury without intention to kill, the most serious charge that could be brought against them.[152]

Liverpool, England—The same year, two preadolescent boys became the youngest Britons to be convicted of murder in more than 200 years. Their crime outraged Britons and garnered sympathy worldwide for the victim and his family. The two 10-year-old boys reportedly kidnapped a 2-year-old boy from a shopping mall in Liverpool. Together, they allegedly clubbed the small child with bricks and an iron bar. Thereafter, they placed the victim's body on a railroad track to be cut in half by a speeding train.[153]

The remaining cases, although involving adolescents, also evoked horror in their respective countries and beyond.

Glasgow, Scotland—Two 15-year-old boys were convicted of killing two people who died in a train wreck caused by them. The two male youths and their girlfriends had been drinking cider and beer near the railroad when the boys allegedly decided to put concrete slabs across the train tracks. The passenger train, whose crew and passengers numbered six at the time, careened out of control for several hundred feet. The four survivors attributed their lives to luck.[154]

Toulon, France—A 16-year-old boy went on a killing rampage considered to be the worst mass killing in France in the 1990s. Before he took his own life, the youth reportedly managed to kill 12 people and wound another eight. The victims slain on September 24, 1995, ranged in age from 17 to 75. The youth allegedly selected a hammer and baseball bat to kill his first three victims—his mother, her husband, and their son. He then took a gun and, according to witness accounts, walked calmly into a village where he randomly fired at townspeople as they went about their daily activities. Although no motive was known, neighbors of the gunman described him as an aloof adolescent with a fascination with Hitler and neo-Nazi topics.[155]

Mass murder committed by juveniles living abroad, as in the United States and Canada, is an exceedingly rare event during times of peace. In countries at war, however, the phenomenon, although rarely discussed, is apt to be far more commonplace.[156] Hundreds of juveniles under 18 years of age reportedly are being detained in prisons in Rwanda on charges of genocide. These youths are believed to have participated in acts that, under other circumstances, would be classified as mass murders.[157]

Widely publicized accounts of juvenile homicides in countries other than the United States and Canada are too few, and the cultures are too diverse, to speak with authority about public perceptions and the society's reactions to these events. It would appear that responses to juvenile violence or its perceived threat range in the extreme from the annihilation of children in Brazil to their symbolic redemption in Rwanda.

Estimates suggest that as many as 200,000 children live on the streets of Brazil. Impoverished and without social services to help them, some prey on the public in an attempt to survive. The government's failure to address the children's crisis has heightened public fear. Death squads reportedly have been hired to find and kill homeless children who are perceived as predatory.[158]

In sharp contrast to the neglectful attitudes and passivity of the Brazilian government, authorities in Rwanda want to know whether children who have participated in mass murder can be reintegrated into society in a few years. Accordingly, they have selected approximately 150 boys, ranging in age from 6 to 15 years, from thousands being detained in jam-packed prisons on charges of genocide. These children have been placed in a children's center, where they are learning academic and vocational skills to equip them for a better future.[159]

CONCLUDING REMARKS

This chapter looked at the characteristics of youth homicide and the faces of young killers, particularly in the United States. Juvenile homicide offenders in the United

States are likely to be male, in their teens, and poor. The majority are members of minority groups and urban dwellers. They are likely to pack guns and use them to kill when they are with other youths. No place is entirely safe anymore. Increasingly, juveniles kill adults and other kids in their homes, in schoolyards and classrooms, on the streets, and in places of business.

The cry of alarm currently being sounded in the United States by practitioners in the criminal justice system, politicians, the media, and the public is warranted. An examination of homicide arrest data clearly indicated that murder by American juveniles has become an increasingly serious problem, particularly since the mid-1980s. Interestingly, Canada, which borders much of the United States and has many similar problems, has recorded only a slight increase in juvenile homicide in recent years. Criminologists maintain that juvenile homicide in Canada, in sharp contrast to that in the United States, has remained quite stable over the past 20 years. The next chapter highlights research findings about juvenile homicide offenders and specifically looks at the factors that have contributed to the escalation in youth murders in the United States since the mid-1980s.

Chapter Two

Ingredients for Juvenile Murder

THREE SEPARATE homicidal incidents occurring in three distinct cities across three consecutive days are encapsulated in the following. These are among an estimated 15 to 25 incidents of homicides committed by juveniles that could be spotlighted in this 72-hour period.

- **Thursday, February 1, 1996, Tampa, Florida**—A 46-year-old accountant was murdered. Three youths—two boys, ages 17 and 18, and a girl, age 16—were arrested in connection with the killing. They were the dead man's neighbors. He was known to have befriended them and loaned them videotapes. The neighbors were shocked by the arrests. They described the adolescents as "good kids." Why would they do such a thing?[1]

- **Friday, February 2, 1996, Moses Lake, Washington**—A 14-year-old boy entered his junior high school with a hunting rifle. He killed a teacher and two students, wounded a third student, and threatened to kill more before he was subdued. What motivated his rampage?[2]

- **Saturday, February 3, 1996, Vista, California**—Five people were killed in a condominium, and a fire was set in an apparent attempt to cover up the mass murder. The prime suspect was a 15-year-old boy. The victims were his parents, sister, and grandparents. The youth was arrested the day after the homicides while cruising around locally in his parents' Mercedes. What type of kid is this?[3]

When youths kill today, adults ask why, just as they have for centuries.[4] The question, however, has become more complex since the mid-1980s because there really are two issues involved: Why are youths killing, and why are more youths killing today in the United States than in previous generations? This chapter synthesizes the literature on clinical and empirical findings related to youth homicide. Thereafter, it addresses factors operating today that appear to be contributing to the escalation in murders by youths.

YOUTHS WHO KILL: A SYNTHESIS OF THE LITERATURE

Many clinicians and researchers have examined cases of youths killing over the past 50 years in an effort to determine the causes of juvenile homicide. Two excellent critiques of the literature by University of Virginia professor Dewey Cornell and State University of New York at Buffalo professor Charles Patrick Ewing have been published in recent years.[5] Both scholars cited a number of methodological problems with most of the available studies on juvenile homicide and suggested that reported findings be viewed with caution.

Much of the difficulty with this literature stems from the fact that most published accounts of young killers consist of case studies. The cases reported often were drawn from psychiatric populations referred to the authors for evaluation and/or treatment after the youths committed homicides. The conclusions drawn from these cases, although interesting and suggestive, cannot provide us with precise explanations regarding why youths kill because it is unknown to what extent the youths examined are typical of the population of juvenile murderers. In addition, in the absence of control groups of any type, it is unknown in what ways these young killers differ from nonviolent juvenile offenders, violent juvenile offenders who do not kill, and juveniles with no prior records.

Research on juvenile murderers has been primarily descriptive. Not surprisingly, psychogenic explanations (e.g., mental illness, defective intelligence, childhood trauma) have largely predominated in the literature given the professional backgrounds of many of the authors. Biopsychological explanations (e.g., neurological impairments, brain injury) have been investigated by some scientists. Data on important sociological variables (e.g., family constellation, gang involvement, drug and alcohol use, participation in other antisocial behavior, peer associations) have been reported by some researchers. However, sociological theories of criminal behavior and crime (e.g., strain/anomie, subcultural, social control, labeling, conflict, and radical theories)[6] have not been systematically investigated in the literature on youth homicide.

It is important to note that statements about juvenile murderers in the professional literature typically are about male adolescents who kill. Although some studies of adolescent homicide have included both females and males,[7] most research has focused on male adolescents because they comprise the overwhelming majority of juvenile homicide offenders.

Girls Who Kill

A few publications report case studies of girls who have murdered.[8] These studies reveal that girls are more likely than boys to kill family members and to use accomplices to effect these murders. Girls also are more likely to perform secondary roles when the killings are gang related or occur during the commission of a felony, such as robbery. Their accomplices generally are male. Pregnant, unmarried girls who kill their offspring at birth or shortly thereafter, by contrast, often appear to act alone. Girls' motives for murder are varied. Instrumental reasons include ending abuse meted out by an abusive parent, eliminating witnesses to a crime, and concealing a pregnancy. Expressive reasons include acting out psychological conflict or mental illness, supporting a boyfriend's activities, and demonstrating allegiance to gang members.[9]

Homicides Involving Young Children as Offenders

Research specifically investigating "little kids" who kill also has been sparse, partly because of its low incidence and the difficulty of obtaining access to these youths.[10]

The importance of distinguishing between preadolescents and adolescents in under-standing what motivates youths to kill and in designing effective treatment plans was recognized by clinicians as early as 1940.[11] However, subsequent investigators have not consistently used age as a criterion in selecting samples of youths who kill.[12] In one frequently cited report, for example, the young killers ranged in age from 3 to 16 years.[13]

Physically healthy children under 9 years of age who kill, in contrast to older youths, typically do not fully understand the concept of death.[14] They have great dif-ficulty in comprehending that their actions are irreversible.[15] Prepubescent children who kill often act impulsively and without clear goals in mind.[16] Preadolescent mur-derers also are more likely than older youths to kill in response to the unstated wishes of their parents.[17] In addition, the incidence of severe conflict[18] or severe mental ill-ness[19] tends to be higher among younger children who kill than among their adolescent counterparts. Adolescent killers are more likely to kill because of the lifestyles that they have embraced or in response to situational or environmental constraints that they believe to be placed on them.[20]

Case Study Research Pertaining to Adolescent Murderers

The literature cited here highlights findings from studies of youths who typically ranged from 12 to 17 years of age, although some research included adolescents in their late teens. In recognition of reporting practices in the professional literature, the terms *juvenile* and *adolescent* are treated as equivalent terms in the discussion that follows. Similarly, the terms *murder* and *homicide* are used synonymously, although the in-tended legal meaning is that of murder. Accordingly, terms such as *juvenile homicide offender*, *adolescent murderer*, and *young killer* are used interchangeably throughout the remainder of this chapter.

The following subsections address various areas covered in case studies of adoles-cent murderers. It is important to keep in mind the caveats discussed previously re-garding the shortcomings of this body of literature.

Psychological Disorder and Youth Homicide

Several scholars also have synthesized existing scientific publications relating to various types of juvenile homicide offenders,[21] including youths who commit sexual murders.[22] Much of the literature, particularly during the 1940s, 1950s, 1960s, and 1970s, suggested that psychodynamic factors propelled youths to kill.[23] These factors included impaired ego development, unresolved Oedipal and dependency needs, dis-placed anger, the ability to dehumanize the victim, and narcissistic deficits.[24]

Many studies have investigated the extent of severe psychopathology such as psy-chosis, organic brain disease, and neurological impairments.[25] The findings, particularly with respect to the presence of psychosis among juvenile homicide offenders, are mixed and might be the result of how the samples were generated. Individuals who are diag-nosed as psychotic have lost touch with reality, often experience hallucinations (seeing or hearing things that are not occurring) and delusions (bizarre beliefs), and behave in-appropriately. Most studies report that juvenile homicide offenders rarely are psy-chotic.[26] Some studies, however, do posit a high incidence of psychosis,[27] or episodic psychotic symptomatology,[28] and other serious mental illness such as mood disorders.[29]

Several case reports have suggested that young killers suffered from brief psychotic episodes that remitted spontaneously after the homicides.[30] This phenomenon, initially introduced by renowned psychiatrist Karl Menninger and one of his colleagues 40 years ago, is known as "episodic dyscontrol syndrome" and is characterized by incidents of severe loss of impulse control in individuals with impaired ego development.[31] Diagnosing psychosis in homicide offenders who kill impulsively, brutally, and apparently senselessly, in the absence of clear psychotic symptoms, has been strongly challenged by some of the leading experts on juvenile homicide.[32]

Examination of the literature indicates that there is considerable variation in diagnoses given to adolescent murderers both within[33] and across studies. Personality disorders and conduct disorders rank among the more common diagnoses.[34] Attention-Deficit/Hyperactivity Disorder also has been noted with some frequency.[35]

Neurological Impairment and Youth Homicide

Significant disagreement also exists with respect to the prevalence of neurological problems in juvenile killers,[36] which may be partly due to differences in assessment and reporting practices used by various clinicians.[37] Neurological impairment may be indicated by brain or severe head injuries, past or present seizure disorders, abnormal head circumferences or electroencephalogram (EEG) findings, soft neurological signs, and deficits on neurological testing.[38] Several researchers have found significant neurological impairment or abnormalities among young killers,[39] particularly those on death row.[40] Others have maintained that neurological difficulties are absent or rare among the juvenile murderers assessed in their studies.[41]

The Intelligence of Young Homicide Offenders

The findings with respect to intelligence also are mixed. Several studies have reported that there were mentally retarded youths (IQ score below 70) among their samples of adolescent homicide offenders.[42] However, there is a consensus across many studies that few young killers are mentally retarded.[43]

By contrast, there is disagreement regarding the intelligence of the majority of young killers.[44] Some researchers have reported that the average IQ scores of the juvenile homicide offenders in their samples were in the below-average range (70-99).[45] Others, however, have found that the IQ scores typically were in the above-average range (100-129).[46]

The literature on juvenile homicide offenders indicates that, regardless of intelligence potential, many struggle in educational settings. As a group, they tend to perform poorly academically,[47] have cognitive and language deficits,[48] experience severe educational difficulties,[49] suffer from learning disabilities,[50] and engage in disruptive behavior in the classroom.[51]

Home Environments of Youths Who Murder

Case studies of adolescents who killed biological parents and stepparents have appeared far more often in the professional literature than have case studies of other types of juvenile homicide offenders.[52] These studies have indicated that youths who killed parents or stepparents, particularly fathers or stepfathers, typically were raised in homes where child abuse, spouse abuse, and parental chemical dependency were common.[53] Recent research on the "adopted child syndrome" suggests that adopted youths who kill their adopted fathers might be driven by other psychodynamic factors including unresolved loss, extreme dissociation of rage, hypersensitivity to rejection, and confusion about their identity.[54]

With few exceptions,[55] published research and case studies have reported that the majority of adolescent homicide offenders are raised in broken homes.[56] Recent studies have suggested that the majority are likely to come from criminally violent families.[57] Parental alcoholism, mental illness, and other indicators of parental psychopathology are commonly found in the histories of juvenile murderers.[58] Child maltreatment and spouse abuse also are encountered repeatedly in the homes of adolescent homicide offenders.[59] Young killers as a group,[60] and youths who kill parents in particular,[61] frequently have witnessed one parent, typically the mother, being abused by the other parental figure. Juvenile murderers,[62] especially adolescent parricide offenders,[63] often have been physically abused. Sexual abuse also has been documented in the lives of juvenile murderers,[64] including those who kill parents.[65]

Involvement in Other Antisocial Behavior

Juvenile homicide offenders typically had engaged in several types of deviant behavior prior to committing homicide.[66] Several studies have reported that the majority of adolescent murderers have had prior arrest or offense histories.[67] Findings regarding whether young killers have had lengthy histories of fighting and other violent or antisocial behavior have been mixed. Some researchers have reported extensive antisocial behavior,[68] others have uncovered little or none,[69] and still others have found that previous delinquency varied significantly by the type of juvenile homicide offender[70] or the nature of the relationship between the offender and victim.[71] Gang participation also has been found among juvenile homicide offenders.[72]

Substance Abuse

The literature on substance abuse among juvenile homicide offenders has been sparse.[73] Examination of available studies reveals that both the percentages of juvenile homicide offenders who reported abusing substances and the percentages of those who indicated that they were "high" at the time of the murder have increased over the past 20 to 30 years.[74] Earlier studies indicated that between 20% and 25% of young killers abused alcohol or drugs.[75] Cornell, Benedek, and Benedek reported in 1987 that more than 70% of the 72 juvenile murderers in their Michigan sample reportedly drank alcohol or used drugs.[76] Zagar and his colleagues compared alcohol abuse among 101 juvenile murderers to that among 101 matched nonviolent delinquents in Cook County, Illinois. They reported in 1990 that juvenile murderers were significantly more likely to abuse alcohol than were those in the control group (45% vs. 28%).[77] Myers and Kemph reported in 1990 that half of the 14 homicidal youths in their study were diagnosed as substance dependent.[78] In a later study of 18 juvenile murderers, Myers and Scott found that 50% were substance dependent.[79] Psychiatrist Susan Bailey reported in 1996 that, of the 20 juvenile murderers in the United Kingdom whom she treated, 75% abused alcohol and 35% abused drugs.[80] Researchers in Finland reported in 1997 that 10 of the 13 young homicide offenders in their study were dependent on alcohol.[81]

Sorrells' study of juvenile murderers in California, published in 1977, indicated that approximately 25% (8 of 31) of juvenile homicide offenders were under the influence of drugs and/or alcohol at the time of the homicidal event.[82] Cornell et al. noted 10 years later that more than 50% (38 of 72) of their sample of juvenile killers had killed while they were intoxicated.[83] A U.S. Department of Justice study, also published in 1987, indicated that 42.5% of juvenile murderers were under the influence of alcohol, drugs, or both at the time of the incident.[84]

Fendrich and his colleagues compared substance involvement among 16- and 17-year-old juvenile murderers to that among four different age groups of adult murderers incarcerated in New York State prisons in a 1995 publication. The groups were compared in terms of regular lifetime use, substance use during the week preceding the homicide, and at the time of the crime. In general, the juvenile murderers had relatively "lighter" use and lower levels of drug involvement than did adults in the sample. Of the 16 juvenile homicide offenders, 8 indicated that they were "substance affected" (intoxicated, crashing, or sick or in need of a substance) at the time of the murder. Of these 8 offenders, 5 acknowledged using alcohol and 3 acknowledged using marijuana. Only 3 young killers reported using cocaine, heroin, or psychedelics. The research team cautioned against concluding that substance use does not present a special risk for violent, homicidal behavior among juveniles.[85]

> Analysis of respondent substance use attribution patterns suggests that when 16- [and] 17-year-old perpetrators use substances, the substances they use tend to have consid - erably more lethal effects than they do on perpetrators in older age groups. Thus, our study suggests that a focus on ingestion and involvement rates may underestimate the risk posed by substances for homicidal behavior among juveniles. [86]

Other Social Difficulties

Studies have indicated that a significant proportion of juvenile murderers do not attend school regularly[87] due to truancy,[88] dropping out, or expulsion.[89] Running away is a common response of adolescent parricide offenders.[90] Enuresis (bed-wetting)[91] and difficulties relating to peers[92] have been found in the histories of youths who kill.

Summary: A Case Study Portrait of Adolescents Who Kill

Given the methodological problems in the literature cited earlier, generalizations from many of these studies to the population of juvenile murderers must be made with caution. However, some consensus among the studies reported suggests that a portrait of the typical adolescent murderer can be drawn. Before sketching his profile, it is important to note that many youths who possess these characteristics do not commit murder. With this caveat in mind, available data suggest that today's young killer tends to be a male who is unlikely to be psychotic or mentally retarded, to do well in school, or to come from a home in which his biological parents live together in a healthy and peaceful relationship. Rather, he is likely to have experienced or been exposed to violence in his home and to have a prior arrest record. He is increasingly more likely to use or abuse drugs and alcohol as compared to juvenile homicide offenders in the past.

Empirical Studies of Juvenile Homicide Offenders

Well-designed empirical studies of juvenile murderers that attempt to compensate for the weaknesses of case studies do exist. However, they are relatively few in number and typically also suffer from methodological limitations related particularly to sample selection and size. Hence, generalizations from these studies also must be made with caution.

In one study, for example, 71 adolescent homicide offenders were matched with 71 nonviolent delinquents with respect to age, race, gender, and socioeconomic class. Both groups were selected from a group of 1,956 juveniles referred for evaluation by the juvenile court. The sample of juvenile murderers represented all youths convicted of homicide in the referral sample. The control group was a subset of the larger sample. Accordingly, the samples were retrospective, were nonrandom, and reflected the selection bias in the referral and adjudication process.

Both groups were assessed on numerous educational, psychiatric/psychological, social, and physical dimensions. Four significant differences were found between the two groups. Compared to nonviolent delinquents, juvenile homicide offenders were more likely to come from criminally violent families, to participate in gangs, to have severe educational deficits, and to abuse alcohol.[93] The same results were obtained when the study was repeated using different groups of juveniles obtained and matched in the same way.[94]

Dorothy Otnow Lewis, a psychiatrist at the New York University School of Medicine, and her colleagues also have conducted several investigations of juvenile homicide offenders.[95] Their research, although groundbreaking, often has consisted of small samples of cases referred to the senior author and her team for evaluation. In one study, Lewis and her colleagues compared 13 juvenile murderers evaluated after the homicides to 14 violent delinquents and 18 nonviolent youths. All three groups were incarcerated at the time of the evaluation and were compared with respect to a set of neurological, psychiatric, psychological, and social variables. Analyses revealed that the adolescent homicide offenders did not differ from violent delinquents. However, the juvenile murderers were significantly more likely than the nonviolent delinquents to be neuropsychiatrically impaired, to have been raised in violent homes, and to have been physically abused.[96]

A recently published Finnish study was similarly designed to assess whether selected risk factors would differentiate young murderers from other violent offenders and nonviolent youths. Sample participants were recruited from among all Finnish male prisoners born after a certain year and ranged in age from 18 to 22 years at the time of the study. The pool of volunteers was asked to indicate their prior criminal involvements on a questionnaire. The participants were then divided into groups from which study participants were randomly chosen. The groups were small; only 13 had committed murder or attempted to do so, 13 had committed less serious assaults, and 11 reported no violent crimes in their offending histories. Several reliable differences were found. Members of the homicide group were significantly more likely to admit having been cruel to animals than were members of the other two groups. The age at which members in the murderer group began abusing alcohol was significantly younger than that among those in the nonviolent group. Relative to the nonviolent offenders, the homicide offenders were significantly more likely to have been physically abused and dependent on harder drugs such as cocaine, speed, stimulants, and tranquilizers. Although other differences were observable among the groups, the findings did not reach significance, which could have been due to the small sample sizes.[97]

Other empirical studies have looked for distinguishing characteristics among youths who commit murder.[98] Corder and her colleagues compared 10 youths charged with killing parents to 10 youths charged with killing other relatives or close acquaintances and 10 youths charged with killing strangers. In addition to the groups being small in size, they were not randomly generated. Individuals in the three groups had been sent to the hospital for evaluation and were matched with one another by age, gender, intelligence, socioeconomic status, and date of hospital admission. The three groups differed significantly from one another on several variables. Those who killed parents, for example, were significantly more likely than those who killed others to have been physically abused, to have come from homes in which their mothers were beaten by their fathers, and to have amnesia for the murders.[99]

Several other researchers, as highlighted earlier, have proposed typologies of youths who kill. Attempts to validate typologies of juvenile homicide offenders, however, often have failed because they consisted of small samples or lacked control groups. By contrast, the typology proposed by Cornell, Benedek, and Benedek has shown remarkable promise. This scheme classifies juvenile homicide offenders into three categories based on circumstances of the offense: psychotic (youths who had symptoms of severe mental illness such as hallucinations or delusions), conflict (youths who were engaged in an argument or dispute with the victim when the killing occurred), and crime (youths who killed during the commission of another felony, such as rape or robbery).

The Cornell et al. typology was tested using 72 juveniles charged with murder and a control group of 35 adolescents charged with larceny. Both groups were referred for pretrial evaluation and were assessed with respect to eight composite categories: family dysfunction, school adjustment, childhood problems, violence history, delinquent behavior, substance abuse, psychiatric problems, and stressful life events prior to the offense.[100] Based on information pertaining to the offense, 7% of the juvenile homicide offenders were assigned to the psychotic subgroup, 42% to the conflict subgroup, and 51% to the crime subgroup.

Analyses revealed significant differences on all eight composite categories between the homicide group and the larceny group. In addition, a number of significant differences emerged among the three subgroups of juvenile homicide offenders. Psychotic homicide offenders were significantly more likely to score higher on the psychiatric history composite and lower on the index of criminal activity than were the nonpsychotic groups. Relative to the conflict group, the crime group scored significantly higher on school adjustment problems, substance abuse, and criminal activity and scored lower on stressful life events. This study provided preliminary support that juvenile homicide offenders could be distinguished from other groups of offenders and from one another. The authors correctly advised that further studies were needed to determine whether the differences among the homicide subgroups will hold up when group assignment is not determined by offense circumstances.[101]

Subsequent research has found significant differences between the crime and conflict groups. The crime group youths had higher levels of psychopathology on the Minnesota Multiphasic Personality Inventory (an objective measure of personality)[102] than did the conflict group youths. The crime group killers also had more serious histories of substance abuse and prior delinquent behavior than did the conflict group murderers.[103] The crime group adolescents were more likely to act with others and to be intoxicated on drugs at the time of the murder than were the conflict group youths. The crime group homicide offenders also showed poorer object differentiation and more of a victim orientation in responses to the Rorschach (a projective measure of personality[104]) than did their conflict group counterparts. The Rorschach responses suggest that crime group youths are more likely to dehumanize other people, to respond violently when frustrated, and to have more severe developmental deficits than are conflict group youths.[105]

Distinctions also emerged within the conflict group between youths who murdered parents and those who killed other victims, none of whom were family members. Juvenile parricide offenders scored lower on school adjustment problems and prior delinquent history than did those who killed others, but the former were higher on a family dysfunction measure. Cornell's findings with respect to youths who kill parents are similar to conclusions reached in clinical case studies and provide further empirical support that these youths might represent a distinct type of homicide offender.[106]

Myers and his colleagues classified 25 juvenile homicide offenders using the *Crime Classification Manual* (CCM) of the Federal Bureau of Investigation (FBI). The murderers involved in their study included children and adolescents. The sample size was too small to test differences among the four categories of motives in the *CCM*. Accordingly, the cases were classified into only two categories: "criminal enterprise" and "personal crime."[107]

Important findings from the Myers et al. study included characteristics common to the young killers as well as those that differentiated the two groups from each other. A total of 10 profile characteristics applied to more than 70% of the total sample. These consisted of family dysfunction, previous violent acts toward others, disruptive behavior disorder, failed at least one grade, emotional abuse by family member, family violence, prior arrests, learning disabilities, weapon of choice, and psychotic symptoms.[108]

Statistical analyses compared the two crime classification groups with respect to psychiatric diagnoses, psychotic symptoms, biopsychosocial variables, and crime characteristics. Statistically significant differences were found between the criminal enterprise and personal crime groups with respect to victim age, victim relationship, and physical abuse. Youths in the criminal enterprise group were more likely than those in the personal crime group to have been abused and to have killed an adult or elderly victim whom they did not know. Personal crime group murderers tended to select child or adolescent victims whom they knew.[109]

FACTORS CONTRIBUTING TO THE RISE IN JUVENILE HOMICIDE

The existent literature on juvenile homicide rarely addresses the factors fueling the recent dramatic rise in murders by juveniles. Several reasons account for the gap. Most of the studies of adolescent murderers were published prior to 1990. These research efforts typically were restricted to the analysis of individual and family characteristics, which were relatively easy to obtain and verify. These studies were not designed to measure many sociological variables of interest and, therefore, did not address the phenomenon of juvenile homicide within the context of broad societal changes that have occurred during the past several decades.

TABLE 2.1   Ingredients for Juvenile Murder in the 1990s

Situational factors	Child abuse
	Child neglect
	Absence of positive male role models
Societal influences	Crisis in leadership and lack of heroes
	Witnessing violence
Resource availability	Access to guns
	Involvement in alcohol and drugs
	Poverty and lack of resources
Personality characteristics	Low self-esteem
	Inability to deal with strong negative feelings
	Boredom and nothing constructive to do
	Poor judgment
	Prejudice and hatred
Cumulative effect	Little or nothing left to lose
	Biological connection

SOURCE: Heide 1997b. Copyright John Wiley & Sons Ltd. Reproduced with permission.

This section attempts to supplement the existing literature on young murderers with a perspective that offers explanations for the shifts to more juveniles being involved in acts of homicide in the United States.[110] I am convinced, after evaluating approximately 90 adolescents involved in murder, that many factors often act in concert when youths kill. Some of these factors are more global and difficult to measure in the individual case, yet their effects on a society and on a generation of children growing up today are more visible. As depicted in Table 2.1, these variables can be grouped into five main categories: situational factors, societal influences, resource availability, personality characteristics, and their cumulative effects.

I present these 15 variables in the hope that the discussion sheds light on why youths today are more likely to kill than in prior years and leads to further research into these factors and their interactive effects. The case commentaries that follow each of the seven case studies in Part II focus on the influence and interaction of these variables in the lives of young killers whose stories are told. Suggestions made in Part III with respect to intervention and prevention are based on finding solutions to the problems highlighted in the following.

Situational Factors

Many of today's youths grow up in families that foster violent and destructive behaviors. Despite a decrease in the number of young Americans, reports of *child abuse* have increased greatly in recent years.[111] Commentators often ask whether the increase is due to a genuine increase in the incidence of abuse or merely reflects an increase in its reporting. Social services personnel and child abuse experts typically reply that some of the increase might be due to the greater willingness of people to report various types of abuse today than in the past. However, they maintain that it is highly unlikely that, given the magnitude of the difference, changes in reporting practices can account for most of the increase. Figures released by the U.S. Advisory Board on Child Abuse and Neglect in 1993, for example, indicated that reported cases of child abuse and neglect had increased from 60,000 in 1973 to more than 3 million cases in 1993.[112]

Although the majority of children who are victims or witnesses of family violence do not grow up to victimize others,[113] a growing body of research indicates that these children are at greater risk of engaging in delinquent behavior. Retrospective studies of violent adolescents and young killers repeatedly have found child abuse, neglect, and exposure to parental violence in their backgrounds.[114]

Well-controlled and extensive research conducted in recent years by several professors at the State University of New York at Albany has helped to clarify the nature of the relationship of child maltreatment to delinquency. These studies were prospective by design, meaning that individuals were selected for reasons other than having delinquent histories, and the individuals were followed for several years to determine the extent of their subsequent involvement in criminal or delinquent behavior. Cathy Spatz Widom used official records to compare the criminal and delinquent involvement of maltreated youths to that of a matched group of nonmaltreated youths. She found that youths who were abused and neglected were at higher risk of becoming juvenile delinquents or adult criminals and of engaging in violent criminal behavior. In comparison to youths with no histories of child maltreatment, abused and neglected children committed significantly more offenses, began their delinquent careers earlier, and had a higher percentage of individuals charged with five or more offenses.[115] Those who had been victimized as children also were significantly more likely to receive a diagnosis of antisocial personality disorder (persistent pattern of violating the rights of others) as adults than were those in the control group, even after demographic characteristics and arrest history were taken into account.[116]

Carolyn Smith and Terence Thornberry investigated the relationship of child maltreatment to involvement in delinquency among students attending public schools in Rochester, New York. Unlike other prospective studies, this research included self-reported measures of delinquency as well as official records. According to the study design, students from the 7th or 8th grades were selected in such a way as to overrepresent those who were at higher risk of delinquency and drug involvement, and these youths were followed over time. Using official measures of delinquency, Smith and Thornberry replicated Widom's findings. More important, they found that "more serious forms of self-reported delinquency, including violent, serious, and moderate forms of delinquency,"[117] were related to child maltreatment. Subsequent analyses confirmed that these results were genuine and not due to factors such as race/ethnicity, gender, socioeconomic class, family structure, or mobility. This study also provided preliminary support that experiencing more extensive childhood maltreatment was related to more serious forms of delinquency.[118]

There is a growing body of evidence that indicates that even young children are traumatized by exposure to parental violence.[119] Research also has indicated that youths' witnessing of parental violence is associated with subsequent violent behavior,[120] particularly by men toward their spouses or partners.[121] Smith and Thornberry found that children who witnessed and experienced many violent acts in their homes (e.g., child abuse, spouse abuse, family conflict) were twice as likely to engage in violent acts themselves.[122]

TABLE 2.2 Definitions of Abuse and Neglect

Type of Maltreatment	Definition
Physical abuse	Inflicted physical injury or the attempt to inflict physical injury or pain that is indicative of the unresolved needs of the aggressor inappropriately expressed
Sexual abuse	Children can be overtly or covertly sexually abused or forcibly raped by parents, guardians, or other adults. *Overt sexual abuse* includes behaviors that involve direct physical contact between the victim and the offender (e.g., fondling, oral or anal sex, vaginal intercourse, simulated intercourse). *Covert sexual abuse* consists of exposing a child to sexual issues that are age inappropriate or raising a child in an environment that is sexually saturated or provocative (e.g., a parent masturbating in front of a child, a neighbor sharing pornography with a child). As illustrated in Table 2.3, the motivational dynamics involved in overt sexual abuse are conceptually distinct from those involved in *forcible rape*.
Verbal abuse	Words spoken to a child, or remarks made in the child's presence about the child, that either are designed to damage the child's concept of self or would reasonably be expected to undermine a child's sense of competency or self-esteem
Psychological abuse	Words and behaviors that undermine or would reasonably be expected to undermine a child's sense of self, competence, and safety in the world
Physical neglect	The failure of parents or guardians to provide food, clothing, a safe environment, and adequate supervision for their children
Medical neglect	The failure of parents or guardians to provide medical care and treatment for their children
Emotional neglect	Encompasses the failure of parents or guardians to meet their children's emotional needs. Children have needs to be loved, supported, and encouraged to develop a sense of themselves as valuable individuals and to obtain basic trust toward others.
Emotional incest	A parent or guardian aligns with a child in a spouse-type role. As a result, the child nurtures the parent, acts as the parent's confidant, assumes parental chores and responsibilities, and occasionally protects the parent.

SOURCE: Definitions are from Heide 1992/1995.

Some children who are physically, sexually, verbally, and psychologically abused kill the abusive parents, who often have alcohol or other drug problems.[123] Typically, these adolescents have been victims of the types of abuse and neglect illustrated in Tables 2.2 and 2.3. They kill because they are afraid or see no other way in which to escape their situations or to end the abuse. Patty was a 17-year-old girl who had been physically, verbally, and psychologically abused by her father for years. In addition, she was sexually abused and forcibly raped by him. After being denied help by the adult figures in her life and failing in earlier attempts to run away and to kill herself, Patty believed that she had no recourse.[124] Early one morning while her father slept, she fired a bullet into his head.

TABLE 2.3 Overt Sexual Abuse Distinguished From Forcible Rape

Overt Sexual Abuse	Forcible Rape
Often characterized by physical gentleness on the part of the adult	Characterized by brute force
Reflects inadequacy of the adult[a]	Reflects rage of the adult
The adult looks to the child to fulfull his needs for nurturance, love, and intimacy	The adult selects the child to vent his anger and to demonstrate his power
The adult does not intend or desire to hurt the child physically or psychologically	The adult intends and desires to hurt and control the child
The child might not be fearful	The child is likely to be terrified

SOURCE: Reprinted with permission, K. M. Heide, copyright, *Why Kids Kill Parents* (Ohio State University Press, 1992; Sage, 1995).

a. The adult chooses the child because the adult's primary orientation is to children (Groth's *fixated pedophile*) or because the adult is under a great deal of stress, loses control, or evinces poor judgment (Groth's *regressed pedophile*). See Burgess et al. 1978.

Living in households like Patty's, many abused youths fail to bond with others. These adolescents often lack attachments to teachers and conventional peers as well as to parents. Consequently, they do not develop the values, empathy, and self-concept that fosters self-control and could inhibit them from killing others.[125] Malcolm, whose story is told in Part II, had been sexually abused and physically, medically, and emotionally neglected from the time he was a child. His father abandoned him as an infant, and his alcoholic mother died when he was 7 years old. At age 12, he was living on the streets, making his living by taking what he wanted by threat or force. I first met Malcolm at age 15 after he had been charged with two counts of murder and two counts of attempted murder, each count resulting from a separate incident.

Rather than being passively indifferent toward the lives of others, some abused youths are angry and in pain and vent their rage through destruction and violence.[126] One of my clients, José, was sentenced to prison for a murder he committed at 18 years of age. The killing was especially brutal; the victim was beaten beyond recognition. The blows to the victim's skull were so severe that brain tissue was found in several areas of the apartment. José committed the crime with the assistance of three friends. The four boys all told me that it was José's idea to commit the murder. José acknowledged a long history of violence toward others. He explained that he wanted to hurt others as he had been hurt.

Neglect frequently accompanies abuse, but it also can exist independently, often manifesting itself as the common failure of parents to supervise their children.[127] During the past 25 years, several significant changes in family structures have contributed to decreasing levels of child supervision and have placed adolescents at greater risk of getting into serious trouble.

As one indicator, the number of children born to unmarried mothers has nearly tripled, from 398,700 in 1970 to 1,165,384 in 1990. Over these two decades, dramatic increases in illegitimate births were apparent among both White and Black women. For every 1,000 births by White women, the number who were born to unmarried women rose from 57 in 1970 to 201 in 1990. The comparable figures for births to Black unmarried women were 376 in 1970 and 652 in 1990.[128]

During the same period, the divorce rate[129] and percentage of single-parent households[130] also increased. Today, more than 50% of all marriages end in divorce. The Carnegie Council on Adolescent Development noted in its concluding report that more than 50% of all children in the United States in the mid-1990s will be raised for at least part of their childhood and adolescent years in single-parent households, a far greater percentage than that of a few decades ago. Almost half of the adolescent children of married parents will experience their parents divorcing or remarrying by 16 years of age.[131]

In addition to the rising number of children born to single mothers, the increasing divorce rate, and the increasing percentage of single-parent families, the number of mothers in the workforce also has increased significantly during the past two decades. In 1970, 30% of married women with children under 6 years of age were gainfully employed; in 1990, 59% of women in this category were working. The percentage of married women with children ages 6 to 17 who were working rose from 49% in 1970 to 74% in 1990. Figures for single mothers with children are not available for 1970 to permit comparisons across the two decades. However, 1990 data indicate that among single mothers, 49% with children under age 6 and 70% with children ages 6 to 17 were working.[132] Increases in the percentages of working wives with children were evident among both White and Black women over the past two decades.[133]

Given these familial changes, the time that youths spend with their parents and the amount of supervision and guidance that they receive have decreased significantly during the past several decades.[134] Experts have estimated that children in the 1990s have lost an average of 10 to 12 hours per week of parental time compared to children in 1960.[135] In 1970, 37% of families with children under 18 years of age lacked full-time parental supervision; in 1992, the percentage had risen to 57%.[136]

Many of the adolescent homicide offenders I examine are not in school during the day and are out late at night. Their parents do not know where they are, in what activities they are involved, or with whom they are associating.

Often accompanying abuse or lack of supervision is the *absence of positive male role models*. In some cases, the identities or whereabouts of fathers are unknown. In others, fathers are present only to be uninvolved, violent, or both. Boys need same-sex role models to define themselves as male. When fathers are absent, young males are more likely to exaggerate their purported masculinity.[137]

Mothers, although typically loved and often revered by their sons, all too frequently cannot control their sons' behavior. Case 1004 told me, for example, that his mother was "a nice lady. . . . She took care of me when I was out there, ya know, but I would avoid every word she was sayin', that why I'm in here now. I wouldn't do what she say." Case 1005 related that his mother was "a very tiny young lady, but I love her more than anything, you know, and like, she give me anything I want. I don't have to go out and do wrong, I just did it. She give me anything. She try to tell me what good and what bad for me. But, I just, I didn't listen."

Societal Influences

On a larger scale, youths who kill today also are affected by our country's *crisis in leadership and lack of heroes*. In the past, U.S. presidents, successful entertainers, and legendary sports figures were presented to the youth of America as people to emulate. In the 1990s, the personal ethics and behavior of many of these individuals have been seriously questioned. Government leaders who break campaign promises and involve themselves in money and sex scandals have shown that many politicians today deny responsibility for their behavior and decisions. When leaders of our country no longer are expected to keep their word and are not held accountable, some youths become cynical about their futures. When police officers are viewed on nationwide television repeatedly beating an African American in their custody and are proven to be lying on the witness stand in the case of another African American man, adolescents from minority groups increasingly lose faith in a criminal justice system that is supposed to protect them and dispense equal justice. When world-class boxing champion Mike Tyson and rappers such as Snoop Doggy Dog[138] are accused of violent criminal acts, some adolescents feel free to adopt similar courses of behavior.

Adolescent deviance and decreased inhibitions to violence also have been correlated to *witnessing violence*.[139] Although authorities debate whether some individuals are more "susceptible" to engaging in violence after repeated viewings due to personality, biological, or environmental factors, two facts are beyond dispute. First, over the past two decades, films and television shows, including the evening news, have become more and more violent.[140] Second, the American public has become increasingly concerned about the effects of violent programming on people in general and on the young in particular.[141]

Experts estimate that the average youth in the United States watches 45 violent acts on television *every day*, with most of them committed with handguns.[142] A study conducted by the American Psychological Association (APA) confirmed that children who view 2 to 4 hours of television violence daily will witness 8,000 murders and 100,000 other acts of violence before finishing elementary school.[143] The APA Commission on Violence and Youth estimated further that if the viewing period is extended to the late teens, these youths will have observed about 200,000 violent acts. The commission cautioned that these figures might be even higher for youths who watch cable programs and R-rated movies on home videocassette recorders.[144]

An impressive body of research spanning more than 30 years indicates that exposure to television violence is related to violent behavior.[145] For example, research shows that aggressive children who have difficulty in school and in relating to peers tend to watch more television.[146] Studies reveal that even limited exposure to violent pornographic movies can lower the inhibitions of psychologically normal adults to engage in aggressive behavior.[147] Researchers in the physical and social sciences agree that repeated exposure to a stimulus results in individuals' becoming habituated to that stimulus. When habituation occurs to a violent stimulus, for example, more intense violent behaviors are needed for the viewers' bodies to react and to register physiological indicators of distress.[148]

Perhaps even more troubling than the thousands of children watching violent programs are the scores of youths who see violence firsthand in their neighborhoods, schools, and homes.[149] The exposure to violence among inner-city youths is particularly alarming.[150] In 1992, Bell and Jenkins surveyed 203 African American students in a public high school in an inner-city Chicago community. Four out of five of these students qualified for some type of public assistance. The area in which the school was located consistently had one of the highest homicide rates and ranked third in homicides during the year in which the study was conducted. As depicted in Table 2.4, 43% reported that they had seen a killing and 59% reported that someone close to them had been killed. The percentages of children who reported exposure to shootings were

TABLE 2.4 Inner-City Chicago High School Students' Reported Experiences Regarding Violence (*N* = 203)

Event	Percentage Reported
Witnessing violence	
Seeing a killing	43.0
Seeing a shooting	61.0
Seeing a stabbing	47.0
Experiencing violence	
Being shot	6.0
Being stabbed	8.5
Being raped	7.0
Being shot at in their lifetime	43.0
Knowledge of close other's violent victimizations	
Close other being killed	59.0
Close other being shot	65.5
Close other being stabbed	45.0
Close other being raped	43.0

SOURCE: Data excerpted from Bell and Jenkins 1994.

even higher, as 61% had seen a shooting, 66% knew that someone who was close to them had been shot, and 48% had been shot at themselves.[151]

To many children and teens, the world is a violent place. This image is particularly extolled in violent videogames and in the music known as "gangsta rap." Rappers (e.g., Ice-T, Spice 1, and Geto Boys) sing about robbing, killing, and raping, which they maintain is part of everyday life in "the hood" for low-income members of society, particularly African Americans. The words in gangsta rap music, similar to the scenes in televised violence, would appear likely to have a disinhibiting and desensitizing effect on those who listen to them repeatedly. Although the link between gangsta rap music and violence has not been proven, a recent study provided some evidence that misogynous (hateful toward women, hate-filled) rap music was related to sexually aggressive behavior against women by men.[152] In several of my recent cases, violent music lyrics appeared to provide the additional impetus needed for unbonded youths to kill.[153]

Most of the inner-city young homicide offenders whom I have evaluated viewed violence as part of everyday life. They carried guns and were prepared to use them. Case 1002 explained that he brought a gun with him on the day of the homicidal event because "you see, that's a real rough neighborhood, and it was rougher than the neighborhood I stayed in. You know, if you don't have a gun around there, something is able to be killed. So I had to bring a gun with me that day."

Life in the project "was like really wild," Case 1005 maintained. There was "a lot of robbing and killing goin' on." People who lived there "growed up in the wild, a faster place, that all they know." Case 2014 stated that there was "a lot of violence" in his neighborhood, "a lot of crime every day, fighting, killing." Case 5030 remembered, "One time I was walking, sidewalk, I saw a man get busted in the head, man get shot. They don't want police come there. Whoever did it get away. I seen a lot of, I seen a lot of violence in my time."

Case 2008 explained that he got in trouble because he "found the wrong people, see them do something, then you want to do it." He indicated that watching people in his neighborhood shooting up or at each other had an effect on him. "I wanted to try it." When asked if the homicidal event was the first time he had ever shot at anybody, Case 2008 replied "no" and indicated that he had shot at people "often." He added, "I really wanted to scare them. . . . They play with me like that, too."

Resource Availability

Not only do our youths grow up in a world that encourages violence, but those in the United States are increasingly finding themselves surrounded with the tools that make acts of violence quick and easy.[154] Recent research has demonstrated that youth involvement in violence has been associated with the frequency of carrying a weapon.[155] Moreover, the increase in murders by juveniles in the United States in recent years has been tied directly to their use of firearms, particularly handguns.[156] Analyses by the FBI indicate that gun homicides by juveniles nearly tripled from 1983 to 1991. By contrast, murders by juveniles using other weapons declined during the same period. In 1976, 59% of young homicide offenders killed their victims with firearms. Approximately 15 years later, 78% selected firearms as their weapons of destruction.[157]

Carnegie-Mellon University professor Alfred Blumstein has argued that the increase in killings by juveniles is a result of the rapid growth in the crack markets in the mid-1980s. Juveniles who were recruited into illicit drug marketing armed themselves with guns for protection. Other juveniles in these communities, aware of what was happening, armed themselves for protection and for status reasons. Consequently, guns became more prevalent in the larger community. When guns are easily accessible, youths who often are impulsive and unskilled in conflict resolution might use them as a means of retaliation. The presence of firearms increases the likelihood that an act of lethal violence will occur under these circumstances.[158]

The majority of juvenile homicide offenders whom I see used *guns*, which were readily available to them, to kill their victims. At the time Case 1004 was arrested for murder and armed robbery, he was carrying three firearms that he had just gotten from a burglary. Case 1004 related, however, that he did not usually walk around on the street with a gun "on me, but I had some I can get. If I didn't have none, I can get some. I can get one or whatever from a brother or my friend." He explained that most of his friends carried guns "once in a while, they'll, like on a Friday night, they'll walk around with 'em, you know, in case something jumps off in the neighborhood." As illustrated in the following exchange, young killers frequently reported that guns were cheap and easy to get in their neighborhoods.

> *Heide:* Okay. How about guns? Were they easily accessible?
>
> *1002:* [laughs] Guns, most people had them. I'd go down the street and get me a soda with a gun.
>
> *Heide:* So you could get guns?
>
> *1002:* Yeah.
>
> *Heide:* Okay. Tell me, if you would, from what you know, from knowledge of the streets, what would a gun cost on the street?

1002: Depends on what kind of gun you're gonna get.

Heide: Okay. Well, give me some examples.

1002: You're talking about a gun at a store?

Heide: No, not a gun at a store.

1002: You're talking about a hot gun?

Heide: Yeah, something you could get on the street.

1002: If a junkie selling it, you could probably get it for about $25. If it's a good gun, it ain't no dude who smoke reefer or nothing, you know, he will probably charge you about $30 to $40. The most I'd ever seen a person sell a gun for would be $120.

Young killers whom I assessed often could provide specific information about the prices of specific types of hot guns. Case 1005 related that the going rate for a .22-caliber gun would depend. "If it [is] hot and is new, get about, some would sell it for $30 or $20. Cheap." For a .38-caliber pistol, "you could spend about $40 or $50." For a .357 Magnum, the cost would be "about, almost $80 or $100."

Many of these youths did not have the physical ability or the emotional detachment to use other weapons of destruction, such as knives or fists. At 12 years of age, Timmy, a boy from a middle-class family, decided that he was going to kill himself. He thought that he would kill his mother, whom he perceived as the person responsible for much of the unhappiness in his family, before killing himself. Although Timmy tried to get his brother to leave the home, his brother did not cooperate. Rather than postpone his plan, Timmy shot his brother with a .357 Magnum. When his mother arrived home, he shot her as well. Overcome by the sight of human carnage, Timmy could not manage to turn the gun on himself. Instead, he aborted his plan and called for help.

Most of the adolescents involved in felony homicides whom I have evaluated are using *alcohol and drugs*. These observations are consistent with findings from a growing number of studies of a substantial relationship between adolescent violence and substance abuse.[159] Interestingly, drug use surveys indicate that the rates of illicit drug use by adolescents, which had declined during the 1980s,[160] are again rising in the 1990s and are much higher than they were a generation ago. This increase has been observed among both younger and older adolescents.[161] The percentage of youths reporting past-month use of marijuana, stimulants, hallucinogens, or inhalants rose from 1991 through 1994.[162] A 1993-1994 survey of junior high (6th through 8th grades) and high school students (9th through 12th grades) conducted by the Parent Resource Institute for Drug Education found a strong link in both groups between use of alcohol and marijuana and several measures of violent behavior, including carrying a gun to school and threatening to harm another person.[163]

Although few of the young killers whom I have evaluated claim that alcohol or drugs caused them to commit murder, it is likely that chemical abuse affected their judgment about engaging in criminal activity and their perceptions during the homicidal event. In addition, it is highly probable, in light of prior research, that the use of alcohol and drugs by many adolescent murderers is "more a reflection of shared influences on a wide variety of deviant behavior than of any causal relationship."[164] Several researchers have found that various types of deviant or illegal behaviors are positively related to one another.[165]

Another teen I evaluated is Peter, a gentle boy who had a serious drug problem for which he had been hospitalized. Peter, whose case is presented in Part II, was diagnosed as having severe marijuana dependence and a history of alcohol and cocaine abuse. One day, after getting high on marijuana and possibly acid, Peter impulsively entered the home of an elderly man intending to steal his car. When the man momentarily appeared, Peter stabbed him with a knife he had picked up shortly before in the kitchen. Peter said that he "freaked out" after he saw the victim's blood. He left shortly thereafter in the victim's car and picked up some other kids to go joyriding. Although he knew what he did was wrong, the drugs helped Peter to forget about the homicide for a while.

Other than guns and drugs, the majority of the young killers whom I have met are *poor and lacking in resources*. This finding is, to some extent, reflective of the rising percentage of Americans under 18 years of age being raised in families with incomes below the poverty line.[166] The percentage of children living in poverty in the 1990s has increased as a by-product of the changes in family structure over the past two decades. The escalation in single-female-headed households occasioned by the rise in births to unwed females and in divorce has resulted in more children being raised in poverty.[167] Research indicates that about three out of four households headed by single females live in poverty at least some of the time, and that one third are chronically poor. As we approach the millennium, it appears that one out of every three children under age 6 lives below the poverty line.[168]

Many young killers are from lower-class areas where violent crimes are commonplace. Robbery and burglary provide a means to acquire money, drugs, and other goods as well as an opportunity for fun.[169] When asked how he could afford to buy drugs, for example, Case 5030 stated matter-of-factly that he was "stealing anything that I can get my hands on" from "anyplace."

Case 1002 reported that whenever he was "out there doing wrong," he was trying to help his mother. "Every time I go out and make money, you know, I would bring it to my momma. Tell her to keep the money. She know that it would be stolen or something, you know, and then my momma didn't like stolen money, you know, she would hardly take it." He related that he gave the money to his mother to help her with "bills, help her get some clothes, something she want, anything, food."

Personality Characteristics

Changes in the personality characteristics of youths over the past two or three decades are difficult to measure. Unlike the variables discussed under situational factors, societal influences, and resource availability, there are no indicators available that systematically chart differences in how youths today perceive the world and respond to it relative to their counterparts 20 or 30 years ago. On the basis of the preceding discussion, it seems fair to say that adolescents today in many ways encounter greater challenges at a younger age than did youths in the past. Many of these juveniles face these difficulties with parents who cope maladaptively themselves. Other youths confront problems alone. Some youths under such constraints fare well. Unfortunately, too many do poorly.

The adolescent homicide offenders whom I have evaluated generally lack a healthy self-concept. They have deficits in communication skills and decision-making ability.

The personalities of youths who kill almost always are marked by *low self-esteem*. They might appear tough and cool, but deep down they typically feel insecure and do not believe that they can succeed in conventional activities such as school, sports, and work. Johnny, who was sentenced to life in prison at 16 years of age, did not like violence. He was an obese youth who hung around with some "tough kids." He explained that he went along with their violent escapades, which eventually resulted in his charge of murder, because he "wanted to be somebody."

Another common trait of adolescents who kill is an *inability to deal with strong negative emotions* such as anger and jealousy. Many of these youths, particularly those who are unbonded, have low frustration tolerance (poor self-control) and a fragile self-concept. When wronged, they become consumed with rage and feel compelled to strike back.[170] In addressing "the young male syndrome" and homicide, professors Margo Wilson and Martin Daly of McMaster University noted, "The precipitating insult may appear petty, but it is usually a deliberate provocation (or is perceived to be), and hence constitutes a public challenge that cannot be shrugged off."[171]

To some male adolescents, nothing less than murder is considered an appropriate response. Derek shot a clerk in a convenience store because the man "dissed" him. Derek explained that he had entered the store, pointed the gun at the clerk, and demanded money. When the clerk allegedly laughed and tried to brush Derek's hand away, Derek fired directly into him.

The perceived affronts do not always come from strangers. Jerry, whose story is told in Part II, methodically planned the execution of his "best friend." The friend had gone out with Jerry's girlfriend, and Jerry believed that the friend "broke a rule" and deserved to die.

Other youths are more *bored* than angry. Engaging in violent behavior becomes a way in which to amuse themselves and pass the time.

Heide: You said that you felt bored a lot in here [prison]. . . . When you were bored on the outside, what did you do?

2008: Sit in the house and listen to music.

Heide: And that would help? [Case 2008 nods in agreement.] Did you ever just go and smash something because you felt so bored and felt like doing something?

2008: I ain't gonna smash something, but just shoot through it.

Heide: You'd shoot, just go out and shoot, because you were bored, kind of have an effect on something? [Case 2008 nods affirmatively.] How often did you do that?

2008: Every time I see a dog, I used to shoot after it and cats.

Heide: Did you hit them?

2008: I don't know, can't tell if I hit them, can't tell if you shoot them unless the bullets stay in them. But if it go through them, you can't tell.

Many of the young killers whom I evaluated were neither committed to nor involved in conventional and prosocial activities such as school, sports, and work. Lacking such "bonds," these youths had the free time and often developed the concomitant belief system needed to commit crimes.[172] They fashioned themselves as "players" in the game of life, and they were out to have "a good time."[173]

For these adolescents, robbing and using guns often seemed like fun and a way in which to reduce boredom. Case 2008 related that he engaged in fewer strong-arm robberies of women as time went on because "that ain't excite me no more. I stop trying to do that. I stop doing that, though I used to do that sometimes to ladies, then I try men like that."

Many young killers explained that on the nights of the homicides, they were hanging out with other boys drinking and doing drugs, when one suggested that they rob somebody. Although most of the boys had participated in robberies several times in the past, these times were different. Something happened in the interchange, typically quite unexpectedly, that turned the robberies into homicides.[174]

Case 3026 related that he was high on marijuana on the night of the homicide.

> I was running around with two friends. They had guns, right. I knew they had guns because they showed it to me before, but that particular night I didn't know they were going to do anything such as to rob somebody. Okay, the robbery or, it turned into a homicide. It wasn't intentional, but there's a saying, if you don't intend to do some - thing, you're not supposed to have it, you know. He had the gun and he was high also and . . . he was so high that it looked like the guy was coming towards him, but he was going toward the guy—subconscious—and he shot, and the guy died en route to the hospital.

Some youths simply have *poor judgment*. They became involved in felony homicides not so much out of anger or reckless thrill seeking but rather because they chose to be at the wrong place at the wrong time. When invited to accompany a group of boys "out for a night of fun," they are sent cues that something bad might happen, but these indications go undetected. One of my clients, Tony, found himself in this type of situation. Tony was a kid who did not have many friends. One evening, Tony saw some boys from his neighborhood riding around in a nice car. They stopped and asked whether he would like to join them. Tony got into the car, which had been stolen a little earlier. A few minutes later, the boys stopped at a gas station. The next thing Tony knew, he found himself in the middle of a robbery that ended with one of the boys shooting and killing the attendant.

Whereas many groups of children and youths commit acts of violence out of generalized anger or "for kicks," others do so out of *prejudice and hatred*. Despite the civil rights movement of the 1960s, the United States has encountered increasing struggles with issues of cultural diversity in recent years. Affirmative action, sexual harassment policies, gender equity, political correctness, and hate crime statutes once were presented as means to move our nation toward a society of peacefulness and equity. Today, these concepts are interpreted by some Americans as threats, reverse discrimination, and detrimental to First Amendment rights.

Youths today, as in the past, search for their identities through causes in which to believe. Those with fragile self-esteem tend to be attracted to groups that accept and exalt them on the basis of superficial characteristics, such as skin color. Two teenage Caucasian brothers about whom I was consulted were members of a Skinhead group. One evening, they came across a homeless African American man who had passed out in a public garage. Unprovoked, they beat him until he died.

■ THE CUMULATIVE EFFECT IN CONTEXT

For many youths, the effect of these factors is cumulative. Put succinctly, many young killers growing up in the 1990s have *little or nothing left to lose.* These are the kids who are angry, frequently in pain, and too often unattached to other human beings due to experiences in their home and neighborhood environments. More than in other generations, adolescents today are growing up in an era beset by "an overall decline of the extent and influence of the family from the extended multigenerational family, to the nuclear family, to the single-parent family, to the 'no parent' family of street children."[175]

Many of these youths lack self-esteem and the resources to improve their lives. They are living in a society experiencing increases in youths having sex and babies outside of marriage,[176] using drugs, engaging in criminal violence, and dying violently whether through homicide or suicide. As a result, many juveniles today are living under extreme stress and are severely alienated.[177] They do not hold conventional values or dreams. Often chronically bored, they use drugs, alcohol, and sex to anesthetize themselves and commit crimes for fun. They live in the moment. To them, thrills—and lives—are cheap.

Case 3017 described his friends as

> the type that like to party and stuff. None of them would do no hard drugs and that; [they would] smoke a little reefer. I had a few of them that were shooting up, but—a couple of them shooting up, you know, doing some hard drugs. But the rest of the ones I went to school with, they skip school, making bad grades, you know, and do nothing in school but mess with the girls, go to lunch, PE [physical education], and that's about it. That's all for school for them. Then, ah, go do some wrong, go break into some houses, robbing, whatever they want to do. Makes them some money. Then they go get high and party. That's about all they do.

When asked, he explained his friends' and his own participation in burglaries and robberies.

> They say that's the only way they can, ah, left to make money, you know. I didn't see it like that 'cause, you know, I [was] used to getting me a job for something like that right there. But since I've got started getting high with them, you know, I didn't want to be called square at all like that, so go along with it. Just do what they do. . . . I'm under the influence, you know, by my friends, you know. They want to do this, you see. I'm drunk, I'm not really thinking about nothing right now. But see, whatever they do, I be game, you know. I be ready to do it with them.

In summary, changes in situational factors, societal influences, and resource availability in the 1990s appear to be significant factors in the rising involvement of youths in homicides. These variables likely interact with the personality characteristics of particular adolescents, making some youths more likely than others to engage in violent behavior.

The Biological Connection

Biological factors have not been considered under any of the variables discussed so far. Yet, in many cases, they might be intricately entwined in the homicidal equation.[178]

Experts agree that all human behavior, including violence and aggression, is the result of intricate processes in the brain.[179] In reviewing the research on biological perspectives of violence, the Panel on the Understanding and Control of Violent Behavior made the following observations:

> Violent behaviors may result from relatively permanent conditions or from temporary states. Relatively permanent conditions may result from genetic instructions, from events during fetal or pubertal development, from perinatal accidents, or from birth trauma. Relevant temporary states may be brought on either by some purely internal activity (e.g., brain seizures) or through responses to external stressors, stimuli that produce sexual arousal, ingestion of alcohol or [an]other psychoactive substance, or some other external stimulus.[180]

A growing body of research suggests that criminal behavior might be linked, at least in some cases, to genetics, neurological factors, and biochemical reactions.[181] Recent findings suggesting an association among violent behavior and genetic influences, the neurotransmitter serotonin, and brain dysfunctions are particularly interesting.

Hans Eysenck, a British psychologist, argued persuasively more than 20 years ago that personality differences between criminals and noncriminals were genetically based. He maintained that psychopaths were extreme extroverts who lacked a "conscience" because they failed to acquire conditional emotional responses of fear associated with rule-violating behavior due to the underarousal of their autonomic nervous systems.[182]

Results from two studies conducted in Israel and the United States and released in January 1996 provided the first replicated association between a particular gene (the D4 dopamine receptor gene) and a specific personality trait, called "novelty seeking." Those who score high on this trait are characterized as impulsive, curious, excitable, fickle, quick-tempered, and extravagant. These studies in concert demonstrated that this association was independent of ethnicity, age, or gender of the study participants.[183]

Of the 50 known neurotransmitters, serotonin is the one that has been studied most intensively in relation to violent behavior by animals and humans. Significant differences in serotonin synthesis, release, and metabolism have been found in violent animals from a variety of species when compared to their nonviolent counterparts. Although caution is advised in generalizing from animal studies to human behavior, several researchers have reported an association between low levels of serotonin and impulsive, aggressive, or suicidal behavior in humans.[184] Some scientists have concluded from these studies that cruelty and brutality to children can lead to changes in brain chemistry. These brain chemistry changes might help to explain why some battered children later become violent adults.[185]

Sociobiologists such as C. R. Jeffrey of Florida State University have long maintained that criminal behavior is influenced by both individual biological factors and social and environmental conditions.[186] In his book *Sociobiology*, E. O. Wilson noted that individuals are born with different potentials for learning. The physical environment (neighborhoods and schools) and the social environment interact to either limit or enhance a particular individual's capacity for learning.[187]

Although no neurophysiological variable has yet been found, several types of indirect data suggest that brain functioning abnormalities increase the likelihood of violent behavior. Many studies have found that neurophysiological deficits in attention, memory, and language/verbal skills are common in youths who demonstrate violent or aggressive behavior. This correlation could indicate a direct relationship between limbic system damage and violent behavior. However, Reiss and Roth reported, "It is more likely to reflect less direct results of distorted social interactions with peers resulting from impaired communication skills or to arise from frustration over the inability to compete successfully with peers in cognitive tasks."[188]

Conclusions drawn with respect to juvenile murderers by Lewis also are consistent with a "diathesis-stress theory"[189] of aggression. She maintained that genetic factors and biological vulnerabilities, particularly when severe, predispose certain individuals to respond violently. Lewis's research findings suggest that if these individuals are subjected to intense psychological, social, and environmental stressors that exceed their ability to cope, then violent expression is more likely to result, particularly among males.[190]

> Individually, each of the vulnerabilities characteristic of juvenile murderers may be present, to a greater or lesser extent, in nonviolent delinquents and even in nondelin-quents. It is, rather, the combination of serious intrinsic vulnerabilities in the combi-nation of an abusive or violent environment that is associated with the development of aggression. The impulsivity, emotional liability, and cognitive impairment often as-sociated with neurological dysfunction diminish the ability to control behavior. A para-noid orientation and a tendency to misperceive reality further lower a child's threshold for controlling aggression. Abuse and family violence, in turn, provide stimulating mod-els for assaultive behaviors and also engender rage in these already oversuspicious, impulsive individuals.[191]

Lewis's theory of neuropsychiatric vulnerability also received support in a larger study involving urban delinquents in Chicago,[192] in a study of 21 juvenile murderers in England,[193] and in a study of 18 juvenile murderers in Florida.[194] Results from a study of young murderers in Finland were consistent with Lewis's theory, although they were not as distinct and definite.[195]

In the next chapter, the legal response to youth homicide is discussed. Attention focuses on juveniles processed in the adult criminal justice system, juveniles sentenced to death, and mental status defenses.

Chapter Three

The Legal Response to Juvenile and Adolescent Homicide

THE PROSECUTOR'S office almost always seeks to bring charges against youths who have been involved in the killing of others. However, the legal response to youths who kill, both historically and currently, varies widely.[1] Prosecution may occur in either a juvenile or adult forum, depending on the law and practice in the jurisdiction. Some young killers are processed in the juvenile justice system, where their sentences may be calculated in months. Other adolescent murderers are tried in the adult criminal justice system, where they can legally be sentenced to life imprisonment or death.

- An 11-year-old boy, recently ordered to stand trial as an adult for killing an 18-year-old male, is the youngest juvenile to be tried as an adult in Michigan. If the boy is convicted, the judge could sentence him in either the adult or juvenile justice system. If sentenced in adult court, the boy automatically would be confined to prison for life. If sentenced in the juvenile court, the youth could be released back to the community at any time.[2]

- A 12-year-old grandson of a famous civil rights leader was considered a behavioral problem. His family sent him to live with his grandmother with the firm belief that she would straighten him out. Shortly after he moved in with her, the adolescent doused his grandmother with gasoline and set her ablaze. After a series of operations and weeks in intensive care, the woman died. The boy pleaded guilty to the juvenile equivalent of manslaughter in New York State. The juvenile court judge recognized that the boy was mentally disturbed and ordered him to participate in a treatment program for at least 18 months.[3]

- The juvenile court in Chicago retained jurisdiction over the two young boys who hung the 5-year-old boy out the 14th-floor apartment window and intentionally dropped him to his death, despite intense public pressure to try them as adults and put them in adult prison. The juvenile court judge sentenced the boys to a period of up to 10 years in a state correctional institution rather than a less restrictive private treatment program. She ordered state officials to devise a long-term, comprehensive treatment program in the hope that the boys could become rehabilitated.[4]

- Three of the four boys initially charged with killing a British man and wounding his companion were indicted as adults in Florida. After two mistrials, a third jury found one of the two gunmen guilty of first-degree murder. This youth was sentenced in accordance with state statute to a life sentence, with a mandatory minimum 25-year sentence before parole eligibility. A second youth was allowed to plead guilty to second-degree murder and was sentenced to 27 years in prison in exchange for testifying against the first defendant. This youth subsequently was convicted of the attempted murder of the female companion and was sentenced to life in prison.[5] The third co-defendant, who drove the getaway car, pleaded guilty to conspiracy to commit armed robbery and accessory after the fact and was sentenced to 8 years in prison.[6] The fourth co-defendant, who was 13 years old when arrested, apparently was not involved and was dropped from the case.[7]

- "Tom Malone," at 19 years of age, had recently been released from prison when he and another ex-con went out for a night of partying. Witness accounts indicated that Tom picked a fight in a bar parking lot with a man who had just celebrated his 26th birthday with friends. Despite the man's attempts to placate Tom and to resist fighting, Tom repeatedly stabbed the victim until he was dead. Tom was indicted for first-degree murder, convicted, and sentenced to death in Florida. A second jury who heard the case on appeal reached the same verdict and unanimously recommended that Tom be sentenced to death in the electric chair. The judge subsequently imposed the death sentence.[8]

JUVENILES AND THE ADULT CRIMINAL JUSTICE SYSTEM

Increasingly, given the current mood in the United States, more juveniles are being prosecuted as adults.[9] Depending on the facts of the case, a prosecutor may file charges ranging from first-degree murder to manslaughter. Determining whether the youth intended to take the life of another human being often is decisive in determining whether first- or second-degree murder is the appropriate charge. The state attorney's office typically seeks to charge the youth with *first-degree murder* if the adolescent appears to have premeditated or planned the killing. In many states, the prosecutor also may file first-degree murder charges if the killing occurred while the offender was engaged in the commission of certain felonies such as robbery or rape.

In nonfelony killings in which premeditation was lacking, the prosecutor may attempt to charge the youth with *second-degree murder* if the adolescent behaved with callous disregard for human life. In such cases, the victim's death resulted from the youth's committing a reckless act that is imminently dangerous to another human being.[10] A youth who recklessly throws a bowling bowl off an overpass onto the highway below, for example, may be charged with second-degree murder if the bowling ball hits a car and causes an auto accident that claims a life.

After examining the circumstances, the state may decide that first- or second-degree murder is not an appropriate charge and may consider filing less serious charges or none at all if the killing appears justifiable (e.g., self-defense). A homicide committed in response to adequate provocation traditionally has been defined as lacking "malice aforethought" (actual or implied intent to kill) and has been considered *voluntary manslaughter.* A homicide generally has been considered *involuntary manslaughter* if it occurred during the commission of an unlawful act not amounting to a felony or if it was the result of criminal negligence.[11] An intoxicated adolescent who killed someone in a car accident may be charged under this statutory provision if the state does not have a separate charge of vehicular homicide.

Young Killers and Provocation in Focus

Young killers often behave impulsively and maintain that they acted out of strong emotions frequently occasioned in some fashion by previous actions by the victim. For voluntary manslaughter to be the appropriate charge, however, four elements of adequate provocation must be proven. The provocation must have caused the youth to kill the victim, and it must have been such that it would have caused a reasonable person to lose control. In addition, the time that passed between the provocation and the killing must not have been sufficient for the passions of a reasonable person to cool, and the defendant must not have cooled off during the period between the provocation and the murder.

The particular situations that cause some young killers to become enraged or distressed have not been recognized by the courts. For example, juvenile murderers have reported becoming very disturbed by something said to them (e.g., "Fuck you, asshole") or minor batteries (e.g., someone bumped or pushed them). They have felt "dissed" (disrespected) by these actions and compelled to redress the perceived affront. Traditionally, however, the courts have not considered words, no matter how vile or insulting, to constitute adequate provocation. Similarly, the courts have not viewed trivial blows, even if technically a battery, as qualifying as sufficient provocation to cause a reasonable person to engage in a killing frenzy.[12]

The Model Penal Code suggested that a murder be reduced to manslaughter if the defendant was acting "under the influence of extreme mental or emotional disturbance for which there is reasonable explanation or excuse." The position of "extreme disturbance" is consonant with the concept of "adequate provocation."[13]

▪ TRANSFER TO CRIMINAL COURT

Each of the 50 states and the District of Columbia has provisions to try juveniles in adult court. Some states specifically mention murder when discussing transfer procedures in the juvenile code. In these states, the minimum age for exercise of criminal court jurisdiction in homicide cases often is lower than in other felony cases.[14]

Transfer mechanisms include judicial waiver, statutory exclusion from juvenile court jurisdiction, and prosecutorial discretion. Any or all of these transfer procedures may exist in a given state.[15] Some states have provisions whereby the criminal court can impose juvenile sanctions instead of, or in addition to, adult sanctions or can transfer the case back to juvenile court for sentencing.[16]

No national data exist with respect to the transfer of juvenile murderers to adult court. In fact, the exact number of juvenile transfers to criminal court presently is unknown. There is evidence that the number has increased with the availability of easier transfer mechanisms largely enacted since the mid-1980s.[17] It has been estimated that as many as 200,000 juvenile cases were handled in adult court in 1990 alone.[18]

The percentage of juvenile cases judicially waived to criminal court in the United States has remained fairly constant at 1.4% of the total number of petitioned cases from 1985 to 1994. The actual number of cases waived, however, rose significantly from 7,200 in 1985 to 12,300 in 1994, an increase of more than 70%.[19] Over that 10-year period, the type of cases waived changed dramatically. Since 1991, cases against persons have outnumbered property charges as the most serious offenses waived to adult courts by juvenile court judges.[20]

Of the youths waived to adult court from 1985 to 1994, between 94% and 96% were male. Over the 10-year period, an increase in younger youths being waived could be observed. In 1985, 6% of juvenile cases waived to criminal court were age 15 years or younger. In 1994, 12% were in that age group.[21]

In contrast to information available on judicial waivers, there are no national statistics kept on the number of juvenile cases transferred to adult court by prosecutorial discretion or statutory exclusion.[22] Recent data reveal that many state attorney offices, however, are using their prosecutorial power to try juveniles in adult court. In a national survey of 308 prosecutors, almost two thirds of prosecutor offices transferred at least one juvenile case to adult court in 1994. Of these offices, 32% reported that they had transferred at least one murder case.[23]

Statistics also indicate that the juvenile population in U.S. jails has escalated in recent years. The average daily population of juveniles in adult jails increased by 384% from 1,629 in 1985 to 7,888 in 1995. Recent advancements in reporting practices reveal that the number of juveniles who were tried as adults or were awaiting trial as adults in jails rose from 3,330 in 1993, to 5,139 in 1994, to 6,018 in 1995.[24]

Evidence also exists that increased numbers of juveniles are being placed in adult prisons. In 1992, 38 states reported committing 5,637 juveniles to state prisons, an increase of almost 40% since 1988.[25]

Juveniles and the Death Penalty

The United States stands alone among Western industrialized nations in permitting the execution of individuals for murders that they committed as juveniles.[26] Although some evidence exists that Americans might be less approving of condemning juvenile murderers to death than of sentencing adult killers to death,[27] executions of youths under 18 years of age have been deemed constitutional.[28] Three U.S. Supreme Court decisions speak authoritatively on this issue. In 1982, the court held in *Eddings v. Oklahoma* (1982) that a defendant's youth, troubled past, and mental and emotional difficulties are relevant factors to consider in mitigation with respect to imposition of the death penalty. The court reasoned that any mitigating factors, whether statutorily based or not, should be weighed against any statutory aggravating factors by the decision maker in arriving at a death determination.[29]

The 1988 case of *Thompson v. Oklahoma* (1988) has been interpreted to prohibit the execution of a youth under 16 years of age only in states where the minimum age of execution is not legislated.[30] The Court specifically held in *Stanford v. Kentucky* (1989), decided 1 year after *Thompson*, that the executing of offenders for crimes that they committed at age 16 or 17 did not violate the Eighth Amendment's provisions against cruel and unusual punishment.[31]

Victor Streib, dean and professor of law at Ohio Northern University and a leading authority on capital punishment, has tracked legislation and court cases with respect to juveniles sentenced to death since 1973, when the death penalty was restored in many states to conform with the Supreme Court's guidelines in *Furman v. Georgia* (1972).[32] Streib reported that of the 38 states and the federal government that permit capital punishment, 24 states authorize executions for individuals who committed crimes when they were under 18 years of age. Of these 24 states, 4 have chosen 17 as their minimum age. The remaining 20 states have set their minimum at age 16, either by legislation or by court ruling. The other 14 states and the federal government restrict the death sentence to offenders who killed at age 18 or older.[33] Streib estimated that over the 24½-year period from January 1, 1973, to June 30, 1997, 160 (2.7%) of the 6,030 murderers sentenced to death were juveniles at the times of the commission of their crimes. During this time frame, the percentage of the total death sentences imposed on youths under age 18 has fluctuated. Since the beginning of the 1990s, it has averaged approximately 2.6% of all death sentences.[34]

As of December 31, 1995, 51 (1.9%) of the 2,661 people on death row across the United States were age 17 years or under at the times of their arrests.[35] Although death sentences imposed on those under age 18 have a high reversal rate, nine executions of juvenile offenders have occurred since the U.S. Supreme Court held in the 1976 case of *Gregg v. Georgia*[36] that current death penalty statutes were constitutional. In the 1980s, three juvenile murderers were executed. From the beginning of the 1990s through December 7, 1993, the death sentence had been carried out on six young killers.[37]

Amnesty International has compiled a list of 22 documented executions of juvenile offenders in other countries from January 1985 to June 1995. Three countries reported executions of 15 individuals who were under 18 years of age at the times of the commission of their crimes during the mid- to late 1980s. Of these 15, only 1 was age 18 at the time of execution; the remainder were age 17 or under. Bangladesh executed 1, Iraq executed 13, and Nigeria executed 1. Four countries executed 7 juveniles during the early 1990s. Iran was responsible for 4 of these; the other 3 juveniles were executed in Pakistan, Saudi Arabia, and Yemen.[38]

JUVENILES SENTENCED TO DEATH: THE CASE OF MARK

Mark was on death watch status and had been on "the row" for more than 8 years when I evaluated him. Prior to meeting with him, I had reviewed extensive case-related materials. Mark's statements to me about the murder were consistent with earlier statements he had made at his trial and those he had written in his 224-page autobiography. His rendition of the facts also was in agreement with those reported in the presentence report and those mentioned in the reports and testimony of the mental health professionals who had examined him previously.

At the time of the killing, Mark was about 2 months away from turning 18 years old, the age at which he intended to enlist in the marines. He desperately wanted to leave home because he was having difficulty with his mother and wanted to be on his own. From his perspective, living at home had become increasingly worse since his father's death approximately 1 year before the homicide. Mark was unable to secure a job and felt unable to wait the 2 months required by law for emancipation into adulthood. He saw robbery as the way in which to obtain the money necessary to solve his problems and discussed this possibility with one of his friends, Tommy.

A few days before the killing, Mark stole two handguns on two separate occasions. On the day before the homicide, he had put the wrong lights on the Christmas tree and left the house. Calling from a friend's house later, he asked his mother for permission to stay there for supper. His mother reportedly told him to go ahead because she said that he would do it anyway. When he returned that night, Mark's mother had thrown the tree across the living room and had put it away.

Mark stated that he did not argue with his mother that night and went into his room and went to bed. The incident, however, was not resolved in his mind; he still was angry the next day. He spent some time at Tommy's house, and when he was not invited for dinner, he left and drove around. Mark went back to Tommy's around 7 p.m.; finding that Tommy had plans for the evening, he left again. Although Mark had no recollection, he was identified later as the person who had, sometime around 7 p.m., exposed himself in a convenience store.

Mark drove around casing out convenience stores. He had just about given up hope of robbing one when he spotted one that looked promising. He parked his car and entered. Seeing no one other than the young female clerk, Mark pulled out one of the stolen handguns and demanded money. The victim offered no resistance and gave him $139.

While the robbery was in process, an adolescent who knew Mark attempted to enter the store. Mark pointed a gun at the youth and told him to leave.

After securing the money, Mark told the victim to come with him. He told me that he intended to leave her somewhere away from a phone so that he could have ample time to get away. As he drove out of the parking lot, Mark recognized that one of his high school teachers had just driven into the parking lot.

Mark turned off the main highway onto a dirt road. He related that he was thinking of letting the victim out along that dirt road. After he drove in about a half mile, his car got stuck in the dirt. During the 10 to 15 minutes it took Mark to get the car unstuck, the victim asked Mark to let her go.

> *Mark:* I was still afraid that if I let her go while I was still stuck, she'd have time to get the police. So I told her [to] stay there while I was getting the car unstuck.
>
> *Heide:* And then what happened?
>
> *Mark:* Ah . . . I think it was while I was trying to get the car unstuck that the idea of se [sic], of having sex with her came. Ah . . . I don't know what triggered it.

After Mark got the car unstuck, he drove down the road a little farther, parked, and ordered her out. As they were walking down the road, he ripped her blouse off and told her to take off her clothes. After Mark vaginally raped her, he allowed her to get dressed again. As they were walking back toward the car, Mark said, he pulled the gun out and shot her. Mark thought that "she might have been [walking] a little bit ahead" of him. He did not think that she was aware that he was going to shoot her.

Mark told me that he shot the victim in the head, about the ear, from a few feet away. Following the first shot, "she . . . gave a kind of grunt and fell." He added, "And then, ah, I think I shot her again. . . . Ah, I don't remember there being any movement. . . . I pulled her off into some weeds alongside the dirt road. I tried to pull her off into the brush." Thereafter, Mark went back to the car and put the gun in the trunk. He was confident at this point that he would not be caught. As he was driving back the way he came, he passed a police car. Mark's attempts to elude the police were unsuccessful and he was apprehended almost immediately.

When I asked him how he was feeling when the car got stuck, he said that he was mad. Mark related that the rape took about 5 minutes. The loss of control is apparent with respect to both the rape and the murder in the dialogue excerpted in the following:

Heide: Do you remember how you were feeling [during the rape], what was going on with you?

Mark: All I remember is anger.

Heide: Anger. Okay.

Mark: Frustration.

Heide: Where was that coming from?

Mark: Ah . . . oh, I think I was . . . I think it was from problems I'd been having at home and . . . ah . . . having things adding, kind of piling on each other and not really being able to diminish them in any way.

Mark indicated that the thought of shooting the victim occurred "within seconds . . . of shooting her. Ah . . . just as you're walking, just began thinking of it, as you're walking towards the car. And, ah . . . I don't know . . . half a minute."

Mark was charged as an adult with armed robbery, sexual battery, and capital murder. He was convicted of all three offenses at trial and was sentenced to death along with two life sentences. The state supreme court overturned the death sentence and ordered a new resentencing hearing 3 years later because the trial court judge did not list the factors in mitigation. Mark was sentenced to death a second time by the same judge without a jury hearing. Two death warrants were signed thereafter and the execution dates subsequently were stayed, first by the state supreme court and then by the federal courts.

The death sentence was overturned again, and another resentencing hearing was ordered. I testified at Mark's third resentencing hearing. Jurors who heard about Mark's troubled youth reached a different conclusion from that reached by the original jury. They voted eight to four in favor of life, and the judge who previously had sentenced Mark to death imposed a life sentence.

MENTAL STATUS ISSUES AND DEFENSES

When a youth is arrested for murder, psychological issues, as well as legal matters, immediately come into play. Attention typically focuses on the young killer's present mental status (competency) and on his or her mental status at the time of the killing (sanity or capacity).[39] In cases involving juvenile murderers, defense attorneys frequently seek the assistance of mental health professionals to evaluate their client's competency to stand trial and the client's sanity during the homicide.[40]

Those who are designated as mental health professionals vary by state law. Individuals with advanced degrees in the social and behavioral sciences (e.g., psychologists, mental health counselors, social workers, marriage and family counselors, nurse practitioners) or medical doctors with specialties in psychiatry (psychiatrists) are generally recognized as mental health professionals.[41] Depending on their credentials ("knowledge, skill, experience, [and] training or education"[42]) and the case law and practices in the jurisdiction, these professionals may be "qualified" to testify in court as forensic experts and to render their opinions regarding the young killer's mental status at varying points in time.

Competency Issues

Juveniles who are processed as adults must be competent to stand trial. Many states have recognized the right of youths who are retained in juvenile court to be competent to stand trial in recognition that adjudication in juvenile court can be punitive and can result in negative consequences.[43] In adult court and in those states that recognize the competency rights of juveniles charged with delinquent acts, it is important that the adolescent understand the nature of the proceedings, that is, that he or she is being tried for allegedly participating in a murder. The juvenile murderer must be capable of comprehending that, if convicted, he or she can be confined or possibly executed, depending on which court retains jurisdiction and the laws of the state. The youth must be able to provide information to his or her attorney so that counsel can prepare a defense, and the juvenile must be able to maintain appropriate behavior in court.[44]

Issues of competency can be raised at any point in the proceedings and can include other matters prior to trial. These may include competency to plead guilty, to refuse an insanity defense, to waive the right to counsel, or to confess.[45] For example, the attorney may question whether the youth was competent to waive his or her Miranda warnings when the youth confessed to the police. Did the adolescent actually understand, when arrested, that he or she did not have to give a statement to police and that any statements made would be used against the youth?

One young killer related that the police "had really messed me up that night for something I totally misunderstood, which I thought I understood at the time but I misunderstood it." He explained that when he confessed, he thought anything that he said could be used *for* or against him. Not talking, he thought, would be akin to an admission of guilt.[46]

Issues of competency can be revisited during the trial if the defendant does not appear to be functioning adequately. In addition, many states have provisions that if the young killer appears to decompensate after he or she is convicted, then he or she can be evaluated for competency prior to the sentence being imposed or during its imposition, whichever applies. In these states, if the defendant or inmate is determined to be incompetent, then provisions are to be made for treatment prior to sentencing or during the sentence, depending on the circumstances operative in the case.[47]

The U.S. Supreme Court has held that a defendant sentenced to death must be competent at the time of execution.[48] If the murderer appears to be mentally ill to the point that the murderer does not understand that he or she is going to be executed and the reason for imposition of the death sentence, then the proceedings legally are to be halted to determine the killer's competency to be executed. If found to be incompetent, then the killer is to be treated to restore him or her to competency. When restored to competency, the murderer can lawfully be executed.[49]

Typically, both the state and the defense will be interested in what was going on in the mind of the killer at the time of the murder as well as his or her present state of mind. The young killer's perceptions, intention, and mental status at the time of the offense might have dramatic consequences, depending on the specific facts of the case. Looking at the total spectrum, in-depth analysis of the adolescent murderer and his or her actions at the time of the killing might mean the difference between the youth being sentenced to death or set free.

If there is substantial evidence that the youth killed the victim or was otherwise involved in the homicidal incident, then defense counsel typically will consider exploring defense strategies based on the youth's mental status or competency at the time of the offense. Defenses available may vary by state law and may be different even within the same jurisdiction depending on whether the young killer is tried in a juvenile or an adult forum.[50] Mental health experts with expertise in forensic matters are likely to explore whether mental status defenses such as insanity, automatism, diminished capacity, or voluntary intoxication are factors in the instant or presenting case, particularly if the youth is tried in the adult criminal justice system. In some cases, particularly when a youth kills his or her parents, the mental health expert will look closely at the defendant's perceptions at the time of the homicide in the context of self-defense.[51]

The Insanity Defense

The insanity defense currently is recognized in federal courts and in 47 states in the United States. In the 3 states where it has been abolished (Idaho, Montana, and Utah), expert testimony still is admissible with respect to the defendant's criminal intent.[52] The insanity defense postulates that an offender should not be held accountable for his or her homicidal behavior if, at the time of the killing, the defendant had a mental disease, defect, or impairment that rendered him or her "insane." In some states, the pertinent legal test is specified by the legislature in state statutes; in other states, it is found in case law or embodied in jury instructions.

Numerous tests have been formulated by courts and legal experts over the years to assist judges and jurors in determining whether defendants should be acquitted because they were insane at the time of the crime. Current insanity tests typically can be grouped into three broad categories depending on whether the alleged defect is in cognition, volition, or mental or emotional processes or behavioral controls.[53] Mental health professionals use these tests to evaluate whether a particular defendant meets the legal standard of insanity in the jurisdiction. Research suggests that opinions reached by forensic examiners may vary depending on which insanity test is used.[54]

To qualify as insane under the first test, represented by the M'Naghten Test (which is law in about one third of the states in this country), the defendant must lack understanding of his or her criminal behavior to the degree that the defendant did not know "the nature and quality of his [or her] act" or that it was "wrong."[55] This test, which was the law in the state in which Mark was indicted, is a very strenuous one and could not be met given the circumstances present in his case. To have found Mark insane, the judge or jury would have to be persuaded that Mark, at the time he entered the convenience store and abducted the clerk, had a mental disease or defect that severely limited his ability to reason in a clear and normal fashion. The cognitive deficit would need to have been so severe that the jurors concluded that Mark did not know that (a) he was threatening the clerk with a deadly weapon when he pointed the gun at her, (b) he was having sex with the victim without her consent, *and* (c) his firing the gun into the young woman's head would likely result in her death. If the jurors concluded that Mark did know what he was doing, then they would have to believe that his actions were consistent with those of an individual who did not know or believe that robbing, raping, and killing the woman were wrong before they could adjudge him insane.

To judge a youth not guilty by reason of insanity (NGRI) under the second test, represented by the Irresistible Impulse Test, the decision maker must believe that the adolescent *could not* (as opposed to *did not*) control his or her behavior because of a preexisting mental disease or defect. This standard is another exacting test, has rarely been adopted, and no longer is the exclusive standard for judging insanity in any state. However, it is important because several states have added this test to some form of the cognitive test.[56] Had this standard been the applicable test, then to find Mark insane, the decision maker would need to have believed that Mark's "compulsion" to rob, rape, and kill was such that he would have robbed the convenience store, raped the woman, and killed her even if he knew that he would be caught and severely punished for his behavior.

A youth is more likely to be found insane under broader tests such as the American Law Institute's (ALI) proposed Model Penal Code. The ALI test is essentially a combination of the two earlier mentioned tests, albeit in softer language. The ALI test was the standard used in the federal courts until 1985 and currently is law in close to half of the states in this country. Under the Model Penal Code test, an adolescent could be adjudged insane if he or she lacked "substantial capacity either to appreciate the wrongfulness of his [or her] conduct or to conform his [or her] conduct to requirements of the law."[57]

The American Bar Association (ABA) truncation of the ALI test replaced the ALI standard in federal courts in 1985 in response to the American public's dissatisfaction with the insanity verdict reached in John Hinckley's attempted assassination of former President Ronald Reagan. Although the ABA test narrowed the scope of the ALI standard, the revised test still remains a more expansive test than the M'Naghten Test. Under the ABA version, a defendant could be found insane if he or she "was unable to appreciate the wrongfulness of his [or her] conduct."[58]

The ALI test and the revised federal test allow mental health professionals, as well as judges and jurors, to consider the emotional factors operating in the adolescent, rather than simply cognitive considerations, in determining whether a particular defendant was sane. Had this standard been the law, it is possible that certain factors in Mark's case might have persuaded the decision maker that Mark should not have been held responsible for his behavior. Strong corroborative data indicated that Mark was "under the influence of extreme mental and emotional disturbance" and manifested an abrupt loss of control. It is very possible that Mark could not (as opposed to did not) control his behavior during the homicidal event due to strong negative feelings raging within him. Records confirmed that Mark had an established psychiatric history as a child and had been deeply affected by the unexpected death of his father almost a year to the day of the killing. During the 6 months preceding the murder, he engaged in negative behaviors that resulted in his termination from three volunteer groups and his subsequent loss of support from others in his community.

The procedures required to raise the insanity defense differ across jurisdictions. A defendant who asserts this defense has the initial burden of producing evidence suggesting that he or she was insane at the time of the crime because a presumption of sanity exists in all jurisdictions. After the threshold requirement has been reached, jurisdictions vary, typically in accordance with the insanity test used, regarding who has the ultimate burden of proof.[59]

The decision as to whether a particular defendant will be held legally responsible for his or her behavior appears to be influenced, at least to some extent, by which test is used to determine sanity and by which party has the burden of proof as to the accused's frame of mind at the time of the crime.[60] Some scholars take the position that juries on occasion acquit defendants on grounds of insanity because they believe it is unfair to convict the mentally ill[61] or because they feel some sympathy for them, given their life circumstances,[62] rather than because the applicable insanity test prescribes a particular result.

Despite the attention that the insanity defense receives, it rarely is used and seldom is successful.[63] When defendants are found NGRI in homicide cases, they are adjudged not responsible for their murderous actions. However, they hardly ever are set free at the trial's conclusion. Instead, they almost always are committed to a mental hospital for assessment of their present mental condition and continuing threat of harm to society.[64]

State statutes differ in the procedures required to commit persons found NGRI. In most states and in the federal system, the trial court or some other judicial body retains jurisdiction over NGRI acquittees who have been hospitalized. Release usually is contingent on the former defendants' proving to the court that confinement for continuing mental illness and dangerousness no longer is appropriate under the governing statute.[65]

About a dozen states that have the insanity defense also have a "guilty but mentally ill" (GBMI) verdict. This verdict allows the fact finder to indicate that the defendant, although mentally ill, is guilty beyond a reasonable doubt of the crime as charged. Accordingly, the offender may be sentenced to any appropriate sentence with the opportunity for treatment in a psychiatric hospital during this period. A GBMI offender who remains dangerous may be legally held until the expiration of his or her sentence, at which point the offender must be civilly committed or released.[66]

Defenses Based on Other Mental Status at the Time of the Offense

Automatism, a defense recognized more in the United Kingdom and in Canada than in the United States, denotes "unconscious involuntary behavior over which the defendant has no control."[67] *Black's Law Dictionary* indicates that this defense may pertain to "behavior performed in a state of mental unconsciousness or dissociation without full awareness."[68] When successfully litigated at trial, this defense excuses the defendant from criminal responsibility. The rationale for acquitting the accused is that, if the defendant did not have conscious control of his or her body at the time of the offense, then no act has occurred sufficient to impose criminal liability.

Automatism that results from internal factors such as a dissociative disorder (e.g., multiple personality disorder, now called dissociative identity disorder[69]) would qualify as a disease of the mind and would be labeled *insane automatism* under Canadian law. The defense of automatism is used more frequently in cases involving unconscious behavior that appears to be caused by external factors such as concussion, medical administration of drugs, involuntary ingestion of alcohol and drugs, and hypoglycemia.[70] Other classic examples of automatism include epilepsy and somnambulism (sleepwalking).[71] Automatism also can result from physical and emotional trauma.[72] As noted by University of Nebraska law professor Robert F. Schopp, "Although the paradigmatic cases of automatism are those involving convulsions, reflexes, or other movements that are apparently performed without any conscious direction, the defense also applies to those who perform complex actions in coordinated, directed fashion but with substantially reduced awareness."[73]

Other defenses, when pleaded successfully, might not completely exonerate the young killer. However, testimony about the defendant's mental status at the time of the crime might reduce the grade of the offense and thereby result in a lesser penalty. *Diminished capacity* and *voluntary intoxication* defenses may be used to indicate that the offender did not have the capacity to form the requisite criminal intent to commit the crime.

Not all jurisdictions recognize the concept of diminished capacity. In those that do, the types of evidence that mental health professionals may testify about during the trial stage vary extensively.[74] The most conservative approaches allow evidence pertaining to the defendant's mental disease or defect to be admissible at trial to show that the offender lacked the capacity to form the requisite mental state to commit the crime. More liberal approaches advocate that the defendant's personal characteristics, such as his or her intelligence, excitability, personality development, and other dimensions that bear on the ability to control actions and understand wrongfulness, should be admissible to the jury in determining the defendant's culpability. The most radical approaches maintain that any factors that might predispose a person to antisocial behavior, such as growing up in a violent home environment, having an abusive childhood, or living in abject poverty, are relevant in establishing a defense of diminished capacity.[75]

The voluntary use (or abuse) of alcohol or other drugs to the extent that they arouse passions, lower inhibitions, or cloud reason and judgment does not excuse a defendant from responsibility for the commission of a criminal act or lead to his or her acquittal. In some jurisdictions, however, voluntary intoxication is recognized in the context of establishing diminished capacity.[76] In other jurisdictions, it has been considered a defense in its own right to crimes that require specific mental states.[77] In some states, evidence presented by a medical or mental health professional that an adolescent was so intoxicated at the time of the crime that he or she was incapable of forming the specific mental state required (say, premeditation) may be introduced to show that the youth did not commit that particular crime (e.g., first-degree murder). The defendant instead may be convicted of a lesser charge.[78]

In many cases, the defendant's mental disorder or intoxication level causes cognitive or volitional impairment, but not of the magnitude needed to result in insanity or the inability to form the specific criminal intent. Testimony about the offender's mental state at the time of the crime in these cases, although generally not permissible during the trial phase, might be appropriate at sentencing to establish *diminished or partial responsibility*. Evidence of diminished responsibility might influence the judge to impose less than the maximum sentence allowable by law.[79]

Self-Defense

Generally, a person may lawfully use deadly physical force against another in self-defense only when under the reasonable belief that the other is threatening him or her with imminent death or serious bodily injury and that such force is necessary to prevent the infliction of such harm. In most jurisdictions, an honest belief on the part of the defendant that he or she was in imminent danger is not sufficient. Some evidence exists that the requirement that one must be in actual danger might be changing.[80] Self-defense usually requires that the appearance of danger must have been so real that a reasonable person, faced with the same circumstances, would have entertained the same beliefs.[81]

Some jurisdictions require that the defendant must have exhausted all possible avenues of retreat before responding to force with force. In jurisdictions that impose a duty to retreat, an exception often is made to permit one to stand one's ground and use force when threatened with imminent harm in situations where one is attacked in one's home. When both the assailant and the victim share the same residence, however, society's expectations appear to be different, particularly in cases where a battered woman kills her abusive spouse or mate.[82]

Similarly, convincing a judge or jury that an adolescent acted in self-defense when he or she killed a parent is difficult unless (a) the parent was attacking the youth and (b) the possibility of the youth's retreating at that moment without sustaining serious injury or death was extremely remote.

The doctrine of self-defense, as formulated almost 1,000 years ago, was designed to address combat situations between men. It did not take into consideration differences in physical size and strength between men and women[83] and between parents, particularly fathers, and their children.[84] In addition, it did not address circumstances related to psychological injury and the perception that aspects of one's self that are deeply valued are being severely damaged, and possibly irreparably destroyed, by another individual.

A compelling argument has been made that the doctrine should be broadened to include psychological self-defense.[85] Like battered wives, children and adolescents who have been severely abused might believe, based on their experiences, that they are in danger of being severely beaten or killed in the near future if they do not take lethal action when it is possible. Abused adolescents who do not believe their physical survival is threatened might feel that their psychological survival compels them to attack the abusive parents. Perceiving that they are unable to engage in physical battle as equals with the abusive parents, abused adolescents frequently strike when the abusive parents are physically defenseless (e.g., sleeping, passed out from drinking).

Peter, a 17-year-old boy, had been severely abused from the time he was a baby. He was terrified one night that his father was going to make good on his threats earlier that evening to kill him. Peter shot his father in the back of the neck and once just behind the ear as the man sat watching television in the middle of the night. There was no evidence to indicate that Peter's dad was aware of his son's presence when Peter trained the rifle on him and fired repeatedly.[86]

Given the circumstances in this killing, defense counsel did not attempt to persuade the jurors that Peter acted in self-defense. Instead, in line with all the mental health experts who evaluated Peter, the adolescent's lawyer argued that the youth was insane at the time of the murder. The jurors, after deliberating for hours, were hopelessly deadlocked. The judge eventually ordered a directed verdict of acquittal on the grounds of insanity. Her review of the testimony at trial indicated that the state had introduced no evidence to rebut the defense's position that Peter was legally insane when he shot his father. She noted further that even some of the state's own witnesses supported the defense's contention that Peter was insane at the time of the crime.[87]

This chapter looked at the legal response to youth homicide. Information pertinent to the processing of juveniles in the adult criminal justice system was synthesized. Defenses involving the young killer's mental state or beliefs at the time of the homicide were reviewed. The next chapter discusses the importance of a thorough assessment. The focus is on understanding why a particular youth has been involved in a homicide.

Chapter Four

Understanding the
Juvenile Murderer

DONNELL, A HANDSOME, 17-year-old African American youth, was charged with three armed robberies of convenience stores and two homicides in connection with them. In all three of these incidents, the youth allegedly fired shots from his handgun. In the past two incidents, Donnell reportedly fired directly at a store clerk in each of the stores, killing both of them. The state indicted the adolescent as an adult with multiple charges, including two counts of first-degree murder, and announced its intention to seek the death penalty. Prior to trial, a plea agreement was reached in which Donnell avoided a possible death sentence by agreeing to plead guilty to two counts of second-degree murder and one count of armed robbery.

Prior to the sentencing hearing, defense counsel contacted me for assistance in gaining understanding of their client and his involvement in these crimes. Defense counsel related that Donnell had been raised for most of his life in a Christian home by his grandparents, who were known to be stable and good-valued people. His grandfather was a hardworking man who provided well for his family. My evaluation verified that Donnell had his own room at his grandparents' home and was essentially raised as an only child by grandparents who loved and doted on him. He lived a middle- to upper-middle-class life. The family lived in a beautiful home on about 5 acres of land with a pool, tennis court, and basketball court. A boy who had a college fund set up for him and a family business to go into was robbing and killing people. The obvious question was "Why?"

ASSESSMENT AND ITS IMPLICATIONS

A mental health professional with expertise in conducting forensic evaluations of youths charged with violent crimes can provide invaluable assistance to the attorney in understanding the youth and the factors contributing to his or her murderous behavior as well as his or her mental state during the crime. Mental health experts are increasingly called on by defense attorneys to testify about an adolescent's state of mind at the time of the killing. Consideration of the youth's mental status during the crime might persuade a judge or jury to excuse the defendant from whole or partial responsibility.[1] A thorough evaluation by a well-respected mental health professional also might assist the defense in other ways. Armed with a favorable report from a qualified forensic evaluator prior to trial, defense counsel might succeed in persuading the prosecution to dismiss or reduce the charges or, at the very least, to forgo seeking the death penalty.[2] In cases of minors, it might persuade the state to retain a youth in juvenile court rather than transferring him or her to adult court.[3]

Testimony by mental health experts also can be enormously valuable at sentencing. If the young killer is convicted of first-degree murder at trial, then defense counsel may use findings from the examiner's assessment to convince the court to choose a sentence alternative to death. Death penalty statutes typically contain specific psychological mitigators. For example, it is a mitigator in certain states if a homicide offender, although legally sane during the commission of the crime, was "under the influence of extreme mental or emotional disturbance." Testimony by a mental health expert that a particular juvenile was unable "to appreciate the criminality of his [or her] conduct or to conform his [or her] conduct to the requirements of the law" when committing the homicide often is another mitigating circumstance.[4] The mental health expert who has completed an in-depth evaluation also could testify to nonstatutory mitigators that might be relevant to understanding the youth's involvement in the murder. These factors might include the effects of egocentrism, child maltreatment, a dysfunctional family, peer pressure, mental retardation, extreme drug or alcohol abuse, or substance addiction on a juvenile's intellectual, emotional, and moral development.[5] In cases where the youth is convicted of something less than capital murder, the defense may present mental health testimony to persuade the court to depart downward from the sentence required or recommended by statute.

In most jurisdictions, if the defense announces that it plans to use a mental status defense at trial, then the prosecution is permitted to have its own mental health experts evaluate the defendant. A thorough assessment by the state's expert is just as essential as one by the defense's expert. In addition to rendering an opinion regarding the defendant's mental state at the time of the homicide, the expert retained by the state may be asked to address particularly whether "aggravating circumstances" apply that might influence a jury or judge to recommend or impose a death sentence in a capital case. Psychologically aggravating factors contained in the statutory guidelines typically involve matters relating to the defendant's knowledge of his or her behavior and the defendant's intentions at the time of the offense. For example, it is an aggravator in certain states if a defendant "knowingly created a grave risk of death" to others such that his or her participation in the crime evinced "reckless indifference or disregard for human life." Another factor in aggravation may apply if a defendant "knowingly directed, advised, authorized, or assisted another to use a firearm" to threaten or injure another person related to the commission of the crime. Aggravating circumstances include whether the defendant intentionally killed the victim, intentionally inflicted serious bodily injury that resulted in the victim's death, or intentionally engaged in conduct designed to bring about the victim's death. Evidence of planning and premeditation of the offense by the defendant also may be considered aggravating conditions.[6]

There are, of course, other pertinent areas of investigation for mental health professionals, regardless of whether they are retained by the defense or the state or appointed to assist the court. These matters may include, for example, whether the defendant appears genuinely remorseful, is amenable to treatment, is presently dangerous, or is likely to constitute a continuing threat to society.

It is not unusual in a complex capital case for several mental health experts to be involved. For example, I was the lead mental health examiner for the defense in a capital case involving a young man, Sammy, whom I suspected was mentally retarded and possibly neurologically impaired. On my recommendation, the young man also was evaluated by a clinical psychologist, a nationally recognized expert in mental retardation, and a neurologist. Based on our findings, defense counsel advised the court that the team of defense experts believed that the defendant was incompetent to stand trial and also was insane at the time of the crime.

Shortly thereafter, my report, incorporating my findings and those of the other defense experts, was given to the state's expert and two court-appointed psychiatrists. The six mental health professionals who examined Sammy all agreed that the defendant was mentally retarded and incompetent to proceed to trial. Five of the six doctors, including the one retained by the state, initially believed the defendant to have been insane at the time of the crime. After 3 years of treatment in a secure mental hospital, the defendant was adjudged competent and returned to jail, where he currently is awaiting trial.

Mental health professionals who perform conscientious evaluations of defendants often find themselves doing research and investigative tasks in addition to their clinical functions. Prior to finalizing my conclusions, I insist on verifying information provided by the young killer so that I can reduce the risk that I am being manipulated by a defendant who is malingering or engaging in deception.[7] Clinicians who assess individuals in prisons and jails, unlike those who treat patients in a therapist's office or a hospital or clinic, cannot assume that patients honestly report their histories, current levels of functioning, and symptomatologies. A murder defendant possibly facing a death sentence, life in prison without parole, or incarceration for 20 or 30 years certainly has reason to lie or to embellish facts.

Valuable corroborative sources include review of case records and clinical interviews with family members and, on occasion, consultation with professionals who have had previous or ongoing contact with the youth. These may include mental health practitioners, schoolteachers, social services staff, and law enforcement personnel. In addition, psychological and neuropsychological testing of the defendant can provide important corroborative data and ideally should be administered by a competent psychologist to every adolescent charged with homicide. On occasion, a neurological assessment by a physician also might be indicated.[8]

Psychological Testing

Although a forensic psychologist may use a variety of tests, he or she almost always administers a revised Minnesota Multiphasic Personality Inventory (MMPI-2). The most widely used psychological test, the MMPI is a 567-item true/false questionnaire designed for use with those age 18 years or over. This test has three validity scales that provide information about the offender's attitude about taking the test and about whether the profile is valid. The MMPI contains 10 major clinical scales and a host of additional scales that provide information about specific problems. The clinical scales and the profile they form provide valuable information about personality, diagnosis, and prognosis.

The MMPI has become one of the most widely used personality tests in forensic evaluations for several reasons.[9] Responses on the validity scales indicate whether offenders are answering the questions honestly or whether they are "faking good" (denying problems and trying to appear better off psychologically than they are) or "faking bad" (trying to appear worse off or more sick than they are). The test provides a reliable, objective portrait of mental health symptoms, and the results can be presented in a relatively clear and understandable manner to legal personnel and juries.

Many repeat offenders, for example, exhibit a "4-9 profile," which means that their responses result in elevations on Scales 4 and 9. This profile suggests that the individual might meet the criteria for antisocial personality disorder (also referred to as sociopathy or psychopathy). An individual with this profile tends to have difficulty with authority figures, is likely to con people, and has difficulty incorporating the values and standards of society. Such an individual might seek immediate gratification of his or her impulses and frequently does not consider the consequences of his or her behavior, which at times is impulsive. Furthermore, an individual with this response pattern usually does not experience much anxiety and generally is not a good candidate for psychological treatment.[10]

In addition to the MMPI, clinical psychologists with whom I consult typically administer the Rorschach Psychodiagnostic Test, Sentence Completion Test, Anger Expression Scale, Coopersmith Inventory (a self-esteem test), and, when indicated, an intelligence test such as the Wechsler Adult Intelligence Scale–Revised (WAIS-R). When a dissociative disorder is suspected, the Dissociative Experiences Scale and/or the Structured Clinical Interview for DSM-IV Dissociative Disorders (SCID-D) also are administered.[11]

Identifying Genuine Versus Malingered Amnesia

The need for corroboration is particularly important in cases where defendants report amnesia, which is relatively common in homicide cases.[12] Although there is no scientifically proven way in which to distinguish malingered from genuine cases of amnesia, significant progress has been made in the development of clinical decision models for the identification of malingered disorders.[13] One threshold model, for example, lists eight events that should alert the clinician to the possibility of malingered amnesia. The more of these factors present, the more likely it is that defendants are lying about their alleged memory deficiencies.

Prior to concluding that defendants are malingering, forensic examiners normally take into account the defendants' presentations, data from their social histories and case-related records, and available information from neuropsychological testing and neurological consultations. Skilled experts who suspect that defendants are faking amnesia typically give them a chance to explain apparent inconsistencies in their presentations. These data are then compared to both real and simulated cases of amnesia.[14]

▨ FORENSIC EVALUATION: FOUNDATION, RESULTS, AND CONCLUSIONS

In preparation for the case studies to come, I highlight areas that I have found to be essential in evaluating defendants. Mental health professionals, defense attorneys, prosecutors, and judges might find this discussion particularly illuminating because it interweaves psychological and legal issues that all must face in dealing with youths accused of homicide. Students and general readers also might be interested in the scientific framework that guides the forensic examiner in understanding the worlds of these young killers, in unraveling the motivational dynamics behind the murders, and in addressing relevant issues such as treatment and continuing threat to the community.

Referral Reasons

Mental health professionals may be asked to evaluate a number of issues. As suggested earlier, these may include young killers' competency to stand trial, their competency to waive their Miranda rights, their sanity at the times of their crimes, their amenability to treatment, or their continuing threat to the community. Under some circumstances, it might be appropriate for examiners to discuss whether young defendants, if they do not represent a continuing threat to the community, could benefit from juvenile sanctions. In capital cases, mental health professionals may be asked to reach an opinion regarding factors in mitigation or aggravation of death.[15]

Unfortunately, it is not always clear to attorneys, judges, mental health professionals, defendants, and jurors what mental health professionals are evaluating. Sometimes, this confusion and lack of specificity can have dramatic results. For example, my review of Mark's case revealed that the mental health experts who evaluated Mark prior to his trial did not address factors in mitigation of death in their evaluations. Depositions taken years later, while Mark was awaiting his execution, indicated that the mental health experts recalled that defense counsel asked them to evaluate the defendant's mental status only at the time of the crime. The examiners limited their assessments to whether Mark was legally insane at the time of the homicidal event and did not consider whether any of the factors in mitigation of death that are concerned with mental status applied.

I, on the other hand, concluded that both statutory and nonstatutory psychological mitigators were present, and I testified accordingly. In addition, I testified that Mark seemed to be a good candidate for rehabilitation when I evaluated him. Although he was arrested three times in the 5 months preceding the killing, Mark did not have a significant history of prior criminal behavior, whether the reference group was youths or adults. He saw himself as responsible for the killing and was very remorseful. Had Mark's appellate lawyers not been as diligent in securing a resentencing hearing, Mark would have been executed. He would have gone to his grave condemned to death by jurors who obviously lacked critical information to render an informed judgment.

Materials Reviewed Pertinent to Evaluation

I prefer to review materials relating to the homicide case prior to meeting with the adolescent homicide offender. When I am thoroughly familiar with the murder, I am better positioned to evaluate the youth's mental state at the time of the crime. Important case information includes initial police incident reports and supplementary interviews with witnesses conducted by law enforcement detectives. Pertinent witness depositions taken by prosecutors or defense attorneys, if available, typically are helpful because these statements are sworn and may be introduced as evidence if the case goes to trial. Statements about the offense that the youth might have made to the police, to the grand jury (if applicable), and to other known parties on record can provide corroborative data, on the one hand, or evidence of malingering or deception, on the other.

Careful review of confessions made to the police can prove invaluable. In the case of Peter, whose story is told in Part II, close examination of the transcript typed from a tape recorder indicated that the purported confession was more reflective of the adolescent's acquiescent response style than a waiver of his Miranda rights and a voluntary admission of guilt to the police officers who questioned him.

In another case, review of videotaped confessions, when combined with extensive case materials, enabled me to reach an opinion that would not have been possible otherwise on the mental status of two defendants at the time of the murders of three individuals. The case involved two brothers accused of killing three family members. I was retained by the prosecution after the boys' defense attorneys filed notice with the court that they intended to pursue insanity or mental infirmity defenses in both cases. Although the court granted the prosecution's motion to allow the state's mental health experts to examine the two defendants, certain restrictions were imposed. The individual evaluations were to be conducted in the presence of the brothers' respective attorneys. In addition, no questions were allowed to be asked about events leading up to the homicides or about events during or after the homicides.

Both youths gave detailed confessions to the police. These statements indicated that each of the adolescents had extensive recall of the events before, during, and after the multiple homicides. Statements made by the brothers indicated that, at the time of the crimes, each knew that he was actively engaged, with his brother and a third party, in killing three people. The youths' extensive recall of events was inconsistent with being in a dissociative state, and there was no evidence to suggest that either boy was psychotic at the time of the homicides or had a psychotic history. The deliberation, choices, and extensive recall of the homicidal events also were inconsistent with either youth being intoxicated to the point that he could not formulate the conscious decision to cause serious bodily harm or death to the victims. Accordingly, I concluded that both defendants were sane under M'Naghten, which was the relevant test in this state, and that the defendants' statements did not support the diminished capacity defense based on intoxication also suggested by defense counsel.

In addition to case-related data, I find it enormously valuable to review pertinent background materials related to the youth himself or herself, preferably before meeting the youth. These include school records, medical records, and social services records with respect to both dependency and delinquency histories. Existing psychological or psychiatric reports or clinical notes from a client's previous mental health interventions also can be helpful in verifying a psychiatric history and in arriving at a correct diagnosis. I list materials that I have reviewed in my report and any additional materials that I would like to see prior to finalizing my opinions with respect to competency issues, mental status, prognosis, or disposition.

Description of the Clinical Evaluation

My clinical evaluations of young killers typically range from 3 to 5 hours. The semistructured interview I have designed provides the means necessary to assess the defendant's level of personality growth. Its format also permits the exploration of the youth's perceptions of the homicidal incident and processing through the adult criminal justice system. In addition, the interview examines other content areas relevant to his or her social history, including family relationships, school, work, friends, drug and alcohol involvement, activities, music and movie preferences, physical and mental health history, feelings and coping strategies, and prior delinquent activity and criminal history.

The responses given by the youth during the interview enable me to achieve a fairly solid grasp of the way in which the youth perceives himself or herself and others and of the youth's characteristic ways of responding to events. The extensiveness of the assessment, particularly when considered in the context of assessments of more than 100 youths charged with one or more violent crimes, provides a solid foundation on which to evaluate an adolescent's statements about the homicidal event, to understand the dynamics behind the killing, to assess his or her mental state at the time of the incident, and to address dispositional factors.

I typically tape-record my clinical interviews with defendants. This procedure has a number of advantages. It allows me to stay focused on the defendant and his or her responses, to keep the pace of the interview going, and to ask pertinent follow-up questions without delay. It provides a record of the adolescent's communications, which may be transcribed verbatim in relevant places. It allows time to go back over an assessment and to deliberate carefully with respect to its content.

Behavioral Observations

Observational data can be invaluable to the forensic examiner. Forensic examiners, as well as many police officers, prosecutors, defense attorneys, and judges, often can get a good sense of whether a defendant is being open and candid by watching his or her body language. Studying the young killer's expressions, movements, and mannerisms frequently reveals whether he or she appears anxious or remorseful at any point in the interview and whether the young killer is being manipulative. Clinicians who have been trained in neurolinguistic programming observe the defendant's eye movements to see how he or she processes information.[16] These data can be helpful in determining the credibility of the youth's statements. In addition, neurolinguistic techniques can be combined with behavioral observations to enhance rapport by matching the defendant's posture, breathing, or movements.[17]

Observational data that I typically address include the young killer's size and appearance. Scars and tattoos are worthy of note and inquiry. During the assessment, I monitor the adolescent's eye contact, degree of alertness, apparent nervousness, ability to concentrate, and level of cooperation. In cases where the defendant's answers are restricted, behavioral data can be helpful in discerning whether the response pattern is indicative of depression, low intelligence, restricted personality development, or the intentional withholding of information.

I routinely inquire whether the defendant is on psychotropic medication, which can affect the adolescent's behavior during the assessment. Mental health professionals often can discern from behavioral data whether the defendant is oriented to time and space, is experiencing active psychotic symptoms, has adequate long- and short-term memory, or currently is depressed.

I exercise care before concluding that a defendant has no affect. The lack of responsiveness by a young killer might be an indication, as in Donnell's case, that an examiner's questions hold little interest for him or her. Donnell was described by a therapist who had seen him on a few occasions as showing no affect. Although his affect was fairly restricted during my evaluation of him, he did become animated and laughed at several points in the assessment, particularly when asked questions that seemed preposterous to him—whether he ever had been sexually threatened in jail, whether he ever had forced sex on any girls, and whether he ever had sniffed glue or other inhalants. He also became animated when I asked him questions related to areas about which he enjoyed talking, such as sexual involvements with girls and sexual history. He laughed when I encouraged him to sing some of the lyrics from one of the rap songs he liked and proudly obliged.

Personality Assessment

An assessment of the adolescent's personality or ego development is essential. Personality assessment reveals how an individual makes sense of the world. In addition to helping interpret behavior, knowing the youth's personality level can aid in determining the credibility of his or her statements. It also is critical in evaluating issues related to the likelihood of continued criminal behavior and in charting treatment strategies and prognosis.[18]

Several frameworks for measuring personality or ego development currently exist.[19] The youths whose stories are told in Part II were classified by the Interpersonal Maturity Level (I-level) classification system.[20] This theory of personality development originated with a group of psychology students at the University of California, Berkeley, in the early 1950s. It has its underpinnings in child development, psychoanalytic theory, Lewinian theory, phenomenological theory, and social perception.[21]

Over the past 40 years, I-level has been widely researched and used with both juvenile and adult offender populations for treatment and management purposes.[22] The construct validity of I-level has been demonstrated using several theoretical constructs, including the California Personality Inventory, Loevinger's ego development system, Eysenck's Personality Inventory,[23] and four other psychological classification systems (Hunt's Conceptual level, Megargee's MMPI-Based Criminal Classification System, Quay's Adult Internal Management System, and the Jesness Inventory Classification System).[24] Research also has shown that although I-level is related, to some extent, to both age and intelligence, it clearly measures more than these two variables and is related to many ego development dimensions such as internalization of values, need for status, tolerance, independence, and flexibility.[25] In addition, several studies have established the predictive validity of I-level in various settings with both juvenile and offender populations.[26]

Research has shown the semistructured clinical interview method to be a more valid and reliable way in which to measure I-level than a structured instrument such as the Jesness Inventory.[27] Studies have reported that agreement on I-level ratings among experienced raters (interrater reliability) using the interview method typically exceeded 80%, even when based on the most difficult cases.[28] Test-retest measures of I-level using the interview method after 8 to 12 months also exceeded 80%.[29]

I-level classifies people into one of seven categories according to the complexity with which they perceive themselves, others, and their environment. The theory postulates that individuals progress from Level 1 to higher levels as they resolve problems encountered at the respective levels. If the developing child has a very stressful or threatening experience, then he or she might resist change and make desperate attempts to remain at his or her present level of development because it seems safer than advancing to the next higher level.[30]

TABLE 4.1 Salient Dimensions of I-Levels 2 to 5

I-Level	Dimensions
2	Typical of very young children
	Others are viewed in terms of whether or not they give them what they want
	Do not know how to predict or influence the behavior of others
3	Typical of young children
	They know that their behaviors affect the responses they get from others
	They see people in stereotypical ways and as objects to be manipulated
	They look for simple formulas to get others to give them what they want
	Their planning is short term
4	Typical of youths by the time they enter their teenage years
	They have a set of internalized values
	They see themselves as accountable for their behavior
	They are aware that they have choices
	They tend to be rigid about codes of correct behavior
	They are aware of feelings and motives in themselves and others
	They can enter into a reciprocal relationship with another
	They are capable of feeling remorse
	They often are concerned with their own uniqueness
5	Not typical in offender populations
	They continue to see themselves as accountable for their behavior
	They are less rigid in their lives and less judgmental toward others
	They can understand viewpoints different from their own
	They can truly empathize with people whose lives are different from their own
	They can play different roles (e.g., mother, employer, sorority sister, graduate student) but may experience role conflict

SOURCES: Warren 1983; Harris 1988; Van Voorhis 1994.
NOTE: I-levels refer to interpersonal levels of maturity.

The maturity levels that have been empirically identified in the offender population range from Level 2 to Level 5.[31] Salient dimensions of these four levels are depicted in Table 4.1. In a population of more than 1,000 delinquents ranging in age from 11 to 19 years, 95% were classified as perceiving at Level 3 (31%) or Level 4 (64%).[32] Among the adolescent murderers whom I have assessed, about 40% to 45% perceive at Level 3 and about 50% perceive at Level 4. Very few perceive at Level 5.[33]

When babies are born, they perceive at Level 1. Infants initially do not see themselves as separate from the world. As they try to satisfy basic needs, they learn to discriminate between self and nonself. For example, they come to realize, in time, that a thumb is part of them, whereas a pacifier is not.

Most infants who recognize differences between self and nonself will move on to the next integration level, where they come to recognize that there are differences between persons and things. For example, a baby learns that a mother and a bottle both provide sustenance. However, an infant boy who perceives at Level 2 knows that when he screams, his mother might come across the room to hold him; a bottle on the kitchen counter will not respond by itself to his crying.

Most children will advance to Level 3, which is considered normal development for toddlers and prepubescent children. Research has indicated that by 14 years of age, 66% to 75% of youths will have moved beyond this level.[34] Adolescents past age 14 who perceive at Level 3 are more likely to get into legal trouble than are higher maturity adolescents in the same age range.[35]

Individuals classified at Level 3 are primarily concerned with identifying who the powerful people are in any given situation. They try to get their needs met by figuring out what formulas to use to manipulate others into giving them what they want. Their formulas consist of conforming to the demands of the person in power at the moment or controlling others through attack or intimidation. They do not feel guilty or perceive a need to make amends for their misbehavior because they do not see that they have done anything wrong.[36]

For example, a 15-year-old boy whom I evaluated was riding his bicycle through the park one day when he saw a man in his late 20s jogging. The man was wearing a large gold chain around his neck. The youth rode the bike up to the man, stopped in front of him, and pointed a handgun at him. The boy reportedly said, "Give me your rope." When the man did not comply, the youth related that he cocked the trigger of the gun and repeated, "Give me the rope." As the man turned away from the 15-year-old and started running, the youth fired four shots into his back. When I asked the youth whether there was any way in which "this whole thing" could have been prevented, he nodded affirmatively and replied, "He should have given me the rope. After all, I asked him twice."

Youths at this level of perceptual development tend to view others in stereotypical ways. They do not yet appreciate that other people have needs and feelings different from their own. When I asked one Level 3 young killer how he was different from his mother, he replied, "She's a lady; I'm a man. I rob people; my momma don't."

Individuals at this socioperceptual level frequently deny that they have strong feelings or deep emotional involvements and are incapable of feeling remorse. A 16-year-old boy, who was convicted of attempted first-degree murder, told me that he shot his best friend and crippled him for life. The youth explained that when he fired the bullets into his best friend, he had mistakenly believed that his best friend had stolen money from him. In light of the circumstances, I asked the adolescent how he would have felt had his friend died. The youth replied, "Better." He explained that "I would not be here today [in prison]. There wouldn't have been any witnesses."

Individuals who move on to Level 4 incorporate the values of "the big people," typically their parents and teachers, and strive to be like them. Unlike individuals at earlier stages, they are able to evaluate their behavior and that of others against an internalized set of standards and have some perception of the role that needs and motives in themselves and others play in behavior. They are aware that behavioral choices are available to them and may experience guilt when they fail to behave in accordance with their values. Those who perceive at this level want to make something of themselves and to be recognized for their ideals, interests, potentialities, and/or accomplishments by those they admire. They have the ability to make long-range plans and to delay their responses to immediate stimuli. They are capable of entering into a reciprocal relationship with another person whose needs, feelings, ideals, and standards of behavior are similar to their own.[37]

Persons at Level 5 are increasingly aware of different ways in which to cope with events. They begin to distinguish roles appropriate for themselves and others for different occasions. Although an individual at this level might sometimes wonder which of the roles is "the real me," the individual is aware of continuity in his or her own and others' lives. Individuals classified at Level 5 are able to appreciate people who are different from them and to understand what they do and how they feel. They are capable of putting themselves in others' roles because they can compare their impressions of events and activities to those of others.[38]

Those who perceive at Level 6 are able to perceive differences between themselves and the social roles they play. They can recognize and accept role inconsistencies in themselves and others because they are able to see continuity and stability. Very few individuals, if any, reach the ideal of social maturity associated with Level 7, the highest level. Individuals at the highest stage of socioperceptual development are able to see the integrating processes in themselves and others.[39]

By maintaining that individuals are accountable for their actions, the criminal justice system implicitly assumes that defendants are at Level 4 or higher. As indicated by the research findings highlighted earlier, many youths have not reached this level of personality development.

Relevant Social History

There are certain areas that I investigate in my clinical interviews with defendants to enable me to get to know them as people. Exploring the following areas gives me information on both structural dimensions of personality (how offenders think) and specific content that might be useful in understanding their worldviews.[40]

Exploring family relationships and dynamics often provides invaluable data about a youth's involvement in crime. Asking an adolescent to describe each of the family members typically gives information related to his or her personality development and bondedness to each member. When a teen is reluctant to disclose negative information about his or her family, sometimes asking how the teen was disciplined will enable him or her to open up. The young killer's answers to questions such as, "If you had children, would you raise them pretty much the way you were raised, or would there be some differences?" often provide insight into the home environment.

Inquiring into the defendant's experiences with school, work, religious organizations, and other activities (e.g., sports, extracurricular activities at school) provides a measure of the youth's involvement in prosocial activities. Questions about friends are good sources of data regarding the adolescent's bondedness to peers and involvement in delinquent or conventional activities. Follow-up questions regarding gang involvement can be asked if suggested by the young killer's responses. Questions about girlfriends and sexual history, as well as about pets and animals, can yield data with respect to bondedness, sociopathy, power and control issues, and destructive traits. Asking about the youth's neighborhood typically provides information about the level of violence that is considered normative in the young killer's environment.

Asking about the youth's movie and music preferences can provide invaluable insight into the adolescent's interests. As discussed in Chapter 2, repeated exposure to violent television and movies, and perhaps even to violent music, might serve to desensitize a particular youth to violence, might act as a disinhibitor, and might even have a hypnotic effect on a youth who is exposed to them repeatedly.

Asking the young killer to describe himself or herself and to indicate things about himself or herself that the youth likes and dislikes often leads to information pertinent

TABLE 4.2 Goldstein's Model of Drug-Related Violence

Psychopharmacological	Some individuals might engage in violent behavior because of the chemical effect on them of short- or long-term ingestion of specific drugs
	Sometimes, the violent behavior is unintended; other times, users intentionally consume drugs to reduce anxiety or to get the courage to do the intended violent act
	Some individuals might become violent due to the increased irritability associated with drug withdrawal
	Some individuals, after taking substances, behave in ways that increase the likelihood that they will become victims of violence
Economic compulsive	Chronic drug users might commit crimes, including violent crimes such as robbery, to secure money to maintain heroin or cocaine addictions
	Sometimes they do not intend to use violence but resort to it as events unfold during the incident (e.g., drug users panic, victim surprises offender in a burglary)
Systemic	Violence associated within the system of drug distribution and use
	This violence is part of doing business in a black market and includes events such as robberies of drug dealers, territorial disputes between drug dealers, and elimination of informants
	It also might include disputes between users over drugs or drug paraphernalia

SOURCES: Goldstein 1985; Goldstein et al. 1990; Goldstein, Brownstein, and Ryan 1992.

to the youth's self-esteem, self-concept, level of insight, and openness to change. Questions about specific types of feelings (e.g., anger, depression, upset, conflict, boredom) and coping strategies typically provide data about the young killer's level of awareness. Inquiries about the defendant's physical health, as well as his or her experiences with mental health professionals, are important data to obtain. The defendant's future goals and "plans," as well as his or her interest in receiving treatment, are helpful in determining prognosis.

I have found that getting an accurate account of drug and alcohol history is critical. Early and extensive drug and alcohol usage can impair the adolescent's development. In addition, exploring how drug and alcohol use affects the life of the youth and his or her interactions is essential. Drug use and drug trafficking appear to be etiological factors in the creation of violence. Paul Goldstein, a professor at the University of Illinois at Chicago Circle, theorized that drugs and violence may be related in three ways: the psychopharmacological, the economically compulsive, and the systemic. These models are highlighted in Table 4.2.

I ask the young killer specific and direct questions about drug and alcohol involvement in relation to everyday life as well as with respect to the homicidal event. I ask detailed questions about the youth's involvement with specific drugs across categories, even in cases where the youth maintains that his or her drug usage has been very limited or nonexistent. Specific questions might jar the memory of a youth who "forgot about that" or is reluctant to reveal information unless a direct question is put to him or her. I routinely inquire about use of stimulants (e.g., cocaine, amphetamines), depressants (e.g., quaaludes, barbiturates), narcotics (e.g., codeine, heroin, demerol), hallucinogens (e.g., LSD, psilocybin, phencyclidine), cannabis (e.g., marijuana, hashish), inhalants (e.g., sniffing glue, gasoline), use of anesthetic gases (e.g., nitrous oxide, ether), and/or short-acting vasodilators (e.g., amyl or butyl nitrate).

I intersperse the street names of various drugs with the classes of drugs to ensure that the youth knows what drugs are being included (e.g., speed, downers, smack, mushrooms, PCP, THC). I also ask specifically about polysubstance use (using two or more substances at the same time or within a few hours). Table 4.3 lists the drugs reportedly used by young killers, their typical effects on users, and the dangers associated with abuse.

The psychopharmacological association of certain drugs with violence is a complex relationship.[41] As noted by professor D. Wayne Osgood of the University of Nebraska at Lincoln, animal studies are the only source of controlled experimental research on the impact of intoxication on violence and are illustrative in this regard.

> A striking finding in this literature is that some illicit drugs, such as marijuana and opiates, lower rather than raise rates of aggressiveness (except during withdrawal from addiction). Other drugs, such as cocaine, amphetamines, and PCP, are associated with violence only as an occasional secondary feature of generalized disorganization in be-havior, which may correspond to paranoia or psychosis in humans. The most definite finding from animal research is that low doses of alcohol produce aggressive behavior in a wide range of species from fish through primates.[42]

Prior Delinquent History

Exploring the youth's prior involvement in criminal activities is relevant to assessing personality development. It also provides important diagnostic information useful to the examiner in making a judgment about the young killer presenting a continued threat to society. Comparing information provided by the youth to prior record data also can provide an indicator of the youth's credibility.

Adjustment in Jail

I ask specific questions about the youth's experiences in jail. In addition to mental health-related questions (e.g., nightmares, sleeping patterns, anxiety level, suicidal ideation or attempts), I inquire whether the youth has been involved in fights, has been physically or sexually assaulted or threatened, or had his or her belongings or food taken. These data can aid the mental health professional in advising whether the youth can adjust to a prison environment, needs to be housed in a special wing, or is a suicide risk.

Motivational Dynamics Behind the Homicide

The use of open-ended questions is particularly helpful in assessing the offender's perceptions of his or her role in the homicide. The defendant's answers to questions such as "What happened that got you in here?" can provide information regarding personality development. Low-level maturity defendants tend to be very event oriented. They will go into detail about how this happened, then this happened, and so on. Higher maturity defendants are more likely to report how they were feeling or

TABLE 4.3 Drugs Reportedly Used by Some Young Killers

	Drug	Street Name	Physical Dependence	Psychological Dependence	Tolerance	Effect on Mood	Other Related Dangers Regarding Abuse	Psychopharmacological Association With Violence[a]
Depressants	Alcohol	Booze	Moderate	Moderate	Yes	Euphoria, relaxation, release of inhibition	Brain damage	Strong
	Barbiturates	Downers	Moderate to high	Moderate to high	Yes	Sedation; induce sleep	Confusion; especially lethal with alcohol	Weak
	Methaqualone	Quaaludes, ludes	High	High	Yes	Hypnotic	Convulsions	Some case reports
	Benzodiazepines	Valium, Xanax (examples)	Low to moderate	Moderate to high	Yes	Sedation; induce sleep	Confusion; effects additive with alcohol	No
Stimulants	Amphetamines, methamphetamine	Speed, uppers, ice	Possible	Moderate (oral); very high (injected or smoked)	Yes	Euphoria, stimulation, hyperactivity	Hallucinations, psychotic episodes	Moderate
	Cocaine	Coke, crack, snow	Possible	Moderate (snorted); very high (injected or smoked)	Possible	Euphoria; excitation followed by depression	Mental impairment, convulsions, unconsciousness	Weak to none

Category	Drug	Slang/Other names	Physical dependence	Psychological dependence	Tolerance	Possible effects	Effects of overdose	Withdrawal syndrome
Hallucinogens	LSD	Acid	None	Low	Yes	Overexcitation, increased emotionality, sensory distortions, hallucinations	More prolonged episodes that might resemble psychotic states, irrational behavior	Rare with exception of PCP (PCP: weak to moderate)
	Psilocybin	Mushrooms	None	Low	Yes			
	Mescalin, peyote	Mesc, cactus	None	Low	Yes			
	Phencyclidine	PCP, angel dust	Very low	High	Yes			
	Amphetamine variants	Ecstasy, doom, STP, MDA, MDMA, MMDA, TMA	Unknown	Unknown	Yes			
Cannabis	Marijuana	Pot, grass, weed	Very low	Moderate	Yes	Euphoria, relaxed inhibitions, impaired memory and attention	Paranoia; at very high doses, a hallucinogenic-like psychotic state	None
	Tetrahydrocannibol	THC, Marinol	Very low	Moderate	Yes			
	Hashish	Hash	Very low	Moderate	Yes			
Narcotics	Opium	Paresoric	High	Moderate (oral) to high (smoked)	Yes	Euphoria, sedation, relieve pain	Convulsions	Weak to none
	Morphine		High	Moderate	Yes			
	Codeine		Moderate	Moderate	Yes			
	Heroin	H, smack	High	Very high (intravenous)	Yes			
	Other narcotics	Demerol, Dilaudid	Varies	Varies	Yes			

SOURCES: Goldstein et al. 1987; Goode 1993; Ray and Ksir 1993; Kuhns 1995; Solomon et al. 1996.

a. Data relating to ingestion of drug being associated with violent behavior.

what was going through their minds at the times of their incidents. By asking a broad-based question, the examiner might also get immediate feedback about whether youths see themselves as accountable for their behavior. There is a big difference, for example, between a young killer who says that he or she currently is in jail "because I caught a murder charge" and another who replies "because I killed a man."

I exercise care not to introduce concepts to the defendant such as "remorse," "victim," or "murder." For example, I never ask defendants whether they are remorseful or sorry for what they have done. If they sincerely feel badly for their homicidal behavior, then it will be revealed in their responses to open-ended questions such as "Thinking about the whole thing now, how do you feel?"

Almost all young killers regret their criminal actions because they are "locked up." There is a significant difference between youths who regret killing their victims because they are now incarcerated and those who are truly sorry for what their actions have done to their victims, the victims' families, and their own families. A large number of young killers feel no remorse. When I ask them how they feel about "the guy who died," many reply that they have no feelings about him and might offer as an explanation, "I didn't know him."

I refrain from referring to the deceased as *the victims* because some young killers see themselves as the victims. Likewise, I avoid using the word *murder* unless defendants use the term because it may suggest that defendants were aware of the illegal nature of their conduct when, in fact, they might not have been. Sammy, the young man mentioned earlier who was charged with capital murder, provides a good example of a defendant whose limited understanding and acquiescent response style made him appear to police and prosecutors to be a good candidate for the electric chair.

My first introduction to Sammy came by way of a videotaped confession taken by the police. The tape opened with the police saying, "We are here to talk about a murder, right?" and Sammy grunting affirmatively. My initial impressions from the defendant's cryptic responses to the police questions was that he was a cold-blooded killer. When I evaluated Sammy later, my clinical opinion was entirely different.

Sammy was a mentally retarded young man from a large family who had very limited contact with the outside world. Records indicated that he had been severely abused by his father since he was a baby. Corroborative data indicated that Sammy's father showed Sammy how to kill by demonstrating a strangling technique and referred to this behavior as "putting someone to sleep." Later, Sammy's father told Sammy to put another family member to sleep.

Sammy did what his father told him to do because he knew that he would be severely punished if he did not. Sammy took his father's words literally and thought that the relative whom he killed would wake up later. In obeying his father, it never occurred to Sammy that this behavior was morally or legally wrong. Sammy first learned that his behavior was "murder" after the police told him.

Neurolinguistic programming training can be invaluable to mental health professionals in helping defendants who report that they are unable to tell the examiners about the homicidal events because they become too upset. Julius, an adolescent who killed his father, had difficulty telling me about the events leading up to the homicide because his mind reportedly would "go blank." He was able to remain focused and to relate details surrounding the killing when I suggested that he step back from the events and tell me about them as though he were watching a videotape.

After the defendant has given a detailed account of the homicide, follow-up questions concerning his or her mental state at the time of the crime are appropriate and often necessary. To the extent possible, I explore what the young killer was thinking and feeling before, during, and after the homicidal event to determine whether a self-defense, insanity, or diminished capacity defense seems pertinent. The defendant's behavior immediately after the homicide often provides data regarding whether the young killer knew his or her behavior was wrong. Answers to questions such as "Did you think about calling the police or an ambulance after you shot him?" typically indicate whether the defendant was aware of the illegal nature of his or her behavior, its deadly consequences, and the potential criminal consequences.

Exploring defendants' voluntary use of drugs and alcohol in relation to the homicides is particularly important in terms of diminished capacity. If young killers mention using drugs or alcoholic beverages during their accounts of the homicidal events, I probe later for where they got the substances, exactly what they took, and when they took it. I include questions regarding what effect, if any, the substances had on their behavior, thinking, mood, and judgment. Additional corroborative data might include who else took these drugs, who else would know about their use of these substances on the days of the homicides, and who else could verify the effects of these drugs on the defendants. Even if the defendants do not mention drugs, I still probe specifically for what drugs, if any, were taken on the days of the homicides.

In every evaluation, I am on the alert for young killers whose acts of destruction appear to be rooted in their characters. Known as nihilistic killers, these murderers represent a grave risk to society. They are individuals who intend to kill and who derive pleasure from watching others suffer.[43] The motivational pattern corresponds to the media depiction, for more than two decades, of "a new breed" of child murderer who appears to kill intentionally, remorselessly, and even gleefully.[44] This pattern also categorizes the adult serial murderer who kills many victims over time for no apparent reason other than satisfaction and release of tension.[45]

A few adolescent murderers who fit this nihilistic pattern truly seemed to enjoy telling me about their murderous activities. For example, these adolescents laughed heartily as they recounted the homicidal events and related that they experienced the victims' dying gestures as "funny." My clinical experiences with young killers have indicated that the best source of data in uncovering this destructive pattern, however, typically was not the adolescents' descriptions of their homicidal activities. Many youths were understandably guarded in their accounts of the murders. Due to the depth of my clinical interviews and the broad array of topics explored, unguarded remarks made about seemingly "innocuous" material provided invaluable data regarding sadistic and destructive character traits. These content areas included girlfriends, pets, activities, careers, and movie and music preferences.[46]

Youths with nihilistic traits often would become animated as they related incidents when they scared others by catching them off-guard, intimidated others by their persona, beat others badly, or destroyed other living things such as dogs, cats, and lizards. Calvin, a young killer who manifested nihilistic traits, related that he would like to be a mortician when he got older because he found death "funny sometimes and just interesting." When probed, the adolescent who was responsible for multiple killings recalled really enjoying a movie in which people died from doing "stupid things" such as bungee jumping. The idea of being a mortician was appealing to Calvin because, as he explained, they make a lot of money, people are always dying, and he has always been fascinated by death.

Other youths who also might manifest nihilistic traits delight in talking about violent and scary movies and music. Donnell, for example, was heavily into "gangsta rap." When asked, he easily described each of the rap singers/groups to which he reported listening. Spice 1 was about "killing a lot of people." MC Eiht was about "killing, making money, fucking whores, and shooting." Eightball and MJG was about "a lot of robbing." Scarface and Geto Boys were about "killing."

Clinical Interviews With Family Members

I routinely speak with family members after evaluating the defendant. Face-to-face interviews are preferable to phone consultations because they enable the examiner to evaluate the source better and they typically result in the party disclosing more personal material. The purpose of these clinical interviews is to determine whether information provided by family members corroborates that given by the defendant, to obtain additional material pertinent to the adolescent's early childhood history, and to get some indication of family dynamics. Parents, grandparents, and siblings often provide information that was not disclosed by the youth because he or she did not know or remember certain events or was reluctant to tell the examiner about them. For example, interviews with family members might provide important information about the medical, psychiatric, or behavioral history of the youth or other relatives.

Evidence of Childhood Maltreatment

I use the Survivors' Coping Strategies Survey, an instrument that I developed with clinical psychologist Eldra P. Solomon, to assess various types of child maltreatment. The instrument has specific indicators of four types of neglect (physical, medical, and emotional neglect and emotional incest) and four types of abuse (physical, sexual, verbal, and psychological abuse), as defined in Chapter 2. Specific questions tap abusive and neglectful behaviors without using labels such as "physical abuse." For example, there are 13 questions that tap physical abuse. One of these questions asks "Did any of your parents ever hurt you physically because they were very angry?" (rather than "Were you ever physically abused?").

The instrument also surveys coping strategies often used by individuals in abusive situations. Examples of these include running away, compulsive behavior, self-mutilation, problems with eating, suicide attempts, and dissociative experiences.

Present Mental Health

As a mental health professional, I use pertinent diagnostic questions to assess whether a young killer has a recognized mental disorder. The diagnoses that I have found most common among this population are conduct disorder, attention deficit hyperactive disorder, substance dependence or abuse, depression, and posttraumatic stress disorder. These mental and behavioral disorders are highlighted in Table 4.4.

TABLE 4.4 Common Diagnoses Among Young Killers

Conduct Disorder	Diagnosis is applicable to children and adolescents under 18 years of age. It is characterized by a long-standing pattern of violating the rights of others or disregarding major societal norms. Diagnostic criteria include specific behavioral indicators of aggression to animals and people, theft or deceitfulness, destruction of property, and other serious rule violations (e.g., truancy, running away). Conduct disorder often is the precursor to a diagnosis reserved for adults who engage in a similar response pattern, Antisocial Personality Disorder. The diagnosis of conduct disorder is to be distinguished from Oppositional Defiant Disorder, often its forerunner. Oppositional Defiant Disorder is a pattern characterized by long-standing defiant, negative, and hostile behavior (e.g., often losing temper, arguing with adults) that is noncriminal.
Attention-Deficit/Hyperactivity Disorder	Diagnosis is based on long-standing difficulties first evident in childhood. Diagnostic criteria include specific behavioral indicators of inattention, hyperactivity, and impulsivity. Established body of research indicates that etiology of disorder is genetically or neurologically based and persists, for many, through adolescence and adulthood.
Substance Abuse	Diagnosis is based on persistent substance use despite negative consequences or distress associated with its use. Negative consequences include failure to fulfill major obligations at home, school, or work; exposure to physically hazardous situations; legal difficulties; and interpersonal difficulties.
Substance Dependence	Diagnosis is based on persistent substance use despite negative consequences or distress associated with its use because of physiological dependence on substance. It is characterized by increased tolerance for the substance and withdrawal symptoms when substance is decreased or depleted in the body. Activities and interest often center around obtaining the substance.
Depression	Diagnosis is based on a noticeable change in previous functioning extending over at least a 2-week period characterized by depressed mood or loss of pleasure or interest. Diagnostic criteria often reflect changes in physiology (e.g., weight loss/gain, sleep difficulties, fatigue) and in cognitive processes (e.g., difficulty concentrating, self-defeating thoughts, suicidal ideation).
Posttraumatic Stress Disorder	Diagnosis is based on symptoms occurring in an individual who has been exposed to life-threatening events (e.g., war, flood, extreme family violence) likely to evoke terror, helplessness, or horror in most individuals. Diagnostic criteria include the reexperiencing of the trauma (e.g., flashbacks, nightmares), numbing of feelings and persistent avoiding of stimuli associated with traumatic events, and persistent symptoms of heightened arousal (e.g., hypervigilance, difficulty sleeping).

SOURCES: American Psychiatric Association 1994; Barkley 1990, 1997.

CONCLUDING REMARKS

Thorough assessment in the case of Donnell, whose case was profiled in the beginning of this chapter, revealed a confluence of factors that contributed to his violent behavior. These factors were brought to the court's attention through my testimony at sentencing.

Donnell's personality development was low. He had not reached the level of personality development where he could see that he was accountable for his behavior and that he had choices. Rather, he thought and acted like a much younger child.

Donnell's restricted personality development was partly due to the chaotic nature of his first few years of life. Donnell experienced early abandonment by both his biological parents and repeated breaks in the bonding process. It is questionable whether he ever bonded to anyone including the grandparents who loved him dearly. There was evidence to suggest that during the short time that he lived with his mother, Donnell might have been neglected and even abused.

As a young adolescent, Donnell lived in several households with different ways of relating and standards for behavior and did not learn responsible behavior. During the 2 to 3 years preceding his arrest for the robbery/homicides, Donnell was living with his father, who was abusing cocaine. While staying with his father, Donnell rarely went to school. He associated increasingly with delinquent youths who lived in low-income neighborhoods known to be violent, and he was arrested for delinquent behavior on a few occasions. Although it was clear to the family, to the school, and to the juvenile justice system that Donnell needed help, no meaningful intervention occurred.

During his middle adolescence, Donnell also became heavily involved in listening to gangsta rap music. The messages in the songs clearly influenced him. When I listened to several recordings after speaking with Donnell, I discovered that some of the responses that he gave to my questions were lyrics from the songs. For example, when I asked Donnell why he shot the clerk immediately on entering the store, he replied that he had gotten "trigga happy," one of the recordings sung by the rapper known as Spice 1.

In addition to the low personality development and unfavorable influences in his early childhood and adolescence, psychological testing revealed that Donnell was of dull-normal intelligence. Donnell also had some brain damage that appeared to have been present from birth.

Under the M'Naghten standard of insanity, however, Donnell unquestionably was sane. At the times of one robbery and of two robbery/homicides, Donnell was aware that he was robbing the stores. When he fired the shots that killed the two victims, he was aware that death could result from his actions. He reported that he was mentally alert when he went into the convenience stores. He was certain that, on these three occasions, he was not high on either alcohol or other drugs because he liked to be in control when he went robbing. His change of clothes, his concern about where the car was parked, and his flight indicated that he was aware that his actions were against the law, although he did not experience them as wrong.

The American Law Institute test was among the mitigating factors enumerated in the state statute. If it had been the test for insanity, then it is possible that, had the case gone to trial, Donnell could have been found to have been insane, particularly when the other factors just highlighted were taken into account. My assessment indicated that "the capacity of the defendant to appreciate the criminality of his conduct" was "substantially impaired." At the time of the offense, the youth knew what he was doing (M'Naghten test), but it is clear from Donnell's remarks to me that he had no emotional appreciation of the consequences of his behavior regarding the victims who died, those who witnessed the crime, his family, and the community at large. Donnell's inability to appreciate the effect of his actions was due to his restricted personality development. Both the clinical psychologist and I saw the defendant as nonevaluative and his actions as impulsive. The psychologist testified further that the defendant did not appear capable of deliberating but rather reacted immediately to stimuli, raising the question of whether his capacity "to conform his conduct to the requirements of the law was substantially impaired" at the times of the killings.

Sentencing guidelines suggested that the defendant be incarcerated for a period of 22 to 39 years. The judge sentenced Donnell to 39 years. Although defense counsel had hoped that the judge would impose a sentence on the lower end, Donnell's attorneys were somewhat relieved that, given the aggravating factors in the case, the judge did not exceed the recommended sentence. Donnell's grandfather offered to use monies from Donnell's trust fund to pay for psychotherapy while Donnell was incarcerated, and defense counsel were investigating ways in which to accomplish this end.

This chapter illustrated the importance of a comprehensive evaluation. In the next part of this book, complete case studies of adolescent murderers are presented. These case studies look at the young killers at several points in time including at the time of arrest, prior to being charged with murder, and after several years in prison.

Part Two

Clinical Portraits

THE NEXT seven chapters consist of case studies of adolescent homicide offenders referred by their lawyers to me for clinical evaluation. All of these youths were convicted of homicide and sentenced to prison. Prior to writing this book, I conducted follow-up interviews with all of them in which they gave me permission to tell their stories.

Three of the seven young killers whose stories are told were convicted of one or more counts of first-degree murder. Although all of these boys initially were charged with capital murder, none was actually sentenced to death. Of the four remaining cases, one was convicted of second-degree murder, two were convicted of third-degree murder, and one was convicted of manslaughter.

The personality development of five of these seven young killers was low. These youths were classified as perceiving at Level 3 of the Interpersonal Level of Maturity Theory, the tenets of which were discussed in Chapter 4.

— Peter, age 17, was convicted of first-degree murder and robbery after stabbing an elderly man to death.
— Jerry, age 17, was convicted of first-degree murder after shooting his best friend.
— Calvin, age 17, was convicted of third-degree murder after participating with sev -
   eral other youths in the beating death of another youth.
— David, age 17, was convicted of third-degree murder of a man he shot at and chased after the man slapped his face.
— Malcolm, 15, was convicted of two counts of first-degree murder for killing two people in two armed robberies. He also was convicted of two counts of attempted first-degree murder in relation to two other robberies.

Among those who perceive at Level 3, three behavioral subtypes have been identified: the *passive conformist*, the *cultural conformist*, and the *manipulator or counter-active to power*.[1] Peter fit the passive conformist subtype, Jerry and Calvin fit the cultural conformist subtype, and Malcolm fit the manipulator or counteractive to power sub-type. David did not fit any of the types. The behavioral response styles of the five Level 3 youths will be discussed in their respective stories.

The two remaining youths perceived at Level 4.

— Joel, age 15, was convicted of second-degree murder for the killing of his high school principal. He also was convicted of several other charges related to the wounding of another principal and teacher and shooting at two police officers.

— Brian, age 18, was present when his friend beat a man to death and was convicted of manslaughter.

Among individuals classified at Level 4, four characteristic ways in which to re-spond to people and events in the world have been empirically identified.[2] The behav-ioral response used by the Level 4 youths whose stories follow is that of *neurotic acting out*, one of two neurotic subtypes. These two subtypes overwhelmingly predominate among offenders who perceive at Level 4.[3]

Individuals who comprise either of the neurotic subtypes, neurotic anxious or neurotic acting out, generally feel anxious and conflicted due to unresolved issues, guilt, and feelings of inadequacy dating back to childhood. Accordingly, they charac-teristically behave in ways that are self-defeating. They might, for example, commit crimes; abuse alcohol, drugs, or food; and remain in situations that are self-defeating. For the neurotic subtypes, criminal or delinquent behavior, including the illicit use of substances, has some private meaning and is part of the neurotic pattern of coping. Instead of trying to resolve long-standing anxieties and pressures, the neurotic subtypes try to deal with their difficulties in one of two ways. Neurotic anxious individuals tend to ruminate about the same events, whereas neurotic acting-out persons attempt to outrun their problems. In a nutshell, neurotic acting out individuals often act out the conflict that they are unable to resolve.

Neurotic acting out individuals have little motivation to understand and resolve their difficulties. Instead, they focus their attention on reducing or overcoming their immediate anxiety and pressures through direct action. In relationships with adults, parents, and other authority figures, they often are concerned with issues of behavioral control. They typically invest in projecting an image of personal adequacy or autonomy to compensate for feelings of inadequacy and test others by acting out behaviorally and sometimes verbally. With adults or peers, they have a preference for nonintimate rela-tionships and tend to choose relationships that are more instrumentally or pragmatically oriented.[4]

Close inspection of the cases mentioned earlier reveals that the seven boys whose stories follow killed friends, acquaintances, and strangers. The dynamics involved in cases of youths who kill parents typically are different from those encountered in nonfamily killings. These dynamics are discussed and illustrated in several clinical por-traits in my book, *Why Kids Kill Parents: Child Abuse and Adolescent Homicide*.[5]

Before presenting the seven stories, it is important to note that the case history method has some disadvantages.[6] Such studies almost always are retrospective, so the data on which interpretations are based might be distorted or selective, particularly if corroborative data are not examined and collateral sources are not consulted. Moreover, each case history is unique and cannot be replicated. One cannot predict how far the findings in a particular case study generalize to the larger population. Causation cannot be determined with this method because the case study method investigates only in-dividuals who have a particular problem or fall into a particular category—in this case, adolescent murderers—and does not focus on those who do not.[7]

Clinical case study, however, has several important advantages.[8] It involves studying actual people with real difficulties and, unlike laboratory experiments, is not contrived or artificial. In addition, the clinical case history can investigate phenomena that are so rare or peculiar that it is unlikely that they could be ethically studied using any other standard method of investigation. Clinical case studies also are essential in generating hypotheses about the causes of and solutions to particular problems and, on occasion, in providing disconfirming evidence for a prevailing hypothesis.[9] They also serve to enhance understanding of particular individuals.[10]

Chapter Five

Peter Daniels

PETER DANIELS, a 17-year-old White youth, had just finished his dinner at his grand-parents' house when he left with permission to visit a friend. His friend was not home, so he proceeded to go to the home of another friend. En route, Peter got tired of walking. At about the same time, a late model car parked in a nearby driveway caught his eye.

Peter easily broke into the owner's home. The sole occupant was Mr. Smith, a 78-year-old widower, who was in the bathroom. Peter took a steak knife that happened to be on the kitchen counter. When the elderly man came out of the bathroom and sat down at the kitchen table, apparently to resume his game of solitaire, Peter thrust the knife into the victim's neck.

Peter ran outside to get rid of the knife. The youth then entered the man's home a second time to get the car keys. He took off moments later in the victim's car. During the next 2 to 3 days, Peter and his friends sped around and had fun in Mr. Smith's car.

Peter was arrested 3 days after stabbing Mr. Smith. Peter's grandmother had called the police because she was concerned about whose car her grandson was driving. Peter subsequently was charged with first-degree murder, burglary of a dwelling, robbery with a deadly weapon, and grand theft. The state announced its intention to seek the death penalty. I was appointed by the court, at the motion of defense counsel, to examine the defendant, particularly with respect to trial preparation related to second phase and to give the report pertaining to factors in mitigation to defense counsel.

THE CLINICAL EVALUATION

My assessment of Peter Daniels is based on a 3-hour interview conducted in adult jail 9 months after his arrest. I consulted with Peter's maternal grandparents and aunt, and with his mother and stepfather and their son 2 days later, for more than 4 hours.

Case materials reviewed included the police investigation reports, autopsy reports, and a transcribed confession given to police on the day of his arrest. I also studied a psychological evaluation, school records, and records from an inpatient drug rehabilitation program in which Peter had participated for a 3-week period 9 months prior to his arrest. In addition, I examined materials provided by Peter's grandmother, Mrs. McEwen. These included correspondence from Peter to Mrs. McEwen, a statement reportedly written by Peter concerning events on the day of the homicide, and a statement allegedly written by another youth implicating one of Peter's friends in the homicide. Newspaper clippings reporting the death of Peter's father and a statement written by Peter's maternal aunt regarding the drug rehabilitation program also were provided by Mrs. McEwen.

BEHAVIORAL OBSERVATIONS

Peter was 18 years old at the time of the clinical assessment. He was approximately 5 feet 10 inches in height and weighed about 140 pounds. Rapport was established fairly quickly, and the youth related in a trusting way. His eye contact was generally very good.

Peter seemed alert, although mildly tense, throughout most of the interview. He experienced noticeable discomfort when asked to answer some questions about the murder and seemed almost tormented as he talked about what could happen to him. His mood could best be described as somber.

Peter was extremely cooperative during the 3-hour period. He listened intently to hundreds of questions and did not refuse to answer anything asked of him. He appeared to work hard to concentrate and let me know when he did not understand the nature of the question. His answers often were restricted due to his level of personality development and his level of intellectual functioning. His ability as an accurate historian regarding family matters appeared limited, making consultation with a family member important for clarification.

Peter's answers clearly indicated that he was oriented in time and space. His short-term memory and, for the most part, his long-term memory were intact. There were no data to suggest that he was responding to private sensory experiences (hallucinations) or that he had delusional beliefs or a delusional network in place.

The youth did not appear to be manipulative during the interview. His responses to questions and his behavior during the interview generally suggested that he was trying to be truthful. I questioned the accuracy of a few responses pertaining to the homicidal event because they appeared inconsistent with prior statements that he had made to police and with his responses to some of my probe questions. When these discrepancies were subtly probed, it was apparent that the youth was not engaged in trying to deceive me.

PERSONALITY DEVELOPMENT

Peter's way of perceiving the world was fairly simplistic, and he met the diagnostic criteria for Level 3 of the Interpersonal Maturity Level (I-level) classification system. The youth's ability to plan prior to the arrest seemed to be limited typically to short-term events, and his behavioral responses appeared impulsive and nonevaluative.

Characteristic of Level 3 youths, Peter operated on the basis of formulas that seemed to provide the structure he wanted and needed to get by in life. Peter's behavioral response style was characteristic of the Level 3 *passive conformist*.[1] The youth described himself in conventional, socially desirable terms during the clinical interview. Peter saw himself as a person who got along with adults and peers. He did not see himself as "a bad dude." He genuinely appeared to see his involvement in the homicide as the result of external forces—particularly drugs—and not as acceptable behavior. He came across as relatively open to listening to authority figures.

Peter had a low sense of self-esteem and a correspondingly high need for social approval. Although his relationships with peers appeared very superficial, Peter wanted their approval. Peter's formula for getting along with people was to conform to their wishes.

Peter described himself as "easy to get along with. I would share alike. I wouldn't argue or fight back." When asked what his friends would say about him, Peter reported, "I used drugs and I liked to goof off sometimes. That's mainly it." When asked whether there was anything about himself that he did not like, Peter said, "Drugs—I'd like to quit that altogether."

RELEVANT SOCIAL HISTORY

Family Constellation

Peter reported that his mother and father did not marry each other. Peter's mother still was living at her parents' home when he was born. At some point—Peter did not remember when—his mother moved out and he remained with his grandparents. He lived with his grandmother and grandfather most of his life.

Peter reported that his mother lived about 20 minutes away from his grandmother's home. He stated that he used to go to stay with her on weekends. Peter did not know why he did not live with his mother when she left her parents' home.

Peter decided to go to live with his mother at 13 years of age because he wanted to see what it would be like. He lived with his mother and her husband for 2 to 3 years. Peter returned to his grandparents' home when he was about 15 because he did not think his mother cared about him.

Peter indicated that his mother was 36 years old and working as a cook in a nursing home at the time of the assessment. When asked to describe his mother as a person, Peter said, "I have no idea." He could not list any ways in which he was like his mother or different from her because he really did not know her well. When asked what it was like for him not to know his mother, Peter replied that it was "difficult. I'd like to know her better."

Peter's mother reportedly married David, a man who was a few years younger than her, about 3 or 4 years prior to the evaluation. Peter described David as "all right," a man who worked in computers. Peter "got along with" David. Peter stated that his mother and stepfather smoked marijuana when he lived with them and that he had smoked marijuana with his stepfather on one occasion.

Peter related that, at the time of the clinical assessment, his mother and David had a 9-year-old son, George. (George actually was 10, almost 11.) Peter stated that George was a "nice little brother" and that they got along together.

Peter was raised with two children who were about his age: Mark and Patricia. Peter said that Mark, his cousin, was like him because Mark really did not know his father either. Mark's mother, Donna, was Peter's mother's sister. Donna, who lived nearby, was married to Frank, who was not Mark's father. Mark's father was living in another state.

Peter stated that Patricia is his grandmother's daughter and his aunt. She was 18 and a senior in high school at the time of the clinical assessment. Peter described Patricia as "a human being. She's up in the world, on top of things. She's smart." Peter stated that their relationship was casual. Peter had not been sexually involved with either Patricia or Mark.

Peter was young—around 2 years of age—when he last saw his father. Peter's father died when he was about 14. Peter did not know why his father had no contact with him. The youth had no memory of his father and felt that he should have known "a little bit more" what the man was like. About the only thing Peter knew was that his father, after whom he was named (Peter Carmichael), was a police officer and had another family who might have lived nearby.

When asked in another context whether there was anyone that Peter looked up to and wanted to be like, the adolescent said his father. "I just knew he was a police officer, and his dad before him was a police officer, and I would have liked to follow in his footsteps, make it a[nother] generation."

Peter described his grandmother as a caring person and said that she was the one who cared the most about him in the family. "She would talk to me if I got in trouble." His grandfather did not talk that much to him but sometimes would watch television with him. Peter expressed some concern about the effect his grandfather's drinking was having on his health. He was concerned that his grandfather might have been an alcoholic.

Peter reported that his mother and brother had been to see him twice during the 9 months he had been incarcerated. The last visit from his mother that he recalled was about 4 months prior to my assessment when she came with Peter's attorney. Peter reported speaking to his mother on the phone about once a week. She would ask him how he was doing and whether he needed anything. Peter's stepfather had been to see him once. Peter's grandfather had been to see him about three times. Patricia had been to see him about five times. By contrast, his grandmother saw him every week on visiting day and always stayed the entire 2-hour period.

Peter had the feeling that his parents did not care about him. He said, "I never really talked to 'em that much." When asked to describe a good mother, Peter said it would be "somebody who would sit down and talk to you about your problems." When asked whether his mother or his grandmother was a good mother, he answered no and yes, respectively. Peter described a good father as "somebody who shares things with you." When asked whether anybody had been a good father to him, Peter replied no.

Peter's grandmother punished him when he did things wrong by spanking him with a wooden spoon. The youth saw these beatings as deserved and not as excessive. He said that he also was grounded for 2 to 3 weeks but that he would not have to do the whole time because his grandparents would let him off.

When probed about possible abuse, Peter's answers suggested that no sexual abuse or physical abuse had occurred. Some psychological abuse or verbal abuse might have occurred. He recalled his parents "once in a while" cussing at him (calling him an "asshole" or a "jackass") when he did something stupid. The alcohol and drug use reported in both homes suggested a strong possibility of emotional and physical neglect (failure to supervise adequately).

School

Peter stopped going to school in the 9th grade because he did not like to go to school. Peter said, "I don't do so good in school." He explained that he had a "slow [specific] learning disability" (SLD) and was assigned to special SLD classes because "I am not as fast as the other kids. It takes me time to work it out."

Although the youth maintained that his learning disability had not given him "any trouble," he could not keep up with all the work required in seven classes every day. School got harder for him when he got into the middle school, around the 6th grade, because the teachers did not help him as much. "The teachers put it on you. The teachers let you be an adult."

Peter saw most of the teachers as "the same." He remembered one teacher, Miss Talbot, who taught him in the SLD program when he was in the 1st or 2nd grade, helping him in science and English. He said that "she would talk with you about your problems."

Peter related that he got along fairly well with the teachers and other students. He had been in trouble in school once or twice but could not recall why. He had been suspended for being a "disruption in class." He explained that he acted like a "smart aleck" about three or four times because he wanted to be "noticeable." He denied getting into fights often at school.

Peter attended alternative school for a couple of weeks after dropping out of regular school. He stopped attending because "I didn't feel like going anymore." When asked why, he said, "No reason."

Work History

Peter worked at two jobs in the months preceding the homicide. First, he worked full-time for about a month with his grandfather at a lumber company building trestles to go on the roofs of homes. Afterward, he helped a neighbor build pools full-time for about 2 to 3 months.

Friends

Peter had a few friends who were "all the same." Peter described his friends as teens who "liked to do what I liked doing." He mentioned skipping school with Charlie and smoking some dope with other youths who would go with them. Peter also would go over to Cory's house frequently and party with him until about 11 p.m.

Peter maintained that his friends were not the type of adolescents who got into a lot of trouble. He noted that several of them (Barnie, Charlie, and the Smith brothers) had been held in the juvenile detention center awaiting hearings in juvenile court or placed in a short-term commitment program after being convicted of delinquent acts. When asked, Peter said that loyalty to friends was not important to him. Peter had not heard from any of his "drug friends" since his arrest. He had heard from his girlfriend and a few other girls.

Girlfriends

Peter had had only one girlfriend, Charlotte, prior to his arrest. They had been dating for about a year. Peter indicated that they got along together and shared things, that he cared about her, and that he would like to see the relationship continue. He also stated that he got along great with her parents. When asked whether sex was a big deal for him, he answered no. He related that Charlotte wrote to him about once or twice a month and had visited him twice.

Activities

Peter enjoyed swimming during the summer and playing basketball and football. He stated that he had played basketball one year while he was in high school. He described himself as an "average" player.

Alcohol and Drug Involvement

Peter began using drugs when he was about 14 years old. "It [marijuana] was going around school, and I just joined a group of kids and started doing it on a regular basis." Peter smoked daily because he "just liked the feeling. You were mellowed out, you didn't disturb nobody or nothing, you caused no problems." When Peter felt bad, he also comforted himself by using drugs. Peter bought drugs with money that his grandmother gave him for lunch or got them from friends would give some to him.

He stated that he had used two other types of drugs: cocaine and acid. He said that he "did" powder cocaine for the first time about 7 or 8 months before the homicide because he and a couple of friends wanted to try it. Peter said that "coke was okay" and that he liked it, but he stopped using it after a month because he and his friends stopped going to the place where they had bought it. He described the high from cocaine as different from the high from marijuana. "Coke is, you are, like, hyper. You want to, like, fight somebody all the time." He explained that if "somebody said something smart, you would turn around and hit 'em. . . . You didn't care if you got hurt or nothing. You would go ahead and do it."

Peter reported dropping acid three times: the day of the homicide and the 2 days following it. When asked initially how he remembered that so clearly, he replied that he just remembered taking it with his friends, Cory and Barnie. He stated that on acid, "you would see things and sometimes you would black out and not know what you were doing." When probed about what one would see, Peter said, "Lil' green men, smurfs, Bambi." He said that he did not see smurfs but did see Bambi and that "you go into a cartoon land. Everything looks like a cartoon . . . different and strange."

When asked whether he ever saw himself as having a problem with drugs, Peter answered yes and related that he had been in a drug rehabilitation program approximately a year before the murder. He stated, "I got kicked out because I left the campus and I wanted to get my drugs." After being discharged, Peter went back to live with his grandmother, who also saw him as having a problem with drugs.

Peter did not see himself as having a problem with alcohol. He admitted that he would drink a couple of beers if he did not have drugs but said that he did not like the taste of alcohol. Peter attended Alcoholics Anonymous meetings in jail. He indicated that he had "gotten nothing out of it" because he did not have a problem with alcohol.

The youth stated that he had not taken any illicit drugs since his arrest. He related that he has thought about using drugs sometimes but that eventually the urge would go away. Peter claimed that he did not intend to resume using illicit drugs because he has come to believe that these drugs made him commit the homicide and that he "would wind up in the same position again."

Mental Health History

Peter reportedly had received no counseling on an outpatient basis or in school prior to his arrest. He saw himself as needing help at the time of the clinical assessment "to get to a level where I am supposed to be at. Some people would have a 10th-grade average; I would have a 5th grade." This deficit made him "feel bad."

Peter recalled taking tests and speaking with a clinical psychologist for several hours about 6 months prior to speaking with me. Aside from this doctor and myself, Peter had not talked to any mental health professionals while in jail. Peter expressed interest in getting some more counseling on drugs.

Peter had thought about killing himself since his arrest. He was not suicidal at the time of the assessment because he was hopeful about the outcome of the trial.

Handling Problems and Affectivity

Peter did not see himself as a person who had strong feelings about things. However, when specifically asked questions relating to anger, Peter acknowledged that he often had experienced angry feelings. His statements suggested that he had trouble discharging anger effectively.

Religious Affiliation

Peter apparently had not been raised with any religious affiliation. Since his incarceration, he had met with the jail's minister, attended some services, and professed to believe in God.

Prior Delinquent Involvement

Peter never had been arrested prior to this incident. He mentioned being stopped for trespassing and getting a ticket for speeding. Peter denied any prior involvement in stealing, home burglary, robbery, or car theft.

Future Orientation

Peter indicated that in the future, he would like to make his living building pools because at the end of it "you can see what you did." He also would like to get married someday and have children because that is "the way I feel." He would raise his children differently from the way in which he was raised; he would "teach 'em to care and to share alike."

Adjustment in Jail

Peter's statements suggested that he had made an adequate adjustment in the 9 months that he had been housed in the juvenile section of the adult jail. After describing the physical location of his cell, he said that it was "nice." Peter was attending a Life Skills program that met for about 3 hours weekly and had a work assignment that consisted of cleaning up the unit.

Peter "got along fine" with the roommate with whom he had been housed for about a month because it was the first time this boy had gotten into trouble and he could talk to him. Peter also could talk to five or six of the youths whom he knew from the outside. His comments indicated that he was not comfortable with youths who were "criminal," that is, youths who had been "in and out of trouble all of their lives."

Peter reportedly had not been threatened, had not had any of his possessions taken by other inmates, and had not been bothered sexually by the other juveniles with whom he had been housed. He "guessed" that he had not had any difficulties with the other inmates because "they are scared of me because of my charges."

■ SYNOPSIS OF CONSULTATION
WITH FAMILY MEMBERS

Two days after examining Peter, I met with his grandparents, Mr. and Mrs. McEwen, and their 18-year-old daughter, Peter's Aunt Patricia, as a group and later individually, for $2^{1}/_{2}$ hours. I met with the defendant's stepfather and mother, Mr. and Mrs. Dalton, and their 11-year-old son, George, again collectively and then individually, for $1^{3}/_{4}$ hours. Information obtained from them was generally consistent with information given by Peter, particularly regarding family constellation, the youth's school and work history, alcohol and drug involvement, friends, girlfriends, mental health history, and lack of previous criminal involvement.

Mrs. McEwen stated that incarceration had been a difficult experience for Peter. A letter dated about 2 months after the homicide from Peter to Mrs. McEwen (addressed "Dear Mom") suggested that Peter initially had felt very stressed in jail. Both grandparents expressed concern about Peter's safety if he was sent to an adult prison.

Mrs. McEwen advised that Peter had difficulties in learning since he began attending school and provided school records in support. Testing conducted when Peter was in the 4th grade and after his arrest indicated that Peter's intelligence was in the dull/normal range (IQ scores = 83 and 82, respectively). Peter's school difficulties and testing conducted by the consulting psychologist suggested possible neurological difficulties. He attended SLD classes through the 6th grade. These classes were not available when he went to live with his mother in another county.

Mrs. McEwen explained the history behind Peter's dropping out of school. Peter liked school and attended regularly prior to being admitted to the drug treatment facility approximately 9 months before the homicide. When he was discharged from this hospital, his high school refused to take him back. He attended an alternative school for a while and disliked it. It was at this point that he began skipping school and then dropped out of school.

Family members generally agreed that Peter started using drugs excessively when he was about 13 or 14 years old. The McEwens believed that Peter started using drugs, skipping school, and associating with "the wrong crowd"—youths who got into trouble—after he went to live with his mother and stepfather. His father died during this same period. The Daltons maintained that Peter already was on drugs and out of control when he went to live with them.

At the time of my evaluation, these two groups of family members essentially functioned as two separate families. There was a great deal of animosity between the two families, and each set was quick to hurl accusations at the other group. Statements by family members in two important areas, however, were consistent. These concerned the family's reaction to Peter's arrest and the pathology of the family system.

The Family's Reaction to Peter's Arrest

Mr. and Mrs. McEwen, Patricia, and Peter's mother all expressed disbelief that Peter committed the homicide. They stated that this behavior was totally inconsistent with Peter's prior behavior. They were convinced that Peter did not act alone because Peter was a follower, not a leader. Although they knew that Peter was in the victim's home during the homicide, they did not believe that he stabbed the victim. Mrs. McEwen reported that Peter seemed "cool as a cucumber" after the homicide. She did not believe that Peter would have acted so calmly if he had just killed someone.

Mrs. McEwen related that when Peter was first interviewed by police about the homicide and was asked basic questions (e.g., "How was the man killed?" "How many times did you stab him?"), he initially replied that he did not know. Later, he answered these questions. When she asked Peter how he knew then but did not know earlier, he replied that the police said the victim was stabbed twice and so he must have done that.

The family members maintained that Peter was covering for another youth, Barnie, who had either threatened Peter or duped him or both. They had some evidence to support this belief and showed me a letter written by another youth alleging that Barnie killed Mr. Smith. The family wanted the public defender's office to depose witnesses who could verify that Barnie had admitted involvement in the homicide.

Peter Was Raised in a Dysfunctional Family

It was clear after speaking with various family members for more than 4 hours that Peter was raised in a dysfunctional family. Although there were points of disagreement, certain facts suggesting family dysfunction were agreed on by family members. In some areas where there was disagreement, the evidence presented made it possible to make some determination of which family members were reporting more accurately.

Bitterness and animosity among the grandparents, parents, and their children were apparent. Even in a time of real tragedy—Peter's arrest for murder—the family members were pointing fingers at one another regarding who was to blame. The data suggested that Peter was raised in a chemically dependent family, was emotionally neglected by his mother, was rejected and abandoned by his father, and was physically abused for a short period by his stepfather.

In this family, the generations and the roles have blurred. Peter was born out of wedlock and raised for most of his life by his grandmother, Mrs. McEwen, whom he considered his mother. Mrs. McEwen raised another grandchild, Mark, who also was born out of wedlock. (Mark's mother was Donna, Peter's mother's younger sister.) Peter regarded his 18-year-old aunt, Patricia, the daughter of his grandparents and with whom he also was raised, as his sister.

Peter did not consider anyone to be his father. At no time in his life did he have a strong, positive male figure with whom to bond or identify. Peter had no contact with his natural father. Although his father lived close by, he did not acknowledge his son. This abandonment and rejection was psychologically abusive. Peter's father contributed nothing to the child's support. Peter was not informed that his father had died until after the funeral.

Peter's grandfather, with whom Peter lived for most of his life, was a practicing alcoholic. Mr. McEwen related that he had been arrested for driving under the influence (DUI), had violated probation for drinking, and had gone to jail as a result. However, Mr. McEwen did not see himself as ever having had a drinking problem.

During the 2 to 3 years when Peter lived with his mother and her husband, he was again in an environment where adults abused substances. The parents smoked marijuana frequently. On occasion, Peter would have observed them using drugs.

Peter's stepfather did not embrace the role of a father in Peter's life. Mr. Dalton acknowledged using an aggressive style with Peter that might have been physically abusive when the boy was younger.

▦ MOTIVATIONAL DYNAMICS BEHIND THE HOMICIDE

In this section, I recap Peter's statements to the police before detailing those that he made to me. Peter's statements to the consulting psychologist were consistent with those he made to me. My conclusions follow.

Peter's Statements to the Police

There were three statements by Peter. The first spontaneous one, "I did it," was followed by a statement apparently given to Detective Williams that was summarized in his report, and the third was transcribed. No mention was made on the tape whether Peter was on drugs at the time of the taped interview. Detective Williams' report indicated that Peter had related prior to the taping of his statement that he had not consumed any drugs or alcohol on the day of the murder.

Peter's transcribed answers to Detective Williams' questions initially suggested that he had been watching the victim, Mr. Smith, for about 4 days because he had been thinking about taking the man's car. He answered twice affirmatively when asked by the officer whether he had decided to steal the car and to kill the man on the Sunday before the homicide. When asked immediately afterward what his reason was for killing the man, the youth replied "to steal the car." Peter described how he entered the home and killed the man. When asked whether anybody else was involved, Peter said no.

Peter's Statements to Dr. Heide

Peter gave a detailed account of his behavior on the day of the homicide and particularly on the 2- to 3-day period following the murder prior to his arrest. He related that on Wednesday, the day of the killing, he stayed at home waiting for his mother. She was supposed to pick him up at 4 p.m. to go shopping for shoes. He claimed that he had "acid left over for the next day" and that he took some at 3 p.m. His mother failed to come.

At around 5 or 6 p.m., Patricia took him to his mother's house, and the three of them went to the shoe store in a nearby city. On the way back, Patricia and Peter stopped at his boss's house, and Peter remembered speaking to him and his wife. He remembered returning home and eating dinner at around 8 or 8:30 p.m.

Peter left his grandmother's home after dinner and went down the street to see a friend, who was not home. He stated, "By that time, the acid was starting to kick in pretty hard and I left." He decided to go to another friend's house. En route, about a block from his house, Peter recalled saying to himself, "I'm tired of walking, I'll steal a car." At that point, he was in front of Mr. Smith's home. He went in through the porch door and saw that one of the sliding glass doors was open. After entering, he saw Mr. Smith.

> He was in the bathroom, and I was gonna pick up something to scare him, and that's when I wound up picking up the knife and I put it in my hand and stepped back out on the porch. He came [out of the bathroom] and sat down and started playing cards [at the kitchen table]. And that's when—I didn't say nothing—I just stepped in the house and I cut him in the neck or stabbed him in the neck. He fell to the floor, and I ran outside and threw the knife in the street, and then I came back in and grabbed his keys, got into his car, and went to the friend's house I was going to go to before I did this.

Peter did not know Mr. Smith and had never seen him before the incident. He stated, "I just wound up at his house." He related that the police had asked him whether he ever had "stalked the house." Peter told me he did not know what that meant when he replied yes. He thought that the police were asking him whether he ever had gone past Mr. Smith's house. "I walked by his house every day. I thought that's what they meant. They meant, did I ever watch him?" Peter maintained that prior to that moment when he was walking by Mr. Smith's house, the thought to steal this particular car—a year-old Thunderbird—had not occurred to him. He did not know to whom the car belonged or who lived in this particular house.

Peter ripped the screen because the screen door was locked. He was able to get into the house because the sliding glass door was open. He picked up a 4- to 5-inch blade steak knife that had been on the kitchen counter. "I picked it up just to scare him, to tell him to give his keys up, and I ended up stabbing him." Peter stated that Mr. Smith did not see him.

When asked what was going through his mind at the time of the incident, Peter replied, "My mind was just blank. I did not know what to do; it just ended up that way." Peter maintained that the thought to kill Mr. Smith did not occur to him. "It just sort of happened." When asked what he was thinking when he was out on the porch waiting for Mr. Smith to come out of the bathroom, Peter said, "Nothing—just to tell him to give his keys up, and that's when I stabbed him."

Peter remembered stabbing the victim once on the right side. When asked what it was like when Peter stabbed Mr. Smith, the adolescent replied that he "freaked out. That's when I ran outside and threw the knife across the street. . . . When I see the blood come out of his neck, it scared me a little bit."

The youth was not sure how far the knife went into the victim's neck. It could have gone right through the man's neck, as far as Peter knew. All he remembered was that he "stuck it in real fast and pulled it out real quick and that was it."

Peter remembered that, after Mr. Smith was stabbed, the victim said "what the hell" and fell to the floor on his side. Peter stated, "They said that they found cuts on his face and that he was stabbed a couple of times." The youth remembered stabbing him only once.

Peter left the house after stabbing the victim because he was "about to throw up." After throwing the knife away, he went back into the victim's house "to get the keys for the car." When asked what was going on with the victim at that time, the youth replied, "I believed he was already dead. He was not moving or anything." When asked whether it ever had occurred to him to call the police, Peter said, "No. I guess, 'cuz of drugs telling me to get the car and leave, somebody might see me." When asked why it would have been a problem if somebody had seen him, Peter said, "They probably would have called the cops." When asked whether he was concerned about leaving because he might get into trouble, he initially said, "No, I wasn't really feeling nothing, sick to my stomach. My mind was still blank at the time, just to get out of there." He indicated that afterward, he had some awareness that his behavior was wrong.

After leaving the house, Peter "forgot about it [homicide] for a while. I blocked it out." He thought about it next when his grandmother called the police "because I was riding in that car." He admitted to speeding around and having fun in the car but denied telling anyone the circumstances behind his getting it. Peter did not think about how long he was going to ride around in the car. He knew that he would not be able to keep the car. He thought that he would be spotted sooner or later because "they" would find out what happened. He indicated that during the 2 or 3 days that he was driving around in the car, the homicide was not bothering him. He stated that he told the police what had happened because he believed that it would have started to bother him.

The youth stated that he dropped off the car in a wooded area on Friday night and that Barnie rode with him while Charlie and Wayne followed in another car. Peter did not wipe the car clean for fingerprints. He maintained that the car was in good condition when they left it. The adolescent admitted that he drove "wild," that the car was a little dented, that he hit the side mirror when driving through the woods, and that a couple of youths broke a window. Peter stated that the radio was still in the car and that the tires had not been slashed when they abandoned the car.

When asked what he was feeling as he thought back about the incident, Peter said that he was "scared. I can't believe I would do something like that. I don't seem the type to do something like that. I don't act that way. I get nervous even talking about it." Peter had no idea why he killed Mr. Smith. He never had wanted to hurt anybody. When asked whether there was any way in which this whole thing could have been prevented, Peter replied, "If I wouldn't have done drugs, if I would have just stayed home."

When asked whether he told me essentially what he had told the police, Peter responded affirmatively. He stated that he told the police that he was on acid. He maintained that he still was under the influence from the night before and expressed concern that the police never had given him a drug or alcohol test.

I explored acid and its effects on people in general and on Peter. Peter indicated that people could tell when others did acid by "the way they are acting. You can tell. They would act funny and goofy—laugh at everything." When asked whether other people could tell that he had been doing acid when he went over to somebody's house, Peter said, "They could tell I was on something. I would be laughing and acting goofy." When asked whether it would be hard for him to hide being on acid, he said yes. When asked whether it was possible that he took acid on the Thursday and Friday after the homicide rather than on the Monday, Tuesday, and Wednesday preceding the homicide as he initially indicated, Peter replied, "Yeah, it could have been possible."

Peter drove around in the victim's car until about 11 p.m. on the night of the murder. He parked the victim's car at a church about a block from his grandparents' house. He then returned home and went to sleep.

Peter gave a detailed description of the events that occurred over the next 2 days. On Thursday afternoon, he did some acid with Barnie and drank some beer. Peter smoked some marijuana with Cory during the evening and nighttime hours and did not go home that night. On Friday, he smoked marijuana with some kids who were skipping school and later smoked dope "all day long" with Barnie.

Peter said he told Barnie that he could take the victim's car because Barnie wanted to run away. Peter stated that as they were driving around at about 8 p.m. on Friday, they went past Mr. Smith's house. Peter saw the police and paramedics there and told Barnie that he had to get rid of the car. After leaving the car in the woods, Peter and Barnie bought a bag of marijuana laced with LSD and smoked it.

Peter stated that it was around 9 or 10 p.m. at that time, and then they went to a party. The boys left the party at around midnight. Peter returned home and went to sleep. Peter was awakened the next morning (Saturday) by his grandmother, who asked him whose car he had been driving. Peter told her the car belonged to Barnie. Mrs. McEwen then called the police. Initially, Peter told the police that it was Barnie's car. He admitted he committed the homicide after the police officers read him his rights. "They asked me if I could show 'em where the car and the knife was, and I showed them both."

Conclusions

There were two matters of discrepancy concerning statements made to the police and statements made to me and the consulting psychologist. These concern whether Peter planned the auto theft and homicide and whether Peter was on drugs, particularly acid, at the time of the homicide. My assessment of Peter and review of this case indicated that it was unlikely the homicide was planned and questionable whether Peter was on acid at the time of the homicide.

I was concerned when I learned that the defendant apparently was questioned at length prior to the tape-recorded statement. This period of questioning might have, in essence, functioned as a rehearsal and signaled to Peter what he was expected to say.

Peter was the type of youth who could be easily intimidated. He was of dull/normal intelligence. His personality development was low, and drugs (possibly acid and almost certainly marijuana) were in his system when he was interrogated by police. In addition, he was frightened that he was in serious trouble. I believed, in light of these factors and Peter's statements to me and to the consulting psychologist, that the homicide was an impulsive rather than a premeditated act.

Close reading of the taped confession revealed that the detective's questions focused on cognitive issues (e.g., what Peter was thinking, what he decided and when). Peter consistently responded by saying what he did rather than what he thought. For example, Detective Williams asked Peter, "When did you, when did you decide how you were going to kill the man?" Peter replied, "I just picked up the knife and stabbed him with it."

The defendant was very acquiescent when responding to Detective Williams' questions. The detective asked leading questions throughout the interview and introduced material the defendant never mentioned.

Detective: Why this man in particular? Did you think it would be easy because he was old?

Peter: Yes.

Detective: Is that . . .

Peter: Yes.

Detective: . . . the main reason? You knew that you, he would not be able to put up a fight?

Peter: Yes.

Detective: And you would be able to kill him easily.

Peter: Yes.

Detective: And just to take his car for a couple of days.

Peter: Yes.

The failure of police to test Peter for drugs shortly after his arrest was a serious mistake. Although it would not establish precisely when the defendant took certain drugs, it would at least indicate what drugs were in his system at the time of arrest.

I had some doubt whether Peter was on acid at the time of the homicide. Several statements made by the defendant were inconsistent with his being on acid at the time of the killing. These statements related to Peter's behavior when on acid, its obvious observability to others, his inability to hide the effects of acid, and his admission that he could have been mistaken when he first took it. In addition, Peter's detailed rendition of the crime did not sound like someone who was high on LSD.

Peter's grandmother, his mother, and Patricia, as well as the two friends whom he visited shortly before the homicide, were questioned about Peter's behavior by police. All indicated that Peter did not appear high before or immediately after the homicide. In addition, Barnie told police that he provided Peter with LSD on Thursday and Friday, the 2 days following the homicide.

■ EVALUATION OF FORENSIC ISSUES RAISED

In this case, there was no question raised by counsel about the defendant's competency to stand trial for capital murder. Peter knew the nature of his charges and was able to assist his lawyers. However, he had difficulty integrating some of the information pertinent to his case. For example, Peter knew that he should get some prison time for killing Mr. Smith, but a 25-year mandatory sentence seemed too much to him. He believed that he should get less time because he was young and never had gotten into trouble before. He did not seem to understand that his desire to get less time was not possible if he was convicted of first-degree murder.

Client's Sanity at the Time of the Crime

Peter was sane under the M'Naghten standard at the time of the homicide. Peter's recollection of the events before, during, and after the homicide was fairly extensive. Although Peter stated that his mind went blank when he stabbed Mr. Smith, he clearly remembered picking up the knife, going out to the porch, stabbing Mr. Smith, seeing

Mr. Smith fall, and the blood flowing out. His rendition of the homicidal incident suggested that he knew the nature and quality of his acts, although he did not foresee their likely consequences. His motivation in fleeing appeared to have been based, to some extent, on the realization that stabbing Mr. Smith was legally wrong.

Making Sense of Murder

The clinical and investigative evidence suggested that the thought to steal the car arose as Peter was walking to his friend's house. He acted immediately and without giving the matter any deliberation. He grabbed the knife because it was there.

To understand why Peter used the knife against Mr. Smith, it is necessary to keep in mind that Peter was an anxious adolescent with a great deal of anger and hurt bottled up inside him. (These conclusions were consistent with those reached after testing by staff at the drug rehabilitation center.) Peter was largely unaware of his anger and pain in the course of his day-to-day living. He also was incapable of discharging strong negative emotion in a healthy way.

The reader will recall that on the day of the homicide, Peter's mother failed to pick him up at his grandmother's home as she had promised. Both Peter and his grandmother related that Peter had been waiting all day for his mother to arrive. It seemed likely that Peter was angered and hurt by his mother's behavior. Given that confrontation was not within Peter's repertoire of behavior, he might have suppressed the anger and hurt that he felt toward his mother. His impulse to steal a car when he had been given one by his mother might well have been unconsciously driven by a desire to be free of her. Interestingly, he told his friends that the stolen car belonged to his mother, suggesting that Peter made some connection between the crime and his mother.

Factors in Mitigation

Eight factors in mitigation of the imposition of a death sentence appeared to apply in Peter's case. Three of these were among those listed in the state statute. The legislature considered a defendant's having "no significant history of prior criminal history" as a mitigating factor. Peter had no prior criminal history.

The legislature also deemed "the age of the defendant at the time of the crime" as a potential factor in mitigation of death. Peter was 17 years old when he killed Mr. Smith. Juveniles' ability to cope and their life experiences typically are less than those of adults.

The state statute indicated that it was a mitigating factor if "the capacity of the defendant to appreciate the criminality of his [or her] conduct or to conform his [or her] conduct to the requirements of the law was substantially impaired." At the time of the offense, Peter knew what he was doing, as indicated by the M'Naghten Test. However, the adolescent had no emotional appreciation of the consequences of his behavior with respect to himself and the victim. He stabbed the victim, ran outside and threw away the knife, came back into the house to get the car keys, took off in the car, and essentially blocked out what happened for 3 days. His statements to me and to the consulting psychologist indicated that his actions were impulsive. It was questionable whether his ability to conform his conduct to the law at that moment in time was possible. His capacity would appear diminished due to his extensive history of drug use, his restricted personality development, and possible neurological difficulties.

I also suggested that defense counsel bring to the court's attention a state statute that delineated criteria for the judge to consider with respect to the imposing of adult or juvenile sanctions when youths were processed as adults. This statute did not technically apply when a juvenile was indicted for a capital or life felony. However, it appeared relevant for the court's consideration given Peter's age, development, and living situation. The legislature indicated that "the sophistication and maturity of the child, as determined by a consideration of his [or her] home, environmental situation, emotional attitude, and pattern of living," should be considered at sentencing. Peter's personality development and behavioral response style were particularly relevant here. Peter was not a criminally sophisticated youth; his perceptions and ways of responding were characteristic of youths much younger than 17 years of age. Peter could not be considered to be mature under any criteria.

Peter's history of significant drug abuse was among the nonstatutory factors in mitigation of the imposition of a death sentence. It was likely that Peter's development was arrested and his judgment affected by the young age at which he began using drugs daily. Records confirmed that Peter's drug usage was so severe that he was committed to a psychiatric facility 9 months prior to the homicide. He was diagnosed as having severe cannabis (marijuana) dependence, alcohol abuse, and cocaine abuse. The existence of alcoholism also was noted in the family by treatment staff.

Peter's being raised in a very dysfunctional family also was pertinent in terms of mitigation. Peter's family clearly was a high-stress, dysfunctional family for several reasons, as described earlier. The significance of being raised in this environment needed to be explained to the court. Growing up in an alcoholic family, for example, has been compared, in terms of stress levels, with being raised in a concentration camp.[2] When Peter was admitted to the psychiatric facility, staff rated his psychosocial stressors as severe.

Peter's long-standing difficulties and the lack of meaningful intervention also were pertinent considerations at sentencing. Peter's school records indicated that he had difficulties in learning since he began attending school. Records indicated that the school board became aware of aggressive tendencies and acting-out behaviors when Peter was 11 years old. He received no counseling to handle his learning difficulties. On admission to the drug rehabilitation center, the psychologist who examined Peter noted that he scored very high on tests measuring anger and anxiety. Within 3 weeks of being at this psychiatric facility, he was discharged as a disciplinary problem because he ran away from the facility on three occasions.

It also was relevant to introduce Peter's self-concept in terms of mitigation. Peter did not have a delinquent self-image. He seemed motivated to take advantage of treatment opportunities afforded to him. He was particularly interested in more drug counseling.

Diagnostic and Treatment Considerations

School records and existing psychological evaluations strongly suggested that Peter had a history of Attention Deficit Disorder with Hyperactivity. His neurological and psychological problems contributed to his learning and behavioral control problems. Peter also met the diagnostic criteria for dependence on marijuana and had a history of abusing cocaine and alcohol in his adolescent years.

At the time of my clinical assessment, the prognosis in Peter's case was guarded. Peter was nonevaluative and impulsive. He did not know how to deal with his feelings in a constructive way and resorted to drugs. His rendition of the homicide suggested a gap in his thinking. One moment he was thinking about scaring Mr. Smith, and the next moment he was stabbing him. Hyperactive children often have difficulty in coming up with verbal mediators between thinking about something and taking action. Although Peter was a passive youth, he remained a potential risk until he gets to the point where he thinks about what he is about to do and its possible ramifications.

CASE PROCESSING AND DISPOSITION

Peter was convicted at trial of first-degree murder, burglary of a dwelling with battery, robbery with a deadly weapon, and grand theft. The consulting psychologist and I were among those called by defense counsel to introduce factors in mitigation of death at the sentencing hearing. We testified regarding Peter's intellectual and personality deficits, his family problems, his long-standing problems in school, his drug addiction, the impulsive nature of the crime, and his lack of criminal sophistication.

Under state law, the jurors could recommend that Peter die in the electric chair or be sentenced to life with a minimum of 25 years to be served before parole eligibility. The jurors recommended that Peter be sentenced to life imprisonment rather than death.

The judge followed the jurors' recommendation for life. However, he showed Peter no mercy. He departed from sentencing guidelines to impose a more stringent sentence. He cited three factors in aggravation to justify his actions: Peter allegedly observed the victim for several days, the victim was a 78-year-old man who was hard of hearing, and the victim lived alone.

The judge sentenced Peter to three counts of life imprisonment for the murder, robbery, and burglary convictions and to 5 years for the grand theft charge. The sentences were to run consecutively. Although Peter will become eligible for parole after serving 25 years, the consecutive nature of the life commitments makes it unlikely that Peter ever will be released from prison.

FOLLOW-UP DATA

I conducted a follow-up interview with Peter 5 years after my evaluation. At that time, Peter had been incarcerated for 5 years 9 months. He had spent 4 years 9 months of this time in adult prison. I spoke with Peter's grandmother 9 months after my follow-up interview with him.

Clinical Interview

I saw little change in Peter since my pretrial evaluation. He presented as a young, passive, and anxious adolescent rather than as a 23-year-old man. He was pleasant and courteous. He seemed lost in a complex world and completely void of insight.

Peter had been in four different institutions since being sentenced to prison. He indicated that he had difficulty adjusting to prison. Peter stated that he had been in trouble about seven or eight times in prison. He indicated that he had been cited for being in unauthorized areas, being disrespectful to an officer, and having contraband (e.g., food from the kitchen). Although Peter denied involvement in any fights, he mentioned getting transferred because he fought with another inmate. He acknowledged being approached by other inmates for sex but denied participation in any homosexual activity in prison. Peter had his foot locker broken into and his personal belongings taken on one occasion.

Although he attended general equivalency diploma (GED) classes for a while, Peter apparently did not score high enough to receive his diploma. Peter has received no vocational certificates. Other than carpentry, Peter has not participated in any vocational programs.

Peter did not seek out counseling in prison. He participated in a drug program for 7 or 8 months. He quit because "it was too hard for me." He did not like the confrontational aspect of the program. It reportedly brought up too many memories for him. He attended Narcotics Anonymous meetings while participating in this program. He stated that he did not go to Alcoholics Anonymous meetings because he did not have a problem with alcohol.

Peter related that his grandmother has visited him every other week. His grandfather sometimes has joined her. Peter's mother and stepfather and their son have visited him about three or four times per year. Patricia has come less frequently than she had in past years because of her family responsibilities. Peter has not seen his cousin Mark, with whom he was raised, for several years. Peter has heard from one girl with whom he went to school.

Peter maintained that he did not commit the murder himself. "I was there, me and another person was there. There was two of us, just me and him." He identified his co-defendant as Barnie. Peter initially related that he told the police about Barnie when first questioned, "but they didn't go for it." Peter had trouble explaining to me why he later confessed and maintained at the time of the trial that he acted alone if, in fact, he had an accomplice. He suggested that he protected his friend as he would protect his brother. He apparently did not see his allegedly telling the police that Barnie was involved prior to his arrest as inconsistent with his allegedly protecting him later.

Peter paused for a long time before explaining Barnie's role.

> Okay. They charged him with grand theft. The way I would see it, if they charged him with grand theft, they should have charged him with the other crimes . . . because in grand theft, the car was taken from one particular spot. Now for him to have been charged with grand theft, he had to have been at that spot. So I don't know how they misinterpretated [sic] that.

Peter's response to my question of how the whole crime could have been prevented was telling. "Could have left, turned around and left, but I didn't." Although Peter evinced no remorse for the victim, he clearly regretted his actions. Peter "felt sorry for doing it." He explained, "I done it when I was 17. I was a juvenile then. I done messed up my life now." Peter objected to the state's portrayal of him "like I was a mass murderer, like they say, Ted Bundy and all them." He insisted, "That's not me. It was just an accident that happened. I wished it never did happen, but I can't change that right now."

Peter acknowledged that being in prison was a constant reminder of his crime. Peter said that the toughest thing about being in prison was "living my life in here." He did not see prison as having done him any good in any way.

Peter did not comprehend the magnitude of his sentence. He expressed hope that he would be released in a few years. He would like to lead "a normal life" when he is released. He wants a house, car, "a wife and kids," and a job.

Review of Peter's Prison File

Review of correctional records revealed that Peter minimized the nature and scope of the problems he has had in prison. On admission, prison officials evaluated Peter's attitude as good but his adjustment and prognosis as only fair. Peter had difficulty adjusting to the prison regime and was transferred to several different prisons, largely because of behavioral problems. His progress reports were uneven and rarely included outstanding ratings.

Peter had received 18 disciplinary reports in less than 5 years. Of these, 9 were for being in an unauthorized area. The remaining infractions included possessing contraband, loaning or borrowing materials, showing disrespect to officers, disobeying verbal or written orders, participating in a drug deal, conspiring to commit a crime or violate the rules, and participating in sex acts or unauthorized physical contact.

Peter has had little involvement in institutional programs. He appeared to have completed only one program during his time in prison. Records indicated that despite written recommendations, Peter had not participated in Alcoholics Anonymous, Narcotics Anonymous, or a drug program. He had not received his GED or elected to take a suggested auto mechanics course.

Peter's grandmother has been his only steady visitor. Peter's file contained correspondence from her to prison authorities when she felt Peter had been treated unfairly. Despite Peter's denials, he appeared to have had at least one homosexual liaison. The relationship appeared to be a consensual one, with the other inmate assuming a protective role with respect to Peter.

Follow-Up Interview With Peter's Grandmother

Statements made by Mrs. McEwen were largely consistent with those made by Peter. Mrs. McEwen confirmed that she, unlike other family members, has visited Peter on a frequent and consistent basis.

She indicated that Peter has had difficulty adjusting in prison. For example, Peter has gotten into trouble several times because he does not understand that he cannot go where he wants. Mrs. McEwen had heard allegations that Peter had been involved in homosexual activity, but she did not believe them. She is aware that her grandson is not "a tough guy" and is likely to encounter trouble defending himself in prison.

Mrs. McEwen's remarks indicated that Peter has not made much progress in prison. He has been unable to complete his GED due to his learning difficulties. He has not completed any vocational programs or received any counseling. Mrs. McEwen related that Peter had just gotten out of lock-up for having "dirty urine." Although Mrs. McEwen believed Peter's story that he had not been using drugs recently, she acknowledged that he has obtained and used illicit drugs while in prison.

Mrs. McEwen believes that Peter has "grown up a bit" in prison and could adjust to a normal life in society with guidance from his family. Mrs. McEwen indicated that she and Peter's mother and stepfather have resolved their differences and are prepared to help Peter when he is released. Asked what it would be like for her when Peter was released, Mrs. McEwen's eyes filled with tears and her voice cracked as she replied, "It would be the happiest day of my life [because] he doesn't belong in there."

Mrs. McEwen remained convinced more than 6 years after Peter's arrest that he did not kill Mr. Smith. Peter told her a few months prior to our meeting that Barnie killed Mr. Smith while Peter and Corey waited outside the man's house. The three boys allegedly made a pact that if they got caught, Peter would take the blame. They believed that Peter would be set free because he was a juvenile and had no prior record. Mrs. McEwen indicated that the police intimidated her grandson into confessing and that he is in prison for something that he did not do.

> I know Peter. He wouldn't hurt anyone. He would go out of his way to help someone. Prior to his being arrested, I've seen him when people got hurt, how he would—his reactions—it worried him to death that they weren't going to get the right kind of help. And he had nothing against old people. He used to help the old people in our neigh - borhood. He'd go over and rake leaves and pull weeds for them. He is just not that type of a child that he would do this. He is not a violent person. I've seen him get mad. Even when he and Patricia would get mad, she'd whack him one, [and] he'd just turn around and walk away from her.

■ CASE COMMENTARY

Peter has changed little over the years. I felt the same sadness when I evaluated him at follow-up as I had prior to his trial. He struck me as clueless. With a prison sentence that extends to perpetuity, Peter hopes every day that he will somehow, some way, be released miraculously from the gates of hell.

The follow-up interviews with Peter and his grandmother raised the question as to whether one or more of Peter's friends had participated in killing Mr. Smith. It is possible that, given Peter's personality development, conforming pattern, and correspondingly high need for approval, he could have covered for others due to misplaced loyalty to friends or fear of police. For the same reasons, it also is possible that he could have lied to his grandmother, who did not want to believe that her grandson killed an innocent man.

Interestingly, Peter told me during the follow-up interview that only Barnie was with him. His grandmother indicated that Peter related to her that both Barnie and Cory were involved. If Peter did not act alone, then why the apparent inconsistency regarding who else was involved?

I did not believe Peter's statement that Barnie was involved in the murder for several reasons. Prior to trial, Peter gave me a fairly detailed account of his killing of Mr. Smith. He did not appear to have the capacity to make this scenario up and specifically denied that others were involved in the killing. As discussed previously, Peter's suggestion at the follow-up interview that he was trying to protect Barnie was unconvincing given his statement that he initially told police that Barnie killed Mr. Smith. When asked how the incident could have been prevented, Peter said that he could have left Mr. Smith's home rather than referring to what Barnie could have done.

In addition, Peter's eye movements at follow-up, when analyzed in terms of neuro-linguistic patterns, were telling in this regard. When Peter was remembering events, he looked up and to the left. This pattern is one that typically has been identified as a visual recall pattern, particularly in right-handed people. When I asked him about Barnie's role in the homicide, Peter did not access information in this visual recall pattern. Instead, his eyes shifted to a pattern normally associated with auditory processing. His pattern was one typically seen when people are talking to themselves and, perhaps, rehearsing what they might say.[3]

How does a youth who was, in many respects, a gentle kid wind up killing a helpless old man? We see in this case a number of factors contributing to Peter's homicidal behavior. These include situational factors, resource availability, personality characteristics, possible neurological vulnerabilities, and their cumulative effect.

Peter's family life was chaotic. He was abused, neglected, and without a positive male influence. He was psychologically abused by a father who rejected him from birth, emotionally neglected for years by his mother, and physically abused on occasion by his stepfather. His grandfather was unable to serve as an effective role model due to his alcoholism.

Peter's mother and stepfather also apparently abused substances. Peter learned from an early age that adults coped with life by using chemicals. It was not surprising that Peter, a boy with low self-esteem, would gravitate to drugs as a way in which to soothe himself and bolster confidence.

Poor self-esteem was only one of the personality characteristics that put Peter at risk of behaving maladaptively. Peter, typical of individuals with low personality development, did not have the inner resources to deal with strong negative feelings. He also did not have the judgment to seek help or the social supports to turn to when he needed help.

Biological factors seemed operative in this case. Peter's dependence on marijuana and his periodic abuse of other substances clearly affected his judgment and development. In addition, psychological testing and school records supported the existence of neurological deficits.

These intrinsic vulnerabilities combined with extrinsic vulnerabilities, such as childhood abuse and neglect, appeared to have ignited into violence on the night of the homicide. Peter was angry with his mother when he left his grandparents' house. There was no conscious decision to kill; there was an explosion of rage at a man who happened along the path of a boy who was impulsively reacting to events as they unfolded.

Prognosis

The prognosis in Peter's case was worse at follow-up than at the time of conviction. Peter is 6 years older, and there has been no demonstrable progress. Peter has not accepted responsibility for killing Mr. Smith. Data suggested that he still is abusing drugs and reacting impulsively.

Peter's lack of progress is a sad commentary on the correctional system. Peter is not oppositional. He is capable of responding positively to authorities. He needs more structure and attention than he has received. He requires strategies to make him stop and process what he is going to do before he can be safely returned to society.

Chapter Six

Jerry Johnson

JERRY JOHNSON, a White youth from a middle- to upper-middle-class family, was a popular kid at school. One night, he and his co-defendant, Marcus, picked up two other friends, Timmy and Shawn. The four boys, who ranged in age from 15 to 17 years, went into the woods together. Timmy and Shawn thought that they had gone there to look for marijuana. Jerry and Marcus, however, had different plans. Jerry shot Timmy to death, and Marcus beat Shawn and left him for dead.

Jerry and Marcus contacted law enforcement officials a short time later. They told police that someone had shot at the four of them when they were in the woods. They said that they had scattered in response and were worried because they could not find the other two boys. Jerry and Marcus led police to Timmy's body. Meanwhile, Shawn managed to crawl to the road. He was picked up by a passing motorist and told authorities what had happened.

Police reports suggested that the killing and attempted killing had something to do with a disagreement over a girl. There was speculation that Marcus was a Skinhead and that this affiliation might have had something to do with it. Both youths were charged with first-degree murder in connection with Timmy's death. Marcus also was charged with attempted first-degree murder for his role in beating Shawn.

Subsequent investigation indicated that Jerry had masterminded the killing of Timmy and that Shawn had inadvertently got intertwined in the execution plot. I was appointed by the court at the motion of defense counsel to conduct a sanity/competency evaluation of Jerry and to give the report to defense counsel.

THE CLINICAL EVALUATION

My assessment of Jerry Johnson is based on a 4-hour interview conducted in adult jail 13 months after his arrest and a 1-hour consultation with his parents about a week later. Case materials reviewed included the police investigation reports and a deposition of Shawn Morris, the youth who survived the homicidal attack.

BEHAVIORAL OBSERVATIONS

Jerry, age 17 years, presented as a tall, thin male. He reported his height as 6 feet and his weight as 140 to 145 pounds.

Jerry seemed alert and fairly relaxed during most of the clinical interview. He did experience noticeable discomfort when asked about the murder. Although he played with one of his shoes throughout most of the interview, his eye contact was generally very good.

Jerry was extremely cooperative and very polite. He answered hundreds of questions and did not refuse to answer anything asked. Jerry exercised care in answering the questions, pausing when necessary to think about his answers. His deliberation seemed to be reflective of his desire to be accurate rather than indicative of the search for a socially approved response. His answers often were restricted, however, and this was more indicative of his level of personality development than of an unwillingness to answer. His answers clearly indicated that he was oriented in time and space and that his short-term and, for the most part, his long-term memories were intact.

The youth did not appear to be at all manipulative during the interview. His responses to questions and his behavior strongly suggested that he was trying very hard to be truthful. His answers to many of the questions, particularly those surrounding the homicide, were anything but self-serving.

PERSONALITY DEVELOPMENT

Jerry perceived at Level 3 of the Interpersonal Maturity Level (I-level) classification system. Typical of individuals at this developmental level, Jerry saw the world in black-and-white dimensions. Although he acknowledged having different groups of friends, for example, he saw everyone in a particular group as being the same. The differentiations that he made concerning people were minimal and were based on external characteristics (e.g., social class, town, into sports or not into sports, Skinhead or not a Skinhead).

At the time of the homicidal event, Jerry did not appear to have internalized a value system by which he judged himself. Rather, he seemed to have operated on the basis of formulas that provided the structure that he wanted and needed to get by in life. Jerry believed, for example, that people ought to follow the rules. If one broke a rule, then one had to pay for it. Why? Because one broke the rule, and that is how it works.

Jerry used a behavioral response style known as the *cultural conformist*.[1] The peer group was very important to Jerry. Although his relationships with peers appeared very superficial, Jerry wanted admiration and approval from his peers. His formula for getting along with many teens was to conform. He considered it very important to keep his word and to do anything for someone he perceived as a good friend. "If you trust me, I won't go back on my word . . . if you *really* trust me." Jerry wanted his friends to trust him, and he wanted to trust them in return. For Jerry, that is how it should be. A friend should be willing to do something wrong for his friend. That is what friends are for.

RELEVANT SOCIAL HISTORY

Family Constellation

Jerry was the youngest of three sons born to Mr. and Mrs. Michael Johnson. Jerry's mother was 49 years old and working as an executive secretary at the time of the clinical evaluation. Jerry described his mother as "a real good woman, good leader," who is good in business and who cares deeply. She made jail a lot easier for him because she visited every evening and asked no questions. The youth saw himself as similar to his mother in that they both got along well with people, made friends easily, handled themselves well in a position of authority, and knew how to get people "to do pretty much what we want them to do in a positive way and sometimes in a negative way."

Jerry felt that he had come to know his father much better since his arrest because his father also visited him in jail every evening. Jerry did not see much of his father growing up because Mr. Johnson worked long hours and the two of them did not get along well. Jerry's father had a position similar to a general sales manager.

Jerry indicated that when he was younger, his father had a drinking problem. Mr. Johnson reportedly argued with Jerry's mother when he had been drinking heavily. He was not physically abusive, however, to either his wife or his son. Jerry suggested that his father stopped drinking several years prior to the homicide.

Jerry had two brothers, Joseph and Julius, who were 11 and 7 years older than him, respectively. Jerry did not know them very well and related that they had visited him on two occasions during his 13 months of incarceration. Jerry was about 9 or 10 when Joseph left home. Joseph was divorced, with three children, employed as a high school teacher, and living several hours away at the time of the clinical evaluation.

Julius went to the same high school as Jerry and was very involved in sports. Jerry described Julius as a "lot like people I stayed away from in high school." Jerry shared a room with Julius for several years and indicated that they fought like brothers often do. Julius recently had moved out of his parents' home and was a golf professional.

School

Jerry was a high school senior when he was arrested. He did well academically (mostly B's and A's). The youth got into trouble only once, and that was for fighting when "some guy" allegedly called one of his friends "a fag"; he received an in-school suspension. Jerry really liked school his senior year because he was a co-anchor on a daily television show at the high school.

Jerry "got along with" his teachers. He thought one teacher, his ROTC instructor, was really concerned about him as an individual and he respected him. Jerry stated that this teacher had written to him on a few occasions. He explained that "I was loyal to him; he was loyal to me."

Work, Career Interests, Military, Fascination With Guns, and Activities

Jerry was both working and going to school at the time of his arrest. His father approved of his plan to go into the U.S. Marine Corps following graduation. Jerry wanted to finish college in the service and become a career officer.

Jerry's interest in going into the military was sparked by his interest in guns that began in junior high school. He had been attracted to law enforcement earlier because of his interest in guns. Jerry was on the rifle team in high school and was an expert marksman. He shot BB guns when he was a young boy. As he got older, his friends got real guns.

Playing "war games" and studying tactics with friends was one of Jerry's favorite activities. Jerry related that he and his friends would dress in camouflage clothing and go into the woods. Ideally, they would have "10 guys," enough to have two teams of 5 each, similar to operations in the Marine Corps. The idea was for one team to go out "on patrols" and the other to ambush them. The point was "to get a high casualty count." The way to win was "to take out the other guys" with BBs or birdshot. Once shooting started, it was over quickly. Getting hurt was part of it.

Friends

Jerry took pride in the number and different types of friends that he had. His friends in junior high usually were quiet, "didn't stand out, and got along with everybody." In high school, his friends were different, "people who stood out more . . . a little unusual."

Jerry maintained that his friends had a better grip on things than did other adolescents. "They knew what time it was. . . . Their values were in the right spot. They were loyal to each other, loyal to the country. . . . They saw things that were right and things that were wrong. Sometimes you have to do things wrong to make things right." Jerry reiterated that you have to "do whatever you have to do to see that right is done."

Jerry was particularly attracted to the military crowd.

> What they believed in, they would do. What they believed in, they really believed in, and I was the same way. If you were friends with somebody, you were friends with them and you'd do anything for them. You had to have goals and values in the right slot. You had to have your stuff wired tight. Be alert and know what's going on.

All of Jerry's friends reportedly believed it was a great country. "If you live here, you should pay it back. The service was a good way."

Girlfriends and Sexual History

Jerry had a girlfriend, Suzie, who had just broken up with him 2 weeks prior to the homicidal event. He started dating her about 2 months prior to the murder and dated her for about 6 weeks. Suzie was the first girl with whom Jerry had sexual intercourse.

Jerry perceived Suzie as moving away from him because his friend, Timmy (later the victim), was "hitting on her." Suzie was a person who took the lead in conversations; she had a "presence." Jerry did not recall discussing his feelings with Suzie and ultimately came to believe that he could not trust her. Jerry had not heard from Suzie since his arrest.

The youth had one other girlfriend, Lynette, whom he dated for about the same length of time. She wrote to him in jail a few times and then stopped writing.

Alcohol and Drug Involvement

Jerry did not drink on a regular basis. He would drink once every couple of months and would get drunk. He drank with friends he trusted, not by himself, and did not see himself as having a problem with alcohol.

Jerry maintained that he did not really smoke marijuana, although he pretended to on occasion. He tried smoking cigarettes for about a week and then quit. He admitted to trying powder cocaine and to free-basing coke on the same day. He used LSD about five times. On these occasions, he would go out to the woods with his friends and go shooting. Jerry had not taken any drugs or consumed any alcohol on the day of the homicide.

Jerry did not see himself as a drug user or as having a drug problem. He never had bought drugs. When asked whether he ever had sold drugs, he seemed momentarily startled. He said that rumors had surfaced after the murder that he sold acid and that they were untrue.

Jerry told me that he had no reason to sell drugs prior to his arrest because his parents gave him money. He volunteered the information that if he had been given the opportunity to sell drugs in jail, then it would have been a difficult decision because of what he had learned while in jail. He vacillated about whether he would sell drugs, having become aware of how much money juveniles could make selling drugs.

Prior Delinquent Involvement

Jerry never had been officially arrested prior to the homicide offense. He estimated that he had about 20 police contacts that resulted in field interrogation forms being filled out by the police. These encounters involved occasions when Jerry and his friends, dressed in camouflage clothing and carrying fake and real guns, would go into the woods.

The youth denied any involvement in burglaries, larceny-thefts, dealing in stolen property, or robberies. He admitted involvement in vandalism on one occasion. Jerry and his friends shot out the windows of the chemistry classroom.

Future Orientation

Jerry was aware that his arrest for murder probably would necessitate giving up his military plans. He eventually wanted to have his own business and live in California because he heard from some military friends that it was nice. He did not want to get married because it is a "lot of responsibility." He explained, "If you are not sure you can do it, you should not do it."

Adjustment in Jail

Jerry maintained that he was doing "okay" in jail. He felt that the 13 months of confinement had been "a good experience" because, similar to the military, it builds character. He reportedly met people that he never had contact with before and learned things that "sheltered" people do not know. Jerry had no problems with inmates approaching him sexually. He noted that it was tense in jail, that people want to kill others for things such as cigarettes, but that he had learned to stay out of conflicts by not letting things bother him.

Although he had been housed in the forensic section of the jail for about 6 months, he had no more than casual contact with any psychologists on staff. He had not seen any mental health professionals prior to my clinical assessment.

■ SYNOPSIS OF CONSULTATION WITH PARENTS

Jerry's parents were extremely cooperative during the consultation. Both responded to questions asked. The information they provided was consistent with information given by Jerry, with one exception. So far as they knew, Jerry did not use drugs or alcohol. I did not find this discrepancy particularly significant given that the youth reported only minimal usage.

Reaction to Son's Arrest for Homicide

Mr. and Mrs. Johnson related that they were "totally shocked" when Jerry was arrested for murder. When Jerry called them to report that he was at the police station, they were not concerned. Jerry had told them that someone had been shooting at them while they were in the woods, and it was their impression that he was helping the police.

They described their son as a "thoughtful, kind, gentle person," a boy who "does what he says," who comes home "on time" or calls them. Both parents characterized Jerry as an "ideal son." Mrs. Johnson stated that he kissed his parents goodbye every morning. He had "no problems anywhere" and no arrest history. In the words of Mr. Johnson, Jerry had the "most boring past." They saw their son (as did I) as "extremely polite and well mannered." Mr. Johnson described his son as very poised and mature, as "17 going on 40."

When asked whether they were aware of anything that would account for Jerry's behavior in the incident, they said no. There was no change in Jerry's behavior prior to the homicide, "absolutely nothing." Jerry was "caring about people." Mrs. Johnson recalled that Jerry took Neal, an abused boy, "under his wing" because he felt sorry for the boy.

The parents agreed that, on occasion, Jerry would show anger, but they did not see their son as having a vindictive streak. They said that a lot of times, Jerry would hold in his anger.

Mr. Johnson was very concerned about Jerry's complete lack of remorse for his behavior. It appeared that his son was treating this whole thing as though "nothing happened," that it somehow was not quite real to Jerry. Mr. Johnson's statements suggested that, although Jerry acknowledged what happened (he killed his best friend), he lacked an emotional appreciation for what he had done. According to his parents, Jerry's emotional reaction would be consistent with his behavior in the past. Jerry admired men such as General Patton who appeared really strong in adversity.

Parents' Reaction to Victim

Mr. and Mrs. Johnson related that the victim, Timmy Collins, was an abused child. Mr. Johnson described Timmy as a "hoodlum" and said that the police considered Timmy "a bad case." At the time of his death, the youth was "on the run," having escaped from the juvenile detention center.

Mr. Johnson related that the police had come to the Johnson home about a month before the homicide looking for Timmy. Although Mr. Johnson did not appear to know the extent to which Jerry had helped Timmy when the boy escaped from the juvenile detention center, it was his impression that Jerry was protecting Timmy in front of the police. Jerry told his father that whenever anything goes wrong, the police blame Timmy.

After this incident, Mr. Johnson told Jerry not to hang around with Timmy anymore. Mr. Johnson indicated that Jerry's continued association with Timmy was the only thing about which Jerry ever lied to him and his wife. When asked whether loyalty was important to Jerry, his parents said yes. They attributed the importance that Jerry placed on loyalty to the military.

Jerry's Physical and Mental Health History

Mr. and Mrs. Johnson reported that Jerry's most major physical illness was a broken arm. Prior to their son's arrest, there was "nothing to give them any concern," and they never felt the need to have him evaluated by a mental health professional. To their knowledge, Jerry never had been evaluated by a school counselor.

Jerry's Adjustment in Jail to Date

Mr. and Mrs. Johnson had seen no real change in their son since his incarceration. They saw him as successfully adapting to the situation by reading, playing cards, and making friends, which they noted he did easily. The feedback given to them suggested that Jerry was regarded as a positive peer influence in jail. Mrs. Johnson noted that Jerry finished his high school requirements in jail and received his diploma from the high school he had been attending, becoming the first and only one to do so from jail.

They related, consistent with Jerry's statements, that he had not been evaluated while in jail and had received no counseling. Mrs. Johnson related a conversation with a state social services counselor who reportedly wanted, in his words, "to get into Jerry's mind" because the counselor opined that there might be "another Ted Bundy" in their midst. Mrs. Johnson stated that she asked the counselor not to evaluate Jerry after the man made this statement.

Parents' Projections of Jerry's Adjustment to Prison

Jerry's parents believed that their son would be receptive to counseling. They believed that he could cope mentally with confinement. Mr. Johnson mentioned that Jerry had "plenty of street smarts." The boy's parents were concerned with their son's ability to defend himself physically in a prison environment given his small stature and the fact that he had lost more than 30 pounds. Mrs. Johnson's major concern was Jerry's physical safety, whereas Mr. Johnson's major concern was Jerry's lack of remorse.

Family Dynamics

Mr. and Mrs. Johnson's statements about the family were consistent with those made by Jerry. Jerry was very fond of his mother and relatively distant from his father and two brothers. Mr. Johnson characterized the two older boys as "jocks" and said that his long hours at work (10-12 hours daily) limited the time he spent with Jerry.

Mrs. Johnson did not drink or use drugs. Mr. Johnson used to drink but quit about 3 years ago. The parents viewed their family as "very close." Mr. Johnson stated that there was no mental illness in the family. He mentioned an aunt and uncle who were alcoholics but said that Jerry would not have been exposed to their excessive drinking.

Jerry's parents indicated that they had moved about five times when Jerry was growing up. However, they had been living in the same area for 10 years prior to Jerry's arrest. Jerry had attended schools in this area from the 3rd to 12th grades.

Mr. and Mrs. Johnson did not report a religious affiliation. They said that Jerry believed in God and that they never had any concern about his values. They saw their son as always truthful.

Jerry's School, Work, and Recreational Activities

Mr. and Mrs. Johnson confirmed that Jerry did well in school (he was on the honor roll during the 6 weeks before his arrest). He had won a student award for his television productions. Mrs. Johnson related that the "teachers loved him" and were very supportive when he was arrested.

Jerry worked for about 2 to 3 months prior to the murder. He worked for about a month at a fast food restaurant, where he might have met Timmy. At the time of his arrest, Jerry had been working at a discount department store for about 1 to 2 months. Mrs. Johnson stated that he loved working at the department store because he liked having his own money. His parents also acknowledged giving Jerry money.

Mr. Johnson stated that Jerry was a loner up until he was about 12 or 13 years old. Jerry reportedly was not involved in team sports but did develop an interest in karate. According to Mrs. Johnson, Jerry liked the types of activities in which he could improve his own skills.

Mr. Johnson related that his son had been fascinated with the marines since he was about 13 years of age. He befriended Vietnam veterans and wrote a letter about joining the marines to the commandant of the Marine Corps. When asked what led to Jerry's interest in guns, Mr. Johnson said that Jerry studied every phase of the military. For a period, Jerry seemed interested in going into the Secret Service or Federal Bureau of Investigation because, his parents thought, he liked to solve things.

Mr. and Mrs. Johnson saw Jerry as a "born leader." He was an Eagle scout, active in the ROTC, and had been a counselor at the Leadership Camp for two summers prior to his arrest. In that capacity, Jerry taught scouts how to survive and how to be good scouts.

Jerry's Friends

Jerry's friends went "from one end of the spectrum to the other." His parents saw Jerry as accepting people for who they were. One boy was attending the U.S. Military Academy in West Point, New York, and another was from a Jewish family. Jerry liked each ethnic group. He drove to South Carolina to see a friend graduate from a boot camp because the boy's parents were not going.

Jerry's parents related that their son was "very well liked." The wrestling team reportedly had reserved a vacant chair for Jerry at their banquet after the youth was arrested, even though Jerry was not on the team.

Jerry's mother had met Jerry's girlfriend, Suzie, but did not know her well. Neither parent had met Jerry's co-defendant, Marcus Stone, and had no sense of him as a person.

▨ MOTIVATIONAL DYNAMICS BEHIND THE HOMICIDE

Jerry gave a very detailed account of events on the day of the homicide. He began by recalling getting angry at a student in his building maintenance class who disturbed him by slamming a book down three times while he was trying to rest. Jerry reportedly told this boy that if he did it again, he was going to kill him and meant it. He recalled, "I was mad. It's unusual. Angry—lot more—and sad. A whole lot of things."

As he discussed the events leading up to the murder, it became clear that Jerry was very upset on the day of the homicide. He perceived that his girlfriend, Suzie, had broken up with him because she was interested in dating his friend, Timmy. Jerry believed that Timmy and Suzie had been sneaking around to see each other during the week to 10 days preceding the homicide. He sensed that they were in the early stages of dating and were lying to him about it. Although Jerry and Suzie had small fights during their 6 weeks of dating, Jerry believed that "it was reparable until Timmy came into it. . . . Timmy added a lot to her breaking up with me."

Jerry stated several times that he had done a great deal for Timmy. When Timmy escaped from the juvenile detention center approximately 1 month before the homicide, Jerry picked Timmy up and helped the boy get set up on the outside. Jerry's account essentially indicated that he was enraged with Timmy because he saw Timmy's behavior as an act of betrayal.

> Timmy was betraying our trust—trying to get my girlfriend to go out with him. That broke all the rules right there. We [Jerry and co-defendant Marcus] decided he needed to die for it. That was the main rule—I mean, *the* rule not to break. After all I did for him, that was the worst thing he could have done.
>
> After I helped him out after he escaped . . . if anything, he should have gone out of his way to help me out. If Suzie was hitting on him, he should have gone out of his way to watch her when I was not around. That was his responsibility—unwritten responsibility—he should have done that. I would do that for my friends. I expected that he would do that for me. . . . He did what an outsider would have done.

When probed, Jerry explained that when he first started to suspect the nature of Suzie and Timmy's relationship, he talked to Timmy and Suzie, Marcus, and two other friends. After a while, he gave up hoping that Suzie and Timmy would tell him the truth. Jerry talked to Marcus "somewhere from a week to 2 weeks, more towards a week . . . that if he was going to go on doing that, we should kill him." Jerry explained that Marcus was willing to help because he was "part of our group of friends." He stated, "If one person does wrong to another person we are all friends with, then he does something to all of us. If he would do it to Marcus, he would sure do it to me."

Jerry said that the day before the homicide, he was really angry and was not sure whether killing Timmy was the way in which to handle it. Marcus provided the "outside viewpoint" that he needed to help him decide to go ahead with the murder. Jerry remembered only one other occasion when he had been as angry as he was in the days preceding the homicide, and that was the time he had got into the fight at school. Jerry's statements indicated that he was so consumed with anger that he could not "blow off things" like he usually did.

> When I'm angry like that, I just couldn't sit there and put it behind me. I think you just have to do something about it. A lot of people aren't willing to—afraid or what not. Sometimes you have to get angry to get things done.

When asked whether he could have waited a week longer to carry out the homicide, Jerry answered in the negative. "No, probably could not have. I was thinking about Suzie and Timmy, and pretty soon they were gonna get together and go out. I had to stop that."

Jerry's rendition of the homicide was very event oriented. He related that Marcus had called around looking for Timmy on the day of the homicide and had indicated that he and Jerry would pick Timmy up to accompany them into the woods to find marijuana plants. He admitted straightforwardly that there really were no marijuana plants; the ruse was used to get Timmy into the woods where he would be killed.

Jerry and Marcus bought ammunition for the shotgun. They put the shells in the shotgun and the shotgun in the trunk before picking up Timmy. Jerry and his co-defendant called for directions to Shawn's house from a convenience store. When they arrived at Shawn's house, they were told that Timmy was over at another friend's house. When they arrived there, Timmy was not there, and they returned to Shawn's house where they found Timmy and Shawn.

When Marcus asked whether Timmy was ready to go, Timmy got up and Shawn followed. Marcus allegedly inquired whether Shawn was coming. Timmy reportedly said yes and asked whether that was all right. Jerry said that Marcus looked at him for an answer. Jerry said yes. Jerry stated that Timmy and Shawn got into the back of Jerry's car. Before entering the car, Jerry said that he and Marcus exchanged glances over the roof of his car. Marcus allegedly smiled and gave Jerry the "throat-cutting symbol." Jerry said that it was understood that Shawn was to die too and that he was Marcus's responsibility.

Jerry described pulling up to the wooded area as Marcus directed him. Jerry never had been there before and did not believe the two victims had been there either. Jerry told Timmy not to wear one of the camouflage jackets in Jerry's car. Jerry left the three boys to turn the car around, took the shotgun from the trunk, and went to join the others. He had difficulty finding them but eventually located them.

When the search for the plants proved unsuccessful, the four boys agreed to leave. As they walked on the trail, Marcus was ahead to the right, Timmy was closer to Jerry to the left, and Shawn was behind him and to the right.

> As we were walking out, I brought the gun over to my shoulder in a standing position. I didn't really aim. I just brought it up and fired, and it hit Timmy, which was what I intended to do—is hit him. He dropped to the ground and he was yelling, and all I could think about was to stop him yelling, so I shot him again. And it's real unusual because I never felt like that—like I was watching it. I didn't really feel like I was doing it. It was like I was watching it, like watching a movie—like I am above it, watching what's going on.

Jerry recalled shooting Timmy twice and running up closer for the second shot. When Jerry heard Shawn screaming, it hit him what was going on. Jerry took pains to explain it.

> I don't want you to get confused. I knew what was happening. It was just weird. I was just numb because this was a big thing. I had him [Shawn] yelling behind me and I turned around and he was scared—real scared—and I turned and raised the gun toward him, and he took off running. He ran fast. I fired a shot, ran after him, he rounded a corner, I fired another shot.

Jerry recalled running toward some bushes. Before he got to them, he stopped and looked to see whether he could see another human figure. Jerry then went through the bushes and trained the gun on Shawn. He was going to shoot Shawn, but started feeling sick. He knew at that time that he was not going to shoot Shawn but that Shawn could not go free either. Jerry grabbed Shawn by the arm and brought him up. Jerry held Shawn until Marcus came over and then let him go.

Jerry related that Shawn started to run. Marcus ran after Shawn and tackled him. Jerry said that he was about 15 feet away at this time. He observed Shawn on the ground; Marcus was punching and starting to strangle him. Marcus called to Jerry for help. Jerry stated that he went over but that he was vomiting at that time. Jerry explained that Shawn was fighting for his life and that it made Jerry ill to watch the struggle. Jerry said that Marcus was stomping on Shawn's throat and kicking him in the head.

When Shawn stopped struggling, Marcus suggested that they leave. Jerry said that he could not run and handed the shotgun and car keys to Marcus. He told Marcus to put the shotgun in the trunk and said that he would meet Marcus at the car.

Jerry thought that both boys were dead when he and his co-defendant left the woods. Jerry stated that he and Marcus took some time in a parking lot to get their stories straight. "We knew that there were two dead guys. We had to call them [police] to cover ourselves." The youths had not given much prior thought to what they were going to do after the killings.

Jerry remembered calling the police and later sitting in the patrol car and watching the computer. As he watched the teletype, it dawned on him that he was a suspect. He related going to the sheriff's office and seeing his parents and brother, Julius. Jerry's father asked him that night whether he had shot anyone and he nodded yes. His father reportedly said, "It was an accident, right?" Jerry shook his head no. Jerry remembered going to the juvenile detention center the next morning. He thought that he was there for about a week before being transferred to the medical section of the adult jail.

When asked whether he perceived the killing of Timmy as the right thing to do given his statement that Timmy had broken a rule, Jerry replied that it was "the only thing to do. There wasn't any other way to punish him. We couldn't lock him up." When asked whether he considered explaining to the police the necessity for the killing, Jerry answered negatively. "The police wouldn't understand. It's against the law for people to kill people, I know that. I know you can't go out and kill people."

EVALUATION OF FORENSIC ISSUES RAISED

Although Jerry's killing of his best friend seemed bizarre to his family, his teachers, and many of his classmates, the homicide indeed made sense when examined from Jerry's view of the world.

Client's Competency to Stand Trial

Jerry clearly was competent to stand trial. The youth was aware of his trial date. At the time of my clinical evaluation, he had been incarcerated for 15 months and appeared to be handling stress well. The youth understood that he was charged with first-degree murder and the nature of the possible penalties for first- and second-degree murder. He also understood the nature of the legal process, that is, the roles of various people within the court system—judge, prosecutor, defense counsel, and jury—as well as his own role. He appeared able to relate well to both of his attorneys and to disclose pertinent facts to them. Jerry could be expected to maintain appropriate behavior in court and to testify relevantly if he took the witness stand, which he quite realistically evaluated as unlikely. He was able to retain and understand what he had learned about the legal process and factors pertaining to his own case.

Client's Sanity at the Time of the Crime

Based on the materials provided by defense counsel and the defendant's statements during the 4-hour assessment, Jerry was sane under the M'Naghten standard at the time of the homicide. Jerry's recollection of the events before, during, and after the homicide was extensive. Although there appeared to be some dissociation when Jerry fired the first and second shots, his rendition of the homicidal incident indicated that he knew the nature and quality of his acts and that such behavior was legally wrong. When probed about the shooting of Timmy, the youth's remarks made it clear that he knew that he was about to kill the victim. "I brought the gun up to him a couple of other times. This time I just went through with it. At that point I knew—I thought the first shot would kill him. I was expecting it to kill him."

Jerry subsequently explained that he meant for Timmy to die on the first shot.

> I didn't want to shoot him and have him lay there. I meant to kill him. . . . He was a good friend of mine. I wouldn't wish that on anybody [lying in pain]. It had to be done [killing], and I was going to do it as quickly as possible . . . without drawing it out. Making him suffer was not the goal.

Making Sense of Murder

Jerry's personality development, that of a low-maturity individual, is helpful in understanding why he killed a youth he characterized as his friend. Jerry conformed to rules and formulas and saw these as the ways in which to succeed in life and to gain social approval from his friends. Jerry perceived Timmy as betraying their friendship and as breaking *the* main rule—"hitting on [his] girlfriend." He was enraged as he thought about the betrayal by his girlfriend and his friend. This behavior had to be stopped, and this wrong had to be avenged. Jerry and his friend, Marcus, saw no other option short of murdering Timmy. The decision to kill Shawn was based on the concern that he would be a witness to the murder of Timmy.

At the time of the clinical evaluation, Jerry had not reached the level of personality development where he truly saw himself as accountable for his behavior. Although the youth regretted the painful consequences that had befallen him, he was not sorry for killing Timmy. When asked whether the homicidal incident could have been prevented, Jerry said yes, it could have if his girlfriend, Suzie, and the victim, Timmy, had acted differently.

> If they would have told me the truth, nothing would have really happened. Trying to trick me, everybody getting over on me. A lot could have been avoided. If Suzie would have spent 5 minutes talking with me, this whole thing would not have happened.

Diagnostic and Treatment Considerations

Prior to the homicidal event, Jerry would not have been identified as a problem youth. Jerry was polite, well mannered, and well liked. He related well to his parents, teachers, and peers. He did well in school, was involved in some extracurricular activities, and had a part-time job. At the time of the clinical evaluation, Jerry did not meet the criteria for Conduct Disorder, which frequently is the forerunner of Antisocial Personality Disorder. A clinical disorder diagnosis often is appropriately given to youths who kill intentionally and remorselessly.

At the time of the assessment, the prognosis in Jerry's case was guarded. He appeared to pose a continuing threat to society so long as his personality development was low and he remained invested in his formulas of intense loyalty and individualized justice.

When asked how he would respond if the prosecutor were to allege that he was dangerous, for example, Jerry maintained that he was "safer than most people walking the street. If I do have a gun, I know how to use it." When asked whether he would be involved in another incident, he said no, "nothing is worth this. I wouldn't risk my freedom for anything." Jerry would not hurt someone unless he had "a very good reason for it."

I recommended to counsel that Jerry also be evaluated by a psychologist. Test data could be helpful in elucidating to what extent Jerry's sense of his betrayal by his girlfriend and Timmy was indicative of paranoid ideation. Prior to scheduling of this evaluation, Jerry entered a plea given subsequent developments in his case.

CASE PROCESSING AND DISPOSITION

Shortly after my clinical evaluation, Jerry was implicated in a scheme to hire a hit man to kill Shawn to prevent his testifying at Jerry's upcoming murder trial. The hitman turned out to be a government informant. Jerry entered guilty pleas to first-degree murder and solicitation to commit first-degree murder. Jerry also provided information to prosecutors about the role of his co-defendant and agreed to testify against Marcus when Marcus went to trial for Timmy's murder. In exchange for Jerry's cooperation, the state agreed to forgo seeking the death penalty.

Jerry was sentenced to life in prison with a mandatory 25 years before parole eligibility on the murder charge. He was sentenced to 7 years on the solicitation charge. The second commitment was to run concurrently with the first.

Jerry was sentenced to another 5 years after being found guilty of possession of contraband, a charge he also incurred while incarcerated in county jail. Jail personnel found a razor blade encased in a plastic handle in Jerry's cell. Authorities thought it was a "shank" (a sharp instrument used for stabbing). Records indicated that Jerry told authorities that he used it to cut paper. This conviction later was overturned on the grounds that Jerry was not given Miranda warnings.

FOLLOW-UP DATA

I conducted a follow-up interview with Jerry approximately 5 years after my evaluation. At that time, Jerry had been incarcerated for more than 6 years. He had spent almost 3 of these 6 years in county jail before going to prison. I met with Jerry's mother approximately 3 months after seeing him.

Clinical Interview

Jerry presented in much the same way as he had when I first met him. He was pleasant, polite, and precise in his responses. He had fared well in prison and showed significant signs of maturity.

Jerry reported that he had taken advantage of vocational training opportunities and had completed courses in cabinetmaking, carpentry, gas engine repair, and law clerking. At the time of the follow-up, Jerry was taking college correspondence courses and working as a clerk in the prison law library. He spent his free time reading books and working out. He watched only one television program on a regular basis: *The X-Files*.

Jerry indicated that he never had been in a fight since being incarcerated. He had not been sexually assaulted or harassed by other inmates. He had been robbed of $6 to $7 by two inmates who attacked him from behind and choked him until he was unconscious.

Jerry recalled receiving only one disciplinary report since coming to prison. He believed that the officer wrote the disciplinary report in retaliation for Jerry being a law clerk, and he was appealing it.

Jerry indicated that the worst thing about being in prison was "not being able to be alone, always having people around." He advised that having 87 bunks in an open bay dorm was "too crowded. I have somebody right on top of me. I can't sit up in bed. There's someone 3 feet to my right, I have a wall to my left, somebody about a foot and a half behind me, and a foot and a half from my feet laying down."

Notwithstanding his apparent discomfort, Jerry acknowledged that prison had been good for him and that he was "thankful in a lot of ways." He related that he had experiences he never would have had anywhere else. He had seen many things, learned a great deal about people, and acquired some job skills. He reflected on his prior thoughts of going into the marines and their current relevance to prison life. "I believe a little suffering can do a lot of good as far as building character."

Jerry shared that his parents had divorced about 2½ years ago. He is on good terms with both parents. He calls his mother and father weekly, and both parents visit him individually every 2 or 3 months. He suggested that his parents were "maybe a little bit embarrassed or humiliated" to tell people that their son is serving a life sentence in prison. Jerry said that he regretted what he had done to his parents. "They have been the best to me. I am really sorry about that."

Jerry has not seen or heard from either of his brothers since leaving the county jail for prison 3 years ago. He has not heard from any friends on a regular basis for more than 5 years.

Jerry indicated that he thinks about the murder "almost every day. Everywhere I look, I am reminded of it." When he looks at his bunk, he thinks about "how I put myself here."

Jerry's thoughts about his involvement in the homicidal event have changed significantly over the past 5 years.

> I can see more of the big picture now. At the time of the crime, I could just see myself, and Timmy was his name. And what we had between us, that was just us and our little situation. But, that whatever I did and whatever he did just affected us—that was

unrealistic, because when I killed him, it affected a lot of people, and I can see it from his family's point of view, from my family's point of view now, and understand. At that time, he was a kid and I was a kid, and we were trying to play like grown-ups, and that was about it.

Jerry now sees "101 different ways" in which the murder could have been prevented. Jerry related that he was wrong for even associating with Timmy given that Timmy was an escapee from the juvenile detention center. Jerry stated that there was nothing for him to have gained by befriending Timmy; he did it for the excitement. Jerry indicated that if he wanted to hurt Timmy or get even with Timmy, then he could have called the police instead of killing Timmy.

Jerry mentioned that he had a lot of Skinhead friends and that Timmy was one of them. Jerry denied being a Skinhead himself. He maintained that the theory that his case was about one White supremacist killing another was untrue.

Jerry stated that he was "under a lot of stress and not able to deal with it" at the time of the killing. He was getting ready to go into the service at the time his girlfriend broke up with him. He had no date for the prom and felt as though he had to go. Timmy had escaped from the detention center during that time. Jerry was worried about helping him when the alleged betrayal happened.

Jerry thought at the time that he was doing the right thing by asking Timmy and Suzie about their relationship. He now sees their apparent lying to him as "natural" because all of them were young. If the same thing happened now, Jerry said, "I could care less. I'd go and find another girlfriend." Jerry emphasized that what bothered him most was Timmy's alleged betrayal rather than the loss of his girlfriend. "I had trusted him, and I had helped him out. I had picked him up when he escaped and introduced him to others. And then, for him to go and do that to me, that's what hurt me."

Unlike 5 years ago, Jerry now appeared genuinely sorry for killing Timmy.

I regret it. I know deep down I didn't have a right to do that, to kill anybody. It changed my view on a whole lot. Before that, I had very low regard for human life. I was focused toward the service. I had read everything I could get my hands on, on Vietnam. And I was desensitized to the killing because you read about people going into the jungles and kill people and come out and become successful people, and there's nothing to it.

I desensitized myself to where I could have done the same thing. And I thought I was doing the right thing as far as focusing that way. I was for the death penalty, believe it or not, the views I had back then. Now I don't think anybody has the right—state, government, whatever—to take another life.

Jerry related that he had adopted an Eastern way of looking at life. At follow-up, he believed in Karma and that "what goes around, comes around."

My suffering in here is nothing compared to the suffering I caused. And it helps me to deal with it a lot more. I only have myself to blame, but all I can do, there is a saying, "that which does not kill me makes me stronger."

Jerry clearly has come to see himself as accountable for killing Timmy. He maintained, "There is no way I can justify the murder. There is no reason I can give as to why." Jerry indicated that at the time of the homicide, he isolated himself and did not feel that he had anyone with whom he could talk. He acknowledged seeking out Marcus because "he was homicidal too, and we fed off of each other." Although Jerry suggested that the killing might not have occurred had he sought out someone "more passive," he quickly added, "It's 100% my fault. I sought out somebody like that. That is the way I wanted to deal with it. I knew this guy had the same kind of views and would probably go for it, so that's why I talked to him."

Jerry testified against Marcus per the plea agreement. Marcus was convicted of second-degree murder and initially sentenced to 20 years. On appeal, the sentence was reduced to 15 years. Mitigation in Marcus's sentence was based on Jerry's being the initiator of the crime.

Jerry felt bad about testifying against Marcus. He indicated that it did not feel like the right thing to do.

> It felt like I was being used by the state to get what I wanted at Marcus's expense. By doing that, I had hurt Marcus's family. But then again, he put himself in that position. I hope he realizes that and learns from it like I have.

Jerry credited reading as being the main force behind the change in his thinking. He referenced Stanton Samenow's book, *Inside the Criminal Mind*,[2] as being particularly influential. Jerry agreed with Samenow's categorization of the motivations that drive criminals: power and control, acceptance, and excitement. Jerry said that he wanted to exert power and control when he killed Timmy because he felt that he had no control and wanted to reestablish control. He wanted "everybody to know you can't do this to me."

Jerry also saw his desire to regain power as the primary reason for his participation in a scheme to have the surviving witness, Shawn, killed. Jerry related that he really did not care whether the supposed hitman killed Shawn. Jerry recognized that he was helpless in jail. Jerry felt that if the hitman did not follow through, he was no worse off. If the hitman murdered Shawn, however, Jerry hoped it might weaken the state's case against him and send an important message to others. Jerry acknowledged, "That seemed like a quick solution to the problem. I would come out smelling like a rose and looking like I was the one in control."

Jerry related that from about 14 years of age, he was focused on the military because it represented power to him and he liked guns. Jerry estimated watching the film *The Green Berets*, starring John Wayne, "a hundred times." He watched the film every day on the videocassette player at home and often would go to sleep watching it.

Jerry admitted, "The whole military thing I was into was twisted from what military life was like." Jerry saw the military "as combat, as a release," and as a way in which to deal with "anger and frustration and everything else." Every weekend, he and his friends would train, engage in BB gun wars, and go out on survival camping trips.

> We were geared more towards shooting at paper targets and thinking of them as hu - mans, to where it turned out, we'd shoot at humans—they were no more than paper targets. . . . I could shoot at a person just as easily as shooting at a tree. You think the same thing. Just get to where you were used to that, even looking forward to getting it over with—killing the first person.

Jerry related that at the time of his arrest, he had a very positive view of government leaders and of the military. He said, "I had more or less a blind faith in leaders in general." His views were very different at the time of the follow-up interview. He remarked, "I am completely anti-government now." Jerry characterized the government as being corrupt and exploiting the people. "I don't trust the government to think they have any genuine feeling for the welfare of anybody in the country. I think it is all self-serving."

Jerry recommended *The Turner Diaries*,[3] which he was reading for the third time, as "essential reading" for understanding the anti-government movement and the rationale for the Oklahoma City bombing. "People get frustrated. It really is corrupt. You can see it from even in here, from the officers all the way up to the secretary of corrections, to the governor, to the president."

Jerry stated that the sentence given to him was fair. "As long as they were in the legal limits of the law," he had no reason to complain. However, he has misgivings about his decision to plead guilty to the murder and solicitation charges rather than go to trial. Although his plea resulted in the sentences running concurrently rather than consecutively, Jerry regrets that he forfeited his right to appeal.

Review of Jerry's Prison File

Correctional records corroborated Jerry's statements. Review of Jerry's prison file revealed that correction officials evaluated Jerry's attitude, adjustment, and prognosis as good on his admission to prison. Jerry did well during his first 3 years of incarceration. Staff initially evaluated Jerry as "above satisfactory." His ratings quickly improved and typically were "outstanding." Records indicated that Jerry took advantage of cabinet-making and other vocational opportunities. He had received two disciplinary reports for minor infractions. One of these was reversed; the other was under appeal.

Follow-Up Interview With Jerry's Mother

Mrs. Johnson's remarks about Jerry's prison adjustment and activities were consistent with those made by her son. Jerry's incarceration, particularly in jail before his transfer to prison, has been a real education for him. He has learned to be on guard to avoid violence, to keep his possessions, and to get his food. Jerry lost about 50 pounds after being locked up; the food was unappealing and occasionally was stolen from him.

Mrs. Johnson has come to believe that Jerry committed the murder because he had been influenced by the people with whom he was associating at the time. She expressed regret that she treated Jerry like an adult when he was growing up and did not ask him more questions about his friends and activities.

Mrs. Johnson indicated that Jerry watched "a lot" of television while growing up. He liked action-packed films. She specifically recalled his enjoyment of army and gangster movies.

Mrs. Johnson related that Jerry "has learned to appreciate friends and family, mostly family," since being incarcerated. He has become "a lot wiser" over the years. "He knows how to spot the con man and the ones the cons will hit on." Jerry has become more reflective about himself and remorseful.

Mr. and Mrs. Johnson both have remained supportive toward Jerry. Their divorce was an amicable one. They talk to one another about Jerry and are prepared to help him when he is released. Mrs. Johnson related that Jerry checks in weekly with both

of them. She has spoken to prison staff on occasion to ensure that Jerry was receiving appropriate medical care and was being treated fairly.

Mrs. Johnson indicated that Jerry has taken advantage of every educational and vocational opportunity to rehabilitate himself. In her eyes, he is ready to be released. "Nothing there is helping him. He knows what he has done, and he's sorry for what he's done. He has tried to do everything he can to make up for it, you know, as much as he can."

▆ CASE COMMENTARY

Prior to his arrest, Jerry was, in many ways, "the boy next door." He was truly a likeable kid. Judging from outward appearances, he was the type of boy who parents would like their daughters to date or their sons to pal around with.

How does a youth from a good family wind up killing his best friend and putting a contract out on another kid who survived the homicidal event? We see, in this case, a number of factors contributing to Jerry's decision to kill. These include situational factors, societal influences, resource availability, and personality characteristics.

Jerry did not appear to have been closely supervised. Both his parents worked, and they trusted Jerry. He was, in his mother's words, "a latchkey child." When he arrived home from school, he watched television until his mother returned home from work. His mother indicated that she did not ask Jerry many questions about his friends and activities. Mr. Johnson worked long hours and did not spend much time with Jerry. Consequently, Jerry did not regard his father as a role model.

The reader will recall that Jerry's personality development was low prior to his arrest. Those who perceive at Level 3 are interested in finding formulas to achieve power. The military, with its rules, provided the needed structure for Jerry.

In fact, Jerry became obsessed with the military. War heroes became his role models. He watched war films repeatedly. He became desensitized to violence. Killing became not only an acceptable solution to problems but also a desirable course of action. He practiced shooting and fantasized killing.

The military code also instilled in Jerry the value of loyalty above all else. Jerry helped Timmy after the boy escaped from the juvenile detention center for two reasons: Timmy was his friend, and hiding him from authorities was fun and exciting.

When Jerry felt that he had been wronged by Timmy and Suzie, he was enraged. Jerry was unable to deal with the strong feelings occasioned by the supposed betrayal. In his mind, the course of action was pre-ordained. Simply put, Timmy broke a rule and deserved to die. Jerry had access to firearms and was mentally prepared to use one.

Jerry felt powerless after he was arrested. He was smart enough to know that if Shawn testified, he would be convicted of first-degree murder. The penalty would be either life in prison or death. When Jerry agreed to pay a supposed hit man $5,000 that he did not have for the man to kill Shawn, he figured that he had little or nothing to lose.

Prognosis

Jerry has made significant strides in prison. His personality development has matured to Level 4. He sees himself as accountable for his behavior and appears genuinely remorseful. He has some empathy for his parents.

Some concerns remain. Before release, Jerry's anti-government beliefs need to be explored. Jerry understandably harbors some resentment toward criminal justice and correctional officer personnel. He allegedly was set up by a hitman who was a government informant. While incarcerated, he reportedly has seen some prison staff engage in unethical and illegal conduct. He is aware of government leaders who are corrupt and ruled by self-interest. Prior to release, it is important that Jerry's negative attitudes toward government leaders be explored further to ensure that they are channeled into appropriate activities and kept within acceptable bounds.

Chapter Seven

Calvin Thomas

A FIGHT ERUPTED between groups of White and Black teens in the yard of an apartment complex in the early morning hours. During the melee, Richard Adams, a White 19-year-old youth, was brutally beaten to death with boards ripped off from a cafe just moments before.

Police reported that Kevin Bateson, a 19-year-old White male, had provoked Calvin Thomas, a Black youth who was one month shy of his 18th birthday, into a fight about an hour before the murder occurred. Several other White youths reportedly joined in the fracas, while many more gathered around to watch. Calvin and the other Black youths were outnumbered and left the area. The prevailing theory was that the Black youths came back armed and looking for revenge.

Calvin was among eight Black youths arrested and charged with first-degree murder. I was appointed by the court, at the motion of defense counsel, to examine the defendant, particularly with respect to trial preparation related to the sentencing phase. The state was seeking the death penalty.

THE CLINICAL EVALUATION

My assessment of Calvin Thomas is based on a $4^1/2$-hour interview conducted in adult jail 10 months after his arrest. On the same day, I also spoke with Calvin's two younger brothers, who were incarcerated at the same facility on unrelated charges. A week later, I spoke with Calvin's parents and his younger sister for approximately 2 hours. Case materials reviewed included the police investigation reports and related depositions, the autopsy report, preliminary psychological data from the consulting psychologist, school records, and statements given to the police by the defendant and by the co-defendants who had agreed to testify against Calvin. Police reports relating to the altercation in which Calvin was involved earlier that night also were reviewed.

BEHAVIORAL OBSERVATIONS

Calvin presented as an African American male, approximately 5 feet 10 inches in height and about 160 pounds. He was missing a center tooth that he said he had lost in a fight.

Initially, Calvin was very apprehensive about the interview and objected to it being recorded. He made it clear from the outset of the evaluation that he believed he was being "railroaded." It took about a half hour to establish sufficient rapport with Calvin to proceed.

Calvin seemed alert and guarded throughout much of the assessment. He appeared angry and particularly agitated when asked to relate details about the homicide. Calvin's eye contact, varying from direct to none, led me to question the veracity of some of his responses.

Calvin was cooperative during the evaluation. Despite his initial distrust, he did not refuse to answer anything asked. His answers often were restricted, which appeared indicative of his overall intelligence and level of personality development. His responses clearly indicated that he was oriented to reality and that he could remember both recent and past events. There were no data to suggest that he experienced hallucinations. Although he talked about being railroaded and expressed considerable doubt about the fairness of the criminal justice system, he did not appear delusional. Rather, his remarks seemed more indicative of his personality development and life experiences.

PERSONALITY DEVELOPMENT

Calvin, typical of individuals who perceive at Level 3 of the Interpersonal Maturity Level (I-level) classification system, made minimal differentiations among people and was focused on power. In his worldview, for example, White people were one way, Black people were another way, and White people were invested in keeping Black people down. When speaking of correctional officers, for example, Calvin stated, "They look at you like they want to say 'nigger' so bad, you can see it in their faces." He made the same remark later regarding his teachers and related how they like to show slavery films in school. He maintained that the police were similarly prejudiced. "The police don't like to see Blacks driving—riding around in a Cadillac."

In Calvin's eyes, at the time of the evaluation, the Whites had the power and the Blacks did not. He related that "White people have the upper hand. They stick together. . . . All they want to do is convict the Black man. The White man always have more power—always have to be right." The adolescent described two cases in which a White man and a Black man were convicted of sex crimes against children. Although the White man had more charges, he was sentenced to 30 years, whereas the Black man was sentenced to 200 years.

Prior to his arrest, Calvin was interested in having a good time and selected his friends accordingly. The adolescent fit the profile of the *cultural conformist*, frequently going along with his friends' wishes to get their approval. Not surprisingly, Calvin viewed his prior delinquent involvements as resulting from hanging around with "the wrong crowd."

RELEVANT SOCIAL HISTORY

Family Constellation

Calvin was the oldest of four children. His parents reportedly had been together about 19 years and seemed to get along fairly well. Calvin had heard that his mother would hit his father if she caught his father "messing up" on something. By contrast, Calvin's father did not hit his mother.

Calvin left home when he was 16 years old because he did not want to do the household chores required of him. He would stay with his aunt, who lived in town. His aunt was not as strict as his mother, and he could get away with more (e.g., he could sell drugs and tell his aunt that he was holding money for a friend).

Calvin described his father as "all right" and stated that he and his father were more "like brothers." They liked to do the same things, such as hunting and fishing. His father was a good father because he worked, paid bills, and came home. Calvin's father reportedly drank about a quart of beer every night and more on weekends and had been convicted of driving under the influence (DUI) in the past. His father would get drunk about three times a year; he had to reduce his drinking because he had ulcers.

Calvin described his mother as "good" because whenever he came to her, she would give him what he needed. She did what she was supposed to do and stood by her children. She did not drink alcohol.

When Calvin did something wrong, he reportedly would get a whipping by his mother, who would use a strap or belt. He recalled receiving frequent whippings as a young child because he did things wrong (e.g., throwing rocks at things or people). As he got older, Calvin's mother allegedly would make him stand 3 or 4 hours with his nose in the corner or in the closet or bathroom. Calvin preferred standing in the corner or in the closet over a whipping because he could go to sleep.

Calvin got along well with his two younger brothers, Julius, age 17 years, and Joey, age 15 years, and with his sister, Tasha, age 14 years. Calvin described Julius as a great kid who liked to participate in many sports and who "beat the charge" on which he had been detained because he was not guilty. He described Joey as liking girls, mowing lawns, and riding skateboards. Calvin suggested that Joey was falsely accused of throwing rocks (firing a deadly missile) on several occasions. He stated that Tasha went to school and played softball. All of them liked sports and were encouraged by their mother, who managed a softball team.

School

Calvin stated that he stopped liking school and had not done well since about the 4th grade. He managed to get all the hard teachers and did not get along with many of them. Calvin perceived that they did not help him when he requested it. Eventually, he refused to do anything in their classes and brought his jukebox to school and listened to music in the back of the classrooms. The teachers reportedly said that Calvin had an "attitude problem" because he would fight with youths who challenged him.

Calvin remembered his 4th-grade teacher paddling him on several occasions. Paddling did not hurt Calvin but made him mad. Calvin got suspended "a lot of times," mostly for fighting, and claimed he was out of school more than he was in school. Calvin stopped going to school in the 9th grade following a suspension at 16 years of age.

Work History

At the time Calvin was arrested, he did not have a job and was not interested in having one. His parents reportedly would give him money when he asked. Calvin was unwilling to work at a fast food restaurant because he did not like people looking at him.

Calvin liked working with plants and had a summer job working for an agricultural firm when he was 16 years old. He worked hard putting sand on the beaches and got along with the people there.

Some time after that job, Calvin went away for approximately 6 months to learn welding in the Job Corps. He initially moved because his cousin was there and had liked it. Although Calvin liked the program, he did not complete it. He was kicked out for fighting with "a dude [to] whom [he] had fronted money." Calvin "broke his jaw or something."

Friends

Calvin related that he had some friends in jail. He considered his co-defendants, whom he initially referred to as friends, as "associates." His only true friend was his dog. He maintained that he got into trouble in the past for selling drugs because he hung around with the wrong crowd. He advised, "If you'd have been in that environment, then you would have done the same thing."

Calvin's friends on the street were "all right." They liked to have a good time and do the things that he did—drink, have fun, and have sex. Calvin reportedly did not hang around with the youths with whom he was arrested. He used to associate with an older crowd—people ages 25 to 40 years—because they did not get into trouble and he had stopped "playing kid games." He liked hanging around older women. These friends had jobs and homes and liked to party on the weekends. He could rely on them when he needed things, and likewise, they could depend on him.

Girlfriends and Sexual History

Calvin had a girlfriend prior to his arrest but reportedly broke up with her because he could not give her the things that he wanted to give her. At the time of the evaluation, however, they were back together. Calvin related that it did not bother him that the baby she had was not his.

The absence of sex has been difficult for Calvin since he has been incarcerated. Having a girlfriend prior to his arrest was very important to him to "satisfy his needs" for sex. Sex was "my hobby" and "like a job." He reported having sex "mostly every day" with different people. He made remarks that "made them feel good," so they would agree to have sex with him.

He reportedly first had intercourse with someone when he was about 11 years old. Some of his partners—all female—were older. When he was 16, one of his paramours was 38.

Calvin denied ever forcing himself on anyone. "If I can't talk her up, I don't want it," he said. He explained, "She was willing to give it up, and I was willing to take it." Probing of prior sexual history revealed no evidence that Calvin had been a victim of either sexual abuse or sexual assault.

Activities

Calvin enjoyed hanging out with friends. He also liked having sex, playing sports, and drinking.

Alcohol and Drug Involvement

Calvin was not sure when he first started drinking; perhaps it was around 10 years of age. He remarked that he drank a lot prior to his arrest and that it had adversely affected his health (he had difficulty sleeping and eating). He drank daily, starting in the morning after he left home. Although he claimed he drank beer all day long, he denied ever having any memory losses. When he was drinking, he would want sex, have sex, and go to sleep.

Calvin admitted to having smoked marijuana on a few occasions (about twice a year) but denied usage of any other drugs, including crack cocaine. Calvin acknowledged having had a problem with alcohol. He did not see himself as having any problems with any other drugs.

Physical and Mental Health History

Calvin said that his health is better since he has been incarcerated because he stopped drinking. He did not recall any serious illnesses when he was a child. He did report two head injuries. (One was sustained when he ran into a chimney). He did not lose consciousness and suffered no memory loss.

Calvin remembered being taken to the hospital and released when he hurt his back while exercising 4 or 5 years ago. At the time of the evaluation, Calvin was experiencing discomfort from this injury and felt that he had not received adequate medical attention in jail.

Calvin claimed that he had been referred by the school to a psychiatrist because he got into trouble frequently. The psychiatrist's records could not be located. Calvin stated that he never had been hospitalized for any physical or mental illnesses. He was not under medication at the time of the assessment interview. Calvin did not express any need for, or interest in obtaining, counseling.

Handling Problems and Affectivity

Calvin described himself as "good. If you give me respect, I give you respect. You treat me like a human being, I treat you like one." When asked about things about himself that he liked, Calvin said that he did not act like "a little kid."

When asked about things he would like to change about himself, Calvin mentioned smoking cigarettes and his bad attitude. He indicated that he had trouble in school because of his temper. "I just go off on you real easy. You just can't say anything to me. You could be joking with me, I just don't like—it's all right, we can play, but I don't like anybody grabbing on me . . . touching me." He explained that if somebody shoved him, he would fight that person because "you can't always walk away from a fight." Sometimes, if somebody made him angry, he might go off and drink.

Religious Affiliation

Calvin has come to know the Lord since being incarcerated. He considered himself a member of the Church of New Jerusalem.

Prior Delinquent Involvement

Calvin reported three prior convictions. He was arrested for selling crack cocaine 14 months before the homicide. He pleaded guilty to selling drugs and was sentenced as a juvenile to 1 year probation. Just 1 month after completing his probation charge, Calvin was arrested on the murder charge.

In the other two prior offenses, Calvin was prosecuted as an adult and maintained his innocence. Calvin was convicted of aggravated battery in a case that went to trial after his incarceration. He maintained that he was not guilty of firing a bullet that hit a Black man. He was sentenced to 7 years in prison on this charge.

The adolescent discussed the circumstances behind his prior conviction of shooting into an occupied dwelling. He "copped out" to shooting into "a house owned by a lady" to help a friend. He was sentenced, shortly before my evaluation, to 13 months in prison on this charge and was given credit for time served.

Future Orientation

When asked what he would do if the homicide charge were resolved in his favor, Calvin said that he would move far away and get a job at a particular supermarket chain. He would make about $230 weekly, "enough for a single man." He maintained that he would not get into trouble again because he has learned not to do the things that he used to do. Instead, he would work and avoid being with "the wrong crowd."

Adjustment in Jail

At the time of my assessment, Calvin had been incarcerated for $9^1/2$ months. He appeared to have made an adequate adjustment to jail. He had not been assaulted by any of the other inmates and had not been bothered sexually by the men with whom he had been incarcerated. He mentioned that he had been threatened by one of his co-defendants but did not take the threat seriously. He maintained, "I can hold my ground."

He stated that he and his co-defendants initially had been treated very badly by the guards. He did not respond to their tactics, and eventually their treatment improved to some extent, but overall "they [guards] treat 'em like dogs." The guards reportedly discriminate against Blacks by denying them "house man jobs." Calvin has responded by filing grievance charges against the guards.

▪ MOTIVATIONAL DYNAMICS BEHIND THE HOMICIDE

Calvin denied involvement in the homicide. His version is recapped in the following and is generally consistent with the statement that he gave to police.

Calvin's Statements to Dr. Heide

Calvin related that on the night of the homicide, he had been drinking and talking to some White girls and Charlie, "a White guy" with whom he used to work, in a shopping mall parking lot. Charlie had been spinning the wheels of his truck, and some other White youths apparently did not like it.

Calvin walked up to Charlie's truck about 11 p.m. and asked him, "What's up?" Shortly thereafter, another White teen, Kevin, whom Calvin did not know but had seen once before buying dope, challenged him, "What you got to do with it, nigger?" Calvin replied, "I ain't got nothin' to do with it." The two men "squared off" and started fighting. Calvin was sitting on top of Kevin when four or five White adolescents joined in because they did not like the fact that Calvin was winning. One White youth hit Calvin in the back with his car and it pushed him up on the hood.

About 100 White people and about 6 Black people were present at the scene. The Black youths did not intervene and got behind the crowd. Given these circumstances, Calvin got in a friend's car, and the Black youths told the crowd that they were "fixing to go." The White adolescents kicked the car as the Black teens were leaving.

After leaving the parking lot, the Black youths went down to the "subs" (subdivisions) or projects. When they got there, "some dude" got Calvin a beer while he was talking to a couple of people and some girls. Hank, another Black adolescent, offered to take Calvin and some other Black youths back to the shopping center to get some liquor. Hank allegedly had told several other Black teens that Calvin had gotten into a fight with some White youths.

After they went to the liquor store, the youths in Hank's car were joined by another carload of Black teens. These youths in concert "tricked" Calvin by bringing him back to a particular area where some White adolescents were drinking. The Black youths went over to the White teens. Once there, one of them wanted Calvin to fight Kevin one-on-one. Calvin maintained that he did not want to fight. Rather, he wanted to go to the Black neighborhood. Then one of the White teens—there were about 10 of them—took a swing at one of the "Black dudes," and they "went to fighting."

Calvin claimed that he did not throw "one lick." He stated, "I was just standing back. I never did do nothing until some gunshots went off." When that happened, Calvin recalled, both Blacks and Whites started running. He ran down to the Black neighborhood—the subs. He did not know what happened from there because he left and the others stayed.

Some of them apparently followed Calvin later, including a youth whose head had been split open. Calvin said that he put the injured youth in the car, went to some girl's house, helped clean the wound out, and took the injured youth to the hospital. Afterward, Calvin was dropped off at the subdivisions and went to his aunt's house, where he had sex with a girl and stayed until the next morning. Later that day, he went to the store, went to the beach with another adolescent, drank a couple of six-packs of beer, and went to a party.

Someone at the party reportedly asked Calvin whether he was up there last night when "the White guy got killed." This individual told Calvin that "they" were saying that Calvin was there when it happened and that some lady apparently had identified him. Calvin did not know anything about it.

Calvin indicated that he was going to go to the police to get it cleared up when about 10 to 12 police units pulled up. The police had their guns out. Calvin recalled going up to them and putting his hands on their car. Nonetheless, they reportedly treated him roughly when they put the handcuffs on him and put him in the car.

When asked whether he knew Richard Adams, he said yes and gestured that he and the victim had been very close. Calvin had known "Richie" for about 4 or 5 years and related that they used to go to each other's houses. Calvin had "good feelings" for him because they would help each other if either was in a bind.

Calvin maintained that he had no contact with the victim that night and did not even know that Richie was there. He thought the victim had been living in another city and had not seen him for about a year. Calvin stated that "a chill ran through my body" when he heard about the victim's death and that he did not want to believe it.

Calvin inquired, however, that if Richie was such a good kid, then why did he have a knife on him? He stated that someone had said that Richie had pulled this knife on someone.

Calvin suggested that the evidence against him was weak. The lady who identified him as being at the apartments and participating in the beating said that the youth she saw was wearing a red shirt and was missing a tooth. Calvin stressed that "some dude" ripped his red shirt off of him in the parking lot and identified another Black adolescent who also was missing a tooth. Calvin denied having any weapons, including sticks, with him that night.

When asked how he felt about what happened, he said he did not like being in jail for something he did not do. He did not believe that his public defenders could defend him adequately given that they kept losing all their cases. At various points, he discussed false statements made against him.

Calvin said he would feel better if he were charged with assault or battery because he did fight Kevin with his hands earlier that evening. He claimed to have forgiven those who beat him up and wanted the Lord to forgive him.

Statement to Police on the Day of the Homicide

Calvin denied involvement in the homicide. He talked about the circumstances of the fight with Kevin and suggested that it was more a matter of him being "pulled into" the fight than of the two squaring off. He told police that he did not have a weapon and did not participate in the fight that resulted in the death of Richard.

SYNOPSIS OF CONSULTATION WITH FAMILY

Per court authorization, I spoke briefly with Calvin's younger brothers while they were in jail. The boys, although somewhat guarded, wanted to speak on behalf of their brother.

I interviewed Mr. and Mrs. Thomas together for more than 1 hour and then met separately with each party for a few minutes. The length of the consultation was approximately 1 hour 45 minutes. Mr. and Mrs. Thomas were very cooperative and pleasant. I also spoke to Tasha privately about her brother. Tasha, although nervous, also was very cooperative and congenial.

Consultation With Calvin's Brothers

The focus of these interviews was on the brothers' relationships with Calvin, how their home life was, alcohol usage by the parents, and whether they were afraid of Calvin. The responses of the two boys were consistent. Both indicated that Calvin treated them nicely, that all the brothers got along well, and that the two did not fear

Calvin. After significant probing, no evidence was presented to indicate that any of the children were abused or neglected. The boys' answers indicated that Mrs. Thomas did not drink alcohol at all and that Mr. Thomas did not drink to excess on a regular basis.

Consultation With Calvin's Parents and Sister

Mr. and Mrs. Thomas reported that Calvin's physical development was normal and that he had no major illnesses, accidents, or injuries as a child. They did not see him as suffering from any type of psychological problems. To their knowledge, he had not been psychologically evaluated prior to his arrest for homicide or received any counseling in the past.

Although they were aware that Calvin had been arrested for selling drugs in the past, they did not believe that he used drugs. The parents were aware that Calvin consumed alcohol on occasion. However, they never had seen him intoxicated and did not believe that he had a problem with alcohol usage.

When asked what it was like to raise children in their community, the Thomases said that it was a concern to keep the children away from drugs. In the area of town known as the subs, which is heavily populated by African Americans, drug selling is common. The older youths reportedly try to get the younger ones involved in selling. Mr. and Mrs. Thomas related that they had lived in this particular subdivision for a number of years and moved to a nicer and more residential area about 5 years ago.

Mrs. Thomas did most of the disciplining in the family. Although she used corporal punishment, it did not appear to be of the magnitude associated with physical abuse. Rather, it seemed to be infrequent and responsive and proportionate to the children's misbehavior. She reported that when the children did something wrong, she would give them a whipping and sometimes take away privileges and ground them. Mr. Thomas was more apt to threaten them with a beating than to give them one. There was no evidence presented to indicate that any of the children were sexually or verbally abused by the parents.

The parents indicated that Calvin dropped out of school in the 8th grade. His grades were below average. They did not see their son's poor performance as due to learning difficulties. Rather, Calvin was more interested in having fun than in studying.

Mr. and Mrs. Thomas did not recall Calvin getting into trouble while he was in school until his final year. They reasoned that he got into trouble to get attention. They did not see Calvin as aggressive and agreed that he would be more apt to "mouth off" than to fight with teens who challenged him. They related that after Calvin quit school, he spent some time in the Job Corps.

Calvin's parents stated that Calvin was a "follower" and that he began getting into trouble after he stopped attending school. He started staying with his aunt, who lived in the subs, because that was where the action and his friends were. Their remarks indicated that this aunt was far more lax regarding setting limits than they were and that she apparently did not provide adequate supervision. The parents' comments indicated that Calvin might have had different types of friends, some with whom he got into trouble and older people with whom he associated who did not get into trouble. His parents verified that Calvin did not typically associate with the youths with whom he was arrested.

Both parents were stunned and upset by Calvin's arrest for homicide. They related that many, if not most, of Calvin's friends were Whites. They knew Richard and reported that he spent more time with their son Joey than with Calvin because Richard was closer to Joey's age.

The Thomases' remarks suggested that they had not seen any evidence that Calvin harbored hatred for Whites in the past. They believed that Calvin's awareness of racial discrimination and inequities in treatment had been bolstered by what had transpired in this case. Mrs. Thomas stressed that she brought up her children to relate to people "as people," not in terms of their color. She has become very sensitive to the reality that discrimination does exist as she has watched the way in which her sons have been treated. She has seen that what happens in the justice system is not always fair. If her son had some involvement in the homicide, then Mrs. Thomas wanted him to be held accountable for his fair share. Both parents expressed concern, however, that Calvin would not get a fair trial in their community.

At the time of my consultation, both parents were employed full-time and had histories of working two jobs at a time. Mrs. Thomas had been a working mother since the children were born. Mr. Thomas reported that even when he was working two jobs, he spent time with his children on the weekend hunting and fishing.

Comments made privately by Mrs. Thomas suggested that she was concerned about Mr. Thomas's drinking. When asked, she stated that Mr. Thomas had been in an accident and subsequently was convicted of drunk driving. Although she was not afraid of Mr. Thomas, she cautiously revealed that he had hit her on occasion and that she told him she was concerned about the effect their relationship could have on the children.

Tasha stated that her brother treated her "okay" and that he acted protectively toward her. She was not afraid of Calvin. When asked what it was like to grow up in her community, she reported that the Black children were treated differently from the White children. Black youths were less likely to be chosen for the sports team and were likely to be disciplined more harshly than White youths. Her experience has been that there were more White teachers than Black teachers and that some White teachers treated the White children better than the Black children. She confirmed that drug selling was common.

▦ PERTINENT PSYCHOLOGICAL REPORT AND SCHOOL DATA

The two measures of Calvin's IQ, the first conducted while Calvin was in the 4th grade and the second by the consulting psychologist after Calvin's arrest for homicide, placed him in the low average/borderline range. Calvin's full-scale IQ at 10 years of age was 85; at age 18, it was 77. There were no large differences between verbal and performance IQ scores.

The psychological evaluation conducted when Calvin was 10 years old noted that he had repeated the 1st grade, failed the 3rd grade, and failed summer school after the 3rd grade but still was placed in 4th grade. In October of the 4th grade, he was placed back into the 3rd grade. Tests conducted at that time indicated that Calvin was performing significantly below grade level. Although classes for specific learning disability were recommended, he was found ineligible because he did not meet one of the criteria.

School records indicated that Calvin was promoted to the 7th grade even though he had not met all the requirements because he "is large and socially mature." His

6th-grade record was very poor, consisting of mostly F's. School records indicated that Calvin was expelled from the 8th grade during the spring semester. The previous semester, his grades all were F's.

▓ EVALUATION OF FORENSIC ISSUES RAISED

The defendant's sanity was not an issue in this case because Calvin denied having had any physical involvement with the victim during the homicidal incident. The defendant's competency to stand trial was not raised by Calvin's attorneys because it was apparent that he knew the nature of his charges and was able to assist his lawyers.

Factors in Mitigation

Given Calvin's stance regarding his noninvolvement in the homicide, none of the psychological mitigators applied. I recommended to defense counsel that if Calvin admitted his involvement or was convicted, then his participation in the offense should be reevaluated prior to sentencing to determine whether any psychological mitigators were present during the commission of the crime.

The only applicable statutory mitigating factor was the defendant's age. At the time of the homicide, Calvin was 17 years old. Juveniles as a group have less life experience and coping ability than do adults. In Calvin's case, this mitigator is particularly appropriate because Calvin's personality development and intelligence both were lower than those of most juveniles of comparable age.

In addition to age and lack of sophistication and maturity, I advised defense counsel to bring Calvin's school history to the court's attention. Calvin's school records indicated that he had difficulties in learning since he began attending school and that no meaningful intervention occurred. Calvin seemed to get into trouble with the law after dropping out of school.

There was some evidence that two other nonstatutory mitigating factors applied in this case. Calvin's responses suggested excessive alcohol use and possible alcohol dependence. I recommended that if Calvin were convicted, then he should be evaluated by an addictions specialist. If evaluation indicated alcohol dependence, then this factor would be important on two fronts: how it might have affected Calvin's judgment at the time of the homicide and how it might have arrested his development given the age at which he reportedly began drinking alcohol excessively.

In addition to Calvin's alcohol involvement, there were data to suggest that Calvin's father might have abused alcohol. This factor was relevant as a factor in mitigation in terms of the dynamics that typically operate in alcohol family systems and their effects on all family members.

Diagnostic and Treatment Considerations

Available data suggested that Calvin probably met the diagnostic criteria for conduct disorder. Despite his proclamations of innocence and "taking the rap" for others, Calvin's arrest history indicated a propensity for violence and violating the rights of others. His oppositional behavior in school and his unwillingness to abide by parental limits at home were consistent with the profile of a conduct-disordered youth. Calvin had a history of abusing alcohol and might have been alcohol dependent prior to his incarceration.

The prognosis in Calvin's case at the time of the assessment appeared poor. Calvin presented during the assessment as angry and explosive. He blamed a racist society for his problems and harbored a great deal of hostility toward the criminal justice system. His pattern of responding violently and resisting limits imposed by others did not bode well for his reentry into society.

CASE PROCESSING AND DISPOSITION

The state tried Calvin first because prosecutors believed that the evidence was strongest against him. Wood fragments found on Calvin's clothes were consistent with the wood found on three boards at the murder scene, including the one believed to have delivered the fatal blow. Jurors were told of the prior provocation by Kevin and the resultant fight between him and Calvin and its escalation.

Johnny, one of the seven other Black defendants, testified as part of pleas negotiations that when Calvin returned to the Black neighborhood, several youths goaded him into retaliating against the White youths. Johnny testified further that Calvin was among the youths who tore boards off the cafe. Johnny stated under oath that although he did not see Calvin strike the victim, Calvin was among the youths who chased the victim with boards and beat him to death.

There were three White people who identified Calvin at the murder scene. A woman who had observed several youths gathered around the fallen victim maintained that Calvin was the one she saw swinging the board over the victim. The two others, both friends of the victim, also identified Calvin as the last youth over Richard's body. One of them was Kevin, the adolescent who had fought with Calvin an hour before the murder.

Two of the three witnesses who identified Calvin made reference to his missing front tooth. Calvin's defense attorney presented evidence that another youth, Tyrone Phillips, had a build and a missing tooth similar to the defendant's. Tyrone was observed with bloody hands in the projects after the homicide by three Black women. In addition, two Black youths who had been at the fight testified that this same youth had bragged that he was the last one over the body. The defense rested without calling Calvin to testify.

Jurors apparently believed that Calvin did participate with the other youths in beating Richard to death. However, the jury decided that Calvin did not intend to cause the victim's death and found him guilty of third-degree murder. The charge of third-degree murder is not commonly found in state statutes of homicide, and its meaning is not uniform in those jurisdictions that provide for this charge. In the state in which Calvin was tried, a defendant could be convicted of third-degree murder if a person was killed while the defendant was committing or attempting to commit a felony other than those specifically enumerated with respect to the felony murder rule. In this case, jurors believed that Calvin was among the youths who engaged in the battery of the victim that resulted in his death.[1]

The judge exceeded the sentencing guidelines and sentenced Calvin to 15 years in prison because of his prior juvenile delinquent and adult criminal histories. The court ordered that Calvin was to serve this sentence after completing the 7-year sentence he received earlier for shooting a man. This aggravated battery charge included a 3-year mandatory sentence for use of a firearm. The 13-month sentence Calvin had received earlier for shooting into an occupied building was to run concurrently with these other sentences.

Within 2 weeks of Calvin's trial, four of his seven co-defendants pleaded guilty to third-degree murder. Two others had entered pleas previously; these included a co-defendant who pleaded guilty to aggravated assault with a deadly weapon and accessory after the fact and another co-defendant who pleaded guilty to manslaughter in exchange for his testimony against Calvin. The seventh co-defendant subsequently was convicted of possession of a firearm with intent to commit a felony. The co-defendants' prison sentences ranged from 13 months to 10 years.

Interestingly, consistent with Calvin's statements, prosecutors credited Kevin, the White adolescent who provoked Calvin into fighting earlier that night, as helping to ignite the spark that led to the fatal beating of the victim. Accordingly, the state charged Kevin with battery and disorderly conduct in connection with these fights. Jurors acquitted him on both charges.

■ FOLLOW-UP DATA

I conducted a follow-up interview with Calvin approximately 4 years after my evaluation. At that time, Calvin had been incarcerated for more than 5 years. I spoke with Mrs. Thomas 1 year after my follow-up interview with her son.

Clinical Interview

Calvin was pleasant and maintained good eye contact during the interview. The hostility and agitation over race relations that had been so apparent during my initial evaluation were noticeably absent. Although animated and responsive, Calvin appeared calm and somewhat subdued.

Some maturation and positive change were apparent. Although Calvin continued to deny involvement in the homicide, he did admit to participating in the other crimes of which he had been convicted: drug selling, shooting at a man, and shooting into a woman's home. He seemed genuinely empathic toward his mother. He seemed to have an understanding of how his criminal behavior and his father's drinking and womanizing over the years had hurt his mother. He appeared to have some understanding of motives in himself and in other family members.

At the time of the follow-up, Calvin had served time in four separate prison facilities. He appeared to experience some psychotic symptoms, including visual hallucinations, early in his incarceration. He reported that things changed back to normal and that he got back to his former self after he was put on medication for a short time.

Calvin has worked at each institution. He has done landscaping, cleaning, cabinet-making, and baking. He completed two programs that focused on drugs and coping skills. He received a certificate in cabinetmaking. At follow-up, Calvin had not completed his general equivalency diploma (GED) or felt a need to participate in counseling or attend Alcoholics Anonymous or Narcotics Anonymous programs.

Calvin stated that he had gotten into trouble a few times for failing to report, allegedly presenting false testimony before a disciplinary team, and exhibiting verbal disrespect to an officer. He related that he had fought with some inmates on a few occasions because they disrespected him but that he was not caught or sanctioned for this behavior.

Calvin indicated that he typically thought about the homicide only if somebody brought it up. He did not believe he received a fair trial. He maintained that he had no physical contact with the victim on the night of the homicide and that there was "no substantial evidence to prove I did this." He related that the co-defendants who testified against him were trying to cover themselves.

Calvin opined that he was convicted because the earlier altercation with Kevin that evening started with him and he was at the scene of the murder later that night. Calvin maintained that he would be a free man today "if I had never asked those guys for a ride to the liquor store." He explained, "I was at the wrong place at the wrong time."

Calvin indicated that the person who delivered the fatal blow was "a compulsive liar" and never was charged because those who knew the truth did not want to get involved. Calvin was portrayed as "the ringleader" because he had earned a reputation when he was on the street as being "wild and young." As a result, some people did not like him.

Calvin maintained that he has put this conviction behind him and holds nothing against anyone. Calvin related that he never has had anything against White people in general. He dated White girls and had a White girlfriend when he was arrested. He lived in predominantly White neighborhoods while growing up. He considered the victim to be a friend.

He has come to believe that he got into trouble because of "peer pressure." He wanted to fit in with a group of people who were into "the negative." His mother told him that he was "doing wrong," but he would not listen to her back then. He explained that he previously had "a really bad temper" and could not control it. "I just reacted." He credited a program in prison as teaching him to evaluate the situation and his behavior before he reacts.

Calvin indicated that prison has been good for him. "It helped me to get in tune with myself, the way I used to be," and to become "more positive." He has positive thoughts regarding the future. He related that he does not want to hang out on the street anymore. He had met a girl while he has been incarcerated, and he wants to be a family man. He related that his family has stood by him and intends to help him get a job and get him settled after his release.

Calvin's mother and sister have visited him every other week. His cousin has visited on alternate weeks. His father has come "every now and then." At the time of the follow-up interview, Calvin's two brothers both were incarcerated, one for violating probation related to a spouse abuse conviction and the other on drug charges. Calvin stated that he believes his brothers were following in his footsteps. Prior to being locked up, Calvin always had "a lot of money," and his younger brothers looked up to him.

Review of Calvin's Prison File

On admission to prison, Calvin denied involvement in all three commitment offenses: the homicide, the aggravated battery, and the shooting into the occupied building. Other information given by Calvin to me, however, was consistent with the content of his prison file, particularly regarding transfers, program participation, and disciplinary report history.

Review of Calvin's prison file revealed that correction officials evaluated Calvin's attitude, adjustment, and prognosis as fair on his admission to prison. With the exception of four disciplinary reports, Calvin generally did well during his incarceration. Ratings of his work performance and adjustment were consistently above satisfactory to outstanding.

Follow-Up Interview With Calvin's Mother

Statements made by Mrs. Thomas were generally very consistent with those made by Calvin. Mrs. Thomas indicated that she has visited Calvin twice monthly and that her husband and other children have visited when they could. Mrs. Thomas related that shortly before my visit, her second son had been mistakenly shot in the stomach with a shotgun during a "drive-by shooting" as he stood outside a church talking. She considered it a miracle that he was expected to recover completely.

Mrs. Thomas remarked that Calvin's relationship with her has improved markedly in recent years. He has seemed genuinely concerned about her. In addition, Calvin has indicated that he wished he had listened to her when he was younger.

Mrs. Thomas related that she was worried when Calvin was first incarcerated in prison. Her son appeared very stressed, and she had doubts whether he would adjust satisfactorily to confinement. He had some of his belongings stolen and was afraid of being sexually assaulted. He also was very angry that he was imprisoned for something he did not do and felt that the police did not investigate his case properly.

Mrs. Thomas firmly believed at follow-up that Calvin was innocent for many reasons. Her son would not lie to her about something so serious. Mrs. Thomas maintained further that law enforcement in Calvin's case, as in other cases involving Black suspects, moved too fast to close the case and that the evidence did not support his involvement. She explained that only one drop of blood was found on his clothing and that was his own. She hypothesized that the wood fibers found in Calvin's socks probably got there from the woodworking he was doing in the two-room extension they were adding to their home. In addition, several youths have told her over the years that Tyrone was "the real killer."

Unlike Calvin, almost all of the other boys who were convicted lived in the projects and came from single-parent families. Mrs. Thomas reasoned that Calvin was arrested because he was present that night and had been in trouble before.

> Once they [police] get your name, you are, like, always picked on. Anytime anything happen and you anywhere around it, so they are always looking at you as, like, part of a suspect because you've been involved in something else, or something like that, and they know your name, whatever.

Mrs. Thomas has seen a dramatic change in Calvin, particularly in the past 2 years. He has grown up in prison, is able to deal better with people, and can handle himself well. "Now he has a bright smile and a bright face." He has let go of the hatred that he felt toward law enforcement and the criminal justice system for convicting him of a homicide he did not commit. Mrs. Thomas credited prayers and her talking to Calvin about the need to forgive those who wrongfully accused him so that the ill feelings he had harbored would not destroy him.

When I spoke with Mrs. Thomas, she strongly believed that Calvin was ready to be released. She was optimistic about his making a successful reentry into the community.

> I don't know what's gonna happen, but I just think the people will accept him—that, you know, he's been gone, however long it's gonna take. Justice has been served, or whatever. He's already paid for whatever the judge has given him, and let that go, because that child is not going to come back from the grave. And he's still alive, so give him a chance. You know, he should already be done changed over the years, which I've seen him change. But give him a chance to live his life.

■ CASE COMMENTARY

This case is a tough one to call given the conflicting evidence presented at trial. Calvin's continued insistence at follow-up that he did not participate in the killing of Richard was noteworthy in light of his owning up to his involvement in the other two commitment offenses. Calvin appeared sincere as he stressed to me 5 years after the killing that he has learned to own up to what he has done. His mother seemed to have no doubt that her son was wrongly convicted of killing Richard.

Making Sense of Murder

This case can be analyzed without taking a position on Calvin's guilt or innocence. Whether Calvin ran with the group of adolescents who chased Richard, and whether he swung the fatal blow, does not change the nature of this killing. Clearly, there were situational factors, issues related to resource availability, and personality characteristics operative in this murder that transcend the role of Calvin.

It is undisputed that crowds of White and Black youths congregated at the shopping mall on the night of the homicide. Who was supervising these youths? Where were the responsible adults when the first fight broke out? When teens piled into cars and rode around the neighborhood in the wee morning hours? When the White and Black youths resumed fighting? When the Black adolescents ran through the subs in pursuit of a lone White youth in the middle of the night?

The co-defendants were generally poor and were products of a poor, Black, drug-infested neighborhood. In addition to drugs, these youths had ready access to alcohol and guns.

The initial fight and the one that followed, resulting in the death of Richard, undoubtedly were sparked by racial hatred. It is possible that some participants were not prejudiced toward the other race but got caught up in the mentality of the mob. Research has shown that some individuals will feel shielded by the anonymity of the group and will commit acts in a group that they never would do alone.[2] The anonymity provides a sense of freedom, and participation in the rampage can be experienced as exciting and exhilarating.

I would hypothesize that most, if not all, of the youths who participated in the frenzied attack on Richard had low self-esteem and were angry and bored given their life circumstances. Most were poor minority group youths living in a rural community in the South. Of the eight who were charged, none was employed and only one had finished high school. Whatever good judgment they might have had probably was impaired on that evening by alcohol or drugs. Given their lack of conventional resources and aspirations, it is unlikely that they thought they had much to lose when they went looking for a fight.

Prognosis

Calvin has made some progress in prison. His personality development has matured and he appeared to be transitional between I-Levels 3 and 4. He appeared calm and showed some insight regarding his behavior. He has continued to maintain his innocence in the death of Richard. However, he has accepted responsibility for his other criminal behavior and expressed remorse for hurting his family.

The prognosis in Calvin's case at the time of the follow-up appeared better than it had 5 years earlier. Calvin had recognized his angry and explosive nature. The strategies that he learned to deal with his "bad temper" apparently were effective given that none of the few disciplinary reports that he received was for violent behavior. Calvin has some conventional aspirations when he is released. Calvin's continued contact with his family and his family's willingness to help him also bode well for him.

I would raise the prognosis given at my initial evaluation from poor to fair given Calvin's changes in prison and the familial support available to him after release. However, several factors concern me with respect to Calvin's reentry to society that affect his prognosis. At the time of the follow-up interview, Calvin did not see a need for postrelease counseling. He did not see himself as having had a problem with alcohol and saw no need to participate in Alcoholics Anonymous or a similar type of program. Although he intended to return to the same southern community, he anticipated no difficulties on his reentry into society.

Calvin's return to this southern community will be headline news. The press has kept this case alive and has followed the reentries, mostly unsuccessful, of Calvin's co-defendants. Although Calvin appears ready to build a future, the question of import is, Will the community allow him to move beyond his past?

Chapter Eight

David Collins

DAVID COLLINS, age 17 years, was riding with his two cousins, Albert, age 24 years, and Casey, age 17 years, through the projects one evening. Albert was driving, David was in the front passenger seat, and Casey was in the back of the car when a 19-year-old man, Jack Turner, approached their vehicle. Jack allegedly accused David of burglarizing his apartment 3 days earlier and of stealing his clothes, his brand-name sneakers, and some money. Then, through the open car window, he slapped David's face.

David reached into the back seat, where he located a .38-caliber pistol and shot Jack. Witnesses recalled seeing Jack running from the scene. David got out of the vehicle and chased after Jack, continuing to fire shots at him. Jack reportedly fell at one point, stood back up, and continued to run toward the rear of the projects. David was observed running back through the projects. Moments later, he got back into his car and fled the area.

The victim was airlifted to a nearby hospital, where he died within a few hours. David was arrested that evening and subsequently charged with capital murder. I was appointed to assist defense counsel in determining what factors could be introduced in mitigation of the imposition of the death sentence if David was convicted of first-degree murder.

THE CLINICAL EVALUATION

This assessment is based on a 2 1/2-hour interview conducted with David Collins in adult jail 7 months after the homicide. Case materials reviewed included the police investigation reports and autopsy report. Statements given to the police by David and witnesses to the shooting, including David's two cousins, were studied. Copies of the youth's school records and information regarding his prior delinquent history also were examined. Consultation with David's parents was not needed due to case developments.

BEHAVIORAL OBSERVATIONS

At the time of the assessment, David was an 18-year-old African American male, approximately 5 feet 8 inches in height and about 150 pounds. He had a medium build and was not on any medication.

David was polite, cooperative, and alert during the evaluation. He generally maintained good eye contact and did not seem to be manipulative. He appeared anxious during the beginning of the assessment and particularly when discussing the events surrounding the homicide. He answered all questions asked. No evidence of psychosis or other severe mental illness was present.

PERSONALITY DEVELOPMENT

David's perceptions were those of a Level 3 individual on the Interpersonal Maturity Level (I-level) classification system. Although he indicated that he got into trouble because he was with the "wrong crowd" prior to arrest, this youth did not appear to use the *cultural conformist*[1] behavioral response as seen in the cases of Jerry Johnson and Calvin Thomas.

In I-level, David's response pattern would be categorized as *undifferentiated*.[2] David's way of looking at the world and behavioral response pattern is one that I have encountered frequently among youths who grow up in the inner city. They are out in their neighborhoods intending to have fun, which often involves participation in criminal activities. These youths see themselves as "players" in a violent society, where one has to be prepared to use violence at any time.[3] They are not roaming around actively looking for violence and typically do not want to hurt or kill anyone. David explained, "I don't put my hand on anybody. I don't have no children, so why should I be hitting on anybody—especially if nobody done anything to me."

RELEVANT SOCIAL HISTORY

Family Constellation

David lived on the outskirts of the city with his mother, stepfather, and two siblings, Barbie, age 14 years, and Nicholas, age 13 years. His 17-year-old cousin, Casey, also "stayed with [the family]."

He described his mother as "loving, kind, understanding." She has been "hurt" by his getting into trouble. David never knew his father. He described his stepfather, Johnny, as "funny, caring, loving. We get along. I enjoy him." Johnny has been in David's life since David was about 4 years old. His mother was employed as a nurse and his stepfather as a maintenance man. Neither of his parents reportedly drank alcohol or used illicit drugs.

David related that he got along fine with both siblings and described them in positive terms. Barbie was "caring, loving, kind. [She] tries to do everything for everybody." Nicholas was "fun, playing, loving, energetic. We play a lot." He also had good feelings for Casey, whom he described as "playful, fun to be around. [He] tries to stay out of trouble. He looks out for me, and I look out for him."

Probing revealed no evidence of physical, sexual, verbal, or psychological abuse. There were no data to suggest that David was physically, medically, or emotionally neglected by his mother or stepfather. David related that his parents gave him everything that he wanted or needed. Spouse abuse or violence in the home was not indicated.

School

David enjoyed school because he liked to meet people and learn. He stated that his grades, although average, went up and down.

David reported attending five schools. He related that he was sent to an alternative school for acting-out youths after getting into trouble for fighting for racial reasons. He did not like being in an alternative school because he did not feel he belonged in that category. Then, when he got into trouble for the first time (for throwing rocks at cars), he went to a youth program. He claimed that he had finished the 10th grade at the time of the homicide and would have been going into the 11th grade.

Work History

David was not working at the time of his arrest. He reported having worked in maintenance during the previous summer.

Friends

David reported that he did not have "friends." Rather, he had "associates," that is, people with whom he talked but to whom he did not feel very close. He liked youths who minded their own business and who were themselves. He disliked adolescents who smoked, drank, or got into trouble.

David related that he did not know many people and that not many people knew him. He maintained that he did not seek approval from others or need any friends because he had Jesus, his family, and his girlfriend. He stated that he could not trust anybody because too many people were back-stabbers. At the time of the evaluation, he felt that he was being railroaded.

Girlfriends and Sexual History

David stated that he had a girlfriend, Shasta. He described her as "loving, caring, fun to be around. I enjoy her." He mentioned that she was White and that they had been together for more than a year. He had a sexual relationship with Shasta that was "loving" and "exciting." She had been supportive of him during his incarceration and had visited him. He said that his family accepted their relationship and that her family generally did, although a brother had voiced some objection.

Activities

David liked to play baseball and football and also enjoyed track. He used to play in the youth league in his city and played some sports in school. He was a good player. He liked to spend time riding around in the car his parents bought for him, seeing nature and other things with his girlfriend. He also liked to play with his brother and sister and to visit his older cousin, Austin, who lived in a large city.

Alcohol and Drug Involvement

David denied any use whatsoever of alcohol or illicit drugs. He never tried alcohol, drugs, or smoking because "they are bad for your health" and he did not believe in them. He saw alcohol, drugs, and cigarettes as potentially affecting his ability to play sports and had stayed away from them because "they just bring you down."

Physical and Mental Health History

David described his physical health as good. He related that he had been hospitalized once at 9 years of age, for 2 or 3 months, when he ran into a pot of boiling water. He reported no head injuries or loss of consciousness at any time.

David stated that he received counseling for two sessions at the mental health center when he had been involved in fighting. He denied taking any psychotropic medications, experiencing any psychiatric hospitalizations, or having thoughts of suicide.

Handling Problems and Affectivity

David described himself as "quiet, very respectful, caring." He added, "I care about people. I try to help people who want help and try to help themselves. I help them." He saw himself as a loner, "as always overprotective of myself."

He described himself in conventional ways. He stated that his family, life, education, and girlfriend were important to him. He did not look for trouble and tried to get along with everybody. He did not see himself as "having an attitude."

He saw himself as different from most Black teenagers in his neighborhood because, unlike them, he did not do drugs or get into trouble. He did not associate with "the wrong crowd." He did not sell crack or have sex with lots of girls because he did not see anything in it. He was "not into the fast lane." He said that others would describe him as "fun, quiet, and playful."

When asked what things about himself, if any, he would change if he could, he said he was "hardheaded, disobedient." Sometimes he would not do what his mother said. He stated that he was happy as a child.

When asked what things about himself he really liked, David replied "everything other than this," referring to his arrest and its aftermath. He liked the way in which he "handles" himself, the way in which he "associate[s] with people, different stuff." David stated, "I know how to take care of myself and how to protect myself . . . to keep myself from being hurt." When asked whether he believed people were out to hurt him, he explained that "every day, you watch the news, somebody gets hurt, shot, killed, car get jacked. I don't want that to happen to me. I guess I'm more paranoid of getting hurt. I like to be protected. I don't want to get hurt, shot up or different stuff like that, beat up or kidnapped." David did not believe that people were out there specifically to hurt him, but "it's out there." Essentially, one has to be ready at all times to defend oneself given the present level of violence in society.

Religious Affiliation

David identified himself as a Baptist. He used to go to church about once a month but had turned away from it prior to his being incarcerated. While incarcerated, he had been reading the Bible.

Self-Reported Prior Delinquent and Criminal History

David was somewhat guarded in the reporting of his prior delinquent history and appeared to minimize his involvement. Available records indicated that he had an extensive prior delinquent history that included 10 felony counts of throwing deadly missiles, possession of cocaine, aggravated battery, and two counts of improper exhibition of a firearm.

David stated that he had been adjudicated on 10 counts of shooting deadly missiles for throwing rocks once or twice at cars when he was about 15 or 16 years old. He said that although he was with five or six other boys, only he and another boy were caught and prosecuted. He spent 7 or 8 months locked up in a detention center and two halfway houses.

David related that he used to view throwing rocks at cars as something fun to do. At the time of the assessment, it seemed "silly and devilish" to him because he was aware that he could have hurt someone.

David reported being arrested on two other occasions. When asked whether he ever had been involved in the selling of drugs, David said that he had been in a car where apparently one person had cocaine and all occupants were charged. He related that about 1 month prior to the homicide, he was arrested for exposing a gun. He said two guys stopped their car and he stopped his car. They said something to him and he said something back. One opened the car door and reached underneath the seat. David was fearful that this individual was going for a gun, so he grabbed from the trunk a gun that belonged to a friend's father. David felt that he had to protect himself at that time. He was processed as an adult and pleaded guilty to the charge in exchange for 2 years probation.

Future Orientation

David did not see himself getting into further trouble because he did not like what had befallen him. He related that he eventually wanted to marry Shasta and have a family. He was interested in getting a general equivalency diploma (GED) and going to vocational technical school. Although he would like to play professional sports, he also was considering becoming an engineer or an electrician as a potential career. He wanted to get involved in church again.

Adjustment in Jail

David appeared to have made an adequate adjustment. He related, however, that he found these 7 months in jail "stressful" because of the "feeling and the effect," the charges pending against him, and the absence of his family.

He spent his time in jail reading the Bible, playing cards, calling home, and talking to his family and girlfriend. His mother, sister, and brother visited him weekly. His girlfriend and cousin, Casey, also have visited him on occasion. His stepfather visited him whenever possible.

▨ MOTIVATIONAL DYNAMICS BEHIND THE HOMICIDE

David gave two statements to police after being given Miranda warnings following his arrest. David acknowledged in both confessions that he shot Jack after Jack slapped his face. When David spoke to me, he claimed to have less knowledge of the events that transpired that evening.

David's Statements to Dr. Heide

David related that on the evening of the shooting, he was riding in a car with his two cousins through an apartment complex in the projects. David and his cousins had to stop their car because the drug dealers "were in the middle of the road." David knew "something was up" at that point. He explained that there was only one way in and one way out of this apartment complex.

When asked how many people surrounded the car, David said that he did not know but that it was at least three. He maintained that "everybody" knew that they were drug dealers. Although he knew their names and they knew his, he stated that he did not know them personally and never had talked to them before the day of the homicide.

> One came around to the passenger area where I was, one was on the driver's side, couple in the back [surrounding the car]. He [Jack] said something. Next thing, he hauled off and hit me in the face barehanded—or if he had something, I don't know—I was dazed. It dazed me, but my reaction was just a sense. I grabbed a pistol. I shot. I ain't aimed it. I didn't look at him to aim. I just grabbed the pistol and shot him.

David did not know whether he hit the victim. He related, "My head was turned [away from him] when I shot. I don't know if he was there or not. I was in shock."

David indicated that he got the pistol by reaching behind the front seat into the back of the car. "You could see and reach through the trunk [because there was no back seat]. The pistol was right there."

David explained the reason he shot Jack in the context of Jack's behavior and the attendant circumstances.

> It was a reaction, you know, a protest. He done hit me in the face. . . . I knew something was up when they stopped me and started surrounding the car. I know they carry guns 'cuz they drug dealers. So, I guess, my reaction was to pull the gun to keep from getting hurt or shot or anything else, robbed.

David viewed being slapped in the face as "bodily harm. I had to protect myself." He stated, "Either you gonna run or you gonna fight."

David maintained throughout his rendition of events that he did not understand how any bullets he fired hit the victim. He could not say for certain that he did not hit the victim because he was not looking at the alleged drug dealer.

The victim started to run away. David got out of the car and also started running. David recalled shooting the gun again while the victim was fleeing. At that point, David thought he might have seen "some gunpowder at the right side of [the victim's] side."

David maintained that the course he ran was different from that taken by the victim. He stated that when he got behind the apartment, he stopped. The victim still was running. David left, turned around, and ran. "I stopped. I guess I started thinking. I came to or something."

When asked why he left the car, David said, "I wasn't even thinking. I couldn't tell you. I wasn't in my right mind. I don't know why I got out of the car. It was something that happened. I was dazed or something."

The youth said it was not true that he was chasing the victim and firing at him. "I just shot twice." The .38-caliber pistol David used was "not my gun. I had it. I got it off the street from a friend. I just had it for a while."

David was puzzled by police reports that claimed the victim was shot by a .38-caliber gun. He related that when he got in the car, the victim's "friend had a gun and was supposedly trying to shoot me or was running behind trying to shoot me. A few days later I heard that his friend said he had shot him [the victim] too with a .22[-caliber gun]." David claimed that the police never investigated the possibility of the victim being hit by a .22-caliber revolver.

On probing, David related that the victim previously had accused him of breaking into his house. "He asked me before, but I said no." David said that the victim's "friends had been drinking and stuff," and one friend pushed the victim to confront him. The youth maintained that he heard after the shooting that "they was going to shoot, fight with me." When asked why the victim accused David, he said that he was accused of plenty but had no idea why. He said people from that section of the city did not know him. He did not know why they believed he burglarized Jack's apartment and guessed that the people there just stick together. "That's just the way Black people is."

From David's perspective, prosecuting him for first-degree murder was unfair for three reasons. First, he did not know whether he shot the victim in the first place. Second, if he did, then somebody else also might have shot the victim and David was getting all the blame. Third, if David did shoot the victim, then it was while trying to protect himself. "I was not trying to hurt anybody."

David indicated that the incident could have been prevented "if we hadn't stopped, if I just had stayed home. I feel like I was caught up in something. Now I am being railroaded" by the police and the state. He stated that if he had been able to retain "a street lawyer," he no longer would be in jail.

When asked how he felt about the individual who died, he said that he was "sorry he was shot. He shouldn't have to go out like that, but I didn't really know him—I can't say. It's difficult, and I know I am in here for it. It's bad on both ends." He described the victim as "just a drug dealer." David speculated that he had girlfriends because most Black girls look for drug dealers because they have money.

David believed that he was being prosecuted as an adult because his last name was Collins. He carried a "bad name—make me look bad." He explained that his uncles and cousins had gotten into legal trouble for drugs, stealing, battery, and other "wild stuff." For example, one uncle killed his wife, one cousin shot somebody, and another cousin was involved in robbery and drugs.

When asked what should happen to him, David maintained, "I was shooting to protect myself" and that he should get "violation of probation" for using the gun. "I did 8 months [in jail since being arrested for this homicide]. That's enough time for anybody."

Conclusions

Before he died, the victim identified David as the person who shot him. Numerous eyewitness statements, including those from David's two cousins, and physical evidence corroborated that David shot Jack. Statements that David allegedly made to his mother and one of his aunts, in addition to those he made to the police immediately after the shooting, indicated that he knew he shot the victim.

◼ EVALUATION OF FORENSIC ISSUES RAISED

Shortly after my evaluation, the state decided not to seek the death penalty after realizing that it could not substantiate the existence of aggravating factors in David's case. Accordingly, my official involvement ended at this time. David's attorneys intended to argue that their client, who clearly was competent to stand trial and sane at the time of the murder, killed the victim in self-defense.

Defense counsel were keenly aware that their defense would need to focus on David's perceptions in those few seconds before the shooting. Did David perceive himself to be in imminent danger of death or serious physical injury when Jack reached through the car window and slapped him? Did David perceive that he needed to use deadly physical force to protect himself? If so, were David's perceptions reasonable under the circumstances?

Making Sense of Murder

David's remarks to me suggested that he was not simply defending himself when he shot Jack. He was extremely provoked by the victim's slapping him. David perceived the physical confrontation as a threat to both his personal safety and his manhood. He was aware of potential danger when the car in which he was riding was surrounded. Moreover, he experienced Jack's hitting him in the face as disrespecting him. Shooting Jack, in the adolescent's words, "was a reaction, you know, a protest. He done hit me in the face."

The youth's statements that he was just reacting and not thinking were very credible. When the victim slapped him, the youth, who had been afraid, suddenly became enraged and lost control. His response to shoot was immediate. His passions certainly had no opportunity to cool when he took off seconds later in pursuit of the victim. However, courts and jurors were unlikely to perceive a slap of this nature as constituting adequate provocation to cause a reasonable person to lose control under similar circumstances.

Diagnostic and Treatment Considerations

Available data suggested that David probably met the diagnostic criteria for Conduct Disorder. His criminal history indicated a propensity for violence and for violating the rights of others. His oppositional behavior in school also was consistent with the profile of a conduct-disordered youth.

The prognosis in David's case at the time of the assessment was guarded. On the positive side, he liked participating in sports, had a steady girlfriend, and reportedly did not use alcohol or drugs. On the negative side, he maintained that he had gotten into trouble repeatedly because he associated with the wrong crowd. His tendency to see the world as a violent place in which one has to be prepared to use violence at any time was another unfavorable prognostic indicator.

▥ CASE PROCESSING AND DISPOSITION

The state argued that David formed the intent to kill Jack when he continued to fire at Jack and therefore should be convicted of first-degree murder. The defense maintained that David was justified in using deadly physical force to protect himself after the victim invaded his personal space and hit him. David's attorney stressed that the victim confronted David while he was sitting in the car and that David immediately reacted to the perceived threat.

The jury rejected the self-defense argument. Jurors apparently believed that David did not intend to cause the victim's death and found him guilty of third-degree murder, an option under the state statute for defendants who kill while engaging in unlawful behavior.[4] The judge elected neither to impose the maximum prison term of 40 years nor to dispose of David as a youthful offender. Instead, he sentenced the adolescent to 15 years incarceration in adult prison with a 3-year minimum mandatory sentence for using a firearm.

▥ FOLLOW-UP DATA

I conducted a follow-up interview with David 3 years after my evaluation. At that time, David had been incarcerated for 3 years 6 months. He had spent 2 years 8 months of this time in adult prison. I was unable to interview David's parents. The phone number David provided was disconnected when I attempted to reach his parents several months later.

Clinical Interview

David was unavailable to speak with me for 6 months because he was in disciplinary confinement on multiple charges. He was pleasant and very accommodating when I finally met with him. He not only agreed to speak with me but also requested that I use his real name in the book, which I declined to do.

Little positive change was apparent. In fact, David appeared to have become more oppositional in prison. David had been housed in two facilities since coming to prison. He was transferred to the present facility for disciplinary reasons. He reported that his custody level was upgraded from medium to close custody because he continued to get into trouble at the second facility. He estimated that he had been on the compound for a total of 2 months out of the 2 years; the rest of the time, he was in disciplinary confinement. David reported at the time of the follow-up interview that he already had lost 990 days of gain time. Accordingly, his sentence length was extended by at least 2½ years because of his acting-out behavior.

David related that he had accumulated 17 disciplinary reports. All of the infractions involved challenges of some nature to the guards. Recent charges included disrespect, disorderly conduct, and disobeying a work order. While in disciplinary confinement, he "caught" two more charges for assaulting the guards. For these particular offenses, he received 180 days in solitary confinement. He was released after serving approximately 130 days.

David did not like disciplinary confinement, despite spending most of his time in it. The food was cold, the conditions were rough, visitation and phone calls were suspended, showers were restricted to three times per week, and recreational opportunities were rare. He related that when he was first put there, he flooded his cell and threw his food tray into the hall. He reportedly was sprayed with a mace-like chemical and put into a dark cell as further punishment.

David showed no real insight into his self-defeating behavior. He explained, "I'm not one to be run over. That's why I stay in trouble. As far as the inmates, I get along with everybody." He blamed the guards for his difficulties, claiming that they abuse their authority. "I guess they feel that we are not human since we are in prison."

David indicated that he did not do very much in prison. "I just hang out all day, work out." He was assigned to a job, but he did not work because there was "nothing to do." He did not participate in any vocational programs because he claimed that there was only one—shoe repair. He did not go to counseling because he said he did not have any problems. He did not attend Alcoholics Anonymous or any drug programs because he said he did not drink or use drugs.

David has had no problems with the inmates. He indicated that prison has been good for him in one respect: He completed his GED. The toughest thing for David about being in prison was missing his family. Although David related that he called his parents and siblings and they visited him, he was allowed no phone calls or visits with family when he was in disciplinary confinement. He indicated that he still hears from his former girlfriend, Shasta, but has not seen her for more than 3 years. He maintained some contact with his cousin, Albert, but none with his cousin, Casey, who reportedly was incarcerated on drug charges.

David related that he tries to blot out the homicide by keeping active. When locked up in solitary confinement, however, his activities have been severely curtailed and his thoughts have focused more on the murder, causing him some distress. He recalled having dreams in which he and the victim were just talking and the victim asked, "Why did I shoot him?" He related a nightmare in which he and his cousin, Casey, had a shootout with Jack and his friend.

David stated that he was aware at the time of the follow-up interview that he could have avoided shooting Jack. "There was no cause of that [shooting], but I guess it happened, so I have to accept it." Accepting it has been "rough because I am in prison." Although David mentioned a couple of alternative strategies, he did not present them as genuinely viable options. He reported that he and his comrades did not have to stop their car. He indicated that it would have been difficult to keep going, however, because the others were standing "in the middle of the street." David added that after Jack struck him in the face, "I could have gotten out of the car and fought." He then stated that it probably would have been six to one against him.

David did not appear genuinely remorseful, although he expressed some sympathy for Jack's mother. He continued to refer to the victim as "a drug dealer." He related that sometimes he has wondered where his feelings were. "I can't bring him back. I feel like I have to move on." David denied that he burglarized the victim's apartment prior to the shooting. He stated that he told Jack he did not break in about 2 days before the homicide. David knew who burglarized Jack's place but did not say or do anything because "it was not my business."

David felt that he both won and lost at trial. He won because he was not convicted of first- or second-degree murder, which could have netted him life in prison. The sentence he received was "a win" because it was less than the 40 years he was offered to plead guilty prior to trial. He viewed being in prison as a loss. David related that 15 years was "too much time for me" and that 8 to 10 years would have been a better sentence.

David was not ready to take responsibility for killing Jack. He maintained that he did not see Jack get shot and that he still did not understand how he shot the victim. He asked how he could have shot Jack in the chest if Jack was able to run 60 or 70 yards afterward? David stated that Jack was not bleeding when the two of them were running.

David readily acknowledged his prior arrest history, as he had during my initial evaluation of him. He continued to minimize his involvement with respect to the drug and assault charges. He did admit throwing rocks at cars because he found it fun and enjoyed the excitement of the cars chasing him.

David maintained that he wanted to be somebody someday. He would like to have a trade, perhaps be an electrician. He was thinking about moving about 1,000 miles away and living with his grandmother when released.

David would like to be a father and related that he would raise his children differently from how he was raised. When he was growing up, drugs were rampant in the Black community in which he lived. "Little kids . . . that's all they see . . . the big drug dealer" with "jewelry, all the girls, a nice car." He explained that many youths wind up dropping out of school to sell drugs and resorting to violence to protect their trade. "There are different ways of growing up now. When I was growing up—really, up until the 1990s—it was fistfighting. Then it's gun shooting. No fistfights, no arguments—it's just gun shooting."

Although David was not at the personality level where he truly saw himself as accountable for his criminal behavior, some movement in this direction had begun to occur. David related, for example, that his mother did "a good job" raising him. "I took it upon myself to do what I wanted."

Review of David's Prison File

David's account of his time in prison was consistent with prison records. Correctional staff evaluated David's attitude at intake as "good but guarded" and his adjustment and prognosis as "good." However, soon after arriving at the first prison facility, he began to get into trouble. His first 6-month progress report reflected that he was evaluated as "unsatisfactory" in his work and housing assignments and had received three disciplinary reports as well as several warnings. A transfer recommendation to a more secure facility was recommended and heeded. At the new facility, David continued his pattern of acting out and spent most of his time in disciplinary confinement. Although most charges involved challenges to the guards, David also received disciplinary reports for having contraband in the form of other inmates' belongings in his possession.

▇ CASE COMMENTARY

This case reflects the random and situational nature of violence for many youths living in the United States today. David was cruising with his two cousins through a low-income neighborhood when their path was momentarily impeded. Violence suddenly erupted. Why? The explanation again is multifaceted, encompassing situational factors, societal influences, resource availability, personality characteristics, and their cumulative effect.

David lived in a world where violence appeared commonplace. Positive male role models were lacking in David's life. His claim that his family name was notorious in the community was true. Several of his relatives were imprisoned for violent crimes. These included an uncle convicted of killing his wife. A juvenile cousin was prosecuted as an adult in connection with multiple charges including armed robbery, armed burglary, aggravated assault, battery, and improper exhibition of a firearm. Another cousin was serving a prison sentence for purse snatching. His cousin, Albert, had been convicted of shooting a youth in one incident and of robbery in another. Shortly after David's arrest, another cousin had been implicated in two burglaries involving batteries of two women.

David truly saw the world as a violent place. Having grown up with the knowledge that violence was commonplace in his family and in his neighborhood, David believed that one had to be prepared to protect oneself at all times. He had a gun within easy reach as he and his cousins were traveling around town. When David felt threatened on the night of the homicide, all he had to do was reach behind him to retrieve a .38-caliber revolver.

Drugs certainly are implicated in this homicide. Blumstein's theory of gun diffusion in response to the infusion of drug markets in poor Black neighborhoods is apropos in this case.[5] Although David denied involvement in drug use or sales, he stressed as significant that those who surrounded the car moments before the shooting were "drug dealers." His rendition of events suggested that he was afraid for his personal safety even before Jack slapped him.

On the night of the homicide, with these existent situational factors and societal influences, David was simply riding aimlessly around the neighborhood. His account suggested that he and his cousins probably were bored and had nothing constructive to do with their time. Their cruising through a low-income area that they knew had limited access in and out evinced poor judgment.

When challenged by Jack, David's fear appeared to turn to rage. David could not tolerate Jack "dissing" him. He could not contain the strong negative emotions inside himself. Without thinking, he exited the car and went to hunt Jack down. In that moment, for David, nothing else mattered.

Prognosis

The prognosis in David's case has become progressively worse with the passage of time. David has become more oppositional in prison. He still was acting like a young man with little or nothing left to lose more than 3 years after killing Jack. His continual challenging of the guards indicated that he has remained unable to deal with his strong negative feelings. At the time of my follow-up interview, he lacked insight into the self-defeating nature of his behavior and believed that his adjustment problems in prison were the result of unfair treatment by the correctional officers.

If David continues this acting-out pattern, he is likely to serve the full length of his sentence. Unless he commits a crime in prison, however, he will be released. If David does not obtain some counseling and learn more effective ways in which to deal with his anger and manage stress, then David is likely to emerge from prison a more angry and violent individual than he was when he entered confinement.

Chapter Nine

Malcolm Farrell

MALCOLM FARRELL was a 15-year-old boy with a string of charges for crimes spanning a 6-week period. The grand jury handed down five indictments, finding that there was probable cause that in four separate incidents, Malcolm had killed two people and would have killed two more had his marksmanship been better. In addition to two counts of first-degree murder and two counts of attempted first-degree murder, Malcolm was charged with two counts of armed robbery and two counts of attempted armed robbery in connection with these same incidents. The boy also was indicted for another armed robbery and grand theft auto in connection with a carjacking incident.

The defense attorney who referred Malcolm for evaluation was distraught. The youth was a poor Black male living in the projects in a southern community. The two homicide victims were White. The boy's family appeared to lack both concern and resources. The assistant public defender believed that if he did not come up with an effective defense strategy, his client would be strapped into the electric chair.

THE CLINICAL EVALUATION

My assessment of Malcolm Farrell is based on a 5-hour interview conducted in adult jail 8 months after his arrest. Case materials reviewed included the police incident and investigation reports pertaining to the five grand jury indictments and autopsy reports in the two murder cases. I reviewed education records from the two states in which Malcolm had attended school. In addition, a presentence report for a probation violation hearing on previous charges, which had been prepared about a month prior to the robberies and homicides, was examined.

BEHAVIORAL OBSERVATIONS

Malcolm was a small-framed youth who, at 15 years of age, stood a little over 5 feet tall. At the time of the evaluation, he had been incarcerated in the juvenile wing of the adult jail for almost 8 months. The boy was cooperative during the evaluation and made some effort to answer every question asked. He had difficulty with some of the questions due to the concrete nature of his thinking, and he often asked for clarification. He was alert, and his concentration was generally very good.

Malcolm was very nervous at first and continued to fidget throughout the assessment. He had difficulty sitting still and played with the microphone of the tape recorder.

His eye contact rarely was good. He looked from side to side and swayed. He was very animated, particularly when denying involvement in one of the murders.

The adolescent appeared manipulative. He seemed to be saying what he thought would be the right thing to say, particularly regarding his descriptions of family members, the reasons he got into difficulties, why he would be "okay" from now on, his stories to the police, and his depictions of offenses. He came across at times as trying to elicit sympathy and as desperate and scared rather than as honest and realistic.

The youth described experiences that sounded like auditory and visual hallucinations. He reported hearing a voice calling his name sometimes and seeing visions of his deceased mother and his deceased brother at his funeral. The context in which he shared this information did not suggest that he was malingering.

During the assessment, I learned that Malcolm had an extraordinary talent. He was able to make noises with his mouth that sounded like musical instruments. On my urging, he proudly demonstrated this ability.

▨ PERSONALITY DEVELOPMENT

Malcolm was another low-maturity youth whose behavioral response style fit the subtype known as the *manipulator or counteractive to power* subtype.[1] Unlike the other Level 3 subtypes on the Interpersonal Maturity Level (I-level) classification system, juveniles who are classified as manipulators are dependent on no one. Their goal is "to take care of number one," meaning themselves. When asked what was really important to him, for example, Malcolm replied, "My life. Nothing and nobody on earth come before me."

These individuals typically see themselves as in control, cool, smooth, and powerful. They are comfortable engaging in criminal behavior and regard it as an appropriate way in which to meet their needs, outsmart others, and give others their due. They attempt to con or intimidate others. When these tactics fail, they might attack. For this subtype, homicide can be the price the victim pays for noncompliance with the young killer's demands.

Those who embrace this behavioral response tend to distrust everyone. From Malcolm's perspective, "You just can't really trust anybody. You can trust yourself. Before my mamma deceased, she told me, she said, 'Your best friend is me.' She said, 'I'm the only friend you got.' . . . [You] can't go around having faith in everybody."

Those classified as manipulator or counteractive to power subtype frequently see the world as a violent place where only the fit survive. Malcolm lived in a lower-income neighborhood where violence was commonplace. He maintained that he did not like his sister going out because a lot of women were getting killed where they lived. He carried a .25-caliber gun for protection. He explained,

> Somebody's always out to try to hurt you and stuff . . . junkies that take that crack, you know, to stop them from slapping you upside the head with something, and killing you, you know, you have to, you know, carry something, do something, you know, to protect yourself. And hands wasn't going to do it, not your hands and stuff, you know, because they walk around in my neighborhood with guns, you know, knives and bats, you know. And to stop you from getting hurt, you got to carry something, even though I knows, you know, you need one . . . but that is for protection.

Malcolm admitted using his gun to intimidate and scare others when necessary. For example, he related an incident in which he refused to give a man one of his tapes.

The man reportedly threw a bottle, cutting the youth on the leg. Malcolm reportedly fired his gun into the air to scare him.

▓ RELEVANT SOCIAL HISTORY

Family Constellation

Malcolm was born in New York and spent his early childhood years in the Bronx. He was the youngest of 12 children born to Millie Farrell and several different fathers. Malcolm's mother reportedly died from high blood pressure when Malcolm was 8 years old. He remembered her as a "nice" and "loving mother" who gave him what he wanted and took care of all of her children. She was "the best human being in the world." Malcolm described her as a heavy drinker and recalled several incidents in which her friends had to carry her home because she was drunk.

Malcolm's father reportedly lived with his mother for a few years when Malcolm was younger. Thereafter, Mr. Farrell apparently lived in the neighborhood and visited his children at their mother's home. Malcolm described his father as "a good daddy." He had not seen or talked to his father, however, in many years.

After his mother's death, Malcolm and several of his siblings moved to a southern city. Malcolm's father remained in New York. Malcolm lived for several years with an aunt, whom he regarded as his grandmother. She was a strong figure in the boy's life. The youth described her as a loving person who wanted the best for him and his siblings. She took them to church, fed and clothed them, saw that they went to school, and encouraged them to do their best. Malcolm reportedly resided with her until she became sick and placed him in a group home.

Malcolm lived in this facility for about 3 months. While he was there, one of his older brothers was murdered following a fight in a bar. Malcolm related that he took his brother's death hard and did not get over it for a long time.

Malcolm attended his brother's funeral and then stayed for a few weeks with his older sister, Josie, who had six children. He claimed that he tried to support her because none of the children's fathers were helping her financially. One of the four men with whom she had children was murdered, two were in prison, and another lived in New York. Malcolm left Josie's home because some of his other siblings were staying there in addition to her own children.

At 15 years of age and having no place to go, Malcolm was living on the street. He related, "I was trying to make it, you know, on my own. I ain't really had nobody to lean on. I didn't have anybody to look up to but me."

The youth described each of his siblings as "nice" and suggested that they took care of, or looked out for, each other. It became apparent through probing that 6 of Malcolm's 10 surviving siblings had not visited him during the 8 months of his incarceration. At the time of Malcolm's arrest, 6 of his siblings were living in the same city. Even these siblings visited him only rarely, if at all.

School

At the time of his arrest, Malcolm reportedly had finished the 9th grade and would be going into the 10th grade in the fall. He maintained that he liked school and never had flunked a grade or quit. He related that he did not find school difficult and that he did fairly well. He described school as a nice place where he could meet others.

Malcolm acknowledged attending a "special school" in New York when he was younger, apparently because of behavioral problems. When he moved to the South, he behaved better in school for a while. Then he started "messing up" because he was staying out late at night with other boys his age and was tired the following day. The youth admitted having some problems with teachers and other students. He estimated that he had been suspended about three times and had been involved in "a couple of fights."

Work History

Malcolm indicated that he had one paid job during the summer when he was 14 years old. He worked on ground maintenance at a school he attended.

Friends

Malcolm used to hang out with other males on the street and apparently engaged in criminal activities with them. Although he maintained that he would be there for his friends, he did not seem to have any close friends. His statement—"If you need something, I give it to you. That's what friends are for"—seemed to be more of a slogan than an accurate depiction of the way in which he interacted with other adolescents.

Girlfriends and Sexual History

Malcolm said that he had a lot of girlfriends, as many as 12 over 2 months. He had only one long relationship, with a girl he knew from the time he was about 9 to 12 years old and then again when he was 15. He reported first having sexual intercourse when he was about 13. When he was about 14, he had a relationship with a woman in her 20s who had approached him.

The youth indicated that he had sex frequently when he was younger because it was part of being young. He did not use birth control and realized that he had to "slow down" when he had to be treated for a sexually transmitted disease. He reportedly impregnated one girlfriend, who later miscarried.

Activities

Malcolm related that he liked sports. He enjoyed making music and took first place in a contest. He wanted to have fun and to act his age but felt that he could not play like kids typically do because of where he lived. He explained that in "today's world, you've got to watch your back."

Alcohol and Drug Involvement

Malcolm stated that he drank alcohol daily from the time he was about 15 years old. He reportedly drank a six-pack of beer and a small bottle of gin every day and drank wine only on special occasions. He drank with others on the street from about 9 p.m. to 3 a.m., drinking to get drunk because he defined that as the purpose.

Malcolm related that he often did not remember what he did when he had been drinking. He recalled fighting and arguing frequently and "fly[ing] off the handle and stuff" because he would get "paranoid many times" when he was drunk. He would just do "weird things." He would pull out his gun, not to shoot, "just [to] be playing." His sister, Josie, told Malcolm that he had a problem with his drinking, and he agreed with her. He did not stop drinking, however, because it was fun.

Malcolm indicated that he smoked marijuana every day as well. Malcolm recalled that marijuana, like alcohol, made him want to fight. He would hit somebody with a stick. He explained, "You all be fighting and stuff. You ain't be meaning to do it." He said that he fought "most every day . . . all them junkies be around and stuff." He admitted to trying powder cocaine but never crack. When asked, he denied using barbiturates, amphetamines, or narcotics.

Malcolm would get money to buy marijuana from his sister or a friend, or he would "just go out and take it." Although he said that it was wrong, he related that he would take it with his hands or "just pull out a gun."

Physical and Mental Health History

Malcolm described his physical health while growing up as good. He remembered two incidents in which he lost consciousness and was hospitalized. On one occasion, he was in a car accident with his mother and her boyfriend, both of whom allegedly had been drinking heavily. He recalled waking up in the hospital with a bandage around his head and his mouth stitched up.

The youth stated that about a week after being released from the hospital, he was hit in the chest while playing basketball with his brother and swallowed the lollipop he was sucking on. His brother slapped him and a man shook him, but neither could wake him up, and he was rushed to the hospital.

The boy reported being "down" because he was locked up and could not see his family, but he did not seem to have a history of major depression. He reportedly experienced a great loss when his brother died and some sadness when he fought with his girlfriend. He never considered suicide. At the time of the evaluation, he thought that talking to a counselor might do him some good.

Handling Problems and Affectivity

Malcolm described himself as "nice to get along with" and "fun to be around." He saw himself as "pretty easygoing." Despite his visible anxiety during the interview, he reported that nothing made him nervous. He recalled being scared as a child but claimed that he would not tell anybody, believing it was best to keep it to himself.

The adolescent related that he would become angry if people lied about him, disrespected him, talked about his mother, talked too much, hit him, or cursed somebody out. When angered, he sometimes would argue with them; other times, he would fight. Malcolm rarely got bored prior to being locked up because he would be drinking or spending time with his family. He acknowledged at one point robbing people on occasion because he was bored and wanted something exciting to do.

Religious Affiliation

Malcolm did not seem to be strongly affiliated with any religion prior to his arrest. The boy defined his difficulties as "living in the fast lane" and maintained that he wanted to straighten out his life. He saw giving his "life to the Lord" as "the only way out" at the time of the evaluation.

Prior Delinquent Involvement

Malcolm freely admitted to robbing men but not women. He explained that he took things from others when he needed them, "not to just be doing it." He also acknowledged selling drugs, "rocks for a dime or 20."

The youth related his prior arrest history fairly accurately. He reportedly was falsely accused of grand theft of a watch, and the charges were dropped. He also was arrested for stealing a bicycle from a shopping mall. He explained that he was "way out there and wanted to get home," so he took a bike from another youth. He was arrested for taking a gold neck chain in a fight, which he maintained he did not do and was found not guilty. He also was taken into custody for running away and staying with a girlfriend.

Future Orientation

Malcolm wanted to make a better person of himself. He indicated that he could have lived a better life and that "it was just my surroundings." Malcolm believed that God would make a way out for him, stop him from going to prison, and keep him out of trouble. He intended to attend church more regularly when he was released. He was interested in getting a job in which he could help people solve their problems.

Adjustment in Jail

Malcolm adjusted fairly well in adult jail. He experienced no difficulties in the juvenile wing and expressed no fear regarding the inmates. He was afraid of what the guards might do to him, however, if he were incarcerated in the general population. He also expressed fear that he might be sentenced to death in the electric chair.

The youth reported having "bad dreams" frequently while in jail, such as getting killed, falling off a building, and having "the devil" riding his back. Malcolm related that he had a recurring dream in which he would call for help as friends passed by, but nobody could hear him.

■ PERTINENT SOCIAL SERVICES AND SCHOOL DATA

Available data indicated that Malcolm was 8 years old when his mother died. He lived for several years primarily with a great aunt, Helen, whom he regarded as his grandmother. She moved the family to a southern city when Malcolm was between 9 and 11. Malcolm spent a short time (perhaps 1 or 2 months) with another great aunt when his "grandmother" no longer could control him.

State social services revealed that Malcolm, at 9 years of age, was enuretic, biting his nails and sucking his thumb on a regular basis. He was observed to be acting out "a good deal of suppressed anger," apparently due in large part to the recent death of his mother following a 3-month hospitalization. Malcolm's great aunt, who assumed responsibility for the boy, his 11 siblings, and 2 grandchildren, was viewed as "extremely overwhelmed and in need of supportive services herself." Conditions in Helen's home in New York were evaluated as presenting "further problems."

> Malcolm sleeps with a brother in one bed. Within that same room, three other siblings share a second bed. Malcolm is said to spend a good deal of time outside the home, and the crowded conditions may be one of the factors. There can be little doubt that Malcolm will need individual and supportive services in his school environment.

School records indicated that Malcolm was retained in the 1st grade. Subsequent testing revealed that Malcolm's IQ was in the low-average range. Clinical evidence suggested, however, that his intellectual potential was likely higher because his performance appeared to be depressed by emotional and developmental factors.

The boy was referred for evaluation in the 3rd grade because he was manifesting "serious behavioral and academic deficits." Prior to his 10th birthday, Malcolm was diagnosed as "neurologically impaired and emotionally handicapped." He was placed in special education classes, apparently in the 3rd through 5th grades in New York. Malcolm appeared to attend regular classes in the 5th through 8th grades in the South. Records indicated that he had to repeat the 8th grade, attended summer school both in the 7th and 8th grades, and had numerous referrals to the principal for disruptive and disrespectful behavior.

At 14 years of age, Malcolm was referred to the state social services agency three times for running away from home in a 1-month period. These referrals predated those for delinquent activities. About 3 months later, the youth was arrested for strong-armed robbery in connection with the bicycle theft and was put in a pretrial diversion program. In less than 2 weeks, he again was referred as "beyond control." This case was closed after counseling 2 weeks later.

Malcolm was arrested 10 days later for petty theft of the necklace and was considered to have violated the conditions of his diversionary program. Then, 4 months after this referral, Malcolm pleaded guilty to taking the youth's bike by force and was placed in a community facility. While Malcolm was in this residence, his brother was murdered. Malcolm's robbery and murder spree came less than 2 months afterward and ended with his arrest 6 weeks later.

▪ MOTIVATIONAL DYNAMICS BEHIND THE HOMICIDE

Here I recap the police report summaries and Malcolm's statements at intake to the public defender's staff prior to reporting those that he made to me. My observations follow.

Indictment 1: Attempted First-Degree Murder and Attempted Armed Robbery

The police report indicated that Malcolm attempted to rob a 29-year-old Black man of a gold chain at gunpoint at 4 a.m. When the victim attempted to flee, the youth allegedly fired, hitting the man in the leg. When the victim subsequently stopped and faced Malcolm, the adolescent reportedly shot the victim in the upper chest. The victim identified Malcolm from a photo pack.

The youth denied to defense counsel any knowledge or participation in this crime. Malcolm told me that he heard about this crime while he was in detention facing other charges. He denied that he could possibly have committed this crime under the influence of alcohol or drugs and forgotten about it. He did not know how somebody could have picked him out from a photo pack.

The defendant's delivery was not convincing. The behavior reported in the police report was completely consistent with something he would do given his personality subtype.

Indictment 2: Attempted First-Degree Murder and Armed Robbery

Police maintained that Malcolm and his 16-year-old co-defendant, Rubio, robbed two Black males, who were in their 20s, of a portable radio dual cassette player at about 11 p.m. This incident occurred 2 days after the first one. Malcolm reportedly shot one of the victims in the back and told the second victim, "you next, fuck nigger." Malcolm was identified as the shooter from a photo pack by both victims, one of whom was 100% sure; the other one was 80% sure. The radio subsequently was recovered in Malcolm's residence after his arrest for another crime.

Malcolm denied to public defender staff any knowledge or involvement in this incident. He told me that he was walking with Rubio, who spotted the victim with the radio. He saw Rubio struggling with the victim and then chasing him. Shortly thereafter, Malcolm related that he saw Rubio coming with the radio and that Rubio "let me hold it." The youth denied having a gun and stated that Rubio had the gun. Malcolm claimed that he had not heard any shots fired.

During his rendition of the offense, Malcolm fidgeted and appeared very strained. When confronted with positive identifications by both victims, he suggested that he might have known one of the victims but was otherwise uninvolved. When I expressed some disbelief, Malcolm's anxiety escalated. He admitted that he was there and that Rubio had a gun, "like the one he gave me, .25 [caliber] or something." When asked specifically, Malcolm denied firing any shots, having a gun, or threatening the second victim. Malcolm struck me as clearly lying.

Indictment 3: First-Degree Murder and Armed Robbery

Police arrested Malcolm and Rubio in connection with the armed robbery and first-degree murder of a White male cabdriver. This incident occurred at about 5:30 a.m., approximately 1 month after the preceding one.

Law enforcement personnel initially suspected that Rubio was involved in this robbery-homicide. The police came to entertain Malcolm's involvement in this incident after three individuals related that Rubio had told each of them that Malcolm had shot the cabdriver. Rubio initially implicated others and changed his story a few times. When confronted by police that he was lying, Rubio told police that he and Malcolm were the ones involved. Rubio related that he called the cab and Malcolm said, "This is a jack." Rubio advised police that the victim said, "I don't have any money" three times and pleaded for his life before Malcolm opened fire with a .38-caliber gun.

A major lead in the investigation came with the police interview of yet another individual, Bruce, who claimed that he had heard about the murder of the cabdriver while in jail. Bruce related that Malcolm admitted his involvement in the homicide over the phone. Bruce told the police that he would help determine who the actual triggerman was and persuaded Malcolm to talk to the police.

Malcolm initially told the police that Sonny, the person first fingered by Rubio, shot the cabdriver. When confronted with Rubio's statement that Malcolm was the killer, Malcolm admitted lying about Sonny but maintained that he did not shoot the cabdriver. Malcolm admitted planning the robbery and getting into the cab from the rear passenger door and sliding over to sit behind the cabdriver. He stated that he had a .45-caliber automatic handgun placed to the rear of the victim's head while Rubio sat in the front seat and had a .38-caliber weapon pointed at the cabdriver's ribcage. Malcolm said that Rubio told the cabdriver to give up the money. Malcolm claimed that the victim made a motion with his right arm, apparently attempting to knock the gun out of the way. At that point, the gun reportedly went off, striking the cabdriver in the ribcage. Malcolm told police that he got out of the cab and watched as Rubio went through the victim's pockets.

Malcolm denied any involvement in this incident when he spoke to the public defender's staff. He maintained that the police came to see him five times in 1 week and that he was unable to contact any family members for advice. He finally told the police that he was at the crime scene to get them off his back.

Malcolm told me the same story as he had told his defense counsel. He was adamant in the face of extensive probing that he was not present or involved. He claimed that he did not even know the date of the incident and that police had said he would not be charged if he admitted being at the scene.

In a nutshell, he explained that he "put it on Rubio" because Rubio had put it on him. When I suggested that the only way in which Rubio's and his statements differed was in who did the shooting, Malcolm said unyieldingly, "And that I can't tell you 'cause I wasn't there."

> Rubio said I did it, so I said he did it. I wasn't there. Rubio said, we called him at 22nd [Street]. He put me in that spot. I put him in that spot. [very angry] 'Cause if I got a shot, I am going to take this shit to trial 'cause I know I had nothing to do with this.

When asked about the likelihood of the jury believing him after the police testified about his apparently having related accurate details of the crime, Malcolm paused for a long time before responding. "Yeah, I see the problem. If I did it, I'm gonna admit it. I'm gonna confess. It ain't no shame. If I did it. I know I ain't do it, so I ain't gonna say I did it." He was not optimistic that the jury would believe that he was not present after he told police he was there. "They gonna look at me like I'm a jackass, stupid, crazy."

Unlike the first two incidents, I had a very solid doubt about Malcolm's involvement in the third one for four reasons. Malcolm was strong, consistent, and adamant about his noninvolvement. He would not budge from his story, in sharp contrast to his wavering with facts in the other stories.

His statement that he "put it on Rubio" because Rubio had put it on him was completely consistent with the perceptions and behavioral responses of low-maturity youths. Those classified at Level 3 would do such a "dumb thing" (i.e., "tit for tat") without taking the time to evaluate the situation more carefully.

Throughout his story, Malcolm appeared fairly calm despite being angry and upset. Unlike his rendition of the other offenses, he was not fidgeting with the microphone. He was more at ease and centered.

I advised counsel that it was important to discern what statements Malcolm was given regarding Rubio's statements to the police. If Bruce had "fed" Malcolm details of the offense, then it is possible Malcolm related what he had heard rather than what he had done or observed.

Indictment 4: First-Degree Murder and Attempted Armed Robbery

According to the police report, a week after the murder of the cabdriver, Malcolm approached a car with the intention of robbing two White males who had just driven to the projects to buy drugs. It was about 2:30 a.m. Johnnie, a drug dealer who sold them crack cocaine, was sitting in the back seat of the car at the time. Malcolm told the two White men to get out of the car and fired two shots through the driver's side window. One of the White males was hit and killed. During this exchange, the car was put into gear, went forward, and crashed. Johnnie agreed to help police identify Malcolm after they learned of the drug dealer's presence at the scene.

When apprehended, Malcolm admitted his involvement. He said that he intended to rob the two because he needed money for school clothes. He claimed that he told the two White males to get out of the car and fired the shots through the open window only to scare them. Malcolm gave the .25-caliber gun to the police.

Malcolm's statements to the public defender at intake and to me were consistent with the police report. I noted his statement to police that he intended to fire only one round but that the gun automatically discharged was inconsistent with the ballistics report; that is, the automatic firing pin was broken.

The youth was extremely anxious during this segment of the evaluation and came across as frightened and desperate. He was adamant that he only intended to rob the victims. He related that he had been drinking that night and that he "kinda had a hangover. I didn't mean to hurt nobody. I never mean to hurt anybody. It was an accident. Nobody ain't perfect."

Malcolm's actions appeared completely impulsive and without direction. Malcolm did not appear clear about what he wanted or expected to get from the two White men. He vacillated from stating that he did not know what he wanted to suggesting that he wanted "to get the car" and "if they had money, I was going to get that too." At one point, he stated, "I wanted anything I could get ahold of."

He maintained that he shot at the two White men who remained in the car after the drug dealer bolted "to make 'em scared, to get out quicker." His statement that he shot to "scare" the victims was indeed plausible given his level of personality development (Level 3) and his behavioral subtype (manipulator or counteractive to power).

Malcolm felt strongly that his being charged with first-degree murder was unfair. He argued that the 30-year-old victim brought about his own death by driving away.

Malcolm: I should be talking manslaughter because when he [victim] got shot he
was driving. I'm the cause of his dying and everything, but I think he

killed hisself [sic] because he was driving that car. . . . He didn't die on that spot where I shot him.

Heide: Suppose the coroner's report were to show that he died from the bullet wound?

Malcolm: How'd he get over there by the tree then, if he weren't driving? He was driving and he ran into a tree and he broke his neck. . . . I know what I seen. I know what I seen. When he got shot, he drove that car. He put that car in gear and drove away. I know what I seen 'cause it was a stick shift. He put that car in gear and drove away.

Heide: What difference does that make?

Malcolm: He kept going straight. . . . He hit the tree. He broke his neck. . . . If he wouldn't have drove, I don't think he would have died.

Malcolm related that he stayed around after the shooting and did not run from the police. He agreed to talk to the police, after being informed of his Miranda rights, because he thought that they would "accept that I didn't mean to do it and let me go." Extensive probing indicated that Malcolm understood the Fifth Amendment privilege against self-incrimination. He intimated that he really did not understand the essence of his Sixth Amendment right to counsel. He claimed that he could not remember being advised that the state would provide him with a lawyer if he could not afford one. However, my review of police records indicated that he had put a checkmark by each of the Miranda statements and had signed the police form.

Indictment 5: Armed Robbery and Grand Theft

The day following the second murder, Malcolm was one of three males allegedly involved in stealing a car at gunpoint from a 15-year-old Black youth. Malcolm's co-defendants also lived in the projects. The carjacking occurred at 3:30 a.m. Malcolm admitted to police that he and 15-year-old Joe helped in the robbery but claimed that only one of them, 16-year-old Troy, had a gun.

Malcolm later told public defender staff at intake that he and Joe were passengers in the rear seat of the victim's car, but he denied having any knowledge that Troy intended to steal this car. Malcolm stated that the victim, known as a "sissy" in the area, voluntarily gave the three of them a ride. He claimed that he had no idea what Troy did with the car after Troy dropped him off.

Malcolm related essentially the same story to me. He said that the youths stopped at a school. While Joe, Troy, and Malcolm were waiting outside the car, Troy reportedly pulled out a gun. Malcolm said that he asked Troy, "Why are you doing this?" and asked Troy to take him home. Malcolm claimed that he was surprised by the robbery and reported that he heard Troy wrecked the car later.

EVALUATION OF FORENSIC ISSUES RAISED

As detailed in the preceding section, Malcolm denied criminal involvement in four of the five incidents in which he was charged. In two of these incidents, he admitted to being at the crime scene but not to participating in criminal activity. In the one incident in which he acknowledged attempting to rob the two White males, Malcolm blamed the victim for bringing about his death after Malcolm shot him. His discussion of the criminal events clearly indicated that he was competent to stand trial and raised no question of his sanity at the times of these crimes.

Factors in Mitigation

Evaluating the psychological mitigating factors was difficult given Malcolm's denial in one homicide and his account in the other. In the one in which he admitted involvement, Malcolm knew what he was doing when he approached the vehicle to rob the men and when he fired into the car. On my probing, he said that he might have had a couple of beers but no marijuana and was not "out of it," that is, "stoned." There were no data to support that Malcolm was "under the influence of extreme mental or emotional disturbance," lacked the capacity to appreciate the criminality of his conduct, or could not conform his behavior to the law at the time of the two murders.

I advised defense counsel that only one statutory mitigator, age, appeared to apply in this case. Several nonstatutory mitigators could be introduced. These included the youth's low personality development and his documented history of neurological, behavioral, and emotional problems that were diagnosed when Malcolm was 9 years old and never were adequately addressed.

In addition to his personal vulnerabilities, Malcolm's familial environment was poor from the time he was born. He spent his early years in an alcoholic family system. The death of his mother, the abandonment by his father, and the murder of his brother were among the traumatic losses faced by Malcolm as a youth. He was emotionally and physically neglected. Documentation existed that he was not properly supervised and was allowed to run the streets as a child and as an adolescent. Malcolm's responses suggested excessive alcohol and marijuana use in the months preceding the alleged crime spree that easily could have impaired the youth's perceptions and judgment.

Diagnostic and Treatment Considerations

Malcolm met the diagnostic criteria for Conduct Disorder. Despite his disavowal of involvement, Malcolm's arrest history and admissions to me indicated a propensity for violence and violating the rights of others. His oppositional behavior in school and his unwillingness to abide by his grandmother's limits at home were consistent with the profile of a conduct-disordered youth.

The prognosis in Malcolm's case at the time of the assessment appeared poor. With the possible exception of the murder of the cabdriver, he appeared to have been involved in several violent episodes in which he posed a severe threat to others. He assumed little or no accountability for his behavior and apparently had no qualms about his actions. His actions suggested extreme alienation from others and a proclivity to attack when what he wanted was not forthcoming. Unlike many other adolescent murderers, the likelihood of successful intervention appeared dismal because intensive treatment programs were lacking in the southern state in which Malcolm lived. In addition, few mental health professionals would advocate that a youth like Malcolm was amenable to treatment at 15 years of age.

At the time of my evaluation, it appeared that Malcolm could hold his own in the adult prison system. He was criminally sophisticated and at home with the inmate population. Judging from his accounts, his adjustment in jail had been smooth.

■ CASE PROCESSING AND DISPOSITION

Malcolm's attorney felt certain that his client would be convicted of multiple charges, including at least one of the two murders, given the evidence against him. Counsel was confident that he could show that Malcolm had a terrible childhood and grew up in a drug-infested neighborhood where violence was the norm. He did not believe, however, that spotlighting Malcolm's troubled youth would have any significant impact on whether his client was sentenced to death. This public defender, having represented defendants for years in the capital division, had no hope that a southern jury would show mercy to a poor Black youth who, in a 6-week span, reportedly had killed two people and seriously injured two others in five armed robbery incidents.

On his attorney's advice, Malcolm pleaded guilty to 9 of the 10 crimes with which he was charged rather than face a possible death sentence if convicted at trial. At 15 years of age, he appeared in the courtroom without any family members present as he pleaded guilty to two counts of first-degree murder, two counts of attempted first-degree murder, three counts of armed robbery, and two counts of attempted armed robbery. The judge sentenced the adolescent to two counts of life for the two murders, of which he would have to serve at least 25 years under state law prior to parole eligibility. The judge imposed four counts of 25 years and three counts of 15 years for the robbery-related charges and ordered all sentences to run concurrently. Rubio subsequently pleaded guilty to the murder of the cabdriver and was sentenced to 35 years for the murder with a 30-year concurrent sentence for the robbery. He also was ordered to serve, on his release, 5 years on probation for another robbery conviction.

■ FOLLOW-UP DATA

I conducted a follow-up interview with Malcolm 8 years 3 months after my evaluation. At that time, Malcolm had been incarcerated for 9 years, more than 8 of which had been spent in adult prison. Then, 6 months after this visit, I received a letter that prompted a return visit. Continuing correspondence from Malcolm indicated that he had significant gang involvement as a juvenile, a factor that had not been known previously.

Clinical Interview

Malcolm appeared very different from the scared and desperate youth I remembered. At 24 years of age, he seemed wiser and more self-assured. He was pleasant, maintained good eye contact, and enjoyed the opportunity to talk. He spoke with apparent ease and candor. He displayed a range of feelings from sadness over the death of his grandmother while he was in prison, to anger over his siblings' abandonment of him during his incarceration, to joy over a child he regarded as a stepson. He spoke passionately of losses he sustained as a child and of a desire to help youths today to make better choices than he did.

Malcolm showed insight into the dynamics of his behavior. Although he had a tendency to try to rationalize or justify his criminal activities, he did acknowledge repeatedly that his actions still were wrong. He frankly admitted involvement in four of the five incidents. He accepted responsibility for both of the attempted murders and robberies and for the murder and attempted robbery of the man who bought drugs in the projects. He continued to deny that he had anything to do with the killing of the cabdriver, maintaining that he confessed to this crime because the police badgered him and he was afraid. His position was convincing; he was willing to take responsibility for crimes he did do but not for ones he did not do.

Malcolm also felt that his conviction for the carjacking was unfair. He related that he knew that his two comrades intended to take the victim's car by force when he got into the car with them. However, he did not personally participate in the robbery. The three agreed that each could have the seized car on different days. Malcolm had the misfortune of having possession of the stolen car on the day that it was spotted, and he subsequently was arrested.

Malcolm stated that he attempted to rob the man of the gold chain because he was "basically looking for fun." He did not need to rob because he had money. He said, "I wanted excitement. I am going to make him run scared. But it turned dramatic when he charged me. I shot . . . I'm laughing, it's all a joke. I'm smoking marijuana." Malcolm could not remember whether he hit the victim or not. At the time, it was "like a prank. I'm young. I'm looking for excitement. I want to see him haul ass, see how fast he can run."

In contrast to the gold chain, Malcolm really wanted the radio that he saw a man carrying. He related, "I didn't have one. I wanted it." Malcolm reported that Rubio was not present and that he committed this robbery alone. He shot the victim in this case because he felt that his manhood was being challenged by the refusal of the two men to hand over the radio.

> I felt that they was trying me because I was so young and fragile-looking and small. They felt, "He ain't serious." I had to prove my point, I was a man. . . . When I had a pistol in my hand, it made me feel strong, invincible, bold, you know. It made me feel like somebody I wasn't, which was a man. At the time, I was a kid trying to be a man. So when I had one in my hand, it was like, I knew I was in control. . . . I wanted power, and you know, the only time I felt I had power was when I had a gun in my hand.

Malcolm said several times that he regretted his involvement in the first two robberies. He had come to realize that the victims had worked for what he had taken and that he would not have wanted someone to take his belongings had the situation been reversed. He also was aware that he had hurt many people, particularly his family.

Malcolm explained that prior to his arrest, he could rob but could not stand to be robbed. He related a series of events that reportedly transpired shortly before his shooting at the White man who had purchased drugs in the projects. Malcolm was standing at a barbecue stand when the three men rolled up in a car looking to buy drugs from him. The boy displayed his stash in his hand, and the driver tipped the youth's hand to obtain the drugs and then sped off. Malcolm took a shortcut through an alley and came across the car. He admitted that he wanted revenge and either the drugs or money to recoup his loss. He told the men to get out of the car. Malcolm saw the driver reach down and was afraid that he might be getting a gun, so he fired at him.

Malcolm indicated that even though he knew that selling drugs was wrong, he was trying to make a living. Over the years, he had come to see the killing as wrong as well.

> I was wrong, you know, when you look at the whole situation. It wasn't worth taking someone['s] life for $20 or $40. It's real wrong. I know the pain I caused this family for losing somebody. Even though he was on dope, hey shit, he was still a human being.

> It was wrong, any way you look at it, you know. All obstacles, all angles, it was wrong.
> And I feel very, very bad about it. This is something I'll never forget as long as I live.

In looking back on his life, Malcolm also saw television as having contributed "a little" to his involvement in criminal activities. He related that he used to watch "a lot of TV." His favorite shows were *Starsky and Hutch*, *Mod Squad*, wrestling, and reruns of *The Untouchables*, which he used to sneak to watch at 1 and 2 a.m. Recalling *Starsky and Hutch*, he explained, "You wanted their car and that big old pistol, a .357, you wanted that." With respect to that series and *The Untouchables*, he added, "You wanted that excitement . . . to be like them."

At the time of the follow-up, Malcolm had served time in three separate prison facilities. He related that he was the youngest of about 800 inmates at the first prison in which he served time. He experienced threats and was "tried" sexually but was able to stand up to these challenges by fighting for his manhood when necessary. He credited the older inmates for helping him to adjust to prison life and to mature.

Malcolm worked in food service, in the dorm, and inside grounds basically doing cleaning or custodial work. He did not work for a period because he was not mentally able to do so after some deaths in his family. Malcolm did not complete his general equivalency diploma (GED) while incarcerated. He did participate in two programs for which he received certificates: wood shop and the Youth Awareness Program. The latter is a program in which inmates stage incidents to demonstrate to students what prison is like. Malcolm indicated that he did not seek out any counseling but did attend Alcoholics Anonymous meetings for about 6 months.

Malcolm related that he had been confined in disciplinary confinement twice for fighting and for disrespect to an officer. He had been placed in administrative confinement on another four occasions. He estimated that he had about 14 disciplinary reports for "minor, petty" infractions such as having somebody's radio, talking during count, verbal disrespect, and fighting. He also had lost gain time once for "snapping at an officer."

Malcolm experienced being away from loved ones as the toughest thing about being in prison. He related that he understood what the victims' families were going through. He recalled being very angry when his brother was murdered and wanting to take his pain out on the whole world. Malcolm saw his criminal behavior as "a cry for attention, for help." It bothered him that society did not care about what he went through prior to his getting into trouble.

> They didn't care my mother died when I was 7 years old. My father, I never seen him.
> I didn't have no dominant mother or father figure in my life growing up. . . . It was
> tough, so everything I get, I had to basically like take it, you know. If I waited on it,
> I'd be waiting a long ass time.

Malcolm saw prison as being good for him "in a lot of ways." He credited prison for changing him because he saw himself as impatient on the street and lacking the resources to turn his life around. From his perspective, prison made him look on the inside and learn responsibility; it helped him mature and become a better man. He has become able to take care of himself and to stand on his own two feet. He also perceived himself as able to read and talk better.

Malcolm expressed bitterness that he had not heard from any of his siblings in years. He remembered his grandmother, Helen, lovingly and as doing her best to raise him. He felt bad that he could not thank her for what she did and let her know that it was not her fault that he did wrong.

Looking back, Malcolm was angry that he had pleaded guilty. He felt that his sentence could not have been any worse had he gone to trial. He believed that the police lied to him and used him to further their careers. In addition, he felt betrayed by his attorney and unsupported by his family.

About 9 years after his crime spree, Malcolm had come to see himself as "a good person who got caught up in bad things." He felt a fair sentence would have been 9 or 10 years. He explained that a 2- or 3-year sentence is not a sufficient time to gain insight. In 6 or 7 years, a person can come to understand himself and change.

Malcolm indicated that when he is released, he wants to help youths who come from similar backgrounds and face the same struggles and temptations that he experienced. He explained that "every kid wants to be in Michael Jordan's spot." They want to have clothes, to get a car when they are 15 years old, to go to DisneyWorld, and to celebrate their birthday every year.

> A lot of kids ain't fortunate enough to do this. A lot of kids don't get nothing for their birthday. A lot of kids don't have a decent pair of shoes. Everything they got on is secondhand. This is constant. This is everyday. It's like they [adults] don't care, you know, until something dramatic and drastic happens. [This] is the only time they dwell on this kid. They only look at the negativism. They don't look at trying to help, give him a chance, anything like that. It's "Damn, he's bad. He did it, he gonna have to pay for it." They don't realize, hey, this kid wants nice things too. If he doesn't have a mother and father, then who is gonna give it to him?

Review of Malcolm's Prison File

Information provided by Malcolm appeared consistent with the content of his prison file, particularly regarding transfers, disciplinary reports, and confinement history. Prison records indicated that Malcolm had received 11 disciplinary reports. Ratings of his work performance and overall adjustment fluctuated from satisfactory to outstanding.

A Second Follow-Up Visit
8 Months After the First One

About 6 months after my follow-up interview, Malcolm requested that I visit him. He indicated in a letter that he had gotten into big trouble and felt his world was closing in on him. Department of Corrections staff told me that he had gravely injured another inmate, necessitating a change in his custody status to close management. He was moved to an even more restrictive facility, where he was locked down 24 hours a day. Central office staff approved my visit reluctantly, expressing fear that the inmate might attempt to harm me physically or manipulate me into seeking favor for him.

Malcolm remained handcuffed and in shackles during our visit due to his custody status. He explained the circumstances behind his putting four batteries in a sock into a pillowcase and seriously beating another inmate with them. He described the victim as "a huge man" who tried to exploit him. Malcolm related, "I gave him a chance to back down, to make amends." The victim reportedly gave him "a look of disgust."

Malcolm became enraged, feeling that his manhood was at stake, and attacked the inmate.

As he expressed appreciation for my coming, Malcolm's lip started to quiver. He related that when the inmate challenged him, he had flashbacks of his being sexually abused at 9 years of age. Tears streamed down his face as he recalled that a man he loved had betrayed his trust and his innocence. Filled with shame, Malcolm never had told anyone. He always feared that others could see that weakness in him, and he felt a need to redress any perceived slight.

Malcolm said with anger, mixed with sadness, that there were no classes in prison to help inmates deal with their anger. With bitterness, he referred to the Department of Corrections as the "Department of Corruption," seeing prison in many ways as hurting rather than helping him. He related that it was difficult being a Black man in society and in prison. "That Black face is always there."

Correspondence From Malcolm

Malcolm expressed his thoughts well in several letters. It was clear from reading his 30-page autobiography that he recalled his early childhood with his mother, her boyfriend Max, his siblings, and his best friend Willie and Willie's mother as "the greatest time" of his life. His life changed dramatically when his mother died. Additional losses followed, some of which he had not discussed previously. As Malcolm's grandmother took over, Max became increasingly less involved with the family, and Malcolm's activities and friendship with Willie were severely restricted. Despite Malcolm's wishes, Helen decided to move the family to the South. Shortly before their leaving, Malcolm learned that Willie had been crushed to death in an elevator accident.

Malcolm saw his years in the South as leading to his downfall. Helen and the children first lived for about 6 months with an aunt, who reportedly was mean and physically abusive, before getting their own apartment in the public housing projects. Malcolm described the area as beset by "shooting, fighting, drugs, prostitutes, all these evil things. Everywhere you look, it was around you." Malcolm wrote that "only the strong survive this area of living" and related that he and his brothers had to fight every day because they were "new" and had to prove themselves. Eventually, Malcolm decided to join a gang, which launched his criminal career.

> I got tired of fighting every day of my life, so I joined in my first gang activity. This was so frustrating because now I was living a double life, one for good when I went to school and was so happy. And the other one, the bad, so I wouldn't have to fight no more.
>
> But when you're involved in a gang or group, you just can't say you're "down" or "I am in," you must show you're "in" or "down" with whatever. I started smoking weed and drinking every day after school. I started hanging out at night, longer than I would or my grandma allowed me to. I started having sex with every girl I could. I used to have to sneak out at night, sometimes by jumping out of my window, to go to our meetings. We would then go around breaking in stuff, stealing, robbing, and beating anyone who tried to stop us or stand in our path.
>
> I was all the way "in" now. I begin to falter in my schoolwork. I begin to have a temper problem when I don't get what I want, when I want it. I did just enough to pass on to the next grade, but I had to attend summer school to do that.
>
> This new life was taking its toll on me slowly. I was now in the 8th grade, and I was now a little older and street smarter of my neighborhood and how things go. I swear I

was grown and could do anything I wanted to do without answering to anyone. I was
smoking heavier now, and I was snorting whenever I got coke and drinking gin. Beer
did me no good anymore. I was now 15 years old.

Malcolm recalled that his gang involvement was halted for several months by his
grandmother's realization that she could not control him and his placement in a group
home. Although he initially felt "hurt, rejected, and betrayed by her" for her actions,
Malcolm came to like the facility, to reform himself, and to enjoy life again. His life
changed abruptly again when he was released from this facility to attend his brother's
funeral.

Malcolm's brother's death hit him hard and reopened his pain at having lost his
mother and his best friend. He felt his "whole purpose of living was a curse," and he
resumed his delinquent activities.

> I told both of them, my aunt and my grandma, I am not living with either of you, the
> way I was treated by you. I rather live in the streets. I begin to turn to my old ways
> again. To help me cope with the tragic death of my brother, I begin to smoke again and
> begin to drink even more now.
>
> I started constantly living and running in the streets again. I return to my duty of
> selling drugs to make ends meet and to feed myself. Since I was deprived of a brother,
> I felt someone was at fault. I felt so powerful and in control when I sold drugs, because
> everybody knows about you, and whatever you ask they would do it because you had
> drugs they like. I liked this control. Everything came so easy from my drugs—jewelry,
> cars, sex, everything a kid my age desired. I was "a top doc" now from drugs.
>
> I felt so hurt and guilty inside, because I felt like I failed. And I gave up, not because
> I couldn't do it, because I felt like I didn't get it done. So I used drugs as an escape
> route of my failure. I portray this image of being able to really deal with it on my own,
> but I needed my father or even Max right now. I just needed anyone to just listen and
> accept me. And I only found this in my gang friends here; among them is where I felt
> loved and wanted. Regardless of what I am, it was them that gave me the pat on the
> back and said, "We're with you always." These are the ones who never ever rejected
> me or made me look or feel stupid. These are the ones who never changed how they
> felt about me because I made a mistake. They was with me right or wrong. They knew
> what I represented and never tried to change me.
>
> After selling drugs for four good months, things begin to change dramatically, be-
> cause my drug supplier had been busted and sent to jail. Now I began to lose my fame
> and power, because I had no more supplier. I began to feel weak and powerless from
> this. My money was running out, and I knew I must do something to regain my popu-
> larity and reputation, so I turn to robbing to build up my reputation once again.
>
> And sure enough, after some sweet licks, I was back again selling drugs, but people
> knew I would rob too, if necessary. I begin selling this "new" drug—"crack" was so in
> demand, one piece could get you anything you want. I felt stronger now with this crack.
> I was exchanging crack for clothes, sex, cars, TVs, VCRs, you name it. From crack
> selling, I was making a lot of money and having a lot of sex, fun, every night.

CASE COMMENTARY

Malcolm represents the urban youths whom Blumstein identified as getting caught
up in the deadly world of drugs and guns.[2] Malcolm was dealing drugs in the mid-1980s,

when crack hit the street. His career ended in 1986 with his arrest on multiple charges including two counts of murder.

Making Sense of Murder

A confluence of factors help to explain Malcolm's predatory behavior. Situational factors, societal influences, and available resources played a role in Malcolm's actions. Available data suggested that Malcolm was physically abused by an aunt and was sexually abused by a trusted male adult. He was emotionally neglected on occasion by an alcoholic mother and was abandoned by his father. He was not properly supervised by his grandmother and was allowed to run the streets. Positive male role models in Malcolm's life were sorely lacking.

Malcolm's family moved to the projects, where violence was routine and guns were easy to obtain. Selling drugs and robbing others became a way in which a poor boy could get money, sex, and status.

In addition to these extrinsic factors, Malcolm had some personality characteristics and intrinsic vulnerabilities that placed him at increased risk of choosing a violent solution. As a youth, Malcolm sustained a number of losses that were not grieved, spawning the seeds of rage. He did not know how to deal with the anger he felt over the murder of his brother. In addition, he was unable to work through the unresolved feelings he had regarding the earlier deaths of his mother and best friend and his separation from loved ones in New York. Drinking alcohol and using drugs numbed the pain but did not extinguish it.

As Malcolm moved into adolescence, he was a boy who had become increasingly unattached and angry. He was looking for excitement and power. His shooting at his victims had an impulsive quality, which might have been due in part to his neurological impairment and his restricted personality development at the time.

Prognosis

The prognosis for Malcolm improved significantly in 10 years. Malcolm has matured from I-Level 3 to I-Level 4 while in prison. He has gained insight into his behavior, sees himself as accountable for his behavior, and appears genuinely remorseful.

Malcolm's violent outburst, however, cannot be ignored. It indicated that his rage at the time was stronger than his ability to control it. Since that episode, he had gained insight into his explosive behavior and had the opportunity to process it therapeutically with me.

Today, unlike 10 years ago, he is a good candidate for in-depth therapy. Malcolm needs to work through his anger and pain and to move beyond the belief that he, more than others, has suffered heartache and loss. If he can learn more socially acceptable ways in which to deal with his feelings and handling stress, then it is possible that he could be released safely back into society. Malcolm expresses himself well in person and in writing, and he could make a positive contribution to children.

Chapter Ten

Joel Westerlund

JOEL WESTERLUND and Jim Maddox, both 15 years of age, were best friends, almost like brothers. With his mother's permission, Jim had moved in with Joel's family. Jim had been living with the Westerlunds for about 6 months when he was suspended from school. When Mrs. Maddox heard about this incident, she told Jim that she would come by the next day to take him back home. Upset by her announcement, the two boys ran away that night.

The next day, the two youths, who were armed with stolen handguns to protect themselves in case they encountered "perverts" on the road, went to school to say goodbye to their friends. Mr. Barnett, an assistant principal, reportedly spotted Jim sitting in a crowded lunchroom. When he approached Jim, the boy ran. Mr. Barnett chased him, and a physical struggle occurred between the two. In the process, Jim fell to the ground, lost his gun, and called to Joel for help. Two other assistant principals, Mr. Abbott and Mrs. Winston, intervened in the melee.

Joel, who had observed this situation from about four tables away, ran to assist his friend. As Joel frantically punched the administrators, a student-teacher, Mr. Burns, physically restrained him from behind. Joel reportedly pleaded with Mr. Burns to let him go, advising the student-teacher that he had a gun. Although Mr. Burns did not release his hold, Joel managed to pull a .38-caliber gun from his pants.

The boy reportedly shouted again that he had a gun and began firing, sending hundreds of students running for cover. Mr. Burns, the first of three to fall, was hit in the leg. Mr. Abbott was hit in the head. Mrs. Winston was shot in the abdomen and in the arm.

Joel fired three shots at two police officers as he ran from the school building, and they returned nine shots of their own. Joel was downed by a bullet that grazed his shoulder, and he was quickly taken into custody. Jim was arrested within a few hours at his girlfriend's house.

Six days after the shooting, Mr. Abbott died. Joel subsequently was indicted by the grand jury with one count of first-degree murder in connection with his death. The youth was charged with two counts of attempted murder for shooting Mrs. Winston and attempting to shoot one of the police officers. He also was charged with aggravated battery for shooting Mr. Burns and for armed burglary with respect to the stolen gun. Shortly after the grand jury indictment, the state announced that it would not seek the death penalty. Although Jim did not fire his gun, the grand jury, in accordance with state law, indicted him for third-degree murder. Jim also was charged with three counts of burglary in regard to the stolen guns.

I was appointed by the court, at the motion of defense counsel, to evaluate issues related to Joel's competency to stand trial and his sanity at the time of the shooting. Joel's attorney also asked me to address the client's amenability to treatment and the likelihood of a successful reintegration into society at a future date with meaningful treatment.

THE CLINICAL EVALUATION

I spent 5½ hours evaluating Joel Westerlund in adult jail approximately 5 months after the shooting. Three days later, I met with Joel's mother for 3 hours. Prior to finalizing my conclusions, I consulted with two mental health professionals who had interacted with Joel after his arrest. Ms. Lumsden, a social worker with the public defender's office, had contact with Joel for a short period of time after his arrest. Dr. Clark, a psychologist, was the head of an inpatient adolescent program in which Joel had been a patient for 53 days. He reportedly had ordered Joel's discharge from the hospital less than 3 months before his arrest. Dr. Clark had visited Joel twice weekly during the 5 months that he had been incarcerated. My purpose in contacting these individuals was to see whether Joel's statements to them were consistent with those that he made to me, particularly with respect to the incident and his recollection of events.

There was no official police report written of this incident. However, extensive case materials provided a graphic picture of the incident. Materials reviewed included more than 40 witness statements as well as the defendant's statements to the grand jury and to his lawyer. In addition to incident-related material, I studied the youth's high school records and his psychiatric hospitalization records. Depositions of the mothers of Joel and his co-defendant, Jim, also were examined closely.

BEHAVIORAL OBSERVATIONS

Joel, a White male, was 15 years 8 months old at the time of the evaluation. He was a lanky adolescent; at 6 feet 1 inch in height, he weighed only 135 pounds. Joel was among the brightest youths I have evaluated; IQ testing confirmed that his intelligence level was in the superior range.

Joel initially appeared slightly nervous, but within a short time, he seemed to relax. Although the adolescent appeared generally at ease during the interview, it was apparent that he was trying to maintain a strong front and not to allow feelings to emerge and overwhelm him. In particular, Joel used humor and flippant remarks to maintain the appearance that the content of our discussion was not upsetting him. Despite the controlled veneer, this boy was scared and confused. Some of the pain and anger that Joel had been experiencing for years surfaced during the interview. However, the pain and anger beneath the surface far exceeded what Joel was prepared and able to deal with effectively at the time of the clinical interview.

Joel was extremely cooperative during the clinical interview. His eye contact was generally very good. He answered hundreds of questions and did not refuse to answer anything I asked, even when it was apparent that my inquiries were a source of pain, discomfort, and even embarrassment to him. The boy's answers at times were restricted, which was more indicative of his level of personality development than of an unwillingness to answer. His answers clearly indicated that he was oriented in time and space and that his short-term memory was intact. With the exception of events during the homicidal incident and immediately following the incident, I found his long-term memory to be adequate.

The youth did not appear to be at all manipulative during the interview. His responses to my questions and his behavior strongly suggested that he was being truthful. His answers to many questions were anything but self-serving. The boy seemed to exaggerate in a few places in the interview. For example, when I probed his remark, "People thought I was a freak," it turned out that only one boy had actually made this remark. In addition, Joel also might have minimized his behavior in some incidents that he related (e.g., fights). The exaggerated statements and minimizations of his behavior were "honest" depictions of the youth's perceptions of events in his life rather than attempts to deceive me. Interview data at several places indicated that one of the values that constituted a core part of Joel's self-definition was telling the truth. The adolescent's statements that he "didn't lie" were consistent with his level of personality development and with his mother's characterization of her son. Ms. Lumsden and Dr. Clark also shared the impression that Joel was honest in his communications with them.

Joel appeared detached and his mood was rather flat throughout most of the evaluation. However, he clearly had the ability to perceive some of the ironies in his responses to questions and to laugh appropriately. In addition, he used humor to protect himself from experiencing some of the strong feelings that were below the surface.

▨ PERSONALITY DEVELOPMENT

Like other individuals who perceive at Level 4 of the Interpersonal Maturity Level (I-level) classification system, Joel had an internalized value system and was aware of feelings and motives within himself and others. Typical of those who adopt a *neurotic acting-out* response pattern, this youth protected himself from pain and anxiety that he could not tolerate by maintaining a position of superiority, waging control battles with adults, and keeping himself distant from others.

Joel compensated for feelings of personal inadequacy by projecting an air of super adequacy. He indicated that he had difficulty relating to teachers who were less intelligent than he was. He reportedly had two math teachers, for example, who did not know how to do math. In spotting their errors on the blackboard, he was suggesting what he believed to be the obvious: He knew more than the people who were empowered to teach him.

Joel's refusal to do his schoolwork and his unwillingness to go to school on occasion also were indicative of a neurotic coping style. He stopped doing his schoolwork because it bored him and he did not like people telling him what to do. He was completely aware of how his refusal frustrated his teachers. No matter how upset they got, the message was clear to him and to them: They could not control him. Obviously, for a boy with an IQ in the superior range, academic failure was self-defeating. But the private meaning was what counted most for Joel. He was in charge of himself and could affect them by doing nothing at all. When he was hospitalized, he cooperated for a short time and then shut down again. It was a control battle, and he was not going to let hospital staff tell him what to do any more than he would let his teachers do so.

Consistent with those who adopt a neurotic acting-out response pattern, Joel took pleasure in challenging authority figures and being oppositional. However, he did not have a delinquent self-image. When asked whether he saw himself as a criminal, he said, "I committed a crime. I don't see myself as a murderer. I killed somebody. *Murderer* is too violent of a word."

Joel also did not see himself as a dangerous young man. He explained that he used to get into a lot of fights because people picked on him. However, he maintained that the fights had been declining gradually. Joel stated, "I am not a violent person. I try to avoid it. But when you can't avoid it, then it [fighting] has to happen."

Joel's preference for nonintimate relationships was clear from his statements about his friends. Joel stated that although he had a few friends, he was really close to only one: his co-defendant, Jim. Before becoming attached to Jim, he had only one other really close friend and acknowledged that this exclusivity in friendships was typical for him. In jail, he was quick to point out that he had "acquaintances" rather than friends. Although he was appropriate and pleasant in his interaction with me, it was apparent that he wanted to keep himself distant rather than to become warm and friendly.

RELEVANT SOCIAL HISTORY

Family Constellation

Joel was the oldest of three children born to the union of Byron and Carol Westerlund. The boy spent the first 8 years of his life living with his parents when they were together and with his mother when his parents were undergoing numerous separations. When Mr. and Mrs. Westerlund divorced, the children stayed with their mother and subsequently moved to another state. Then, 2 years later, Mrs. Westerlund relocated to another county in the same state. At the time of this move, Joel was in the 6th grade and was about 11 years old.

Joel's memories of his early childhood were filled with bitterness. He depicted his father as an alcoholic and a drug addict who was physically abusive to the boy's mother. (The boy's characterization of Mr. Westerlund was consistent with the mother's statements.) Although Joel did not remember his father being physically abusive to him or his siblings, he was afraid of his father and feared that his father would hurt his mother.

Joel reported very limited contact with his father after the family moved away. Over the past 7 years, he had talked with his father on the phone but had not seen him. In the 5 months that he had been incarcerated, Joel's father had sent him one letter, enclosing some papers and pictures.

Joel's bitterness toward his father was apparent. His father was "like a stranger" to Joel and did not mean much to the youth. Joel related that he had "nothing to say" to his father anymore. His statements underscored the pain the youth has felt for years. "I can't ask why? There are too many whys. Why did you beat mom? Why did you drink? That's what caused the beating."

In contrast to the characterization of his father, Joel's description of his mother was positive. When I asked Joel whether there was anyone he admired, he paused, initially said no one, and then said his mother. He related that although he argued with his mother about school, he always liked her and did not wish that she was different in any way. He perceived himself to be a lot like his mother and seemed pleased that, like him, she did not judge people. His statements suggested that he trusted his mother and that she related to him as a confidante and respected his opinion.

Joel related that his mother was the agent responsible for his psychiatric hospitalization. When I asked the youth how he felt toward his mother after she took him to the hospital, his answer was brutally frank as he recalled his feelings at that time. "I hated her. I was disgusted with her. I didn't know why I was sent there. I still don't know why. I disliked her a lot."

Mrs. Westerlund has been visiting Joel every day since his incarceration with the exception of the 2 days a week that personal visitors are not allowed. She has been bringing her other two children with her as well as many of Joel's friends and schoolmates. Joel's descriptions of his 13-year-old brother, Jeff, and 9-year-old sister, Debbie, both were positive. Joel related to his brother as one of his friends and indicated that neither of his siblings ever had really gotten into any trouble.

Joel's description of his mother's fiancé, Buddy Spohn, was marked with ambivalence. Both Joel and his mother related that Buddy also was an alcoholic who drank continuously to excess until about 3 months before the shooting. Buddy stopped drinking 1 week before Joel was released from the psychiatric hospital.

In recalling the 4- to 6-year period in which his mother lived with Buddy, Joel stated that he never was close to the man. In fact, the youth admitted that he "hated" Buddy, that he "disliked him severely" because Buddy drank. The youth described his "stepfather" as a "dirtbag" because he was "loud, all sweaty from the yard, eyes bloodshot or yellowish. He was always red, had a beer belly."

Joel's statements did not suggest that Buddy had been physically or psychologically abusive to him or to his siblings. The youth recalled an incident in which he got into an argument one night with Buddy, who allegedly was drunk. The argument escalated into a physical altercation. Joel reportedly threw Buddy into a wall when Buddy grabbed him. He hit Buddy after the man hit him. During this incident, Joel picked up a wrench and, when goaded by Buddy to hit him, did so. Buddy reportedly called Mrs. Westerlund at work and related the incident. Joel recalled his mother telling him to "get the hell out of her life." At that point, Joel took $30 from Buddy, left the house for a couple of hours to blow off steam, played video games at one of the stores, and walked around for a while. He eventually went home because he was fairly confident that his mother was not serious and was only angry because she had been upset by the call at work.

Joel maintained that although he was not afraid of Buddy, he was worried about Buddy hurting his mother. His fears appeared to spring more from memories of his father's behavior toward his mother than from Buddy's behavior toward her. Unlike his father, who "tried to kill people," Buddy was "more or less a grabbing person, who would shake you." Joel maintained that if Buddy ever hurt his mother, he (possibly aided by his brother) would make sure that Buddy would "get hurt." He told me, "I don't like people messing with my mom."

Joel stated that when Buddy stopped drinking, he started to like the man. At the time of the interview, the youth said that he liked Buddy a lot and that the man was visiting him fairly frequently at jail. Joel did not think that Buddy ever had undergone counseling for his drinking or attended Alcoholics Anonymous meetings. The youth recalled that his mother had attended a few Al-Anon meetings, which are targeted at relatives and friends of alcoholics. Joel related that his mother tried to interest him in attending Alateen meetings, which are designed for teenagers whose parents have alcohol problems. Joel said that he was not interested because he was not an alcoholic and did not consider Buddy a parent at that time. The boy's feelings toward Buddy prior to the time the man stopping drinking were similar to those he held toward his father. "He was nothing to me. I don't like people who drink."

School

Joel maintained that he liked school. He was aware that he had a very high IQ and knew that he could do the schoolwork but did not like to do so. He claimed that teachers generally did not like him because he did not do their assignments. The youth stated that he did not "yell back" at the teachers or otherwise get upset when he was reprimanded. School disciplinary records supported the boy's statements that he was not disruptive in class.

Joel's feelings appeared to be fairly neutral with respect to his teachers. Joel identified three teachers whom he liked. He selected them because they did not get on his case. In Joel's mind, teachers who made rules set the stage for students to break them. He found it easier to relate to those who were more laid back about what students did. When asked whether there were any teachers to whom he ever had felt really close, Joel named two of his elementary school teachers.

When asked whether there were any teachers he disliked, he named two. One was a female math teacher whom he described, in essence, as very controlling and lacking in personal hygiene. The other was a female language arts teacher whom he found to be very "hostile" the one time that he went to her class. He stated, "I hardly didn't dislike any of my teachers. I just didn't feel for some of them. I just didn't care less what they did."

In discussing his attitudes, relationships, and experiences with teachers, Joel did not mention any of the victims. It appeared that these individuals were not salient to him in this context because none of them had taught him. Joel did not know any of them in any but the most superficial way, that is, pretty much by sight only. When the youth was discussing the homicidal incident later in the interview, I probed Joel's feelings specifically toward Mr. Burns, Mr. Abbott, and Mrs. Winston. The adolescent reported that he had minimal interaction with all three and held neutral attitudes toward them prior to the incident. He stated that he knew Mrs. Winston essentially by sight and had recalled speaking to her only once. The boy remembered speaking to Mr. Abbott once when Mr. Abbott had told him to go to class. However, he was not sure whether he would recognize Mr. Abbott by sight.

Joel apparently had no interaction with Mr. Burns prior to the homicidal event. However, he perceived his encounter with this man at the time of the homicidal incident in a very negative light. His feelings toward Mr. Burns, in contrast to those toward Mr. Abbott and Mrs. Winston, were very negative at the time of the evaluation.

Work History

Due to his age, Joel did not hold any regular employment. He did some odd jobs for money (e.g., mowing lawns), but not on a regular basis.

Activities

Joel appeared to be primarily involved in conventional activities. He enjoyed playing video games, listening to music, walking, talking on the phone, going to the store and sitting there, sleeping, and eating. After enumerating how he spent his time, he concluded that he did not do much.

Friends

Joel saw himself as having a few close friends, all of whom he felt he could trust. Joel preferred girls as friends because many boys had "attitude problems." Of the five boys he currently named as friends—Robbie, Bob, Matt, his brother Jeff, and Jim—Jim clearly was the one he considered his best friend.

Joel met Jim in the 7th grade, and the two became friends when they were in class together in the 8th grade. Jim was living with his grandmother then and would ride his bike over to the Westerlund home. Joel related that he and Jim did everything together. Jim moved into the Westerlund home approximately 6 months before the shooting.

Joel's descriptions of his friends suggested that they were conventional rather than delinquent in orientation. Although some of the boys might have drunk alcohol and tried pot, Joel's statements clearly implied that they were not a drinking- and drug-oriented group. Joel indicated that he did not like teens who had attitude problems, were loud and rowdy, and were "two-faced people, backstabbers, liars." When he disliked someone, he reportedly ignored them.

Girlfriends and Sexual History

Joel's heterosexual experience appeared to have been very limited. Sex was not "a big thing" for Joel. He reportedly was attracted to girls who appeared intelligent and did not smoke. He tried to avoid getting involved because "it messes things up." He related that he had a few girlfriends over the years but that there was "nothing spectacular" about these relationships. He had been going "not officially" with a girl, Angelica, whom he had known about 2 months at the time of the incident. He had heard from this girl "once in a while" since his incarceration.

Alcohol and Drug Involvement

Joel's use of alcohol appeared to be minimal. He did not like the taste and did not want to be out of control. He said, "I want to know what I'm doing." He reportedly never had been drunk. He mentioned drinking some wine on New Year's Eve with his whole family.

Joel denied any drug usage, claiming that, with the exception of marijuana, he never had even been exposed to drugs. Drugs, similar to alcohol, did not appeal to him. He reiterated, "I like to know what I am doing." Given his personality development and neurotic acting-out response style, his statements were believable. Joel was not under the influence of alcohol or drugs at the time of the homicidal incident.

Physical and Mental Health History

At the time of the interview, Joel reported feeling "okay." However, he has continued to experience pain and discomfort from the gunshot wound in his shoulder.

He told me about his 53-day psychiatric hospitalization that ended less than 3 months before the shooting. He maintained that "the hospital made me worse." He "hated" the rules, going to groups, attending meetings, getting up at certain times, and being confined. He stated that he became more rebellious and that, after about 3 weeks, he just stopped doing everything. He recalled being confined to his room for a time (at least 3 days on one occasion) and hitting the wall in frustration. He reportedly had been threatened by one staff member, when he did not take his medication, that he could be put in restraints and given drugs intravenously.

He liked many of the adolescent patients there and some of the staff. He did not recall having individual counseling sessions. He hated one of the counselors in the group because he saw her as making statements about him that were not true. He related an incident in which he started screaming and cursing. He said, "I don't like when people lie, and I went nuts." He said that he apologized later. He recalled seeing a psychologist at one other time about schoolwork but could not recall whether it was before or after he was hospitalized.

Prior Delinquent Involvement

Joel told me that he never had been in serious trouble before. Although he had no police record, Joel stated that he had more police contacts than he could count for minor transgressions. These activities included instances of violating curfew and trespassing, for example, walking through somebody's yard and walking through a retirement village.

The youth's attitude toward the police was very negative. He felt as though he had been hunted down by them for doing nothing and blamed for things he did not do. His characterization suggested that he saw police officers as volatile, power wielding, and unnecessarily confrontational. With few exceptions, he did not like police officers. Joel's recounting of his experiences with his hometown police suggested that he had viewed these interactions as particularly negative.

Joel admitted to involvement in petty thievery (e.g., stealing a lollipop for Jim) and to stealing $30 from his stepfather under circumstances that he considered were extenuating. In admitting to these acts and explaining the background, Joel made his position clear: "I am not a thief by any means." He also related an incident in which he and some of his friends broke into a school by going through the roof and another occasion on which he keyed a car for no apparent reason.

When asked whether he ever had been involved in vandalism, he discussed an incident in which he had been unjustly accused of "trashing a house." Joel and the other boys he was with did nothing to the house they had entered. However, they were blamed for vandalism committed by three girls who entered after the boys had exited.

At different points in the interview, Joel claimed that he had been unfairly blamed for things he did not do. He said that he always was made out to be the ringleader and that one of his friends' mother called him "a juvenile delinquent." The youth related that a boy got beat up on one occasion and that Joel was blamed for it because he was there. When asked how he felt to be blamed for something he did not do, he said that it made him want to go out and do it.

Joel might have minimized his behavior on occasion. However, he could have been unjustly accused of being "a bad guy" given his neurotic acting-out behavioral response style of acting in control and behaviorally challenging others. Unfair accusations would increase anger in a youth with a neurotic acting-out behavioral response style. Joel's remarks revealed the anger below the surface. "I hate when people lie. I dislike liars."

Future Orientation

Joel said that there is "not a chance" he would get into trouble again. He saw the homicidal event as something that just happened.

Joel's thoughts about the future are conventional in orientation. Prior to the incident, he had considered being a police officer or going into the military. His objection to the military, however, is that he would be subjected to taking orders. He also has thought about being a veterinarian due to his fondness of animals.

Adjustment in Jail

Joel seemed to be adjusting satisfactorily in jail. At the time I examined Joel, he had been removed from the medical wing and put into the general population. He acknowledged experiencing depression, pent-up anger, and some hatred at being confined. He stated that in the earlier months of confinement, he had experienced nightmares very frequently and was afraid to sleep, which is not surprising given the nature of the incident. At the time of the interview, the nightmares were not as frequent.

The youth did not appear to be a suicide risk. He admitted that he had thought about suicide but maintained that he would not do it. "I still have a life ahead of me," he said.

He said that he felt safe inside and that the other inmates generally left him alone, although a few maintained that they were afraid of him because of his charges. He had not had anything stolen from him and had not been in any fights. He reported that although "sex games" went on, he was not personally harassed by other inmates.

The youth also stated that he liked most of the guards and thought that this type of job was a good one in terms of career choices. His remarks suggested that he tended to get along well with institutional staff. In fact, Joel said that he related so well to some staff that they had stated they wished they could take him home with them.

■ SYNOPSIS OF CONSULTATION WITH MOTHER

Mrs. Westerlund's statements were consistent with those made by Joel with respect to his limited drug and alcohol use, his school problems, his exclusivity with friends, and his description of family dynamics. Joel's mother's recollection of her son's childhood indicated that he had been a witness to spouse abuse. In addition, Joel had been emotionally neglected by his father and a victim of emotional incest by a mother who related to him increasingly as a confidante over the years.

Mrs. Westerlund indicated that she and her husband were divorced when Joel was about 5 years old. However, for the subsequent 3 to 4 years, she and Mr. Westerlund periodically would get back together for a few months in an attempt to reconcile. She recalled that during these years, Mr. Westerlund was drinking heavily, using drugs, and was physically violent toward her. She recalled at least one beating by her husband that Joel observed. On this occasion, she called the police and was taken away in an ambulance. Although she did not believe that Mr. Westerlund physically abused the children, she said that living with him was "like walking on eggshells" for all of them.

When asked, Mrs. Westerlund admitted that she and her former husband had been arrested for distributing marijuana. She explained that she was not involved in this activity and that charges against her subsequently were dropped. Mrs. Westerlund confirmed that her former husband did not visit Joel and the other children after they relocated to another state.

Joel was in the 4th grade when they moved away. Mrs. Westerlund recalled that her son did very well from the 4th through 6th grades. When Joel was in the 7th grade, the family moved to another county so that they could live with Mrs. Westerlund's present partner, Buddy. Joel's school problems began in the 7th grade, gradually got worse, and were the reason why Mrs. Westerlund signed her son into a psychiatric hospital.

Mrs. Westerlund also characterized Buddy as an alcoholic. She indicated that Joel and Buddy did not get along prior to her son's arrest. She said, "I don't know that Joel's ever had a relationship with an adult male that he felt close to. I think probably the closest he's felt now has been with the guards in the jail."

To her knowledge, neither Mr. Westerlund nor Buddy had any counseling to deal with his addictions and the problems associated with his chemical abuse. Although Mrs. Westerlund did not abuse alcohol, she related that alcoholism was common among relatives on both sides of the family. She had some counseling when she was being abused by her former husband.

Mrs. Westerlund indicated that Joel was a healthy child. She recalled some minor head injuries related to falls as a child, but only one to which she attached any significance. Joel lost consciousness in the 7th grade when another youth hit him.

MOTIVATIONAL DYNAMICS BEHIND THE HOMICIDE

Joel spent more than an hour discussing the events that led up to the homicide and his subsequent charges. He began by relating that Jim had stolen a gun the day before the homicidal incident. Joel did not know why Jim had stolen the gun because Joel did not enter the house when Jim stole the gun. Jim subsequently gave the gun to Joel, who unloaded it, putting the five bullets it contained in his pocket.

Later that night, Mrs. Westerlund told Mrs. Maddox that her son, Jim, had been suspended from school for about 2 days. Mrs. Maddox reportedly had told Jim previously that if he missed another day of school, he would have to move out of the Westerlund home. When Mrs. Maddox said that she would pick Jim up the next day, the two boys decided to run away that night.

Jim and Joel took refuge in a recreation room in an apartment complex that night. Neither boy slept well. The next morning, Jim reportedly told Joel that he was going to steal another gun. Both youths entered a home, and Jim stole the gun. After Jim took the gun, the boys rode their bikes over to the middle school to see Joel's brother. A teacher chased them out of this school, and they left and went over to their own high school.

Joel remembered almost falling asleep in a class and being very concerned because the gun was in his pocket. He remembered sitting with friends at the cafeteria table and telling them that he was going to run away. He left lunch a few minutes early to find Jim. Joel went to physical education (PE) class, where he saw Jim talking to another student. Joel told Jim that he was going back to the middle school. Jim told Joel that he would be at all three lunches if Joel needed him. Joel was expecting to be back in 1½ hours.

Joel next recalled sitting in the auditorium unloading the bullets out of the gun. He had put the bullets back in the gun sometime between the night before and that day. Someone turned on the lights while Joel was in the process of unloading the gun, and the youth put the bullets and gun back in his pants.

Next, Joel recalled three teachers coming and saying "There he is" in reference to Jim. Jim went down the hall. Joel ran from them back over to the middle school. Jim came up in front of the school complaining that Mrs. Winston was looking for Jim.

Later at the high school, Joel, Jim, and another youth, Zach, were sitting in an alcove talking. Robbie came up and said he had a knife. Although Joel said he had a gun, he said it jokingly and did not think that Robbie believed him. The boys noticed that a man, whom they did not know was a detective, walked past them. Joel asked Robbie to take a sweater back to Joel's brother, Jeff. Robbie said "okay" and put the sweater in his locker.

Zach, Jim, and Joel went back to the lunchroom because Zach was hungry. Some teachers who had been looking for Jim walked up and told Jim that he had to come with them. Joel recalled the incident as follows:

> He [Jim] gets up, starts walking, takes off running. Teachers grab him, um, pick him up, throw him down. I jump up, it was like, this is my best friend in the world, I'm not going to watch him get beat up by a bunch of teachers [Mrs. Winston and Mr. Barnett were there at first, and Mr. Abbott joined them at some point]. So I run in there and start punching all these teachers and trying to pull them off of him [Jim], and then the PE teacher [Mr. Burns] hits me. He picks me up and throws me into a table and starts squeezing me in the stomach, in the ribs and like that. I'm telling him to let me go. I'm trying to get to Jim, and he wouldn't let me go or anything, so I'm sitting there, trying to fight him off of me. Then I remembered I had a gun. I told him I had a gun, I told him I had a gun, I told him I had a gun. He started laughing at me. He wouldn't let me go, so I shot him inside of the leg. He let me go. It was that simple. It was stupid of him. I asked him to [let me go].
>
> And then I pointed the gun at Mr. Barnett—he was the guy who threw Jim down—and I told him to get away from Jim, and then I fired a shot in the air. *Then I blacked out from one point* because I was behind all these teachers, and then I was in front of them again when I remembered, and Mr. Abbott was lying there. He had been shot already, or he had just got shot. And then I started yelling at everybody and everything, "Get the hell away from me," but none of these teachers would get off. So, I started screaming, and I shot Mrs. Winston—I never even knew I shot her—I couldn't hear by then 'cause the first two times the gun was fired, I couldn't hear anything after that anyway. It was too loud and . . . then . . . *I blacked out again* right after that.
>
> And then, the next thing I know, Jim pushed me out the front door of the school. Um . . . cops were standing there looking at us, bunch of kids ran around this big white bench. Two cops were standing there, go for their guns. So I started running and they were ready to pull their guns. So I turned around and took two shots off at the cop. I didn't try to hit him or anything. I just tried to scare him, then I threw away my gun. I was pretty sure it was out of bullets and I threw my gun, so I kept running. So they started shooting at me. I got hit and then arrested [few words inaudible]. Just one, I don't know, stupid of them, one cop was trying to kill me more or less. [He] jumped up and down on me, yelling at me. I can understand in a way. I don't remember, *I blacked out when I was shot, too.*

I probed regarding the meaning of blackout and where Joel had heard the term. The youth defined it as not being able to remember, like unconsciousness, "a gap in your memory." The adolescent did not know how he had come to know this term; he had heard people use it before.

He said that he had experienced this type of occurrence before. His definition was a broad one and did not suggest that he was trying to be manipulative or deceptive by giving a textbook definition.

> Like when you get hit in the head, like semi-unconsciousness. You get hit, you don't just flob out, you're still standing there, you don't see what happens, you don't hear anything. It's happened to me before, getting hit in the head or something.

Joel described three occasions on which he had been hit in the head. On one occasion, another child hit him with a pole on a bicycle, and he required stitches. On a second occasion, he hit his head walking into a tunnel. The third time, he got hit in the head with a stick when he was about 13 or 14 years old. Joel also associated the term with "getting the wind knocked out of you, passing out," the confused state resulting from a concussion.

Throughout my detailed probing of the incident, Joel's story remained consistent. In essence, Joel remembered shooting Mr. Burns. The youth related that he pulled the gun out and stuck it up in Mr. Burns's face. When the teacher did not heed his warning and appeared to be laughing at Joel, the youth lowered the gun and shot the man inside the leg. When he shot Mr. Burns, he said that he was "trying to get him off me 'cause he wouldn't let me go."

Joel remembered pointing the gun at Mr. Barnett and yelling at him and other people to get away from Jim. After Mr. Barnett ran away, Joel remembered pointing the gun up in the air and firing a shot, "and everybody started running everywheres." When asked what would have happened had Mr. Barnett not complied, Joel said that he did not know. "He [Barnett] wasn't doing anything. He was just standing above him [Jim] like Mr. Abbott."

Joel stated that *after he fired the gun in the air, he blacked out.* He did not remember getting from behind the teachers. He estimated that he was about 15 feet away from them and then, in a flash, was anywhere from a couple of feet to maybe 5 to 10 feet in front of them. He saw Mr. Abbott "on his knees like he was still sitting there, but he was already shot. He just fell over." Joel said that he had "a good idea" that Mr. Abbott had been shot because he was bleeding from the head. Joel indicated that he was not aware that he had shot Mr. Abbott. He said, "I thought Jim did or something because I didn't think I did."

He recalled looking at Jim and then looking at Mrs. Winston. He remembered yelling at her to get off of Jim while he still had the gun in his hand. Mrs. Winston was either sitting or kneeling up by Jim's head, and Mr. Abbott was down by his feet. He recalled seeing her get off of Jim, but he did not remember shooting her. "She just got off him. That's all it looked like to me, that she let back, 'cause I didn't recall shooting her." In fact, Joel said that when he was told that he shot a lady, he did not know to whom they were referring. He claimed that he did not know who the female victim was until Jim told him at the juvenile detention center.

The next event that Joel recalled was Jim pushing him out the doorway, telling him to hurry up, and practically climbing over him. Joel remembered coming back into consciousness then "because my ears were ringing. I could hear the tingling noise in my ears. That's when the gun was being fired and then the cops were standing there in front of us."

Joel said that when he saw the cops, he was "panicking." When I asked him why he was panicking, he told me "'cause of everything that had already happened. All thoughts were racing through my head and everything. I didn't remember anything that happened. I think the whole thing might have took 30 seconds because the thing went so fast once the first shot was fired."

When asked why he was running from the police, the youth said he remembered firing the gun in the school and seeing Mr. Abbott laying on the ground. He knew he had a gun in his hand when he ran out of the school, and he saw the cops standing there and perceived them as going for their guns. He claimed that he did not remember shooting the gun four times in the school building.

Joel remembered shooting the gun at the police but could not remember initially whether he had fired two or three shots. Joel indicated that he fired at the police to scare them, to get them to take time to cover, and to effect his getaway. When I asked the youth whether it had occurred to him that he could have hit one of them, he replied, "I wasn't thinking, I was trying to survive, I was running." When asked whether he had aimed at the police officer, he said no, but he agreed with my suggestion that he had "more or less" left it to fate.

When discussing the shooting of the police, he said,

> It was like having a dream. Whole thing was like a dream. Even stuff I remember was like a dream 'cause it went so fast. Everything was happening so quick, and even then firing their guns at me nine times, I had no idea of that. All I remember was seeing the gun muzzle flash, the barrel, how it lights up. That's all I remember seeing from them shooting. I don't know how many times they shot at me. When I got hit, I went down.

Joel remembered turning around and looking back at the police after he threw his gun. Jim was right behind him. The police had drawn their guns and started shooting at him. Joel said that he turned his head away and kept feeling little things hit his arm, which turned out to be concrete chips from the wall where the bullets had hit. He kept thinking, "What the hell is this?" as the chips hit him. Then he was hit by the bullet.

Joel said that he did not remember being hit. He remembered hitting the ground, landing on his face, Jim jumping over him, and hearing Jim yell his name over and over again. *He stated he blacked out at this time.* He looked up and could not see Jim.

> Everything was black. I started to turn my head, and my vision started clearing at me. There was a cop staring at me. He was up in the air, and he had a gun in his hand and he lands on my back. And I seen Jim a little bit 'cause I seen him running, and then they were arresting me. I kept yelling "Oh shit! Oh shit! I'm hit" over and over again while Jim was yelling my name.

Joel said that he did not remember very much when he was put in the police car and later taken to the police station. His statements suggested that the police treated him roughly and that he returned the hostility that he perceived. The youth reportedly yelled and cursed "up a storm" at the cops and threatened "to beat the shit out of them when I got ahold of them again."

Joel discussed at length that he was angry because the police had shot him and because of the way in which they treated him. He remembered the police reading the Miranda rights but stated that "everything was like a dream." Joel said that he tried to remain calm. However, his statements clearly indicated that he perceived the behavior of police in a very negative way and responded accordingly.

Joel related that he was angry during the incident because he perceived that the teachers were hurting Jim. He stated that they did not deserve to be shot. He said that he was scared and used the gun to scare or intimidate others into releasing his friend. He recalled trying to scare Mr. Burns and Mr. Barnett. He did not know why Mr. Abbott and Mrs. Winston stayed after Mr. Barnett ran. He remembered firing two shots at the police to scare them and "to make them cover up." When asked whether it had occurred to him that he could have hit one of them, he replied, "I wasn't thinking, I was trying to survive, I was just running."

After his arrest, Joel learned what had happened from statements made by one of the detectives and by Jim. He indicated that his memory of some of the events has come back since the event.

Client's Statements to Others

I was particularly concerned about Joel's claim that he could not remember parts of the incident. Accordingly, in my consultation with Mrs. Westerlund, I explored in depth her knowledge of the homicidal incident. Mrs. Westerlund indicated that Joel had discussed very little with her about the offense. What she related to me was consistent with what her son had told me.

I also inquired extensively about Mrs. Westerlund's thoughts on defense strategy. It did not appear as though Mrs. Westerlund had had extensive discussions about trial strategy with Joel or his attorney. She did not mention the possibility of an insanity defense and seemed to believe that Joel probably would get convicted of second-degree murder. Accordingly, I found no evidence that mother and son had joined in a conspiracy to deceive the mental health examiners.

I reviewed the grand jury testimony of Joel and the deposition of Mrs. Westerlund taken by the state 2 weeks after the shooting. Joel's statements in these accounts were consistent with those he made to me. Interestingly, Joel's account to me was more extensive than were earlier accounts. The youth's statements suggested that he could recall different scenes in the incident. His claim that he could remember more as time passed is very credible and convinced me even further that the boy was telling the truth. If he was malingering (i.e., trying to fake that he was insane), then I clearly would not expect him to "remember more." If Joel actually had been malingering when he said in earlier accounts that he could not remember anything from the time that he shot Mr. Burns until the time he hit the door, I would expect him to stand by his first account and not to risk appearing inconsistent.

Statements made by Joel to his attorney, Mr. Davison, about the incident following his arrest also were consistent with earlier accounts. In essence, Mr. Davison stated that Joel did not recall the shooting and thought that Jim had shot the victims. Mr. Davison related that Joel recalled struggling with Mr. Burns and then hitting the door. When asked 4 months after the homicide whether he had shot Mr. Abbott at point-blank range, Joel told Mr. Davison that he did not recall the shooting. However, he thought from what others had told him that it had been from about 10 feet away.

Before finalizing my clinical opinion, I met with two mental health professionals who had contact with Joel after his arrest. Statements made to Ms. Lumsden by Joel after his arrest, although less detailed, were consistent with those he made to me. Ms. Lumsden saw Joel as a youth who was remorseful and an excellent client for treatment.

Dr. Clark had visited Joel a total of 28 times during the 5 months he had been in jail, going at the rate of 2 to 3 times a week during the first 2 months and 1 to 2 times a week thereafter. He was the person who told Joel that Mr. Abbott had died. Dr. Clark said that Joel had been amazingly consistent about the offense. Dr. Clark related that as time went on, Joel remembered more of the details of the offense. The account that Joel gave him was completely consistent with the account he gave me. Dr. Clark strongly believed that Joel was telling the truth and was not trying to deceive him.

■ EVALUATION OF FORENSIC ISSUES RAISED

Although Joel had gaps in memory, he was able to assist his attorney in preparing a defense. Joel's sanity, unlike his competency to stand trial, was at issue. Did Joel intend to kill or seriously injure the teachers he shot? Did he intend to kill anyone who stood in his path and attempted to thwart his actions?

Making Sense of Murder

No evidence existed that Joel had considered hurting any of the teachers when he went to school on the day of the shooting. Unfortunately, neither Joel nor Jim gave much, if any, thought to the harm that could come from having weapons with him. Having the weapons could have bolstered the youths' sense of security, given their plans to run away that day, and their fragile sense of self-esteem. The bringing of guns to school evinces the poor judgment of these boys, not felonious intent.

When Jim was grabbed by the teachers and called out for help, Joel panicked. Joel felt compelled to protect his friend, whom Joel perceived as being victimized by the teachers. When Mr. Burns restrained Joel, the youth was near his breaking point; he was being physically thwarted in his attempts to come to the aid of "his best friend in the whole world." Joel's behavioral response style, neurotic acting out, indicated that he was sensitive to issues of behavioral control under typical conditions. Under extreme conditions such as those presented in this case, Joel was extremely vulnerable to losing the control he so desperately wanted to maintain.

When Mr. Burns failed to heed Joel's warning that he had a gun, the youth felt increasingly frustrated by his powerlessness in the situation. The youth's statements suggested that he was angry with Mr. Burns due to the man's conduct. The youth perceived that he had given Mr. Burns a choice and that, given the teacher's failure to release him, the adolescent had no choice other than to shoot him. Joel's statements suggested that he purposely moved the gun from Mr. Burns's face and lowered it so as not to kill the victim.

Joel's account suggested that he was experiencing more stress as events in the incident unfolded and that he was becoming increasingly more vulnerable to breakdown. Following the shooting of Mr. Burns, the stressors remained present as he noted that the teachers still were holding Jim. After he pointed the gun at Mr. Barnett, who subsequently fled, he fired the gun into the air, causing an uproar in the cafeteria as scores of people ran for cover. At this point, the events overpowered his ability to retain his hold on reality, and he entered into a dissociative state. He remained in this state until after he was arrested.

Client's Sanity

Based on the materials reviewed and Joel's statements to me and others, I had substantial doubts as to the youth's sanity during the homicidal incident. Joel appeared to have been in a dissociative state shortly after he fired the gun into the air until after he was arrested. In my opinion, he did not know what he was doing when he shot Mr. Abbott and Mrs. Winston. Accordingly, under the M'Naghten standard, he would appear to have been insane at the time that he shot these two people.

Joel's sanity with respect to his firing at the police officers as he attempted to flee afterward is less clear. Unlike the shooting of Mr. Abbott and Mrs. Winston, the boy knew the nature of his act; that is, he knew that he was firing a gun. Shooting at the police officers appeared to be a by-product of the dissociative experience. The youth, however, did appear to know the nature and quality of his act and that shooting was wrongful conduct. Although he would not appear to meet the M'Naghten standard, it is doubtful that he possessed the intention to kill. Given his confused mental state, it is even questionable to what extent Joel was aware of the risk to human life created by his firing wildly at the police officers.

The shooting of Mr. Burns, however, was markedly different from that of the others. It is important to recall that the first time that Joel fired the gun, he shot Mr. Burns. This shooting appeared to have an emotional component that the others lacked. Mr. Burns is the only victim to whom Joel harbored any negative feelings during the incident and afterward. Joel recalled pointing the gun at Mr. Burns and then altering its direction and firing the weapon in an attempt to get the man to release him. This injury, in contrast to the others, appeared to have been an intentional act.

Diagnostic and Treatment Considerations

On admission to the psychiatric hospital, Joel was diagnosed as being depressed and oppositional. At discharge less than 2 months later, he was diagnosed as being *conduct-disordered, undersocialized,* and *aggressive and* as having an *oppositional disorder.* Criteria in the *Diagnostic and Statistical Manual of Mental Disorders* are quite clear that a youth cannot be diagnosed with both behavioral disorders.[1] Neither Dr. Clark, the psychologist who had extensive contact with Joel in the hospital and in jail, nor I saw him as conduct disordered. The responses that Joel gave to the Minnesota Multiphasic Personality Inventory (MMPI) administered during his hospitalization did not reveal the "4-9" pattern typically found among conduct-disordered youths. In addition, Joel did not evince a pattern of disregarding the rights of others. He had a very limited prior delinquent history and did not meet the behavioral criteria associated with this diagnosis.

Joel was bonded to his mother and siblings and had friends about whom he cared. He was not typically a violent, confrontational, or destructive youth. He got involved in fights when he perceived others as challenging him. He did not seek out fights or see aggression as a way in which to achieve his objectives.

Joel's way of relating was more consistent with the diagnosis of Oppositional Defiant Disorder. Joel was negative and defiant. He often actively defied his parents and teachers and refused to comply with their requests and rules. He derived pleasure in being his own person and in doing what he wanted.

The chances for a successful reintegration for this adolescent appeared very good with appropriate treatment. Given his personality development, Joel was capable of working through the conflict areas in his life and making changes. At the time of the clinical evaluation, he saw himself as accountable for his behavior and clearly was remorseful. He was haunted by flashbacks and nightmares in which he saw Mr. Abbott bleeding on the floor and had symptoms of Posttraumatic Stress Disorder.

The youth's empathy for Mr. Abbott was apparent to me as well as to Ms. Lumsden and Dr. Clark. Joel knew the serious nature of the man's condition and actually was relieved when the man died because "he would have been a vegetable." Joel was more concerned about the quality of Mr. Abbott's life than about the change in his personal circumstances occasioned by a first-degree murder charge.

Without treatment, the prognosis in this case appeared guarded. Joel had a great deal of anger and pain due to the psychopathology that had existed in his dysfunctional family, largely as a result of the addictive disorders. This anger and pain needed to be worked through and released in a safe way. The youth needed assistance in separating from his mother and achieving a sense of identity that was prosocial and positive. He also needed help in learning to cope more effectively and in maintaining control when he was particularly vulnerable as a result of various stressors in the environment. A period of institutionalization in a facility with a strong and effective treatment component would have been the optimal setting for Joel.

■ CASE PROCESSING AND DISPOSITION

This case made front-page headlines on every day of the trial. The state maintained that Joel intentionally shot the teachers, killing Mr. Abbott in the process and wounding the two others, because he was an angry youth who hated teachers and had problems with authority figures. The defense pursued an insanity defense, arguing that the events were so intense for Joel that after he shot Mr. Burns, he "snapped" and no longer knew what he was doing.

As Mrs. Winston testified about being shot, seeing Mr. Abbott bleeding from his head and scooting over to comfort him, Joel was observed bowing his head and crying. Later, Joel testified that he neither intentionally shot Mr. Abbott nor wanted to kill anyone. He told jurors that he "blacked out" after firing the shot at Mr. Burns and had no memory of shooting Mr. Abbott or Mrs. Winston.

Dr. Clark and I both testified that Joel was in a dissociative state when he shot Mr. Abbott and Mrs. Winston. The anxiety experienced by Joel was so extreme that it pushed him to a breaking point as events in the cafeteria unfolded that day. After he fired the first shot, Joel was on "automatic pilot." He no longer was capable of making rational decisions and distinguishing right from wrong.

The defense maintained through its expert testimony that Joel did not remember shooting Mr. Abbott and Mrs. Winston because he was in a dissociative state. The state's expert, by contrast, contended that Joel had deliberately suppressed memories of the shooting. The state's witnesss claimed that the boy did not have severe emotional or mental problems and clearly knew what he was doing throughout the entire incident.

The jurors deliberated for more than 9 hours over the course of 2 days before deciding that Joel's actions were not premeditated when he shot Mr. Abbott, wounded Mrs. Winston, and shot at the police officers. However, they did not acquit him by reason of insanity. The jury found Joel guilty of the second-degree murder of Mr. Abbott, two counts of attempted second-degree murder, and one count of aggravated battery. The judge had dismissed the burglary charge earlier.

The sentencing hearing was almost as charged as the trial had been. The Department of Corrections asked the court through its presentence investigation to sentence Joel to life for the killing of Mr. Abbott. The department also asked the judge to impose the maximum amount of time for the other three counts and to run them consecutively to each other and to the life sentence. The state called witnesses to inform the court of the suffering and terror caused by Joel's conduct and asked the judge to sentence the adolescent to life. Prosecutors also called the psychologist who testified for their side at trial to persuade the court that Joel was a conduct-disordered and dangerous youth who warranted a lengthy prison sentence.

The defense, by contrast, urged the court to impose juvenile sanctions in the hope that the youth would get treatment. Joel's attorney asked that Joel be spared the victimization and degradation in prison that would reduce his rehabilitative chances. I advised the court that Joel was a good candidate for treatment given his personality development, his genuine remorse for the suffering he had caused, and his empathy for Mr. Abbott.

The judge sentenced Joel to 17 years in prison, the minimum period recommended by the state's sentencing guidelines, with a 3-year mandatory period imposed for use of a firearm, to be followed by 20 years on probation. In pronouncing this sentence to a packed courtroom, the judge related that she had agonized more over this case than over any other case during the past 25 years. She indicated, in a prepared memorandum, that she understood the victims' pain and the community's anger. The judge advised, however, that she was compelled to consider the defendant's age, his lack of a criminal record, and his family background.

From the court's perspective, Joel "possessed only the wisdom, knowledge, and experience of a 15-year-old child" when he committed these crimes. The judge saw him as a troubled youth who could overcome his emotional and behavioral problems with the proper psychological treatment. The judge related that she would have liked to put Joel in a juvenile facility but that "what he did warrants more than that." In sentencing him to adult prison, the judge indicated that she would recommend that Joel be placed in a youthful offender facility where inmates under 25 years of age serve their time and are provided with psychological counseling.

Three weeks after Joel's sentencing hearing, Jim was sentenced by the same judge. He was given 6 years in adult prison as the result of a negotiated plea to one count of third-degree murder and three counts of burglary in connection with the theft of three guns on three different occasions. Agreement was reached that he would serve his prison sentence in a youthful offender facility. The court further ordered that Jim would serve a 15-year probation term after release.

FOLLOW-UP DATA

I conducted a follow-up interview with Joel 7 years after my evaluation. Two staff members with whom I spoke while waiting for Joel described him as a "model inmate."

He was 22 years old and had been incarcerated for almost 7½ years at that time, including jail time.

Clinical Interview

Joel was expressive and pleasant during the 3-hour interview. He seemed fairly relaxed, and his eye contact was excellent. He was candid in his responses and showed a wide range of emotions, ranging from laughter to tears.

Joel had been housed in two facilities during the 6 years that he had been in adult prison. He spent approximately 3½ years in a maximum-security prison before being transferred to a less secure forestry camp. Joel attributed his having few problems with inmates at either institution to his willingness to stand up to other inmates who challenged him and to the nature of his charges. He reported receiving two disciplinary reports, both of which were dropped as unfounded. He never spent time in disciplinary confinement and lost only 16 days of gain time over the years for not showing initiative on the work squad.

Joel took advantage of available prison resources. He received his general equivalency diploma (GED) in prison and completed a vocational clerk typist (business education) course. He also worked for 2 years in the print shop learning the business and attended a vocational drafting course. At the time of the interview, Joel was working in the warehouse doing an inventory job. He spent his free time playing volleyball and basketball, walking around the track, and reading.

Joel reported talking to prison psychologists on several occasions over the years. Initially, psychological services sent for him. Later, he made appointments when he felt the need to deal with strong feelings.

Joel did not see prison itself as bad. He related that it is the officers and the inmates who, on occasion, choose to make it bad by provoking one another. When asked in what ways prison had been good for him, Joel replied "in just about every way." He explained,

> It's made me look at situations better before I get into them. Basically, I look at them, assess and evaluate them before I get into it. I have learned to control my temper way better. There have been a few times when I have come close to losing it, but fortunately, I haven't had any real problems with it. It made me respect education a lot more. . . . I am a bad example in that situation because I was so rebellious towards all of it. . . . I was intelligent and I didn't do anything. I just did nothing. I made absolutely no effort to put anything into it.

Joel's mother, siblings, and grandparents and Buddy have visited him regularly. His relationship with Buddy has continued to improve over the years. Joel related that his mother and Buddy married while he was incarcerated but have since separated. Joel has had no contact with his biological father since receiving correspondence from him shortly after the shooting. Joel has maintained limited contact with some friends from high school. When he is released, Joel would like to resume his friendship with Jim if it is allowed and if Jim is interested in doing so.

Joel's eyes welled up with tears as he discussed the aftermath of the shooting. Sometimes, he would be just sitting quietly and the event would come into his mind. Although he could see Mr. Abbott bleeding and falling over, he reported having no memory of shooting Mr. Abbott or Mrs. Winston. He recalled "bits and pieces" of the event; they were not always in order, and some of them, such as the encounter with the police, were in slow motion.

Joel related that he feels bad when he thinks about the death of Mr. Abbott and the suffering caused to the victims' families and his own family. Joel understood the loss felt by the Abbott family and the hostility felt by Mrs. Winston, and he felt no bitterness about their negative feelings toward him. He could see "a million ways" in which the homicide could have been prevented, beginning with Jim's not stealing the guns. He acknowledged that it was a mistake for the youths to bring the guns to school.

Joel became visibly upset when he recalled stupid remarks made by inmates who expressed approval of his homicidal behavior. He recalled being very angry when an inmate who "fancied himself as a paramilitary guerilla" referred to the shooting in the cafeteria as a "combat situation." He told him, "I wasn't in a combat situation. I was shooting people that were not armed. I was shooting unarmed people. That's not a fucking combat situation, you idiot."

He experienced remarks such as "We need you to come down and kill our principal" as also upsetting. "It doesn't matter what his job is. He is a person, period. He worked as an assistant principal. It wouldn't have mattered if he was a vagrant bum, he would still be dead."

Joel felt he was treated fairly by the criminal justice system. He was aware of the chance that the judge gave him by following the sentencing guidelines. He appreciated that she had dropped the burglary charge because he did not steal any of the guns.

Joel expressed interest in participating in work release. He would like to get a computer job and intended to live with his mother when released.

Review of Joel's Prison File

Correctional records corroborated Joel's statements. Review of his prison file revealed that Joel had received no disciplinary reports. His quarterly reports were consistently "outstanding" in all areas. After his being incarcerated for a year, staff noted, "He is courteous to the staff and is thought to have adjusted well when considering his length of sentence and age." Records verified Joel's completion of his GED and his vocational program participation.

Follow-Up Interview With Joel's Mother

I spoke with Mrs. Westerlund 6 months after speaking with Joel. The interview took place within a few days of the eighth anniversary of the shooting. Her remarks were consistent with those made by Joel regarding his adjustment in prison, his program completion, and the family's continued involvement and support.

Mrs. Westerlund indicated that Joel adjusted to prison "surprisingly well" given that he was a 16-year-old, criminally unsophisticated youth when he was sent to a maximum-security prison. To her knowledge, although he had witnessed homosexuality and been propositioned, he had not been victimized. Joel's mother related that the "bravado, tough guy" role that her son had when he was first incarcerated had been "diluted." Mrs. Westerlund indicated that her son had "matured a lot" and become "self-sufficient." She was pleased that he had availed himself of educational and vocational opportunities and that he recently had completed a 40-hour prerelease course.

Mrs. Westerlund felt bad that her son was prosecuted as an adult and will carry a felony conviction for the rest of his life. However, she believed that his sentence was fair under the circumstances. She related that she felt no bitterness. She had encouraged Joel to ask God for forgiveness for killing Mr. Abbott and to take advantage of educational opportunities in prison as a way in which to respect Mr. Abbott. She related that she had some contact with Jim over the years and still had warm feelings toward him.

Mrs. Westerlund related that the toughest thing for her about Joel's being in prison was "him growing up outside of the family unit." She was anxiously awaiting his release, which she anticipated would occur within the next 6 to 9 months. Joel's mother expressed concern that she had been diagnosed with cancer and that her life might be shortened. She wanted desperately to see her family reunited and to be there to support Joel's reentry into society.

■ CASE COMMENTARY

This case personally affected the lives of scores of people. The surviving victims, the Abbott family, hundreds of students at lunch, and Joel and his family were forever changed when shots rang out in a 4- to 10-second period in a high school cafeteria. A nation took a painful step forward in its evolution as it confronted the bitter reality that children and teachers no longer could expect safety in their schools.

What caused a gifted youth to open fire at school personnel and to exchange rounds with police officers? Joel was not a mean, predatory youth. In this case, situational factors combined with personality characteristics and, once again, the ready availability of a firearm help to explain this deadly rampage.

Joel lacked a positive male figure while growing up. He harbored strong negative feelings toward his father for years and recalled with bitterness his father's drinking and abusive behavior toward his mother. The youth also had a strong dislike for his "stepfather," Buddy, who also was an alcoholic.

Joel's way of dealing with his anger, pain, and anxiety was to withdraw into himself. He did not deal with his feelings and buried them deep within himself. Joel's strong front was an act. He tried to escape from these feelings by challenging others through noncompliance and maintaining a superior stance.

Jim was the person to whom Joel felt the strongest bond. Joel was willing to run away with Jim rather than to face separation. Joel went along with the theft of guns for protection because it seemed like a good idea at the time. Taking the gun to school and loading it is indicative of his poor judgment.

When Joel saw Jim being restrained by the teachers and heard Jim calling to him for help, Joel was overwhelmed with emotion. He was flooded with anger, fear, and anxiety from the present situation as well as with a barrage of feelings from the past. Joel felt compelled to help Jim. Unfortunately, Joel had a loaded gun on his person. When restrained by Mr. Burns, the youth's anxiety reached the level of panic. Joel was like a rubber band that had been stretched too far and snapped.

Prognosis

Joel had matured significantly in prison and was aware of how he had changed over the years. His perceptions were characteristic of a person who perceived at I-Level 5.

Joel showed an ability to step back and evaluate situations from different perspectives. He perceived differences in others and seemed capable of genuine empathy.

Joel appeared to have a very good chance of making a successful reentry into society given the strong familial support available to him and his personal changes. His prison record indicated that he had discarded his oppositional stance toward authority figures. His willingness to talk with the prison psychologists when upset showed a movement away from the neurotic acting-out pattern that he had displayed as an adolescent. His respect for education and his active participation in instructional programs represented another dramatic change.

At the time this book was being published, Joel was the only one of the young killers whose stories are told who had been released from prison. He rejoined his family, maintained steady employment, and made a successful adjustment to the community during his first year of reentry. Joel was looking forward to going to college and making a positive contribution to society.

Chapter Eleven

Brian Clark

BRIAN CLARK, age 18 years, and Mike Harper, age 20 years, had been friends for years. They were riding in Brian's car with Mike's girlfriend and Brian's young cousin after a hard night of drinking and partying when the car suddenly went off the road, hit a tree, and blew a tire in the process. No one was injured. The two young men left the other two in the car and headed down the road at about 2 a.m. on a Sunday looking for a replacement tire.

Roger Parks, a 49-year-old man, heard the commotion from the accident and left his home to investigate. The man allegedly exchanged some words with Mike. Mike did not like what the man said and beat the man repeatedly with his fists and a tire iron while Brian watched. Brian and Mike went back to the car and drove off, leaving the man for dead. Brian and Mike both were arrested and subsequently charged with the first-degree murder of Roger Parks.

THE CLINICAL EVALUATION

This assessment is based on a 3-hour interview conducted with the defendant, Brian Clark, in adult jail 8 months after the homicide. Case materials reviewed included the police investigation reports, the autopsy report, and a post-offense psychiatric evaluation. Statements given to the police by Brian and his co-defendant's girlfriend, Kim, were perused. Copies of Brian's school records and his violation of probation form also were examined.

Despite my repeated attempts by phone and by mail, Brian's parents would not make themselves available for consultation. The lack of cooperation from Brian's parents was very unusual given that their son was facing the death penalty. Their reluctance to meet with me was not due to a lack of understanding of the purpose or importance of this meeting. I spoke to Mr. and Mrs. Clark separately about the nature of my evaluation and my need to speak with them regarding information that they could provide about their son. I explained my role as a confidential defense expert. I related that my report would go to defense counsel and that there would be no financial cost to them in meeting with me.

BEHAVIORAL OBSERVATIONS

At the time of the assessment, Brian was an 18-year-old White male, approximately 5 feet 11 inches in height and about 150 to 155 pounds. He had a slight to medium build. He was not on any medication at the time of the evaluation.

Brian was polite, cooperative, and alert during the 3-hour evaluation period. He maintained good eye contact and good concentration. His answers often were brief. However, when asked to elaborate, he was willing to do so. He answered hundreds of questions and did not refuse to answer any, even when it was a source of discomfort for him to do so. He showed little anxiety during the assessment, and his affect was appropriate to the content of the interview. His answers indicated that he was oriented in time and space and that he was aware of what was happening with his case.

The youth did not appear to be at all manipulative during the evaluation. His responses to questions and his behavior strongly suggested that he was trying hard to be truthful. He did not readily disclose troubling information about his family. When probed, he revealed information pertinent to childhood trauma without using it as a forum in which to discuss its effect on him and its possible role in his subsequent criminal behavior.

■ PERSONALITY DEVELOPMENT

Typical of Level 4 individuals on the Interpersonal Maturity Level (I-level) classification system who adopt a *neurotic* pattern of coping, Brian's self-defeating pattern appears reactive to long-standing pain, anger, and anxiety resulting from childhood difficulties. Brian's involvement in drugs and alcohol began at 14 years of age, about the time he learned that his stepfather was not his biological father.

■ RELEVANT SOCIAL HISTORY

Family Constellation

Brian was raised by his mother, Wilma, and his stepfather, Bob Clark. When Brian was 16 years old, his mother and stepfather divorced. They both remained in the same community, and Brian maintained contact with each of them. He was living with his mother at the time of his arrest.

Brian related that he was "upset" when his mother and stepfather got divorced because he did not want it to happen. At the time of the divorce, his parents argued frequently and Brian was not getting along with his stepfather. He was "a little bit afraid" at times that one of them might hit the other because each reportedly had threatened to do so.

Brian described his mother as "sweet." She would listen to Brian. Regarding his stepfather, Brian said that he liked him a lot. "To me, he's dad." Mr. Clark had been in Brian's life since he was about 1 year old. Brian liked to do things with his stepfather. He appreciated that Mr. Clark would listen to his problems and help him straighten things out.

At the time of my assessment, Brian was just getting to know his biological father. His father, who lived in Wisconsin, had visited him in jail recently. Brian did not remember when, if ever, he had seen his biological father prior to this visit. He indicated that it was "different" and "strange getting to see him after $17\frac{1}{2}$ years." When asked whether Brian had wanted to see his biological father before, he said, "I didn't think about it." He described his biological father as a "good guy." He related that his mother did not keep in touch with his father and that his father had lost track of them. When asked whether it bothered him that he had not heard from his biological father while growing up, he said "not really, not that much."

Brian said that he found out that his stepfather was not his biological father when he was 14 years old. Brian had gotten into trouble at school, and he and his stepfather were arguing. Mr. Clark was angry and "slipped up and said it, he ain't my real father anyway." When he heard this remark, Brian said, "It hurt. I left the house. I did not come back for a couple of weeks."

When Brian returned, his stepfather apologized and they straightened the matter out. Brian indicated that they had a good relationship at the time I met with him.

Brian had a younger sister. He expressed concern that she was starting to grow up like he did. She was out partying and trying to be by herself. His mother, sister, and stepfather had visited him about every other week since he had been incarcerated. Brian also had an aunt, Diane, and an uncle, Dave, to whom he felt close.

Brian's answers to many questions tapping various indicators of abuse and neglect revealed little or no evidence of verbal, psychological, physical, or sexual abuse by parents, other relatives, or non-family members. Brian's physical, medical, and emotional needs appeared to have been met by his mother and stepfather. Emotional neglect occurred by the biological father, who had no contact with Brian from infancy until 3 months after the homicide (more than 17 years). The stepfather's blurting out in anger that he was not Brian's real father was a psychologically abusive act. Brian's answers suggested that this verbal explosion was an isolated act.

When asked about his parents' drinking and drug habits, Brian indicated that his stepfather drank "very occasionally," generally on holidays, and not to excess. Brian's mother started drinking "quite a bit after the divorce." She reportedly would go out drinking with her friends about twice a week and sometimes would get drunk. Brian believed that his mother had a problem with alcohol.

Brian reported that his mother and stepfather had both smoked marijuana on a daily basis for years. He believed that both of them had problems with the use of marijuana when he was growing up. At the time of the evaluation, Brian indicated that his mother currently was not smoking much, if at all. He did not know about his stepfather.

School

Brian did well in elementary school. He quit school in the 9th grade because he did not like going to classes. His grades were failing. He did not find the schoolwork too difficult. "I was wanting to run the street with all my friends instead of going to school and doing something with myself."

Brian got along with the teachers and reported liking several of them. However, he got into trouble "all the time" for "skipping school, just minor disbehavior [sic]." He reported getting into about four or five fights since the 6th grade. He fought over issues such as girlfriends, who was going where, and people talking about others. He denied ever fighting for the sake of fighting. He was "not a good fighter but not the worst" either. He did not like to fight because he did not like to feel pain. He got into these fights because he was "acting like a big shot in front of everybody else. I was trying to look big in front of my friends. I was trying to impress everybody."

He challenged the teachers verbally, saying that "their class stunk, they were worth nothing, or they wouldn't run me." He thought of hitting the teachers but never did because he knew that it was not right, "that I shouldn't take something that far just to make everybody think something."

Brian attended a vocational school for a few months but was discharged from the program for irregular attendance. He decided to get his general equivalency diploma (GED) because he saw that he needed it after he began working. Getting it was "real easy" for him.

Work History

Brian reported working at four jobs. He worked for 9 months as a bag boy in the 9th grade, then as a cook at a country club for 1½ years. He quit working for several months to attend vocational school. He next worked for about a year herding cattle at a cattle auction until quitting to get his GED. He did not work for a period because he was in jail on prior charges. At the time of his arrest on his present charges, he had been working as a luncheon cook for a few weeks.

Friends

Brian defined his friends as mostly "troublemakers," boys and girls who would be "getting into trouble" and "doing something they shouldn't do . . . to prove that they could do it." He liked such adolescents because "they were on their own" and "doing their own thing."

Brian stated that he had many friends prior to his arrest but has outgrown them. "All they wanted to do was party." With the exception of Steve, a boy he had known since they were "babies," "all the rest would turn on you real quick." They were not true friends, and he did not hear from them anymore.

Girlfriends and Sexual History

Brian mentioned that he was going with a girl, Marlene, at the time of his arrest. He described her as "kind of immature" and said that he was trying to straighten her out because he did not want her to get into trouble like he had done.

Brian previously had dated a girl, Shannon, who broke up with him because she wanted to settle down and he wanted to party. He thought her decision to break up with him was "smart of her." Brian mentioned another girl, Hillary, with whom he partied. She was like him and was on the "wild side."

Brian said that he had several other girlfriends who did not mean much to him. He went around with them because he wanted to be like the other guys. When asked whether sex was a big thing for him, he indicated that he, like the other guys, would talk about it a lot but that the stories were not true.

Brian reportedly liked girls who were attractive and had a "little bit of smarts, know what life is about." He did not like girls who threw themselves at him. "I am more like a person who wants a challenge. If it is hard to get, I want it."

Activities

Brian liked to play softball, ride horses, swim, and race cars with his friends to see who had the fastest cars. He also liked to "party a lot—drink all night, smoke dope, or whatever."

Alcohol and Drug Involvement

Brian indicated heavy involvement in drinking alcohol and in smoking marijuana. He normally would drink a case (24 cans) of beer or a pint of whiskey a day. He liked getting drunk because he liked the feeling. "When I was drunk, I didn't care." He got drunk "just about every night." He would start drinking around noon and kept going. "Every once in a while," he would drink in the morning if he had a headache. He reported craving alcohol every day. Occasionally, he drank alone.

Brian began drinking when he was around 14 years old. He wanted to do what he wanted and would not listen to his parents. He was hanging around with youths about 19 or 20 years old who drank. He was able to drink higher quantities of alcohol over the years. He reported feeling sick in the morning at first, but his body got used to alcohol. He missed school because of drinking and had many "blackouts" (periods of time when he could not remember what he had done).

He knew that he had a problem with alcohol "when I started getting in trouble with the law and everybody started turning away from me." Although he was aware of the bad consequences, he would not stop drinking and did not try to do anything about it. Others, including his mother, relatives, girlfriends, and Steve, thought that he had a problem with alcohol.

Brian smoked marijuana "every day." He started when he was about 14 years old. He smoked about an ounce a week. When asked whether he thought he had a problem with marijuana, he said "in a way, but I wasn't really concerned about it." He reported doing other "natural drugs" such as mushrooms. He denied using other drugs such as amphetamines, cocaine, crack cocaine, and heroin because "I didn't see no reason to it."

Brian did not define his drug or alcohol usage as a problem at the time of my evaluation because he had been drug free during the past 7 months due to his incarceration. However, he indicated that if he began drinking alcohol or smoking marijuana, he would do it to excess. He recalled craving alcohol for the first month after his arrest. Then he started to feel better.

Physical and Mental Health History

Brian described his health as good when he was growing up. He did not recall being hospitalized for any illnesses. Other than talking for a few minutes to a juvenile probation officer on a monthly basis, Brian had no counseling. Brian reported no psychiatric evaluations or hospitalizations.

When asked, Brian expressed some interest in seeing a counselor. He was open to talking about his alcohol and drug problems, skipping school, partying, and not listening to his parents.

Brian reported feeling good at the time of the assessment. He was eating well and sleeping about 10 hours a day. He had experienced a few nightmares but did not indicate being disturbed by them.

Handling Problems and Affectivity

Brian described himself as "normally easygoing. I try to get along with everybody. If I like somebody, I'll do whatever I can." Maintaining control of his emotions was important to him. However, he acknowledged that he could get very angry on occasion and that some people had expressed concern about his bad temper.

Brian was aware of using a number of coping strategies. He thought about running away sometimes and did on two occasions to be on his own. He sometimes turned to alcohol and to drugs to feel better. He also saw his hunting, fishing, and playing outdoor sports with his stepfather and uncle as other ways in which he dealt with his difficulties.

Brian stated that he had about the same number of friends as did other adolescents. Relative to other youths, he got into more trouble at school and engaged in more illegal activities. When asked what he liked best about himself, he said that he was active, enjoyed sports, and could do things with his hands. When asked what, if anything, he would like to change about himself, Brian said "getting in trouble with the law, drinking, drugs—try to straighten myself out."

Religious Affiliation

Brian attended a Baptist church when he was younger. He stopped going when he was 10 or 11 years old because he lost interest. He participated in the church service in jail every week because it "helps you think straighter." He related that he believes in God and prays "occasionally."

Prior Delinquent Involvement

Brian reported that he had been arrested about three times as a juvenile for burglary. He associated his getting into trouble with alcohol. He would ride around with others and break into people's houses to steal things to get money to buy alcohol. He would burglarize the homes of people when the people were not there. He selected homes of people he did not know and always had someone with him.

He did not take a weapon to burglarize because "I didn't see no reason for it." He admitted that he had on occasion carried a gun when "trying to act big." He liked shotguns and rifles for hunting; he did not like other types of guns.

When he was 17 years old, he was caught stealing a television, a microwave, and jewelry and was adjudicated as an adult for burglary and grand theft and sentenced to 2 years probation in one county. He started drinking again, stole a three-wheeler, and was convicted in adult court of burglary of a conveyance and grand theft in another county. He served 3 months in jail and was sentenced to 2 years probation in the second county.

Brian denied any arrests for drugs. At the time of his arrest, Brian was on probation for convictions in two counties.

In comparing information provided by Brian to prior record data, I noted that Brian correctly reported his arrests at 17 years of age, his processing as an adult, and his dispositional history. His rendition of his offenses as a younger juvenile (ages 13-16) was not entirely accurate. He did not mention two arrests for misdemeanor possession of marijuana and retail theft. His failure to tell me about these offenses could have been because he did not remember them as arrests but rather simply as police contacts.

Of the 13 charges referenced in the probation violation report, 12 were criminal acts; only 1 charge, truancy, was a status offense. Of the 12 charges, 4 consisted of some type of burglary with associated charges of grand theft (3) and dealing in stolen property (2). The remaining charges consisted of 1 retail theft and 2 misdemeanor marijuana possession charges.

Future Orientation

Brian expressed interest in going to "career school" and someday having an auto mechanic or auto body shop. He related that he likes to work with his hands and to do things that involve art.

Brian indicated that he wanted to have a good relationship with a girl, settle down, and raise a family. He did not see himself getting into trouble again. He had seen "the worst there is" this time. He lost interest in partying because all it did was get him into trouble.

Adjustment in Jail

During his 7 months of incarceration, Brian had been housed in a two-man cell. He reported no difficulties and appeared to have made a satisfactory adjustment to jail. He was getting along with both the guards and inmates and had gained about 30 pounds.

▨ MOTIVATIONAL DYNAMICS BEHIND THE HOMICIDE

Brian denied that he had any direct physical contact with the homicide victim. His version is recapped in the following and is generally consistent with the statements that he gave to police.

Brian's Statements to Dr. Heide

When asked about the instant or presenting offense, Brian stated, "We went to a party and got a little drunk, got drunk. I let a friend of mine [Mike] drive and he wrecked the car, and he ended up getting in a fight with a guy that came to help us. . . . He killed him."

Brian initially was charged with second-degree murder by the police. He later was charged with first-degree murder because the state seemed to believe that he was more involved in the offense than he was. He was unaware at the time of the clinical evaluation that the state was seeking the death penalty.

Brian maintained throughout the interview that he was not involved in the fight. He indicated that he did not hit the victim, that the victim did not try to hit him, and that he had no physical contact with the victim whatsoever.

Probing of the offense indicated that Brian and Mike left a party around 1:30 a.m. They had with them Mike's girlfriend, Kim, Brian's 8-year-old cousin, Eric, and two of Brian's friends. Brian drove the two friends home. After the two boys were dropped off, Mike wanted to drive, so Brian let him.

Mike was driving fast, ran off the road, hit a tree, and blew out one of the back tires. Mike and Brian exited the car, leaving Kim and Eric in the car. It was about 2:30 a.m. as the two young men walked together. "We were gonna go get a tire to fit the car, and then the guy came out to see what was wrong, and he started bad-mouthing Mike. Then they got into a fight, and Mike ended up killing him." Brian indicated that he and Mike were not in the process of taking a tire when the victim approached them. The victim was "in a way bad-mouthing both of us, but he was talking more to Mike. Them two was talking. I was off to the side." Brian stated that, from where he was standing, he could hear what the victim was saying—"young punks like us don't need to be driving down his road, going fast the way we was."

When asked how the physical fight started, Brian replied "'cause the guy said people like Mike need to get their butts kicked every once in a while, and Mike didn't like that too much and swung at him." Mike allegedly asked the victim "if he was gonna be the one that done it." The victim did not have a chance to say anything more because Mike swung at him immediately. "He beat him [the victim] down in the street and picked him up and carried him in the woods and killed him."

At the time, Brian was "standing there by the edge of the road" approximately 8 feet away, possibly farther. Brian said that from where he stood, he could see Mike hitting Mr. Harper. The victim did not have a chance to strike back. "It all happened so fast. I don't think the guy [the victim] knew what happened." Mike hit the victim in the head with his fist. When the man fell down onto the street, Mike continued beating him. Mike picked the victim up and carried him into the woods by himself. Brian described the victim as of average size, perhaps a little bigger than himself. Mike, unlike the victim and Brian, was "a big guy," about 6 feet 4 inches in height and 240 pounds.

Brian observed Mike beating the victim with a tire iron "quite a few times"—more than 10 times—after he carried the victim into the woods. Mike had the tire iron with him the whole time "stuck in his belt loop." Brian was about 15 feet away and close enough to see. The victim did not scream.

Brian described himself as "stunned" and "scared" during the incident. He recalled standing there. Neither he nor Mike said anything to each other. "I was scared and ready to leave, to get out of the area." Brian indicated that he had not encouraged Mike in any way to beat up the victim. Brian did not know what was going to happen next. When asked, Brian acknowledged that he and Mike previously had talked about beating somebody up as guys often do but that it was just talk, "more like jokes."

Brian did not know why Mike beat the man to death. He said that both he and Mike had been "drinking a lot" at the party. "We were drinking out of a keg, so I don't remember how much. It was quite a bit, though." Brian had not been smoking marijuana at the time. He did have a "buzz." He stated, "I was getting pretty . . . I felt very high." Brian indicated that when he left the party, he knew who was with him. He was awake and thought he was "drivin' good."

When asked why he did not tell Mike to stop beating the victim or intervene to stop Mike, Brian replied, "I was scared and everything was happening so fast. It was, I didn't see nothing I could do."

After Mike had beaten the victim in the woods, the two young men went back to the car and left. When asked what he was thinking when they left the scene of the homicide, Brian replied, "I thought about it. I knew he was killed . . . by the way, the sound of everything that was, I could pretty much see what happened." He also heard sounds "like a banging sound, like a hammer hitting." As they were leaving, Brian felt "really scared. I didn't know what to think. It's shocking to see something like that happen. I didn't know what to do."

Brian managed to drive the car to a store in spite of the bad tire. After they arrived, Mike and his girlfriend left the area because Mike thought it would be better if they split up. Brian subsequently called his aunt to pick up him and his cousin.

Brian mentioned that a deputy stopped when they were at the store to see what the problem was. Brian did not explain what had happened. He gave the deputy some identification. Brian was able to talk straight to the deputy, explaining that his tire was flat and he did not have a spare. The deputy left in response to a call. Brian's aunt picked up him and his cousin shortly thereafter, and he got home around 4:30 or 5 a.m.

Brian was arrested the next day at around 5 p.m. The police traced the car to him. Brian gave a statement to the police at around 1:30 a.m. (about 8 hours later). "I told them [the police] everything." During the time that he was picked up by the police and confessed, Brian took them to where Mike lived. Brian indicated that the police gave him food and something nonalcoholic to drink. When asked, Brian stated that he told the police "more or less the same" things that he had told me. When he gave the police his statement, he told them that he, rather than Mike, was driving when the accident occurred. He did not know why he lied about the identity of the driver. "I was so scared and shaky, I don't know what I told them." He explained that he was "scared. I didn't actually know what was actually going on at the time."

Brian was not afraid of the police because he had dealt with the police before. The police initially tried to intimidate him "a little bit" by telling him that if he did not help them, they would "lock me up for a long time, put me away for life." He related that these strategies did not work and that they were straight with him afterward.

When asked, Brian indicated that he did not discuss the homicide with anyone from the time that he left the murder scene to his arrest. "I was scared, now that I just seen somebody get killed and didn't know what to do about it." He was also afraid that Mike might do something to him because he, unlike Kim and Eric, had witnessed the killing.

Brian had known Mike for about 13 years and used to party with him all the time. Brian knew his co-defendant well from growing up with him and had seen him get into fights before. He described Mike as having "always been on the violent side." Mike "put a boy in the hospital once, broke a boy's jaw."

Brian wished that he could go back to when he started drinking and turn it all around. When asked how he felt about the man who died, Brian said, "I feel bad for him and his family. I feel it should never have happened. . . . There wasn't no sense for something like that to happen. Man came out to try to help us and then Mike, being drunk, didn't understand everything the way it should have been understood." Brian explained that the victim "was kinda upset the way we was driving down the road, but I think he was more or less coming out to see if anybody was hurt, to see if anything was wrong. If he could help, then he was gonna help."

Brian did not see himself as a violent person. When asked what would be a fair outcome, he said that it would be fair for Mike "to get a little bit of time, not a lot of time." He explained, "They try to say it was premeditated. It might have been, but I don't think so. He was drunk. He didn't know what was going on himself. It was something that automatically happened. . . . Everything was happening so fast, nobody could understand what was going on."

Brian had difficulty coming up with an appropriate sentence for himself. It was "hard to say because I didn't do nothing wrong that night. I did violate probation, which I understand; if I get time for violating that, I understand. The other charges, I don't see any reason for that."

Defendant's Statements to the Police

There are a few discrepancies in the statements that Brian made to the police and those he made to me, in addition to who was driving the car when the accident occurred. In the taped statement to the police, Brian vacillated regarding how far he was from the place where Mike was beating the victim—from 20, to 30, to 300 feet away. He also appeared to have changed his story to the police regarding whether or not he saw Mike hit the victim with the tire iron.

He did maintain throughout the police interviews that he never had touched the victim. He also held his position that he was scared, "flipping out."

Others' Statements to the Police

Kim and Mike both told the police that Brian did not have physical contact (i.e., in terms of beating) with the victim. Kim stated that she observed no blood on Brian, whereas she observed a lot of blood on Mike. She also told police that Mike stated that he (Mike) had beaten the man and that "Mike and Brian both said that . . . all Brian did was sit there and watch . . . and when Mike started beatin' the guy up, Brian jumped back 3 or 4 feet." She indicated that Mike had picked the victim up "over his shoulders by himself and carried him into the woods."

Conclusions

Statements made by Brian, his co-defendant Mike, and his co-defendant's girlfriend Kim, who was with the offenders moments before and after the homicidal event, indicate that Brian did not have physical contact (i.e., in terms of beating) with the deceased victim. A lie detector test indicated that Brian was telling the truth when he said that he did not hit, kick, or move the murder victim. Physical evidence further corroborated that Brian's participation in the homicidal event was restricted in scope.

EVALUATION OF THE FORENSIC ISSUES RAISED

Brian's competency to stand trial was not an issue because it was apparent that he knew the nature of his charges and was able to assist his lawyers. The defendant's sanity also was not an issue because he denied having had any physical involvement with the victim during the homicidal incident. If Brian admitted at some point that he participated in beating the victim in the incident, then his mental status at the time of the crime would need to be reexamined.

Factors in Mitigation

I advised defense counsel to consider the application of 15 potential factors in mitigation of death in this case. A total of 7, and possibly 8, of the 8 statutory mitigating factors appeared to apply in Brian's case.

Close inspection of Brian's arrest history revealed that *"The defendant had no significant history of prior criminal activity."* Available data indicated that Brian was arrested on approximately six occasions. Of the 12 criminal charges, 9 resulted from apparent involvement in four burglaries with the associated charges cited earlier. Official data confirmed that Brian never was arrested for committing any violent acts. There was no evidence that Brian was armed when committing his burglaries and, hence, prepared to use violence.

"*The capital felony was committed while the defendant was under the influence of extreme mental or emotional disturbance.*" Given Brian's role, this mitigator needed to be qualified as follows: The capital felony was committed *by the defendant's co-defendant* while the defendant was under the influence of extreme mental or emotional disturbance.

Taped statements made by Brian to police after his arrest (12 midnight to 1 a.m.) indicated that, *as Brian watched Mike beating the victim*, he was "under the influence of extreme mental or emotional disturbance." He stated five times in response to police questions (What was going through his head? Did he think there was a chance that the victim would die? Was his mind preoccupied with something else when Mike was hitting the victim with a tire iron so that he did not see it? How come he was not focused on what Mike was doing? How come he did not see whether the victim was wearing shoes?) that he was "flippin' out."

Brian's statement to the police that he was afraid to stop Mike or get in Mike's way because of Mike's size and reputation as well as Mike's behavior at that time is consistent with Brian's claim that he was extremely agitated. Brian stated that Mike "went nuts. He worried me . . . 'cause he flipped out."

Brian's insistence to police that he was focused on getting his 8-year-old cousin home in the midst of this homicidal incident is consistent with his statements that he was "flippin' out." People who are exposed to severe trauma often focus on some detail to hold themselves together. Brian's focusing on what would appear to be a minor issue rather than dealing with the magnitude of what was happening is further evidence that he was not able to process information clearly.

Brian's statements to me also suggested that, at the time of the homicidal event, Brian was "under the influence of extreme emotional or mental disturbance." When asked why he did not tell Mike to stop beating the victim or intervene to stop Mike, Brian replied, "I was scared, and everything was happening so fast. It was, I didn't see nothing I could do." As they were driving away from the scene, Brian figured that the victim had been killed and related that he was "really scared. I didn't know what to think. It's shocking to see something like that happen. I didn't know what to do."

"*The defendant was an accomplice in the capital felony committed by another person, and the defendant's participation was relatively minor.*" Brian's actions in the homicidal event can be summarized as follows. He picked up the victim's flashlight and handed it to Mike, who threw it, causing it to break. He transported Mike away from the murder scene and failed to report the killing to the police officer who asked him for identification shortly thereafter at a local store.

"*The capacity of the defendant to appreciate the criminality of his conduct or to conform his conduct to the requirements of the law was substantially impaired.*" In addition to being flooded with anxiety as he watched Mike beat the victim, it appeared that, at the time of the murder, Brian was under the influence of alcohol and was unable to process information clearly. He and Mike reportedly had been "drinking a lot" at a party that they had just left, and Brian remembered feeling very high.

"*The age of the defendant at the time of the offense.*" At the time of the homicidal incident, Brian was 18 years 4 months old. Although no longer a juvenile, he was still an adolescent. Adolescents' ability to cope and their life experiences typically are less than those of adults.

"The defendant could not have reasonably foreseen that his conduct in the course of the commission of the offense would cause or would create a grave risk of death to one or more persons." When Brian exited the car with Mike to steal a tire to fix his car, he could not have reasonably foreseen that he and Mike would be confronted by a home owner who would challenge Mike and that Mike would beat this home owner to death.

"The existence of any other factors in the defendant's background that would mitigate imposition of the death penalty." There were at least seven factors. Brian was remorseful and did not have a criminal self-image. The adolescent appeared to have had both alcohol and drug problems. Data suggested that he was raised in a chemically dependent and severely dysfunctional family. Brian's difficulties were long-standing, and it appeared that no meaningful intervention had occurred.

Brian appeared to be genuinely remorseful for his actions. He indicated that he felt bad for the man's family. Brian saw the victim as intending to help them and saw Mike's beating him to death as senseless.

Brian did not have a criminal self-image and did not appear to be a violent person. Brian reported that he had gotten into about four or five fights at school since the 6th grade. He maintained, however, that he did not like to fight and did not fight for the sake of fighting. He stated that he burglarized people's homes to get money to buy alcohol and did not take a gun because it was not necessary.

When asked what talking about the homicide was like for him, Brian paused for a few seconds and replied, "It's weird. It's strange. I never seen myself to be in a predicament like this . . . never seen myself as that much of a violent person. . . . I didn't see myself as being able to see something like that happen or being around anything like that." When asked to see himself as he was during the incident, he said that he was "stunned" and "scared."

Brian had an internalized value system that was conventional. Although he had engaged in prior criminal behavior, he saw this type of behavior as wrong. His personality development was sufficiently high that he was capable of seeing himself as accountable for his behavior. His behavioral response style was to run from anxiety and pain by leaving a situation or by anesthetizing his consciousness with alcohol or drugs.

Brian had some awareness that his response pattern was self-defeating. He has some interest in examining his life and redirecting it, and he expressed some interest in seeing a counselor. He was willing to talk about his alcohol and drug problems, skipping school, partying, and not listening to his parents.

Brian appeared to be physiologically dependent on alcohol. Given that Brian began using alcohol daily at 14 years of age, it was likely that his development was arrested and his judgment affected.

Brian also had a history of significant use of illicit drugs. Information provided by Brian indicated that he also was a frequent and heavy user of marijuana. Given that Brian began smoking marijuana daily at about the same time that he began drinking alcohol daily, it was even more likely that his development was arrested and his judgment affected.

Brian appeared to have been raised in a chemically dependent family. In addition to Brian's alcohol and drug involvement, there was some evidence to suggest that Brian's mother might have abused alcohol and that both parents might have used illicit drugs. Brian reported that both parents smoked marijuana for years. This factor was relevant as a factor in mitigation in terms of the dynamics that typically operate in chemically dependent family systems and their effects on all family members.

There were other data to suggest family dysfunction in addition to parental chemical dependency. In an apparent fit of anger, Brian's stepfather had told Brian at about 14 years of age that he was not his biological father. Brian did not have any contact with his biological father until several months after the homicide. The mother's and stepfather's inability or unwillingness to meet with me at a time when their son needed their help also was symptomatic of severe family dysfunction.

Brian's difficulties were long-standing, and it appeared that no meaningful intervention had occurred. Brian's school records indicated that Brian began having academic problems in the 7th grade and had to attend summer school. He was retained in the 8th grade. After repeating the 8th grade, he was administratively promoted to the 9th grade. He failed all courses in the 9th grade. He withdrew from school in the 10th grade when he was 16 years old. His academic problems were a clear signal that something was seriously wrong.

In addition, his daily use of alcohol and marijuana also was evidence that Brian needed help and was trying to run from his problems. Finally, his arrests beginning at 13 or 14 years of age provided further evidence that Brian was acting out. However, there was no evidence that meaningful help was provided to him.

There were some data to suggest that the remaining statutory mitigating factors also might have applied in this case: *The defendant was under extreme duress or under the influence of the substantial domination of another person.* Although Mike did not threaten Brian, Brian indicated to the police and to me that he was afraid of Mike. Mike, in contrast to Brian, was "a big guy," about 6 feet 4 inches in height and 240 pounds, and had a violent history. Accordingly, Brian's unwillingness to stop Mike during the beating was, to some extent, due to his fear that Mike might harm him.

Diagnostic and Treatment Considerations

Brian met the diagnostic criteria for alcohol dependence and possibly for cannabis (marijuana) dependence. At the time of the clinical assessment, Brian's prognosis was good. He did not participate in the killing of Mr. Parks and in no way appeared to encourage the violence. Brian had neither a history of violent behavior nor a criminal self-image. The adolescent was aware that he had both alcohol and drug problems and was amenable to treatment.

■ CASE PROCESSING AND DISPOSITION

Brian's attorneys negotiated a plea bargain with the prosecutors wherein the adolescent was allowed to plead no contest to being a principal to manslaughter in exchange for his willingness to testify against his co-defendant at trial. The court, on the recommendation of the state, sentenced Brian to 10 years in prison. Brian also received prison time for violating probation in connection with the three prior burglaries and their associated charges. Although the burglary commitments were to run concurrently with Brian's homicide commitment, correctional authorities extended Brian's release date to the maximum allowable in response to the court's request on three grounds: the inmate's multiple separate offenses, the extent of psychological trauma to the victim, and the escalating or continuing pattern of criminal conduct.

Brian did not testify against Mike because the case did not go to trial. Prosecutors allowed Brian's co-defendant to plead guilty to second-degree murder after Kim, Mike's former girlfriend, recanted her earlier sworn statements that Mike killed the victim. The court sentenced Mike to 25 years in prison. Prosecutors charged Kim with perjury.

■ FOLLOW-UP DATA

I conducted a follow-up interview with Brian approximately 2 years after my evaluation. At that time, Brian had been incarcerated for $2^1/2$ years. I made no attempt to meet with Brian's parents given their previous lack of cooperation.

Brian was pleasant and maintained good eye contact. He functioned at the same level of personality development. As in my prior contact with him, Brian's answers and his affect were restricted in range. His lack of introspection suggested that he has continued to avoid thinking about painful events in his life. He did not think about the homicide, for example, because "it's in the past. It's over with." His fidgeting with his hands throughout the interview suggested that, despite his calm veneer, he was mildly anxious.

Brian had been housed in a youthful offender facility during the 17 months he had been in adult prison. Despite his slight build, he reportedly had experienced no problems with inmates other than the theft of a few inexpensive items. He related that he had maintained a discipline-free record by "just keeping my mind right, just knowing the only way you are going to get out [of prison] is to stay out of trouble."

Brian received a certificate in cabinetmaking while in prison. He had not gone for counseling because the prison psychiatrists reportedly just give the inmates drugs and do not really help them with their problems. He did not participate in the few remedial educational programs because he stated that he had completed his GED prior to arrest.

The toughest thing about being in prison for Brian was "being away from home." He acknowledged that prison had been good for him because "it's made me grow up more. It makes you realize what life's about." He no longer thought about life as "hanging out" and partying. He related, "You've got to get out and make something of yourself."

Brian reportedly has had regular visitations from his mother, stepfather, sister, and grandparents. He has not had contact with his co-defendant, former girlfriend, or friends since his imprisonment.

Brian indicated that he harbored no bad feelings toward his co-defendant. "He made a mistake. We both made mistakes. My feelings are the same. He's got to do his time, and I've got to do mine."

Brian told me that there were a number of ways in which the killing could have been prevented. "I could have never drove him out there. I could have never went with him that night, or I could have just stopped him before he did it . . . probably grabbed ahold of him and pushed him back and told him to stop."

The young man, however, had some ambivalence regarding the sentence he received. He believed that he deserved to be punished because he was a convicted felon and had violated his probation when he was arrested for the murder. However, he did not think he deserved 10 years of prison time because he did not commit the crime and the sentence he received exceeded the typical manslaughter sentence of 5 to 7 years. He related that his being at the scene where the victim was murdered was "something that just happened. It could have happened to anybody, being at the wrong place at the wrong time."

Brian indicated that he had committed other crimes because it was exciting. He acknowledged that he had used both alcohol and drugs excessively and that his substance abuse also contributed to his getting into trouble. "They altered the way I was thinking, and I wasn't in my right mind. That's probably why I was out there that night" when the man was beaten to death.

Review of Brian's Prison File

Correctional records corroborated Brian's statements. Staff evaluated Brian as "outstanding" with respect to his job and cabinetmaking. He received no disciplinary reports and was described as "a model inmate."

CASE COMMENTARY

Although Brian did not actively participate in the killing of Mr. Parks, several factors contributed to his being present at the murder. These included a history of substance abuse and dependence, apparent boredom and nothing constructive to do, and obvious poor judgment. Resource availability and personality characteristics, particularly when intertwined with the biological effects of alcohol and drugs, also help to explain the killing.

Making Sense of Murder

This homicide seemed completely senseless. As inebriated as Brian was, the adolescent could tell that, despite the victim's apparently brusque style and angry words, the man came out to see whether they had been hurt and needed help. It adds little to say that the man was murdered because these adolescents were "drunk out of their minds." Polls of drinking habits by high school students suggest that drinking and getting drunk at least once are common experiences among the youth of America. Obviously, relatively few of all those who imbibe to excess commit murder.

Mike reportedly consumed Valium, as well as excessive amounts of alcohol, shortly before the killing. These drugs in concert could have had a disinhibiting effect and clouded Mike's judgment. Although I did not evaluate Mike, I would hypothesize that he must have had a torrent of rage within him that exploded that night when he perceived the victim as challenging him. Mike's sense of self-esteem must have been poor for the man's remark to have triggered such a strong negative reaction from him.

Brian's failure to intervene to physically restrain Mike or to dissuade Mike from beating the victim apparently was due to extreme fear and anxiety combined with alcohol intoxication. He did not summon help for the victim for two apparent reasons. First, he was fairly certain that the victim was dead. Second, he remained flooded with fear and anxiety occasioned by witnessing the traumatic event of seeing his friend beat another human being to death.[1] He transported Mike away from the homicidal scene and failed to report the homicide to the police officer who asked him for identification shortly thereafter at a nearby store for similar reasons.

Prognosis

The prognosis for Brian remained good at follow-up. He has accepted some responsibility for the death of Mr. Parks by acknowledging that he did not attempt to restrain his co-defendant. He also was aware that excessive use of alcohol and drugs affected his judgment in general and on the night of the murder in particular. Although he felt that the sentence he received for being an accessory to manslaughter was too harsh given the circumstances, he did not seem to harbor negative feelings toward anyone. He indicated that he has made conscious decisions to maintain an exemplary record in prison because he has realized that it is up to him to make something of his life.

Part Three

The Challenge of
Juvenile Homicide

THE ESCALATION in juvenile homicide in the United States since the mid-1980s is a painful societal problem. Whether we measure the problem in the number of dead bodies or the number of young offenders spending much, if not most, of their lives behind bars, the situation is tragic. If we include those who have been affected by the increase in killings by adolescents, then the numbers rise exponentially. How do we count all of the family members and friends of the victims who must deal with the permanent losses of their loved ones? How do we estimate the number of family members, friends, teachers, and acquaintances of the killers who anguish over whether something they could have done or said would have stopped this course of destructiveness? How do we put an actual number on the people who experience terror when they see a group of juveniles walking down the street or congregating in a shopping mall? How do we comprehend the extent to which thousands, and perhaps millions, of children and adults go to sleep at night in terror and begin their day with apprehension, occasioned by the perception that the world in which they live is increasingly populated by young "super predators"?

If we as a nation and a people are in pain, then there is hope. Looked at dispassionately, pain is our friend. It signals us that something is wrong and needs immediate attention. If juvenile homicide is conceptualized for a moment as a traumatic injury, then the United States is in the intensive care unit of a hospital. If we do not do something fast and meaningful as a nation, then we will continue to suffer, we will come to despair, and, yes, we might eventually self-destruct as a society.

The beauty is that we can identify multilevel factors that have contributed to this crisis situation. Although these variables are primarily psychological and sociological, they can, and on occasion do, interact with biological factors. The final two chapters take into account the previously discussed situational factors, societal influences, resource

219

availability, personality characteristics of juvenile murderers, and their cumulative effects in responding to the problem of juvenile homicide.

These two chapters are among the most important in this book and hold the key to success in reducing adolescent violence in the 21st century. They address the treatment of juvenile murderers and the implementation of prevention strategies to reduce the phenomenon of adolescent homicide. These chapters focus largely on psychological and sociological measures to decrease youth violence because these approaches have the most potential to effect change on a widespread level. Taken together, the remaining chapters provide hope that youth violence can be decreased through better socialization of children and more effective resocialization of young lawbreakers. They discuss how parents, our social and legal institutions, and our communities can improve the means that each employs to socialize children and resocialize those youths who have broken laws and transgressed other important social norms.

Chapter 12 presents data that indicate that most juvenile murderers will be released back into society. The young killers' reflections about life in prison suggest that if prisoners today rehabilitate themselves, then they do so in spite of prison rather than because of it. The chapter reviews the treatment literature pertaining to juvenile homicide. Thereafter, I am joined by Eldra Solomon, a licensed psychologist, as we extrapolate from successful interventions with serious delinquents to discuss components that need to be included in designing effective treatment strategies for young killers. The bottom line is that the likelihood of juvenile homicide offenders reoffending after they are returned to society is lessened with a multifaceted treatment approach. From a public safety perspective, treating young killers makes sense.

The final chapter addresses what can be done to reverse the upward surge in murders by today's juveniles. The solutions discussed in Chapter 13 are based on theoretical considerations, empirical demonstrations, and the insights of the young killers themselves. It is clear from these sources that for societal change to be significant and lasting, it must include parents, the educational system, communities, government leaders, medical and mental health professionals, the media, and individuals joining together to raise a healthier next generation and to build a more peaceful society.

Chapter Twelve

Treating Young Killers

with Eldra P. Solomon, Ph.D.

A TROUBLED 15-year-old girl who had been arrested for car theft was released from the local juvenile detention center after a brief stay on Thanksgiving Day. While many in her community were gathered happily with family and friends over a holiday meal, this adolescent was celebrating her reentry into society by driving her boyfriend around in another stolen car. The police spotted her driving recklessly through the streets and, when she did not stop the car, they gave chase. Moments later, the girl ran a red light and smashed her car into a vehicle carrying three people, killing two of them and seriously injuring the third.

Subsequent investigation revealed that this teenager had been considered "a good kid" and a model student up until about 2 years prior to the traffic fatalities. At 13 years of age, however, her life began to unravel. She started hanging out with older adolescents, lost interest in school, and ignored her parents' dictates. She reportedly drank alcohol and smoked marijuana on a daily basis and experimented with cocaine, LSD, PCP, and psilocybin (mushrooms). During a 14-month period, she racked up 16 charges, the most serious of which had been for auto theft and burglary. In response to these delinquent behaviors, the youth was detained for brief periods at the juvenile detention facility and was repeatedly placed on probation. Meaningful treatment, however, was not part of the intervention package.

In the instant or presenting case, the girl was tried as an adult and convicted of two counts of vehicular homicide. Her tears and anguish over the senseless deaths that she had caused appeared genuine. The judge who presided over her trial, however, showed her no mercy. He sentenced her to 35 years in prison in a state where, by law, adult violent offenders must serve 85% of their sentences. In signing a commitment order that would ensure that the girl spent at least 29½ years in adult prison, the judge proclaimed that it was too late for rehabilitation when two people have died. He maintained that the girl needed to be seriously punished and "taken out of circulation."[1]

The disposition given to this adolescent might strike some readers as extreme. It is an excellent example, however, of the "get tough" approach increasingly being taken

AUTHORS' NOTE: This chapter is based on a paper titled "Intervention Strategies With Juvenile Homicide Offenders," presented by the authors at the 1996 annual meeting of the American Society of Criminology, Chicago, November.

by judges presiding over cases of youths convicted of violent crimes. Uppermost in the minds of many judges today is the need to protect members of a society who are frustrated over the escalation in juvenile violence and who increasingly report fearing their young.[2]

Decrying rehabilitation for violent teens is now a popular stance in the United States.[3] However, this position is, in many respects, shortsighted. In his attempt to send a message to society, the judge did not account for the fact that this youth, like most young killers, is going to get out of prison someday.

It is true that more adolescent murderers today are being transferred to stand trial in adult court than in the past. However, very few youths who are found guilty of homicide in the adult criminal justice system are sentenced to life in prison without the possibility of parole, and even fewer are sentenced to death.[4] The reality is that, whether juvenile or adult sanctions are imposed, most adolescent murderers will be eligible for release back into society.[5] Will these individuals be better equipped to handle life stressors and to resolve conflicts peacefully when they return to the community months or years later? Or, will they pose an even greater risk to the public on reentry?

Follow-up data that I collected on 59 juveniles who were committed to the adult Department of Corrections in Florida for murder or attempted murder during the period January 1982 through January 1984[6] are telling in this regard. These data indicated that by May 1995, although many of these adolescents had received lengthy sentences, only 19 never had been released from prison. Of this group, more than one third had incurred additional commitments while incarcerated. In addition, 5 had escaped from prison and 2 had acquired additional convictions for violent crimes.

Of the 40 juveniles who had been released, more than half (21) had been recommitted to prison during the available follow-up period. Of these, 4 had been returned to prison for violations of parole, and 15 of the remaining 17 had been recommitted to the Department of Corrections for violent crimes. Collectively, these 15 individuals were found guilty of one second-degree murder, two manslaughters, four robberies, six battery offenses, and three charges of carrying concealed weapons. The remaining 2 offenders were returned to prison for drug-related offenses. Interestingly, 8 of the 15 violent offenders also were convicted of drug-related charges.

LIFE IN PRISON

The young killers whose stories are profiled in this book, although incarcerated at many different institutions, painted a similarly disturbing picture of prison. Some readers might question the reliability of this information, given its sources, and wonder about its generalizability to prisons nationwide. As shocking as it might seem, their depiction of life behind bars is consistent with the research literature available on prison life. This literature, which now spans more than 40 years, indicates widespread abuses in the system and very little rehabilitation of prisoners.[7]

The Conditions of Confinement

The young killers related that alcohol typically is easy to get in prison. Although usually made by the inmates themselves, in some facilities it is smuggled in by inmates on work squad or by visitors. Drugs, particularly marijuana, also often are readily obtainable. Correctional officers were identified by several of the young men as the primary source of the drug trade in prison.

Consistent with the existing research literature on prison environments,[8] the threat of violence loomed large in the life of the young killers throughout their incarceration. Malcolm related that he had seen "major violence at every institution" in which he had been incarcerated and considered violence as "a part of being in here." Peter related at follow-up that there had been three stabbings, as well as several fights, at his prison during the previous 7 months.

Mark's comments were especially illuminating. The reader will recall from Chapter 3 that Mark had spent 8 years on death row before his sentence was commuted to life in prison. Mark indicated that violence is "a daily concern but not a daily occurrence," adding that there is "always a potential for it."

The young killers maintained that inmates must be prepared to use violence when necessary. Calvin explained that "in here, you can't let anybody take advantage of you. One do it, another will try." David related that violence is "all about respect" and necessitated when "somebody [is] trying to get over" on another. Jerry divided the prison population into "predators and prey" and "people who are off to the side." He stressed that "you have to be rude and mean or you get walked all over."

Fights often were sparked by small incidents blown out of proportion. Joel stated that inmates fight over "mundane, stupid, ignorant things." He recalled an incident in which two inmates fought after one stepped on the other's foot. Both men had been drinking.

Several of the young killers noted that small fights often escalated into group fights. Sometimes, the opposing sides were members from different gangs. More often, inmates from one city were battling against those from another locale. Fights were seen as affected by race rather than caused by it.

The young men depicted homosexual conduct as widespread in prison. Although much of it was consensual, violence was involved in many instances. Joel saw homosexual behavior as "predominantly consensual or fear gets the best of him [the other person]. Most people don't want to fight." Mark acknowledged that when he got off death row, he got "pressured and caved in." After 6 months, Mark got disgusted with himself and checked into protective confinement. When he was transferred to another institution, this news went with him and he had to let it be known that he was willing to fight. Malcolm maintained that if an inmate does not fight, his manhood will be taken from him.

The young killers noted that young inmates, particularly those who were White and small, were the most at risk for homosexual victimization. Calvin explained that three or four inmates will force sex on an inmate, who gets "turned out." The next time, he will submit rather than be taken by force. David saw violence as also growing out of homosexual liaisons because men become possessive of their male lovers. Mark noted that inmates often talk about homosexual behavior, particularly as inmates with AIDS have become more common in prison.

Some of the inmates reported theft as a major problem. Peter found it to be an "everyday occurrence." Brian related that "it happens all the time." Malcolm also saw theft as a frequent event and indicated that inmates had two choices: fight or accommodate. Jerry believed that theft was more common in juvenile dorms. Mark viewed inmates as most vulnerable for theft when their status is new in prison or at a new institution.

Rehabilitation in the Prison Environment

The young killers did not see prison as a rehabilitating force. As Mark noted, "It's not the prison system that is gonna change anybody, it's the individual." Mark felt that the prison system could do more to help inmates by providing comprehensive educational opportunities and paying them a reasonable wage for their work. "Pay us and let us contribute to our upkeep. . . . Most of us want to be responsible, but we are not allowed to be responsible."

Mark's mother related that "the longer he stays there [in prison], the less ready he will be" and "the worse off it is for society." She pointed out that if Mark is released when he becomes eligible after serving a 25-year mandatory sentence, he will be over 40 years old. He will have no work history, no social security benefits, no college degree, and no significant vocational education. He will return to a community that consisted of horse farms when he left it at 17 years of age. Today, it is a metropolis.

As a group, the young men felt that long sentences were inconsistent with treating offenders and preparing them for reentry into society. Jerry explained,

> You have to rehabilitate yourself. If after 10 years in prison, somebody is still getting into trouble on a regular basis and still shows the same pattern of behavior, they are never going to get right. I believe that after 10 years in this situation, and then if after 10 years somebody has shown good and they are trying and learning from it, [they are on the right track]. Anything over 10 years is just counterproductive.

It has become fashionable since the 1970s to decry treatment efforts as futile. Martinson's claim in 1974 that "nothing works" when it comes to the rehabilitation of juvenile delinquents was embraced by many criminal justice agents, politicians, and the public. However, more rigorous analyses conducted in the late 1970s and 1980s indicated that rehabilitation can be effective and that many treatment programs do work. Palmer's synthesis of these "meta-analyses," published in 1992, indicated that "behavioral, cognitive-behavioral, skill-oriented or life skills, multimodal, and family intervention" were the most successful treatment strategies among those studied.[9]

As we approach the 21st century, there is a heightened awareness of the need for effective treatment for violent youths. The Office of Juvenile Justice and Delinquency Prevention (OJJDP) has maintained through the 1990s that "effective programs for rehabilitating violent juvenile offenders must be developed."[10] The OJJDP devised a "Comprehensive Strategy for Serious, Violent, and Chronic Offenders."[11] The initiative incorporated both prevention and intervention components in an effort to reduce juvenile delinquency and to manage juvenile crime more effectively.[12] The experts who devised the comprehensive strategy conceptualized an effective model for treating juvenile offenders as combining "accountability and sanctions with increasingly intensive treatment and rehabilitation."[13]

Following a brief review of the treatment literature, attention in this chapter focuses on the theoretical tenets that differentiate types of adolescent murderers. One of my colleagues, a licensed psychologist, and I discuss treatment strategies for young killers based on our clinical experiences and empirically based programs that work and those that do not. In so doing, we are mindful of the words of Susan Bailey, a British psychiatrist, who has successfully treated juvenile murderers in England.[14]

While others debate the issues of whether those children facing charges of murder, manslaughter, or attempted murder should be locked up, whether treatment is worth - while, what their rights are and how these balance against those of the victim and victim's family, whether we have adequate legal and administrative procedures, and finally, what the appropriate interventions post-trial may be, the individual clinician and immediate responsible caretakers have to set about the long-term task of rehabili - tation.[15]

■ THE TREATMENT OF YOUNG KILLERS: A SYNTHESIS OF THE LITERATURE

The literature on treating adolescent murderers is sparse and suffers from the same problems as does the general literature on juvenile homicide[16] and violent juvenile delinquents.[17] Most of the treatment results are based on clinical case reports of a few cases referred to the respective authors for evaluation and/or treatment.[18] The extent to which these cases of juvenile murderers are representative of the population of young killers is unknown.[19] In addition, the interventions used often are not based on established therapeutic principles or on empirically documented successes.[20] In addition, programs frequently are not tailored to the type of juvenile murderer.

Despite the fact that most young killers will be released back into society, few receive any type of mental health treatment following the homicides. In fact, the likelihood of juvenile murderers receiving intensive psychiatric intervention appears to diminish as they enter adolescence.[21] University of Florida psychiatrist Wade Myers summarized the literature on the treatment of homicidal youths by focusing on four main areas: psychotherapy, psychiatric hospitalization, institutional placement, and the use of psychopharmacological agents.[22]

Psychotherapy with aggressive youths generally has been viewed with pessimism.[23] The overriding assumption among many clinicians has been that juvenile homicide offenders are antisocial and, hence, are not good candidates for psychotherapeutic interventions. It is important to remember, however, that not all young killers have extensive delinquent or violent histories or antisocial character structures. Available evidence does indicate that psychotherapy can be effective with some adolescents who have engaged in violence,[24] even murder.[25] Preliminary data suggest that psychotherapy may be an effective treatment for conduct-disordered youths who meet the diagnostic criteria for the undifferentiated type, have prior emotional relationships with their victims, and are suicidal.[26]

Among those who have worked with juvenile homicide offenders, psychotherapy, including art therapy,[27] generally is considered to be an important component of treatment with this population. Offenders likely to benefit from interventions of this nature are higher maturity youths, particularly those who are capable of self-examination and introspection and of forming emotional relationships with others. Youths unlikely to do well with this approach include those with low intelligence, limited insight, and aggressive behavioral response patterns. Therapeutic gains typically do not come quickly, even among those who are amenable to psychotherapy, because these youths generally have been raised in chaotic and abusive environments and are slow to trust the therapist.[28]

Psychiatric hospitalization, although commonly used for "little kids" who kill, rarely is used for adolescent murderers. Unlike the homicidal child who typically is viewed as psychologically disturbed,[29] the adolescent killer generally is regarded as antisocial and is likely to be institutionalized in a facility for juvenile delinquents or adult criminals. Adolescents are more likely to be hospitalized if they appear psychotic, remain homicidal, or need intensive psychopharmacological management. Inpatient treatment can be particularly helpful in stabilizing the youths, redirecting their homicidal impulses, and reducing their internal conflicts.[30] In addition, it can provide an optimal setting for evaluating the youths, assessing their potential for continued violent behavior, and understanding the family systems of which they are members.[31]

Institutional placement in juvenile offender programs is a more typical disposition if the adolescent murderer is retained in the juvenile justice system rather than transferred to the adult criminal justice system to stand trial. Mental health care in juvenile facilities, as well as in adult prisons, typically is minimal due to financial constraints and limited awareness of the psychological needs of this population. Despite the lack of treatment, institutional placement appears to have been effective in many cases, as measured by the lack of commission of serious crimes after release.[32]

Myers discussed four reasons for the apparent success of these "preventive detention" programs. Two of these reasons involve normal maturational processes. First, while the youth is institutionalized, "further neurodevelopmental, cognitive, and emotional growth" may occur, thus enabling the adolescent to acquire "better control of his [or her] emotions and aggressive impulses."[33] Second, youths who are contained in a safe and prosocial environment may simply "outgrow" their antisocial behavior over time. Third, for some youths, the homicidal acts of violence were atypical and isolated events, largely the result of extreme circumstances and/or psychological difficulties, and "would never be repeated" regardless of the court disposition or treatment provided. Fourth, for other youths, the program components, treatment agents, and therapeutic setting had a positive effect on their character structures and behavioral responses. For example, Muriel Gardiner, a psychiatrist who worked extensively with homicidal youths, found that those who made successful adjustments to society when released had learned vocations, had strong social support systems and had developed meaningful relationships, and did not return to the unhealthy environments in which they had lived prior to the killings.[34]

Several researchers have expressed concern that institutional programs emphasize behavioral control and conformity to the institutional regime, rather than individualized and specialized treatment of the youthful offenders, as a measure of progress and success.[35] Myers argued persuasively for the development of a "corrective emotional experience" for a subgroup of juvenile murderers who have killed as a result of interpersonal conflict (Cornell, Benedek, and Benedek's conflict group) as opposed to furtherance of another crime (Cornell, Benedek, and Benedek's crime group).[36] This subgroup consists "primarily of youths with some degree of psychological problems (e.g., adjustment disorders, depression), disturbed family functioning, and concomitant stressful life events."[37] Myers recommended placement of these youths in a "therapeutically designed institution" staffed by sincerely interested, empathic, and supportive adults who would function as "prosocial role models" and set appropriate behavioral limits. The program should be tailored to ensure that each youth receives quality mental health care as well as educational and vocational programs that are consistent with his or her ability.[38]

Psychopharmacological management of some juvenile murderers holds promise, although empirical studies are lacking.[39] Researchers have hypothesized that several different neurological processes and biological conditions are linked to violent behavior. These include genetic influences, neurophysiological abnormalities, and malfunctioning of neurotransmitter systems and steroid hormones.[40] Myers, noting that many juvenile homicide offenders are conduct disordered, reviewed studies that evaluated the effectiveness of various drugs in reducing aggressive symptoms among this population.[41] There is some evidence that haloperidol (an antipsychotic drug), methylphenidate (a psychostimulant [Ritalin]), imipramine (a tricyclic antidepressant), and propanolol (an antihypertensive drug), as well as lithium and carbamazepine (both mood stabilizers), might be useful in treating certain conduct-disordered and aggressive children and adolescents.[42] The newer class of antidepressants known as selective serotonin reuptake inhibitors ("the SSRIs," e.g., Prozac, Zoloft, Paxil) also have been used with good results with violence-prone individuals.[43]

Benedek, Cornell, and Staresina discussed four classes of drugs that might be considered in the treatment of the homicidal adolescent, depending on the previous psychiatric history of the youth and his or her current clinical functioning. These consist of antidepressant, antianxiety, antipsychotic, and antimanic (mood stabilizer) medications. The authors advised that these medications, summarized in Table 12.1, must be carefully monitored for occasional paradoxical effects and for possible side effects.

Benedek, Cornell, and Staresina indicated that other medications, including "beta- and alpha-adrenergic blockers, anticonvulsants, calcium-channel blockers, and antiandrogen hormones," have not been proven to be effective in the treatment of violent adolescents or adults.[44] These authors advised that long-term use of psychotropic medication is most appropriate for youths who are severely mentally ill. Short-term use of antianxiety drugs may be correctly prescribed for youths who have killed due to interpersonal conflict. Use of medication for youths who have killed during the commission of felonies should be carefully considered in the context of possible histories of drug abuse and addiction.

Myers maintained that each of these four interventions can play an important role in the treatment of young killers. He advised that effective treatment planning for this population should include all of the possible factors that lead to murder. The family system, as well as the adolescent homicide offender, needs to be thoroughly evaluated. Intervention needs to target chemical abuse/dependency and neuropsychiatric vulnerabilities (e.g., language disorders, learning disabilities, psychomotor seizures) where indicated. Myers' conclusions in 1992 still can appropriately be taken as a call to action.

> Currently, there are no well-designed studies that have evaluated the use of any of these treatments for juvenile murderers. Research studies with long-term follow-up of more clearly defined subgroups of juvenile murderers are needed to determine the optimum treatment strategies for this heterogeneous group and also to help guide the juvenile and criminal justice systems in their handling of this population. [45]

Benedek, Cornell, and Staresina summarized the literature with respect to long-term outcomes of juvenile murderers.[46] They concluded that "with few exceptions, the limited follow-up information is surprisingly positive."[47] Young killers tend to make a satisfactory adjustment in prison and in the community after release from custody and tend to relate well to their families.

CHALLENGE OF JUVENILE HOMICIDE

TABLE 12.1 Medications That Might Be Appropriate in the Treatment of Homicidal Adolescents

Drug Category	Examples	Actions/Comments
Antidepressant	Imipramine, Zoloft, Prozac, Serzone	Preferred treatment for severely depressed young killers, whether their depression is long-standing or reactive to the homicides and their aftermath
Antianxiety	Valium, BuSpar, Xanax	Most effective with anxious and agitated adolescents
		May be prescribed on a short-term basis to facilitate youths' adjustment to confinement or to help calm them down
		May be appropriately prescribed for long-term control of agitation associated with more severe mental disorders, specifically schizophrenia, schizoaffective disorder, and bipolar (manic depressive) disorder
Antipsychotic	Phenothiazenes (e.g., Thorazine), Haldol, Clozaril, Risperdal	Typically prescribed for schizophrenia and mania
		May be properly given for the short-term control of aggression, agitation, paranoid ideation, or nonspecific psychotic disorder
		Use of these drugs for long-term sedation or behavior control or for sedating youths who present management difficulties is inappropriate
Antimanic	Lithium, Tegretol (Carbamazepine)	Also known as "mood stabilizers"
		Used to control manic symptomatology and to prevent the recurrence of bipolar episodes
		Although not well understood, these medications appear to have beneficial results when prescribed for individuals who explode with rage associated with hyperactivity, attention deficit disorder, or aggressive conduct disorder

SOURCES: Benedek, Cornell, and Staresina 1989; Preston and Johnson 1990; Myers 1992; American Psychiatric Association 1994.

Benedek, Cornell, and Staresina advised caution in extrapolating from these studies to the entire population of juvenile homicide offenders. These case studies frequently report on criminally unsophisticated youths who were involved in what appear to be isolated acts of violence, often involving intense interpersonal conflict with the victims.[48] Many specifically involved family members as victims. Perusal of follow-up reports on adolescent parricide offenders indicate that they typically make successful reentries into society.[49] Accordingly, the authors hypothesized that the outcomes for chronic delinquents who killed in the course of committing other crimes would be much less favorable in terms of recidivism and readjustment to society than for youths who killed in response to interpersonal conflicts. Extensive follow-up research on Canadian adolescent homicide offenders by Toupin confirmed that the 18 individuals in the "crime group" committed significantly more offenses, violent offenses, and serious offenses than did the 23 youths in the "conflict group" per year of stay since returning to the community.[50]

▥ TREATING TODAY'S ADOLESCENT HOMICIDE OFFENDER

The important question to ask is how treatment agents can decrease the likelihood that juvenile murderers (including those in the "crime group") who are charted for release will continue to commit crimes and to pose a threat to society. Successful intervention requires that treatment be tailored to youths' development and special needs. At the same time, effective programming must take into account the times and places in which youths live and the influences to which they are exposed.

In Chapter 2, 15 factors were identified that appear to have contributed to the escalation of juvenile homicide beginning in the mid-1980s. *Effective intervention and prevention strategies will take these variables into account.* The reader will recall that these variables were grouped into five categories: *situational factors* (the increase in child abuse and neglect and the absence of positive male role models), *societal influences* (the crisis in leadership and lack of heroes and the increased exposure to violence), *resource availability* (easier access to guns, the increasing involvement in alcohol and drugs, and the rise in poverty and lack of resources), *personality characteristics* of juvenile murderers (low self-esteem and the inability to deal with strong feelings, boredom, poor judgment, and prejudice and hatred), and their *cumulative effects* (little or nothing left to lose and the biological connection).[51]

These variables, particularly those subsumed under situational factors and societal influences, can have a negative effect on children's development and behavior. Accordingly, *personality development might be restricted and negative personality characteristics might be acquired.* For example, children who are abused or neglected might not bond with their caretakers or develop empathy for others. Instead, they might suffer from low self-esteem and vent their rage by attacking innocent people in society. Violent solutions are more likely to be used if mistreated youths have witnessed such behavior and have no adult role models in their lives who deal appropriately with their feelings. Concomitantly, the incidence of behavioral problems, often associated with the diagnoses of Conduct Disorder and Attention-Deficit/Hyperactivity Disorder (ADHD), is likely to increase, especially when these variables are combined with substance abuse and neurological deficits.

The Need for Differential Treatment

It has long been established in the correctional literature that not all juvenile and adult offenders are alike. Positive outcomes are more likely to occur when individuals are classified in ways that increase understanding of them and are then assigned to treatment programs appropriate to their developmental needs.[52]

Psychologist Vicki Agee worked extensively with chronic and serious delinquents, including some juvenile murderers, at the Closed Adolescent Treatment Center in Colorado. She designed an effective treatment program to work with youths she called "aversive treatment evaders" (ATEs). These are the kids within the population of disturbed youths who "combine hostile, aggressive, acting-out behaviors with an amazing resistance to change, usually to the point that some frustrated treater terms them 'incorrigible' or 'untreatable.' "[53]

Agee found the Interpersonal Maturity Level (I-level) classification system to be the most relevant diagnostic system in working with ATEs. The reader will recall that the I-level system was discussed in Chapter 4 and used as a diagnostic tool in each of the case studies presented in this book. Agee classified the I-level subtypes into expressive and instrumental categories and separated ATEs into these two subgroups for intervention purposes. Evaluation indicated that the program was successful, when measured against a control group, in meeting treatment goals and in reducing recidivism. It also was cost-efficient.

The treatment process for juvenile murderers, although consisting of the same phases as the program for other ATEs, differed in focus and was more intense. *Agee's experiences indicated that youths who killed differed in some important ways from other violent youths.* Young killers typically minimized their homicidal and delinquent behavior, presented with strong defenses that protected them from painful feelings, and had fragile egos. Intervention strategies were designed to help these youths to truly acknowledge responsibility for their homicidal behavior, to identify and process feelings associated with the killing and the course of their lives (e.g., remorse, pain, sadness, fear, anger), and to rebuild their egos through education in life skills and social skills training.[54]

Components of Effective Intervention

In 1995, Agee identified 11 components of effective intervention with juveniles in correctional settings. She selected these elements based on her review of the literature[55] and on more than 20 years of clinical experience with residential treatment programs for juvenile delinquents, many of whom she characterized as emotionally disturbed. These components are (1) effective and extensive assessment using a variety of data sources; (2) comprehensive cognitive behavioral programming or restructuring; (3) prosocial skills training; (4) positive peer communities; (5) anger management; (6) empathy training; (7) clear, firm, and consistent discipline; (8) drug and alcohol abuse counseling and education; (9) transition, including family counseling when appropriate; (10) intensive and extended aftercare; and (11) medication when necessary. We add a 12th component to Agee's list: educational and vocational programs and other activities that promote prosocial opportunities for success.

These 12 strategies are consistent with the therapeutic recommendations discussed by Bailey[56] and the conclusions drawn by researchers who evaluated the effectiveness of treatment programs specifically targeting violent juvenile delinquents.[57] The components can be blended easily with one another in several ways. Most can be implemented in individual, family, or group therapy. Some components, such as social skills training and empathy training, can be taught in psychoeducational forums and also used in therapy sessions. Examination of these components also suggests that beneficial interaction effects can be expected. For example, peer communities will likely be more positive influences on their members when the discipline is clear, firm, and consistent and when members know how to deal with anger and are equipped with prosocial skills.

When dealing with adolescent murderers, in most cases, it is therapeutically desirable that treatment take place in a secure and structured facility.[58] The community must be protected while the youth is facing the effects of his or her actions on others and learning more adaptive coping strategies and ways of looking at life.

TABLE 12.2 Information Needed to Design Appropriate Treatment
_____

- Degree of disclosure to interviewers of offending behavior
- Personal responsibility for offending behavior
- Degree of aggression and level of violence
- Frequency and duration of offenses
- Targets of the offender/victim characteristics
- Other abusive, addictive, or compulsive behaviors
- Length and progression of history of emotional disturbance
- Medical history, with special emphasis on any brain trauma or other neurological problems
- Social relationships
- Family system functioning
- History of sexual, physical, and emotional victimization
- Criminal arrests, convictions, and incarceration history
- School and employment history
- Treatment history
- Intellectual functioning
- Educational achievement
_____
SOURCE: Agee 1995, 178.

Effective and Extensive Assessment

Data need to be gathered from a variety of sources to ensure accurate evaluation and sound treatment planning. Relevant sources include clinical interviews with the client and his or her family, consultation with previous treatment agents, staff observations, psychological tests, medical charts, school records, and dependency history. Police and court data concerning the current offense and case processing, as well as prior record delinquent history, also are important.

Agee enumerated 16 factors, listed in Table 12.2, that should be obtained in the evaluation process. These data naturally include characteristics about the present offense and prior delinquent and dispositional history. Gang affiliation and the extensiveness of gang involvement also should be assessed in designing appropriate intervention strategies.[59] Given prior research findings, it is particularly important that young killers be medically evaluated, with particular emphasis on any brain trauma or neurological deficits. Intellectual functioning and educational achievement, as well as school and employment history, also must be assessed. Although rare, those juvenile homicide offenders who are mentally retarded or psychotic are best served in residential facilities specializing in these types of disorders.

Effective treatment planning requires that emotional and mental health issues, including those that involve drug and alcohol use, and treatment history also be carefully examined. The functioning of the youth's family system and the quality of social relationships should be explored. The possibility of sexual, physical, and/or emotional victimization needs to be skillfully investigated in light of previous studies.

The youth's history of victimization, as well as his or her offending behavior, must be addressed in the therapeutic process. One of the most consistent findings across studies of adolescent murderers, as discussed in Chapter 2, is the high prevalence of child maltreatment and other forms of trauma in this population. Psychological problems, drug and alcohol abuse, and delinquency are well-documented outcomes of victimized children and adolescents.[60]

Understanding the extent of trauma and its effects is important in forensic assessment and in treating offenders. Psychological trauma can be defined as the psychological effects of an event(s) that causes intense fear, helplessness, or horror and that overwhelms the normal coping and defense mechanisms. Elsewhere, we discussed the levels of trauma and their implications for assessment and treatment.[61]

Although the psychological effects of trauma are not always obvious, they are present both immediately and after many years.[62] Severe psychological trauma in childhood interferes with normal development and typically leads to symptoms of Posttraumatic Stress Disorder (PTSD), anxiety, fear, depression, anger, lack of trust, a negative view of the world, and little or no belief in a future.

Children who sustain severe trauma often are diagnosed as having Conduct Disorder, Attention Deficit Disorder, or Major Depression. After 18 years of age, they frequently are diagnosed as having Antisocial Personality Disorder or Borderline Personality Disorder (a long-standing pattern characterized by instability in interpersonal relationships, self-image, and emotions and by marked impulsivity). Some are diagnosed as schizophrenic (a psychotic thought disorder) or as having Bipolar Disorder (formerly manic depressive disorder).[63] In our clinical experience, when the trauma has been resolved by appropriate psychotherapy, many of the symptoms disappear.

Symptoms of PTSD are a common effect of psychological trauma. Adolescents with untreated PTSD typically show high anxiety, depression, increased aggression, and decreased restraint and impulse control. High levels of PTSD have been reported in abused youths[64] and in adolescents living in high-crime urban districts.[65] Studies indicate that more than half of adolescent violent offenders exhibit PTSD symptoms.[66]

Agee's intervention strategies—including cognitive behavioral programming, anger management, empathy training, and prosocial skills training—help youths to work through their own trauma rather than to anesthetize their consciousness with alcohol or drugs or to act out their rage with violence.[67] These intervention strategies can be used effectively in individual or group therapy.

Consistent with Agee's approach, we recommend that the youth's level of personality development be assessed at the beginning of therapy. Knowing how youths perceive themselves and their relation to others and to outside events often is critical to understanding the dynamics that led to the homicide. In general, the higher the level of personality development, the better the prognosis. Knowing the adolescent's developmental level also is very important in charting realistic and effective treatment goals and objectives.[68] Treatment strategies often need to be structured differently for low- versus high-maturity youths. For example, before low-maturity youths can feel remorse for their crimes and empathy for the victims and their families, they must come to see themselves as accountable for their actions and realize that they had choices available to them when they committed their homicides.

Comprehensive Cognitive Behavioral Restructuring

Adolescent homicide offenders need to become aware of the nature and content of their thoughts. They also need to know how their thoughts affect their behavior. For example, many juvenile offenders, particularly those who are gang members, have the belief that the world is a violent place. Given their negative perceptions of others, they believe that it is appropriate to carry weapons and to use them when they perceive it is necessary to do so. Some young killers believe that murder is the appropriate response to being "dissed" (disrespected) by someone. Others believe that killing is required when someone "breaks a rule" or does not follow their orders.

Juvenile homicide offenders must be encouraged to examine their beliefs about themselves, others, and the world. Negative, hostile, and violent beliefs must be challenged using cognitive strategies that have proven to be successful.[69] A youth who believes that he must fight someone who insults him, for example, would be encouraged to explore different ways in which to interpret the event and respond to it. Rather than perceiving that his manhood has been challenged and that he must fight, the youth might come to see the aggressor as stupid, insecure, and/or immature. Viewed in this way, the adolescent might then consider walking away, ignoring the remark, or shaking his head as alternatives that a smart, self-secure, and mature man might select in this situation. The youth might define these alternatives as superior options to punching the aggressor in the mouth and risking an escalation in violence and other potentially negative consequences such as serious injury, death, or incarceration.

Prosocial Skills Training

Confronting the juvenile's belief system is not sufficient to engender prosocial behavior. Adolescents who reach for a gun to end a dispute often lack self-control and do not possess adequate social skills or good judgment. Accordingly, they must be taught how to respond appropriately across situations and how to solve conflicts in a peaceful manner.[70] Goldstein developed a curriculum that teaches youths how to solve problems, manage feelings, and relate in interpersonal situations. Skill alternatives taught to deal with aggression, for example, include asking permission, sharing something, helping others, negotiating, using self-control, standing up for one's rights, responding to teasing, avoiding trouble with others, and staying out of fights.[71]

Positive Peer Communities

The treatment milieu is very important in the rehabilitation process. Young killers typically reflect the negative thoughts and behaviors of similarly situated peers. Accordingly, they are more likely to change their thoughts and behaviors in the desired prosocial direction if they are part of a positive peer environment. Staff must structure the treatment environment so that a positive peer culture can thrive. Juveniles are focused on what their peers do and say. Research indicates that youths are likely to behave responsibly and morally when they perceive that other adolescents are acting in a similar way. A positive peer culture can foster healthy role models and moral leadership and can encourage tolerance and respect for others.[72]

Anger Management

Many young killers have difficulty in dealing appropriately with strong feelings, particularly anger. Agee suggested that delinquent youths be taught to manage their anger rather than to express it. Agee made this recommendation based on research findings that suggested that venting anger might lead some people to become angrier. We agree that all juveniles need to learn adaptive ways in which to manage anger. Goldstein's techniques are effective in helping individuals to recognize the antecedents of anger and its physiological indicators, to learn alternative coping skills to use when provoked, and to become comfortable using these strategies through role-playing and other exercises.[73]

We make a distinction between anger management and emotional release. Some youths, particularly those with histories of severe trauma, also need to be encouraged to express their feelings, including anger, in a safe environment. Emotional discharge can be conceptualized as a three-phase process: facilitating the feeling; encouraging its recognition, acknowledgment, and expression; and validating its expression. Techniques to encourage emotional discharge require specialized training by a therapist.[74]

Empathy Training

Young killers often have no feelings for their victims and their families. Low-maturity offenders often see their victims not as people but rather as objects to overcome in their paths to gratification. Even many high-maturity youths might appear fairly unconcerned about "the guy who died." A frequent response to how they feel about the person who died is, "I don't really have any feelings about him. I didn't know him."

Empathy enables a person to feel what another is feeling and to understand what another individual is feeling and why he or she is feeling that way.[75] Empathy training is designed to help an individual feel a sense of connection with others. The juvenile delinquent is encouraged to see the victim as a human being, as someone's son/daughter or father/mother. Several approaches to teaching victim empathy currently exist.[76] Empathy training, as well as cognitive behavioral programming, prosocial skills training, and anger management, is optimally implemented in a positive peer culture.

Clear, Firm, and Consistent Discipline

Juvenile homicide offenders often have not had limits imposed on them and have not been exposed to positive male role models. As a result, they often lack self-control and self-discipline. Mark commented on the need for sanctions for wrongdoing by parents and by the juvenile justice system. He was one of many young killers who believed that if something had been done to help him when he was involved in minor delinquency, his criminal behavior would not have escalated to the level of armed robbery and murder.

> As a juvenile, there were no penalties. I would shoplift, go before a judge, and he would send me home. I would shoplift again and go before a judge, and he would send me home. . . . The greatest extent that was done to me, I was told to go to group therapy, and then the therapist got locked up.

Mark related that when he was caught shooting into a building and charged with criminal mischief, he was fined. His mother paid the money because he did not have it. Mark recalled, "That didn't mean anything to me," and he continued to believe that he could do anything he wanted without negative results affecting him.

Setting boundaries and enforcing limits are critical for the personal growth of the individual youth as well as for the success of the program. Agee advised against providing "the nurturing, nonconforming model" found in traditional mental health settings to emotionally disturbed youths or those with histories of severe behavioral problems.

Agee maintained that effective programming requires that the structure of a program and the group norms designed to promote socialization be clearly stated. In addition, major and minor offenses need to be explicitly indicated, including those that will not be tolerated.

> Juveniles need to know the consequences for unacceptable behavior. Consequences must be prompt, relevant, effective, humane, and *extremely consistent.* Because many juveniles in this population have had success in avoiding consequences by intimidating others or by manipulating others to rescue them, consistency is perhaps the most important component.[77]

Drug and Alcohol Abuse Counseling and Education

Research has indicated that chemical abuse and dependency are common among adolescent homicide offenders. Thorough assessment and effective intervention are critical with this population. Youths need to be informed about direct and indirect effects of alcohol and drugs from the standpoint of users and often from the perspective of children of alcoholics or drug addicts.[78]

Transition, Including Family Counseling When Appropriate

Provisions must be made to prepare the young killer for increased responsibility and freedom attendant with his or her reentry into the community.[79] Depending on the youth's sentence, release may take place when the young killer still is an adolescent or when he or she is well into the adult years. Prior to the young killer's return to society, family counseling might be advisable, particularly if the homicide offender is going to resume living with family members. The youth and family members should have the opportunity to work through the anger, shame, and blame that they share and feel about the murder and each other.[80]

Participation in overnight or weekend furloughs, work-release programs, or halfway house programs can assist in making the transition to the outside world easier for the offender. The offender, regardless of age, probably will need assistance in basic life skills such as interviewing for a job, managing a checkbook, budgeting, making friends, dating, explaining the interval in his or her life due to incarceration, and other "routine" activities.[81]

Intensive and Extended Aftercare

Provisions for continued supervision are essential. It must be remembered that juvenile homicide offenders often have long-standing multifaceted problems. Residential treatment or institutionalization ideally will help them understand their difficulties more clearly and develop more effective prosocial coping strategies. However, many of these offenders still will require substantial services and support on release. Intensive aftercare programs are needed to help high-risk offenders to develop the skills and opportunities needed to interact successfully in the community with "targeted community support systems" such as peers, schools, employers, and families.[82]

Medication When Necessary

Medication could be added to this list in cases of youths with ADHD, Major Depression or Bipolar Disorder, psychotic disorders, or Substance Dependence. Agee advised that when youths are diagnosed with Conduct Disorder or Oppositional Defiant Disorder, effective intervention requires that a clinician determine the cause of the behavior. "It is important to find out whether the juvenile is reacting to a situational conflict (such as family conflict), is being influenced by a negative subculture, or is responding to an underlying organicity such as ADHD, depression, substance abuse, or organic brain syndrome."[83] As pharmacological therapies advance, the use of medication that reduces craving for nonopiate illegal drugs and the potential for violent behavior during withdrawal from opiate addiction also might be explored in working with drug-addicted homicidal youths.[84]

*Educational and Vocational Programs
and Other Activities That Promote
Prosocial Opportunities for Success*

Many young killers are illiterate, are academically deficient, lack job skills, and have few, if any, recognized positive accomplishments. Effective intervention requires that they know how to read and achieve their high school general equivalency diplomas (GEDs). They need to learn viable legal ways in which to earn an economically sufficient living. In addition, they need to be able to participate in other activities in which they can succeed. Involvement in prosocial activities can raise the self-esteem of these youths and provide something constructive for them to do. In addition, their participation in conventional activities can lead them to have "stakes in conformity" and result in their thinking that they have something to lose in going back to criminal activity.[85]

▪ CONCLUDING REMARKS

Recently released government reports also have concluded that there is a need for specialized treatment programs for different types of juvenile offenders. In its March 1996 report titled *Combating Violence and Delinquency*, the Coordinating Council on Juvenile Justice and Delinquency Prevention maintained that graduated sanctions for delinquents are appropriate. These sanctions, described at length in the June 1995 *Guide for Implementing the Comprehensive Strategy for Serious, Violent, and Chronic Juvenile Offenders*, range from "immediate intervention for first-time delinquent offenders (misdemeanors and nonviolent felonies) and many nonviolent repeat offenders"; to "intermediate sanctions for many first-time serious and repeat offenders and some violent offenders"; to "secure corrections for many serious, violent, and chronic offenders."[86]

The coordinating council noted that "as the severity of sanctions increases, so must the intensity of treatment."[87] It did not embrace "large, concrete-care juvenile facilities such as training schools, camps, and ranches" because of their demonstrated ineffectiveness in rehabilitating juvenile delinquents. Rather, "small, community-based facilities providing intensive treatment services and special programming in a secure environment" were viewed as "the best hope" for youths who needed a structured facility. These services include "individual and group counseling, educational and training programs, medical services, and intensive staff supervision." Community-based programs allow for regular family participation in the treatment process, independent living, and a gradual reintegration into the community.[88]

The coordinating council reserved placement in training schools, camps, and ranches for youths who could not be safely contained in a community-based facility. In addition to being accredited by the American Correctional Association, these facilities should provide "comprehensive treatment programs that focus on reversing criminal behavior patterns through education, health, skills development, victim impact awareness, teen parenting, and vocational or employment training and experience."[89]

Treatment programs will not succeed when there is client or institutional resistance. As noted by Bailey, "Any programme, regardless of theoretical base, has to be vigorously and properly implemented with planning for content, resources, and trained staff that can undertake assessment and move onto a programme that has treatment integrity."[90] A few treatment programs that target the violent juvenile offender in secure correctional settings have been shown to be effective.[91] One of these, the Capital Offender Program, appears unique in its exclusive focus on juvenile murderers and is described in Box 12.1.

There undoubtedly are some youths who never should be released. These are the ones who are so badly damaged that rehabilitation appears highly unlikely. These are the adolescents who, if released to society (even as adults), are likely to kill again. Can these youths be successfully identified at the times of assessment? Our clinical experiences suggest that they cannot be.

It takes years for some youths to get to the point where they acknowledge what they have done and begin the long road to recovery. Without treatment, the odds are against young killers rehabilitating themselves. With treatment, the outcome, at least at the onset, is unknown in many cases. Continuing assessment of need and risk is necessary and imperative prior to releasing violent offenders from incarceration.[92]

It is unequivocal that society fears the return of young killers to the community. What might be surprising to many is that the young killers also expressed fear about their getting out of prison. David expressed anxiety that society would look at his past behavior. He noted that his prison number always would be with him, and he anticipated that his murder charge would make it even harder for him to be accepted back into the community. Malcolm was worried that he would receive fewer opportunities because he had been to prison. Joel thought that it might be difficult for him to interact easily with "free people." Mark was concerned about finding work because the skills he learned in prison were limited in a technologically complex society. Jerry expressed apprehension about getting established and becoming independent and self-supporting. Brian related that it would be difficult to be able "to be your own self, do what you want to do, instead of having somebody over top of you all the time."

When asked what could be done to make it easier for them to return to society, the young killers and their mothers repeatedly mentioned helping them get jobs on release. Providing more educational opportunities in prison also was identified as important. Participation in work-release programs and living in halfway houses were viewed as effective ways in which to bridge the transition from prison to the community. Calvin hoped that people would accept that offenders like him had paid their debt to society and would give them a chance to prove themselves. Malcolm appeared to speak for the group when he said he wanted "a fair shot at surviving" and for "people to believe I can change."

BOX 12.1   Capital Offender Program

The Capital Offender Program (COP), located at Giddings State Home and School in Texas, is designed for juveniles committed for homicide. Most program participants spend 2½ to 3 years at this facility. To participate in COP, youths must have been incarcerated at Giddings for a minimum of 1 year. They must have at least 6 months of time prior to discharge from Giddings to participate in the program. In addition, they must be at either a senior or prerelease level. Those who are diagnosed as being mentally retarded, psychotic, or having a pervasive developmental disorder (e.g., autism) are ineligible.

COP is an intensive group treatment program involving two groups of eight juveniles and two or three staff members per group. Each group of youths lives together in a cottage. They meet twice a week for approximately 3 hours per session over a 16-week period. Each group is run by a Ph.D.-level psychologist and a master's-level co-therapist who receive special training prior to program involvement. Psychologists also provide individual counseling for youths on an as-needed basis.

COP's primary goals are "to promote verbal expression of feelings, to foster empathy for victims, to create a sense of personal responsibility, and to decrease feelings of hostility and aggression" (Howell 1995b, 157). Treatment consists of group therapy with an emphasis on role-playing. Participants are required to role-play their life histories and to reenact the murders from both the offenders' and victims' perspectives.

The Texas Youth Commission has evaluated personality changes of the youths while in the program as well as postrelease outcomes. Youths became significantly less hostile and aggressive, assumed more responsibility, and had more empathy for their victims during program involvement.

Recidivism was measured by comparing rearrest and reincarceration rates of COP participants to those of a control group of untreated juvenile homicide offenders who were not treated due to space limitations at 1- and 3-year intervals. Known initial differences in recidivism propensities were statistically removed to ensure that differences between the groups were due to treatment effects. The Texas Youth Commission reported, in its first annual report released in December 1996, that specialized treatment for juvenile homicide offenders reduced the likelihood of capital offenders being arrested for a violent crime within a year after release by 52.9%.

Subsequent data indicated that juvenile homicide offenders who received treatment were less likely to be rearrested and reincarcerated than their nontreated counterparts at 1- and 3-year follow-up periods. Compared to controls, treated capital offenders were 16% less likely to be rearrested at both 1- and 3-year intervals. Juvenile homicide offenders in the treated group were 70% and 43% less likely to be reincarcerated within 1- and 3-year periods, respectively, compared to untreated capital offenders.

SOURCES: Howell 1995b; Texas Youth Commission 1996, 1997.

Chapter Thirteen

Reducing Youth Violence in the 21st Century

REVERSING THE increasing trend toward death and destructiveness by juveniles in the United States is a difficult task. As demonstrated in the case studies in this book, the conditions that lead to homicide are multifaceted and must be confronted if change is to be effected. On a macro level, situational factors, societal influences, and the resources available to youths must be addressed to curtail youth violence, of which homicide is the most extreme form.

In the 1990s, we have seen child maltreatment reach an epidemic proportion. Positive male role models have become fewer in number in American families and in neighborhoods across the country. As we approach the millennium, strong moral leaders and heroes have become harder to identify. Our society has become increasingly saturated with violence. The number of children growing up in poverty has increased. Sadly, many youths today have far easier access to violent images, gangs, guns, and drugs than to prosocial role models, good education, and part-time jobs.

Against this societal backdrop are literally millions of youths, each of whom has a unique biology, developmental history, and personality. On a micro level, individuals' personality characteristics and biological vulnerabilities must be evaluated in the total equation.[1] The effect of these extrinsic and intrinsic variables, as we have seen, often is cumulative. Youths who have low self-esteem, who cannot deal with strong negative feelings, who exercise poor judgment, who are chronically bored, and/or who are prejudiced toward others are at higher risk of acting maladaptively than are emotionally healthier, happier, and more confident youths. Adolescents who are genetically or neurologically impaired (e.g., Attention-Deficit/Hyperactivity Disorder, brain injury) are more likely to behave impulsively than are youths who are biologically normal.

In the midst of the dire predictions of a U.S. epidemic in juvenile homicide in the near future, there is hope, commitment, and, most important, a blueprint for action. In 1993, the American Psychological Association's Commission on Youth and Violence drew the following conclusions after an exhaustive study of the causes of youth violence and potential solutions.[2]

> Psychology's message, however, is one of hope. The commission overwhelmingly con - cluded, on the basis of the body of psychological research on violence, that violence is not a random, uncontrollable, or inevitable occurrence. Many factors, both individual and social, contribute to an individual's propensity to use violence, and many of these factors are within our power to change. Although we acknowledge that the problem

of violence involving youth is staggering and that there are complex macrosocial, biomedical, and other considerations that must be addressed in a comprehensive response to the problem, there is overwhelming evidence that we can intervene effectively in the lives of young people to reduce or prevent their involvement in violence. [3]

The public health community also has taken a leading role in understanding the violence problem and in dealing with it effectively. The Centers for Disease Control and Prevention, schools of public health, state and local health departments, and other public health organizations are actively involved in developing effective policies, programs, and interventions for preventing violence. These efforts are being implemented in many communities in the United States in collaboration with a number of institutions, agencies, and groups, including law enforcement agencies, judges, businesses, medical care providers, schools, and community residents.[4]

In September 1994, President Bill Clinton signed into law the Violent Crime and Law Enforcement Act, legislation that expands federal assistance for comprehensive, community-based efforts to prevent crime. These programs reflect the importance of linking crime and violence prevention to local efforts that foster personal responsibility and enhance opportunity.[5] In October 1995, thousands attended the National Violence Prevention Conference Program titled "Bridging Science and Program" in Des Moines, Iowa. Participants included legislators, practitioners, educators, academicians, researchers, health care professionals, members from the law enforcement and justice communities, and private citizens.[6]

As we enter the 21st century, science has enabled us to identify risk factors associated with violence and delinquency at various developmental periods in children's lives, ranging from birth to adolescence.[7] Programs that have demonstrated effectiveness in reducing delinquency and that show promise for stemming the tide of youth violence have been recognized.[8] In addition, several reviews of methodologically sound evaluations of preventive interventions aimed at risk factors associated with delinquency, violence, and substance abuse are now available.[9] Research clearly indicates that reducing juvenile violence requires a multifaceted, coordinated approach in which the importance of early intervention is recognized.[10]

Several researchers have developed thorough and systematic approaches to curtail youth violence.[11] Some programs are geared to parents and their children from conception to 6 years of age,[12] whereas others are more appropriately targeted at children from age 6 through adolescence and at the communities in which they live.[13] It is beyond the scope of this chapter to discuss the many promising strategies aimed at high-risk youths at various developmental stages. The Office of Juvenile Justice and Delinquency Prevention's *Guide for Implementing the Comprehensive Strategy for Serious, Violent, and Chronic Juvenile Offenders*[14] and another document completed under its auspices, *Combating Violence and Delinquency,*[15] are invaluable publications to consult in designing and implementing programs to address risk factors associated with youth violence at the individual, family, school, peer, and community levels.

Another excellent resource, a special issue of the *American Journal of Preventive Medicine* titled "Youth Violence Prevention," contains descriptions and baseline data from 13 theoretically driven projects that employed strategies on one or more of four levels. On the *individual level*, strategies included social skills training, cognitive-behavioral training, mentoring, and manhood development. On the *proximal interpersonal systems*, interventions focused on family and peers, including activities such as peer mediation, parent education, family counseling, shifting peer group norms and per-ceptions, and preventing association with antisocial peers. In the *proximal social settings*, interventions were organized in the schools and neighborhoods and consisted of increasing community awareness, changing institutional practices, improving student motivation, increasing recreational opportunities, changing teacher practices, changing school climate, and changing community worker knowledge and practices. *Societal macrosystem* approaches involved entrepreneurial training and job training and placement.[16]

Realistically, neutralizing or eliminating the variables that contribute to youths becoming involved in serious crime might take a generation or longer to accomplish.[17] The California Attorney General's Policy Council on Violence Prevention adopted the public health model of prevention in recognition that a successful effort would require a long-term focus on prevention at all levels.[18]

- Primary prevention fosters and maintains healthy individuals, families, and com - munities.
- Secondary prevention addresses the attitudes, behaviors, conditions, and environ - ments that place individuals, families, and communities at risk of violence or expose them to violence.
- Tertiary prevention targets violent populations and their victims through the use of treatment or deterrent to reduce or prevent the risk of continued violence. [19]

The council identified 10 major initiatives for preventing violence. Council members recommended more than 100 targeted strategies and policies with respect to media, firearms, alcohol, community, family, relationships, youths, respect for diversity, personal and social responsibility, and research and evaluation.[20]

▣ PARTNERS IN CREATING A SAFER, HEALTHIER SOCIETY

My clinical experiences evaluating youths charged with murder underscore many of these research findings and recommended public policies. *As the cause of youth violence is multifaceted, so too must be its solution.* Parents, the educational system, communities, government leaders, the media, and individuals must work together to foster a healthy next generation. Individuals and institutions must collaborate to create a more peaceful society before a significant reduction in youth violence will be realized.

Given the changes that have occurred in families and in Western society since the 1970s, the concept of partnership is a critical one now and will remain so in the 21st century. Parents today, possibly more than at any time in history, need help in raising moral sons and daughters who can function well in a global and technologically complex world. The schools ideally build on the foundation that parents have laid.

The educational system, however, must provide a safety valve in the form of a backup plan for children whose parents have failed to instill the personal discipline and qualities needed to succeed in school, work, sports, and other prosocial activities. When parents do not equip their children with the social skills and strategies needed to interact harmoniously with others, it is in society's interest for the schools to assume these functions. Children who are subjected to ineffective child-rearing practices and who are poorly socialized typically lack self-control and a sense of strong attachment to others, including parents and teachers. Unbonded youths with poor self-control are at higher risk of committing criminal acts and engaging in other acts that can result in harm, such as drinking, using drugs, and reckless driving.[21]

Communities, the government, and the media also are potentially important institutions in the socialization of children. They give youths a sense of connection with others and "stakes in conformity." Youths who are bonded to others, committed to school, and involved in prosocial activities in their communities have a sense of "buy-in" with respect to conventional goals and the means to achieve them. Adolescents who trust their leaders and believe that they themselves can make a positive difference in the world are far less likely to engage in violent behavior than are youths who feel a sense of alienation from others and hopelessness about the direction of their lives.[22] Individual adults who interact positively with young people increase youths' sense of connectedness with older members of society and build bridges to a brighter and more successful future for them. This partnership of people and institutions, with 50 recommended strategies for reducing youth violence, is encapsulated in Table 13.1 and discussed in the following.

Parents

First, parenting must once again become a priority for Americans. Key findings from the National Longitudinal Study on Adolescent Health, published in 1997 by the American Medical Association, underscored the important role that parents and families play in the lives of today's youths. "Parent-family connectedness" was one of two variables that consistently protected youths from engaging in high-risk behaviors that threatened their health. Youths who felt love, warmth, and caring from one or both parents, in contrast to those who did not, were significantly less likely to engage in violent behavior; to use cigarettes, alcohol, or marijuana; and to begin having sexual intercourse at a young age. Youths who felt connected to their parents and were satisfied with their relationships with their mothers and/or fathers also were less likely to report being emotionally distressed and having a history of suicidal ideation and behaviors than were adolescents who did not feel close to their parents.[23]

When asked in follow-up interviews how parents could help their children, the young men whose stories are told in this book repeatedly emphasized greater parental involvement. Peter felt that his parents never talked to him. Malcolm advised parents to sit down and give their undivided attention to their children. Parents need to do fun things with their children, be "the kids' role model," and "hear [them] when [they're] not talking." Calvin stressed that parents need to keep their word and support their children in positive activities such as sports and cheerleading. Jerry related that parents should draw their children out and develop a relationship "where the kids are not afraid to tell you the truth."

The mothers of the young killers echoed similar thoughts. Mark's mother stressed that youths need "more parental involvement" to grow up well in today's society. Jerry's mother advised parents to "be realistic about what they [your children] are doing and who they are with. Find out more about their everyday lives. . . . Question them more." Peter's grandmother emphasized, "Know where they are and who their friends are." Joel's mother warned parents to instill in their children that guns are dangerous. Her son listened to her when she counseled him with respect to drug and alcohol use, but she never said anything to him about touching guns.

TABLE 13.1 Partners and Strategies in Reducing Youth Violence

A. Parenting: A priority concern
1. Greater parental involvement
2. Limit setting by parents
3. Parenting classes for parents
4. Participation by parents in support groups
5. Child development and parenting courses in high schools

B. Educational system
6. Design courses to identify child maltreatment (kindergarten through 12th grade)
7. Provide information on the effects of parental chemical dependency
8. Allow support groups such as Ala-teen in schools
9. Improve communication skills
10. Foster self-esteem
11. Provide social skills training
12. Teach conflict resolution
13. Give techniques to deal with feelings and to develop self-control (e.g., anger management, stress management)
14. Develop moral reasoning
15. Encourage understanding of cultural differences
16. Set appropriate limits regarding acceptable behavior
17. Provide a supportive network (e.g., Child Advocate Program)
18. Encourage greater involvement by teachers

C. Communities
19. Greater involvement by adults in the lives of children
20. Mentors
21. Medical community
22. Business community
23. Law enforcement
24. Religious organizations
25. Neighborhood centers or recreation halls
26. Organized community sports
27. Community organizations
28. Volunteer work in the community
29. "Youths helping youths" programs
30. Artists and art organizations

D. Government leaders
31. National commitment to children
32. Future-oriented legislation
33. Supportive services for parents
34. Quality health care for children and their families
35. Research to prevent brain dysfunction
36. Expanded national leave policy
37. Incentives for business regarding day care
38. Prevention programs
39. Early intervention programs for youths with substance abuse and behavioral problems
40. Educational programs targeted to assist disadvantaged children and those with special needs
41. Programs aimed at truancy reduction and dropout prevention
42. Shelters/drop-in centers
43. Gun policy (numbers, access, and lethality)

(continued)

TABLE 13.1 Continued

E. The media

    44. Greater public awareness about community programs to reduce violence

    45. More responsible programming regarding violence

    46. Public service announcements denouncing violence

    47. Continuing campaign to deglamorize drugs

F. The individual

    48. As taxpayer

    49. As voter

    50. As human being

The young men also stressed the importance of setting limits. Brian related that "a lot of parents let their kids do what they want to do" and that "more discipline" and "more control is needed." Mark felt that the lack of parental sanctions, when coupled with the nonresponsiveness of the juvenile justice system, encouraged him to do whatever he wanted without fear of punishment.

> I was raised to think I could do what I wanted to do. I remember my parents telling me I could do what I wanted to do, I could be what I wanted to be. I know it's not what they meant, but that's the way I took it. And then, going outside the house, when I did something wrong and not having anything done to me reinforced that thinking that this applies to everything.

Mark's mother was among those who indicated that she should have been more strict with her son when he was growing up. Calvin's mother cautioned parents to teach their children right from wrong from the time that they are very young. She urged parents to follow through consistently with discipline.

Joel expressed sympathy for parents trying to raise children today. He wryly commented, "Parenting doesn't come with a self-instruction manual." David related that it is particularly hard for single mothers because they have to play two roles.

In light of the difficulties of raising children, particularly those with special needs, parenting classes should be made available to help mothers and fathers.[24] Research shows that increasing parental awareness about home and child management enhances the development of communication, emotional ties, and parent-child bonding. These factors, in turn, help prevent child maltreatment.[25]

Parents also should be informed about the benefits of attending support groups. Self-help groups that may be helpful include Parents Anonymous (for mothers who have abused their children) and Tough Love (for parents whose children are acting out). Other support groups led by professionals include Parents United International Inc. (for parents whose children have been sexually abused) and Parental Stress Services (for children and parents from stressful environments).[26]

Many cases of maltreatment are a result of parental ignorance. Reducing this ignorance through education and parental training can go a long way toward increasing parental involvement and ending today's high rates of child abuse and neglect. With this end in mind, child development and parenting skills courses need to be incorporated into high school curricula for both boys and girls and also made available in the community.[27]

Educational System

The prevention of domestic violence—child maltreatment, spouse abuse, and the witnessing of violence—is the keystone to the prevention of overall violence in society. Parent education about child abuse and neglect should be effectuated both directly (through courses for mothers and fathers) and indirectly (through children who might be in abusive or potentially abusive situations). *There are many ways in which the educational system can help youths rebound from unhealthy influences in their homes and neighborhoods and develop into healthier human beings.*[28] Elementary, junior high, and high schools need to develop courses on child maltreatment. The curricula should help students recognize abuse and encourage them to take appropriate action if they are victimized or threatened.[29]

Similarly, the education system also should provide information to children about the effects of parental alcoholism and chemical dependency. Youths need to learn how to differentiate functional from dysfunctional families and to understand that abuse and neglect often are a consequence of the latter. Children and adolescents from substance-abusing families should be aware that they themselves are at greater risk of chemical dependency and violent death in the home than are youths whose families do not have this malady.[30] They should learn about how to address the problems in their home lives through support groups such as Alateen, which helps youths cope with living with alcoholic or drug-dependent parents. Such groups should be allowed and encouraged to meet in the schools during lunch, during free periods, or immediately following classes.[31]

The schools also are the ideal place in which to improve the communication skills of students, to encourage increased self-esteem, to promote prosocial behaviors, and to teach peaceful methods of conflict resolution.[32] Dissension often is the result of misunderstanding. Schools can help eliminate this ignorance and once again become the safe places they were a generation ago. Classes can be constructed to help students understand and respect cultural differences, which in turn will foster empathy and encourage students to interact with their peers and others in harmonious ways.[33]

In addition to tolerance, children and teens need to be taught communication skills and how to deal with their feelings. Anger management, stress management, moral reasoning, social skills training, and conflict resolution skills could easily be implemented into school curricula from kindergarten through high school.[34] Children and adolescents need to learn self-control. They need to know how to make good and moral decisions and how to fight fair. They need to learn that an argument is not won by silencing the opposition with an insult, a raised fist, or a bullet.

Youths also need limits set for them and consequences for disregarding rules and standards for appropriate behavior. Two national studies recently revealed that principals and students both supported tougher discipline policies. Fully 90% of principals surveyed in the National Association of Elementary School Principals' study identified strict disciplinary policies as essential to keeping schools safe. In addition, 70% of the high school students surveyed in the Public Agenda's report, *Getting by: What American Teenagers Really Think About Their Schools*, indicated that disruptive students were a serious problem, and more than 80% believed that they should be removed from class.[35]

All schools should make some provision to ensure that there is a supportive network available for children who need help. This network, perhaps fashioned as a child advocate program,[36] would be designed to ensure that appropriate referrals to mental health and social service agencies are made. The current system of school guidance counselors is not adequate. Access to guidance counselors often is encumbered by the excessively high counselor-student ratio. In addition, the tasks assigned to guidance departments usually reflect academic goals rather than the psychological or social needs of students. School counselors are expected to assist in course selection, provide college and career advice, and handle conflicts that students have with teachers and with one another. Consequently, they often have little time to assist youths with family or adjustment problems.

Teachers were seen as potentially important figures by the young men and their parents during follow-up interviews. Teachers were depicted as "role models" and as individuals who could have a significant impact on youths. As a group, the young men and their mothers stressed that teachers need to get more involved in their students' lives in spite of increasing class enrollment and related demands. Peter's grandmother advised teachers to pay more attention to seeing whether their students are having problems. Jerry's mother advised teachers to observe their students "very closely." Calvin's mother stressed that teachers need to provide moral guidance when necessary. "Let them know if somebody is doing wrong, you don't have to do that."

Malcolm related, in addition, that teachers need to communicate that "they care about the kid[s], how they turn out." Mark advised that teachers should help their students accept and deal with their emotions. Peter added that teachers should "counsel with 'em one-to-one, not in a group." Brian suggested that teachers should arrange for activities and programs for youths to engage in during and after school that are exciting such as "clubs, dances, sports for just anybody, bungee jumping, rollerblading, rappelling."

The National Longitudinal Study on Adolescent Health found that "school connectedness" was the other variable that was significantly correlated to several adolescent health risk behaviors. Youths who felt that teachers treated them fairly and who felt close to people at school were significantly less likely to be violent, to smoke cigarettes or marijuana, to drink alcohol, and to have had sexual intercourse than were youths who felt disconnected from school. Adolescents who felt part of their schools also were less likely to be emotionally distressed and to have engaged in suicidal thoughts or behaviors than were youths who felt estranged from the junior and senior high school experience.[37]

Community

The community also can play a potentially pivotal role in helping youths make prosocial choices, particularly if many groups, including residents, become actively involved in developing the strategies to reduce youth violence.[38] The increasing proportion of juveniles involved in homicide is indicative of a breakdown in the community. The old African proverb encapsulated in the title of Hillary Clinton's book, *It Takes a Village*, is particularly apropos today[39] in an era besieged with a loss of a sense of community.[40]

Peter's grandmother lamented that adults "just don't want to be involved anymore." Mark's mother stressed that "parents have to form the community that helps children." Calvin's mother advised that all adults—not just parents and teachers—should take responsibility for guiding juveniles. She said, "Every chance you get, talk to them, not [to be] put[ting] them down or fussing at them. Just talk to them. Sometime that's all they need is to talk."

Male and female mentors are needed to guide children who do not have healthy parents who care about them. Mentors can help youths with their difficulties and encourage them to achieve and make a positive contribution to society. They can assist teens in learning leadership skills and in resisting peer pressure to use drugs, commit crimes, or join gangs.[41] Physicians, particularly those involved in primary care, often are in an excellent position to counsel high-risk youths about homicide prevention including firearms.[42] They can play a critical role in educating the public about violence prevention and in encouraging participation in a variety of activities including gun amnesty programs.[43]

Leaders from the business community also must take action to help youths to feel a part of their community and to learn responsibility. Employment opportunities for youths provide a legitimate way in which for them to earn money and acquire desired goods and services. Neighborhood businesses need to provide meaningful part-time employment, summer jobs, and training programs for youths to develop their skills and confidence.[44] Partnerships of private employers, schools, and government, such as the national Jobs Corps, have succeeded in providing intensive, community-based job training programs for youths.[45]

Law enforcement also can provide leadership in the community by working with residents and neighborhood groups, as well as organized institutions and agencies, to reduce youth violence.[46] As noted by the National Crime Prevention Council, "Fruitful partnerships between law enforcement and citizens are promoted by community policing, with law enforcement becoming acquainted with community residents, learning about problems in the neighborhoods, and enlisting support for preventing crime and improving neighborhood safety."[47] Groups that can benefit from partnerships with police include area schools, youth groups, neighborhood associations, community service and social clubs, home/school organizations (e.g., Parent-Teacher Association), tenant groups, religious organizations, associations of home owners or merchants, and taxpayer or political groups.[48]

Religious groups can help youths to make good choices. In poor and minority areas, the church often is one of the strongest and most visible institutions. Churches, synagogues, and other religious organizations need to develop programs to meet the spiritual, emotional, and social needs of adolescents and their families. Religious beliefs can help to dissuade teens, who are easily and powerfully influenced by ideology, from engaging in antisocial behavior. Research indicates that youths who are low in religiosity, as measured by infrequent church attendance, are more susceptible to a variety of adolescent problems including delinquency, teen pregnancy, school failure, and substance use.[49]

At follow-up, the young men and their mothers repeatedly mentioned the need for neighborhood centers or recreation halls. Brian, for example, suggested that youths need places to go where they can play pool and ping-pong, talk, and listen to the radio. Adults should be present to enforce rules, such as no drinking or using drugs, but "not to run 'em off. . . . Give them [instead] the excitement of being there." In the words of Jerry's mother, the community should "have more places they [youths] could go and gather without being reprimanded."

Adolescents need a safe place available where they can hang out, play sports, listen to music and dance, and interact with peers and adults.[50] Youths who have available a supervised location where they are welcome and where there are constructive things to do are less likely to be bored with life and become high on drugs and alcohol than are adolescents who are hanging out in the streets day after day. Teens with attractive prosocial alternatives also are unlikely to be drawn to gangs and hate groups and to feel that they have little or nothing left to lose.[51]

Joel's mother noted with dismay that in her community, there are few, if any, activities available for teenagers that are not costly. David suggested that the community organize football leagues. Malcolm opted for races, explaining that competition was viewed as a way in which to "take your mind off something negative." He envisioned parents watching their children excel at sports and youths being recognized as "Student [or Athlete] of the Week."

There are data to indicate that lower-income male youths who are involved in community sports are significantly less delinquent than their nonathletic counterparts. Studies suggest that youths who play sports also demonstrate achievement in other areas. Participants in the Midnight Basketball program in Chicago, for example, showed positive gains in education and job placement while avoiding criminal involvement and remaining drug and alcohol free.[52]

The community can do more than provide recreational centers and organized sports to help adolescents use their time and talents wisely. More than 400 community organizations have been identified nationally. These include recreational (e.g., YMCA), character-building (e.g., Girl Scouts, Boys and Girls Club of America), career- or avocation-based (e.g., 4H, Junior Achievement), politically focused (e.g., Young Democrats), and religious-oriented organizations (e.g., Christian youth groups) as well as those that instill ethnic pride. Research indicates that many benefits accrue to youths who participate in community organizations including improved social skills and competencies, enhanced educational achievement, positive peer relationships, and increased social responsibility.[53]

"Tom Malone," who was sentenced to death for a murder he denied committing at 19 years of age, related that in poor areas, "being tough" is the only accomplishment available for many juveniles. He suggested giving youths recognition when they do something good. He proposed, in addition, that the community form groups of adults and adolescents to fix up the neighborhood or the homes of the elderly. Community involvement or service of this type fosters trust, facilitates learning, and builds self-esteem. Youths who participate in community volunteer programs, such as VISTA or the National Youth Conservation Corps, gain a greater understanding of others and connection to the community while reducing their feelings of alienation and isolation.[54]

Setting up programs in which older youths help younger children also appears to reap benefits. Adolescents have served effectively in the roles of tutors and Big Brothers and Sisters. They have performed well as advocates for other troubled youths and as mediators in youth conflicts in schools. Studies have indicated that teens benefit from being in the position of helping others and of being needed and respected by other children and adolescents.[55]

A number of communities across the United States have effectively involved youths in using art to address teen problems. Artists, art organizations, and community groups have received assistance from the National Endowment for the Arts, the 56 state and jurisdictional arts agencies, and the 7 regional art organizations in recognition of the role that the arts can play in the lives of children and their families. Mediums used have included dance, music, storytelling, mask making, painting, film, sculpture, pottery, photography, and theater.[56]

Recent research has indicated that collective efficacy, as measured by community involvement and trust among residents, is linked to reduced violence in neighborhoods. These findings held when the effects of individual-level characteristics, prior violence, and measurement error were controlled. Collective efficacy also was shown to mediate the effects of concentrated disadvantage and residential instability on violence levels.[57]

Allegheny County, Pennsylvania, provides an excellent example of a community that successfully mobilized its resources to reduce juvenile crime including violent crime.[58] The antiviolence effort involved the "coordination, collaboration, and involvement of all parts of the community, resulting in positive systemic changes and collaboration across socioeconomic, ethnic, and political lines."[59] The mobilization process was achieved through Law Enforcement Agency Directors (LEAD) meetings, the Youth Crime Prevention Council (YCPC), and Mass Community Education.

The 17 federal, state, county, and local law enforcement leaders who comprise the membership of the LEAD meetings have worked together to develop aggressive interventions aimed at individuals and structures that expose youths to violence, drugs, and guns. The YCPC consists of leaders from government, law enforcement, juvenile justice, health and human services, the media, education, and the religious community. Membership on the YCPC also includes neighborhood representatives, grassroots community activists, youths, and families. Tasks undertaken by the YCPC include assessing the juvenile crime problem, developing strategies to combat the factors underlying juvenile crime, and working with pertinent agencies and groups to implement crime reduction initiatives. Box 13.1 encapsulates 15 YCPC initiatives that Allegheny County is undertaking to reduce juvenile crime. YCPC members are using mass community education in an effort to inform every individual about the county youth crime problem and "to mobilize the entire community to be actively involved in raising its children and ensuring public safety."[60]

Government Leaders

Ideally, initiatives such as those implemented in Allegheny County will become increasingly common in the United States and other countries experiencing serious juvenile crime problems. Interestingly, the young men whose cases are profiled in this book, although generally positive about increased community involvement, did not share similar optimism about the potential role of the nation as a whole to constructively affect American youths. When asked what they would advise the president and Congress to do with respect to today's children, their answers almost uniformly expressed distrust and despair.

Jerry, for example, would not tell legislators anything. He explained, "I don't trust the government to think they have any genuine feeling for the welfare of anybody in the country. I think it is all self-serving." He believed that government leaders who were moral do not survive in politics; they get corrupted over time or weeded out. Calvin could not think of any action to recommend. It bothered him that "they're telling you to do right and they doing wrong." Brian indicated his belief that "there are more criminal acts in politics than there is on the streets." Mark laughed before replying, "I think what the government could do is have the people in government live within the laws themselves. . . . That's the one thing we see on TV all the time. The politicians make the laws and go out and break them." Tom Malone wanted to ask the president how he could do the things he allegedly does and come out "smelling like a rose." From

BOX 13.1   Initiatives to Reduce Juvenile Crime: Allegheny County, Pennsylvania

Aftercare safe places	Create a network of safe places with constructive activities for youths in high-risk neighborhoods
Sports leagues	Create sports programs in at-risk neighborhoods
Jobs	Create and find jobs for young people
Family support centers	Provide prevention, healthy child development, and economic self-reliance support for at-risk families
Mentoring	Increase the number of trained volunteer mentors to meet the demand
HeadStart/ day care	Increase the enrollment of underprivileged children in quality early education and family support programs
Juvenile justice	Ensure appropriate consequences for serious and violent juvenile offenders
Leadership development	Promote the development of leadership skills in youths
Community accountability	Involve community residents in decision making about the youth crime reduction strategies for their neighborhoods
Gun proliferation	Stop the spread of illegal guns and target law enforcement efforts against those who make guns available to youths
Health/wellness	Promote healthy behaviors through home visitation, pre- and postnatal training, and other means
In-school activities	Encourage students to participate in existing in-school activities and provide school-based probation and other services within more schools
Substance abuse	Develop public education campaigns to spread substance abuse prevention and intervention messages
Police response	Expand community-oriented policing emphasizing prevention, problem solving, and intervention
Domestic violence prevention	Increase countywide shelter capacity for domestic violence victims and evaluate the local impact of domestic violence on juveniles

SOURCE: Hsia 1997.

his perspective and life experience, some of the legislators are "worse criminals" than his comrades on death row. Joel did not believe that there was any action that, if implemented on a national scale, would make a difference. He emphasized individual choice as paramount in whether a person engages and persists in crime and suggested that legislators look at their own morality.

The young men's comments are testimony to the cynicism that has become increasingly pervasive in the United States. If juvenile violence is going to decrease in America, then the conditions that breed alienation, isolation, poverty, rage, and resignation must be effectively tackled. Strong and moral leadership is needed. If society wants to hold youths accountable for their behavior, then those in power must act responsibly. Whether we look at personal responsibility from the top down or from the bottom up, the result is likely to be the same. Youths are more apt to make responsible choices if they live in a nation where government leaders, communities, parents, teachers, and adults see that each has a responsibility to contribute to the moral growth of children.

The United States must make a national commitment to improve the lives of today's children or risk that its citizens will live increasingly in fear of its young. Government leaders need to propose legislation that looks to the future for all youths. Parents must have access to supportive services to ensure the physical and mental health of their children as well as their own medical needs.[61] The government needs to join with health professionals in funding research and programs to prevent brain injuries; children's exposure to lead; substance abuse by pregnant women; and other prenatal, perinatal, and postnatal events associated with brain dysfunctions and an increased potentiality for violence.[62]

The national leave policy that permits parents to take needed time off from work to care for a newborn child, a newly adopted child, or a seriously ill child without risk of losing their employment was a big step forward for U.S. families and their children.[63] Initiatives to expand this policy to make more parent employees eligible should be pursued. The nation also must explore incentives to make it feasible for businesses and organizations to operate quality day care facilities on their premises or close by at a cost affordable to their employees.[64]

The parents of the young men emphasized the need for better education and more effective intervention. Peter's grandmother advised that youths today need early intervention, specifically "drug treatment and education and [vocational] training, not juvenile hall." Jerry's mother recommended that the government ensure that "special counseling for troubled kids and kids in certain circumstances" is available.

Research has indicated that opportunities to intervene in the lives of juvenile murderers prior to their killing often were ignored. *A 1998 publication indicated that few of the juvenile murderers in the study had received any type of mental health treatment prior to the killing despite having "long-standing and conspicuous emotional and behavioral disturbances antedating their crimes."*[65]

Programs aimed at prevention and early intervention must be implemented on a grand scale with the knowledge that the direct results might take 20 to 30 years to see. Effective programs for low-income children and their families need to be made available with the foresight that most of the youths arrested for violent crimes are poor.

> Although violence in adolescence affects us all, it does discriminate, and its effects are felt most deeply by the poor and minorities. Without a basic standard of living for all

teens and their families, the cycle of violence cannot be broken. This standard would include, at a minimum, access to jobs, nutrition, housing, income, and services to meet special needs.[66]

Funding of programs such as HeadStart is important in ensuring that poor children are on the same playing field when they enter school with their more affluent counterparts. Early diagnosis of children with Attention-Deficit/Hyperactivity Disorder and learning disabilities is essential to increase the chances that these youths will obtain the educational opportunities needed to reach their potentials. In addition, programs aimed at truancy reduction and dropout prevention need to be implemented in recognition of the correlation between school failure and delinquency.[67]

Federal and state governments also must ensure that shelters and drop-in centers are easily accessible to youths across the country. High-risk youths, particularly homeless teens and runaways, often need crisis intervention, individual counseling, alcohol and drug counseling, transportation, long-term foster care, recreation, and job training.[68] *Denying mental health benefits, social services, and educational resources to children today to save money ensures that our prison population, already at a record high in terms of the number and rate of persons incarcerated in the United States, will continue to grow.*[69]

Given that the majority of homicides are committed with guns, Congress should provide funding to develop, implement, and evaluate school-based programs to inform youths regarding the prevention of firearm violence.[70] The federal government, as well as the individual states, must take meaningful action to regulate firearms.[71] In addition, *the federal government must prioritize reducing the number of guns in our society and restricting their access to juveniles.*[72] Research has shown that the dramatic increase in juvenile homicides since the mid-1980s has been directly due to gun-related homicides.[73] Recent studies also have shown that juvenile homicide offenders like to equip themselves with newer and more powerful weapons.[74] Accordingly, restrictions on assault weaponry must be imposed.[75] Stricter handgun policies have been shown to reduce both homicide and suicide among adolescents.[76]

Some might argue that the United States, and other countries facing similar problems in juvenile crime, cannot afford to implement policies and programs such as these on a widespread scale. The focus in the past few years has been on cutting costs, reducing benefits, and "downsizing." Those who maintain that the United States cannot and should not accept this financial and moral challenge need to look back to the savings and loan crisis of the 1980s. Congress appropriated billions of dollars to resolve the savings and loan troubles. A few government officeholders and businesspersons walked away "big winners" while approximately 250 million Americans picked up the tab. In 1992, the Congressional Budget Office estimated the cost at $800 for every man, woman, and child in the United States based on a bailout figure of $200 billion.[77] In July 1996, the General Accounting Office study put the price tag at more than $480 billion.[78] If the federal government could find the money to redress a situation created by government irresponsibility and human greed, surely funds can be allocated to act responsibly and to reduce human suffering on a national scale.

Media

Although the media's influence in a few cases was observable, none of the young killers blamed the media for the murders they committed or called for censorship.

Their reflections on violent programming are nonetheless provocative. Jerry, who acknowledged watching military films repeatedly, did not believe that violent movies would influence a nonviolent person. He opined that "a person who is violent to begin with would go out and look for that type of thing" and perhaps would use films "to feed on." Mark, who watched little television while growing up, suggested that media violence "is like a sedative. It makes us not notice it [violence] as much. You get used to it. You learn to expect it. It's going to happen. There is nothing you can do" to stop it.

The media, including the record industry, have enormous power and resources available to reduce youth violence in the 21st century.[79] The media can increase public awareness about the nature and scope of the violence problem. They can publicize groups and initiatives in a community organized in response to violence and encourage participation from all of its citizens. The media also can reinforce the lessons of school and community programs designed to reduce conflict, improve communication skills, and change institutional arrangements or policies that appear to contribute to violent solutions.[80]

Efforts currently are under way by the entertainment industry to limit gratuitous violence. In addition to more socially responsible programming, the media have begun to release public service announcements denouncing violence.[81] Provocative posters and billboard displays that promote violence prevention themes for at-risk youths have been designed and widely disseminated.[82]

The media can do more to effect positive social change by continuing their campaign to deglamorize drugs. The electronic and print media also can contribute to violence reduction by promoting acceptance and respect for diversity through accurate portrayals of various groups including age, gender, and class as well as racial, ethnic, religious, cultural, and sexual orientation minorities.[83] The media were extremely successful in educating the American public about child abuse and in changing societal attitudes in this regard in less than 20 years.[84] In the 1990s, talk shows such as those hosted by Geraldo Rivera, Maury Povich, and Oprah Winfrey have done a great deal positive in informing the public about the relationship between child maltreatment and adolescent violence. The media's potential in raising public consciousness about constructive solutions and the richness of diversity during the next decade is almost limitless given today's technology and the widespread availability of media resources to the U.S. population.

Individuals

My recommendations look for people in their roles as parents, educators, organizational members, government leaders, and media personnel to work in collaboration with one another. *The discussion of roles and systems, however, is not intended to obscure the power of the individual to influence the lives of children in our country.* The young killers whose cases were profiled in this book and their mothers each had words of advice for today's youths.

If he had the chance to address millions of youths, Joel would say, "Go to school, be good, respect people." Brian would instruct them to "pay more attention to what their parents have to say to them." Jerry would emphasize education in the context of school but, more important, learning from their life experiences. Peter would talk to youths about "the purpose of what life is for, drugs, alcohol, school, parents, all of that . . . not to get involved in peer pressure."

Calvin would tell the youths of America how he went wrong by dropping out of school and by listening to his peers. Mark would let them know that "no matter what anybody says, you are responsible and there are consequences. Maybe not right away, but there will be consequences." David would tell teens that there is "nothing cool [about being] in prison. Stay in school. Be somebody." Malcolm would advise them further that they have only one life to live and to stay away from the wrong group and avoid temptation. He would emphasize to youths, "Anything you set your mind to, you can do it or get it. . . . If you walk a straight line and work hard for yours, it will pay off in the long run."

The mothers stressed similar themes. Jerry's mother would warn youths to be "very careful" when it comes to choosing friends. Peter's grandmother would caution teens to take responsibility for their bodies and minds and to avoid pressure from friends to use drugs. Calvin's mother added that adolescents need to recognize right from wrong and to "take good advice from family and run with it." Joel's mother would tell millions of youths straight up, "Don't look for an easy out and a fast solution to it." Mark's mother laughed as she suggested that perhaps youths should go to church because nowadays it seemed like many were living in hell.

Individuals have an impact as voters, as taxpayers, and, most important, as human beings. Studies of abused children who did not grow up to abuse or hurt others are instructive in this regard.[85] These adults, in recalling their lives as children, often identify adult figures in their lives who were nice to them. Such a person could have been the lady next door, the man down the street, a teacher or coach in school, or a clerk in the town deli. The exchanges often were brief and not at all dramatic. In these moments, the youths were aware of being acknowledged by adults who communicated, whether intentionally or inadvertently, that they believed in the children and cared about them.

Notes

PART I

1. Sickmund 1994.

Chapter 1

1. Silverstein 1994; Pazniokas 1995; Yeomans 1995.
2. Kantrowitz 1993.
3. Snyder 1994; Fox 1996.
4. Heide 1992; Butts and Snyder 1997, note 1.
5. Bortner 1988; Sickmund 1994.
6. Federal Bureau of Investigation 1997.
7. Solomon, Schmidt, and Ardragna 1990; see also Lee, Lee, and Chen 1995.
8. Solomon et al. 1990.
9. Cornell 1993; Blumstein 1995; Lee et al. 1995; Fox 1996.
10. Flewelling 1996; see, e.g., Abrahamse 1996; Brewer, Damphousse, and Edison 1996; Olson 1997.
11. Heide 1996, 1997b. The rate at which juveniles were arrested for murder also increased substantially during this time frame. The juvenile murder rate peaked in 1993 at 14 per 100,000 and was more than twice the level of the early 1980s (6 per 100,000). The juvenile murder arrest rate in 1996, although the lowest in the 1990s, still was more than 50% greater than the rate in the early 1980s. See Snyder 1997.
12. Ewing 1990; Gest and Friedman 1994; Heide 1994b; Blumstein 1995; Fox 1996.
13. Gest and Friedman 1994; Fox 1995, 1996; Abrahamse 1996.
14. Fox 1995, 1996.
15. Snyder and Sickmund 1995.
16. Smith and Feiler 1995.
17. Ibid., 330.
18. Zimring 1984; Cheatwood and Block 1990; Altschuler 1995; Howell, Krisberg, and Jones 1995; Snyder and Sickmund 1995.
19. See, e.g., in general, Ewing 1990; Cornell 1993; Price 1995; with respect to parricide, see Heide 1993b, 1995.
20. Diaz 1993.
21. Rimbach 1994, A1.
22. Stephens 1994.
23. "Lotto Win" 1995.
24. Jaeger 1995.
25. LeDuc and St. George 1995.
26. "Boy Murdered Mother" 1995.
27. See, e.g., Heide 1995, 165, note 2.
28. Ewing 1990.
29. Federal Bureau of Investigation 1995.
30. Heide 1993a.
31. Levin and Fox 1985; Fox and Levin 1994.
32. Crawford 1995a; Romero 1995.
33. "Lincoln Teen" 1995.
34. "Teen Charged" 1995.
35. Bjerregaard and Smith 1995; Howell 1994, 1995a; Johnson, Webster, and Connors 1995; U.S. Department of Justice 1997.
36. See, e.g., Sanders 1994; Los Angeles Sheriff's Department 1995; Chin 1995.
37. See, e.g., Sanders 1994; Bjerregaard and Smith 1995; Howell 1995a; Johnson et al. 1995; Thornberry and Burch 1997.
38. See, e.g., Sanders 1994; Block and Block 1995; Sheley and Wright 1995.
39. Meehan and O'Carroll 1995; Block and Christakos 1995.
40. Block and Christakos 1995, 29.
41. Howell 1994; Sanders 1994; Blumstein and Heinz 1995; Howell 1995a; Howell, Krisberg, and Jones 1995; Meehan and O'Carroll 1995; Sheley and Wright 1995.
42. "2 Teens Charged" 1995.
43. Whitely et al. 1994, A1.
44. Landau 1993; Moore 1993; Hamm 1995.
45. Holmes and Holmes 1994, 53.
46. Holmes and Holmes 1994; Hamm 1993, 1995; Zellner 1995.
47. Anti-Defamation League 1995a.

48. Anti-Defamation League 1995b, *U.S. Newswire*, quoted with permission.
49. Anti-Defamation League 1995b.
50. Crawford 1995b.
51. McGinniss 1991.
52. "19-Year-Old Murderer" 1994.
53. "Kids Who Kill Their Parents" 1997; Hewitt, Harmes, and Stewart 1997; Moehringer 1997.
54. Fox 1996.
55. See also Blumstein 1995.
56. Heide 1994b, 1996.
57. Federal Bureau of Investigation 1995.
58. Rowley, Ewing, and Singer 1987.
59. Folks 1994.
60. Ommachen 1995.
61. Gersham 1994.
62. See, e.g., O'Keeffe, Brockopp, and Chew 1986; Bergman 1992; Weston 1994.
63. Bergman 1992.
64. Gamache 1991; Levy and Lobel 1991.
65. Weston 1994.
66. Robinson 1995.
67. LeBlanc 1995.
68. "Pre-teen Charged" 1995.
69. Hackett 1988; Leslie 1988; Nordland 1992; Toch, Gest, and Guttman 1993; Maynard 1994; Sautter 1995; Sheley and Wright 1995; Bowles 1997; Sharp 1997; Lawrence 1998.
70. Sautter 1995.
71. Ibid.
72. Nordland 1992, 23.
73. Chachere 1995.
74. "Substitute Teacher Dies" 1995.
75. "Suspended S.C. Student" 1995.
76. Block 1977.
77. "Boy Allows Burning" 1995.
78. Lorente and Bustos 1995; "Girl 'Scared'" 1995.
79. See, e.g., Florida Statutes §790.174 published in *West's Florida Criminal Laws and Rules 1995* (West Publishing 1995, 433).
80. "Shooting Accident" 1995.
81. Troyer 1995.
82. Clary 1994.
83. Morgan 1975; Heide 1986; Annin 1996.
84. Kantrowitz 1993.
85. Wilkerson 1994.
86. Harker 1994.
87. Eftimiades et al. 1997.
88. Hewitt, Alexander, et al. 1997; Hewitt, Harmes, and Stewart 1997.
89. See, e.g., Fallstrom 1993; Baxter 1994; "Crime May Be Down" 1993; Miller 1995.
90. See, e.g., Chiricos 1994.
91. Ewing 1990.
92. Wilson 1994.
93. See, e.g., Harris 1993; Goldberg 1994a; Harker 1994.
94. See, e.g., Glovin 1994; Shirk 1994; McCarthy 1995.
95. See, e.g., Harris 1993; "What Can Be Done" 1994; Schiraldi 1995.
96. Harris 1993; "Save Youths Worth Saving" 1993; Goldberg 1994b; Pazniokas 1995; Spitz 1995.
97. Silverstein 1994; Torbet et al. 1996; "Virginia Governor and Lawmakers" 1996; Dighton 1997; Gray 1997.
98. Torbet et al. 1996.
99. See, e.g., Heide and Pardue, 1986; Mahoney, 1987; Heide, 1988; Lee 1993; Walsh 1993; Davey 1994; Lopez 1994; Mayers 1995; Ganey 1995; Candisky, 1995; Fiagome 1995; "Pennsylvania State Sen. Fisher" 1995; Spitz 1995; Coordinating Council on Juvenile Justice and Delinquency Prevention 1996; Torbet et al. 1996.
100. Fiagome 1995; Coordinating Council on Juvenile Justice and Delinquency Prevention 1996.
101. "Violent Youths" 1994; Spitz 1995; VandeWater 1995.
102. Mannies 1994; Pommer 1995; Torbet et al. 1996.
103. Finch 1994; Spitz 1995.
104. Goldberg 1994b.
105. McCarthy 1995.
106. Spitz 1995.
107. Hirth 1994; "Expulsion Isn't a Vacation" 1994.
108. "The Crisis at Juvenile Hall" 1994; Spitz 1995.
109. Walsh 1993; T. Still 1994; Pommer 1995; Spitz 1995; Torbet et al. 1996.
110. Walsh 1993; Silverstein 1994; Candisky 1995; Spitz 1995; Torbet et al. 1996.
111. See, e.g., Schiraldi 1995.
112. See, e.g., Spitz 1995.
113. Rojek 1996.
114. Calculated from Federal Bureau of Investigation data, 1985 to 1997 publications.
115. Eitzen 1995.
116. Prothrow-Stith and Weissman 1991.
117. Meloff and Silverman 1992; Turner 1994.
118. Jimenez 1994; Kaihla 1994; Hustak 1995.
119. See, e.g., Bagnall 1994b; Turner 1994; Upton and Buchanan 1994; Bergman 1995; Blanchfield 1995; Farnsworth 1995; Hustak 1995.
120. Turner 1994; "Slayings by Teenagers" 1995; Onstad 1997.
121. Silverman 1990; Bagnall 1994a, 1994b; Creechan 1994; Hustak 1995.
122. Farnsworth 1995; Onstad 1997.
123. Meloff and Silverman 1992; Silverman and Kennedy 1993.
124. Chard 1995.
125. Hum and Bohuslawsky 1994; Nunziata 1994; Riga 1995; Roth 1995a.
126. Hustak 1995.
127. "Teen Murder Suspects" 1995.
128. Contenta 1995.

129. " 'What's Going On?' " 1995.
130. Jimenez 1994; Hustak 1995
131. Wyatt 1993.
132. Bagnall 1994a, 1994b.
133. L. Still 1994.
134. See, e.g., Dolik 1993; Bagnall 1994a; Kaihla 1994; Upton and Buchanan 1994; Turner 1994; Contenta 1995; Onstad 1997.
135. See, e.g., Taub 1994; Dranoff 1997; Onstad 1997.
136. Orwen 1993; Kaihla 1994; Prashaw 1994; Scott 1994; Vienneau 1994; Humphries 1995; Tustin 1995; Vansun 1995; Onstad 1997.
137. Ovenden 1995.
138. Turner 1994; Harper 1995; Roth 1995a; Onstad 1997.
139. Dexter 1995.
140. Onstad 1997.
141. Rusnell 1995.

142. Nunziata 1994; Vienneau 1994.
143. Kaihla 1994.
144. Blassnig 1994.
145. Kaihla 1994.
146. Rusnell 1995; Vienneau 1995.
147. Ember and Ember 1993.
148. "Youth Accused of Murder" 1994.
149. "Youths Accused of Murder" 1993.
150. See, e.g., "Youth Remanded in Murder Case" 1995.
151. Ibid.
152. Ibid.
153. Hustak 1995.
154. Grylls 1994.
155. "Death Wears a Boy's Face" 1995.
156. Ember and Ember 1993.
157. "Youthful Killers Given 2nd Chance" 1995.
158. Harris 1994.
159. "Youthful Killers Given 2nd Chance" 1995.

▦ Chapter 2

1. Nicholson 1996.
2. "Teacher Hailed" 1996.
3. "Boy Held in Deaths" 1996.
4. Zagar et al. 1990.
5. Cornell 1989; Ewing 1990.
6. For discussion of sociological theories, see Bynum and Thompson 1995.
7. See, e.g., Malmquist 1990.
8. See, e.g., Medlicott 1955; McCarthy 1978; Gardiner 1985; Russell 1986; Benedek and Cornell 1989; Ewing 1990; Heide 1992.
9. Ewing 1990.
10. See, e.g., Bender 1959; Carek and Watson 1964; Tooley 1975; Pfeffer 1980; Petti and Davidman 1981; Goetting 1989, 1995; Ewing 1990.
11. Bender and Curran 1940.
12. Easson and Steinhilber 1961; Sargent 1962; Goetting 1989; Myers et al. 1995.
13. Sargent 1962.
14. Bender and Curran 1940; Cornell 1989; Heide 1992; O'Halloran and Altmaier 1996.
15. Bender and Curran 1940.
16. See, e.g., Carek and Watson 1964; Adelson 1972; Goetting 1989.
17. See, e.g., Tooley 1975; Tucker and Cornwall 1977.
18. See, e.g., Paluszny and McNabb 1975; Bernstein 1978.
19. Bender 1959; Tucker and Cornwall 1977; Zenoff and Zients 1979; Pfeffer 1980; Heide 1984; "Incompetency Standards" 1984.
20. Sorrells 1977; Zenoff and Zients 1979; Heide 1984, 1992.
21. Adams 1974; Haizlip, Corder, and Ball 1984; Lewis et al. 1985; Lewis, Lovely et al. 1988; Cornell, Benedek, and Benedek 1987b, 1989; Busch et al. 1990; Ewing 1990; Myers 1992.
22. Myers 1994; Myers et al. 1995.
23. Lewis et al. 1985.
24. Cornell 1989. See, e.g., Bender and Curran 1940; Smith 1965; Scherl and Mack 1966; Malmquist 1971; Mack, Scherl, and Macht 1973; Miller and Looney 1974; McCarthy 1978; Washbrook 1979; Malmquist 1990.
25. For a discussion of their findings, see Cornell 1989 and Ewing 1990.
26. See, e.g., Patterson 1943; Stearns 1957; Hellsten and Katila 1965; Malmquist 1971; Walshe-Brennan 1974, 1977; King 1975; Corder et al. 1976; Sorrells 1977; Russell 1965, 1979; Petti and Davidman 1981; Yates, Beutler, and Crago 1983; Cornell, Benedek, and Benedek 1987b, 1989; Myers and Kemph 1988, 1990; Cornell 1989; Ewing 1990; Bailey 1994; Myers et al. 1995.
27. See, e.g., Bender 1959; Sendi and Blomgren 1975; Rosner et al. 1978; Lewis, Pincus et al. 1988.
28. Lewis et al. 1985; Lewis, Lovely et al. 1988; Myers et al. 1995; Myers and Scott 1998.
29. Malmquist 1971; Lewis, Pincus et al. 1988; Malmquist 1990.
30. See, e.g., Smith 1965; Mohr and McKnight 1971; Sadoff 1971; Miller and Looney 1974; McCarthy 1978; Cornell 1989.
31. Menninger and Mayman 1956.
32. See, e.g., Cornell 1989; Ewing 1990.
33. See, e.g., Malmquist 1971; Rosner et al. 1978; Russell 1979; Myers and Scott 1998.
34. Malmquist, 1971; Schmideberg 1973; Sendi and Blomgren 1975; Sorrells 1977; Rosner

et al. 1978; Russell 1979; Yates et al. 1983; Myers and Kemph 1988, 1990; Ewing 1990; Bailey 1994; Myers et al. 1995; Santtila and Haapasalo 1997.

35. Myers et al. 1995; Santtila and Haapasalo 1997; Myers and Scott 1998.
36. Cornell 1989; Ewing 1990.
37. Restifo and Lewis 1985. See, e.g., Thom 1949; Podolsky 1965.
38. Myers 1992.
39. See, e.g., Bender 1959; Michaels 1961; Woods 1961; Lewis et al. 1985; Lewis, Lovely et al. 1988; Busch et al. 1990; Zagar et al. 1990; Myers 1994; Myers et al. 1995; Bailey 1996a.
40. Lewis, Pincus et al. 1988.
41. See, e.g., Hellsten and Katila 1965; Scherl and Mack 1966; Walshe-Brennan 1974, 1977; Petti and Davidman 1981; Russell 1986.
42. Patterson 1943; Bender 1959; Solway et al. 1981; Lewis, Pincus et al. 1988; Busch et al. 1990; Zagar et al. 1990.
43. Ewing 1990.
44. See, e.g., Ewing 1990.
45. Hays, Solway, and Schreiner 1978; Petti and Davidman 1981; Solway et al. 1981; Lewis, Pincus et al. 1988; Busch et al. 1990; Zagar et al. 1990.
46. Patterson 1943; Bender 1959; King 1975.
47. Stearns 1957; Hellsten and Katila 1965; Scherl and Mack 1966; Sendi and Blomgren 1975; Bernstein 1978; Myers et al. 1995; Myers and Scott 1998.
48. King 1975; Myers and Mutch 1992.
49. Busch et al. 1990; Zagar et al. 1990; Bailey 1994.
50. Patterson 1943; Bender 1959; King 1975; Sendi and Blomgren 1975; Lewis, Pincus et al. 1988; Myers et al. 1995; Myers and Scott 1998.
51. Myers et al. 1995; Bailey 1996a.
52. Zenoff and Zients 1979; Ewing 1990. See, e.g., Wertham 1941; Sargent 1962; Scherl and Mack 1966; Duncan and Duncan 1971; Kalogerakis 1971; Sadoff 1971; Anthony and Rizzo 1973; Tanay 1973, 1976; Cormier et al. 1978; McCully 1978; Post 1982; Russell 1984; Mones 1985, 1991; Mouridsen and Tolstrup 1988; Heide 1992.
53. Heide 1992, 1995.
54. Kirschner 1992.
55. See, e.g., King 1975; Fiddes 1981.
56. Ewing 1990. See, e.g., Patterson 1943; Easson and Steinhilber 1961; Woods 1961; Smith 1965; Scherl and Mack 1966; Sorrells 1977; Rosner et al. 1978; McCarthy 1978; Petti and Davidman 1981; Russell 1986.
57. Busch et al. 1990; Zagar et al. 1990.
58. Ewing 1990. See, e.g., Hellsten and Katila 1965; Corder et al. 1976; Sorrells 1977; Petti and Davidman 1981; Lewis et al. 1985; Lewis,

Lovely et al. 1988; Lewis, Pincus et al. 1988; Heide 1992; Bailey 1994, 1996a; Myers et al. 1995; Santtila and Haapasalo 1997.
59. Ewing 1990; Myers et al. 1995.
60. See, e.g., Woods 1961; King 1975; Myers and Scott 1998.
61. Patterson 1943; Sargent 1962; Duncan and Duncan 1971; Malmquist 1971; Corder et al. 1976; Tanay 1976; Post 1982; Russell 1984; Heide 1992, 1994a.
62. See, e.g., King 1975; Sendi and Blomgren 1975; Lewis et al. 1985; Lewis, Pincus et al. 1988; Bailey 1994, 1996a; Santtila & Haapasalo 1997; Myers et al. 1995; Myers and Scott 1998.
63. See, e.g., Scherl and Mack 1966; Duncan and Duncan 1971; Malmquist 1971; Corder et al. 1976; Tanay 1976; Heide 1992, 1994a.
64. See, e.g., Sendi and Blomgren 1975; Corder et al. 1976; Lewis, Pincus et al. 1988; Bailey 1994, 1996a.
65. Heide 1992, 1994a.
66. Ewing 1990.
67. See., e.g., Sorrells 1977; Rosner et al. 1978; Fiddes 1981; Cornell, Benedek, and Benedek 1987a; Ewing 1990; Myers et al. 1995; Bailey 1996a.
68. See, e.g., McCarthy 1978; Lewis et al. 1985; Lewis, Lovely et al. 1988; Myers et al. 1995.
69. Patterson 1943; Malmquist 1971; Walshe-Brennan 1974.
70. See, e.g., Zenoff and Zients 1979.
71. Corder et al. 1976.
72. Busch et al. 1990; Zagar et al. 1990.
73. Ewing 1990.
74. Ewing 1990; Myers 1992. See, e.g., Lewis, Pincus et al. 1988; Busch et al. 1990; Myers and Kemph 1990; Zagar et al. 1990.
75. Malmquist 1971; Corder et al. 1976.
76. Cornell et al. 1987a.
77. Zagar et al. 1990.
78. Myers and Kemph 1990.
79. Myers and Scott 1998.
80. Bailey 1996a.
81. Santtila and Haapasalo 1997.
82. Sorrells 1977.
83. Cornell et al. 1987a.
84. U.S. Department of Justice 1987.
85. Fendrich et al. 1995.
86. Ibid., 1363.
87. Ewing 1990.
88. See, e.g., Smith 1965; Bailey 1994, 1996a.
89. See, e.g., Cornell et al. 1987a.
90. See, e.g., Scherl and Mack 1966; Sadoff 1971; Tanay 1976; Heide 1992.
91. See, e.g., Easson and Steinhilber 1961; Michaels 1961; Sendi and Blomgren 1975; Russell 1986; Myers et al. 1995.
92. See, e.g., Marten 1965; Corder et al. 1976; Zenoff and Zients 1979.
93. Busch et al. 1990.

94. Zagar et al. 1990.
95. Lewis et al. 1983, 1985; Lewis, Lovely et al. 1988; Lewis, Pincus et al. 1988.
96. Lewis, Lovely et al. 1988.
97. Santtila and Haapasalo 1997.
98. See, e.g., Corder et al. 1976; Cornell et al. 1987b; Cornell, Miller, and Benedek 1988.
99. Corder et al. 1976.
100. Cornell et al. 1987b, 386.
101. Cornell et al. 1987b; Cornell, Benedek, and Benedek 1989.
102. Cornell et al. 1988; for a discussion of various personality measures, see Sarason and Sarason 1996.
103. Cornell 1990.
104. For a discussion of various measures of personality, see Sarason and Sarason 1996.
105. Greco and Cornell 1992.
106. Cornell 1990; Heide 1992.
107. Myers et al. 1995.
108. Ibid., 1488.
109. Myers et al. 1995.
110. Portions of this section originally were published in the *Stanford Law and Policy Review,* 7(1), 43-49 (1996); in the *Proceedings of the Fourth Annual Meeting of the Homicide Research Working Group* (National Institute of Justice, 1995, pp. 29-34); and in *Behavioral Sciences and the Law, 15,* 203-220 (1997).
111. See, e.g., Florida Center for Children and Youth 1993; Snyder and Sickmund 1995; Willis 1995; Sickmund, Snyder, and Poe-Yamagata 1997.
112. U.S. Advisory Board on Child Abuse and Neglect 1993; Willis 1995.
113. See, e.g., Gelles and Conte 1990; Scudder et al. 1993; Smith and Thornberry 1995.
114. See, e.g., Sendi and Blomgren 1975; Lewis et al. 1979, 1983, 1985; Lewis, Lovely et al. 1988; Lewis, Pincus et al. 1988; Cornell 1989; Ewing 1990; Heide 1992.
115. Widom 1989a, 1989b, 1989c, 1989d.
116. Luntz and Widom 1994.
117. Smith and Thornberry 1995, 468.
118. Smith and Thornberry 1995.
119. Osofsky and Scheeringa 1997.
120. Thornberry 1994.
121. Hotaling and Sugarman 1986; Browne 1987; Briere 1992; Gelles and Conte 1990; Silvern et al. 1994; Thornberry 1994; Howell, Krisberg, and Jones 1995.
122. Smith and Thornberry 1995.
123. Heide 1992.
124. Ibid.
125. Reckless 1961; Hirschi 1969; Magid and McKelvey 1987; Bailey 1996a.
126. Magid and McKelvey 1987.
127. Heide 1992.
128. U.S. Department of Health and Human Services, Centers for Disease Control and Prevention, National Center for Health Statistics 1990, 198.
129. U.S. Department of Health and Human Services, Centers for Disease Control and Prevention, National Center for Health Statistics 1990; Bynum and Thompson 1995, 235.
130. Magid and McKelvey 1987, 187.
131. Carnegie Council on Adolescent Development 1995, 36.
132. U.S. Department of Commerce, Economics and Statistics Administration, Bureau of the Census 1994 (U.S. Bureau of Labor Statistics 1993, Table No. 626, p. 402).
133. Ibid. (U.S. Bureau of Labor Statistics 1993, Table No. 627, p. 402).
134. Carnegie Council on Adolescent Development 1995, 36.
135. Resnick et al. 1997.
136. Fox 1996.
137. See, e.g., Silverman and Dinitz 1974; Messerschmidt 1993.
138. Dunn 1996.
139. Prothrow-Stith and Weissman 1991; Bailey 1996a; Resnick et al. 1997.
140. Levin and Fox 1985; Prothrow-Stith and Weissman 1991; Fox and Levin 1994; Lacayo 1995; "Crime May Be Down" 1997.
141. Lacayo 1995.
142. Myers 1992.
143. Study called "Big World, Small Screen" discussed in Wheeler 1993.
144. Sleek 1994.
145. Wheeler 1993.
146. Sleek 1994.
147. See, e.g., Donnerstein 1984; Donnerstein, Linz, and Penrod 1987.
148. Fromm 1973; Solomon, Schmidt, and Ardragna 1990.
149. Jenkins 1995; Osofsky 1995; Marans and Berkman 1997.
150. See, e.g., Jenkins and Bell 1994.
151. Bell and Jenkins 1994 (testimony by Bell, November 29, 1994).
152. Barongan and Hall 1995.
153. Heide 1997a.
154. Sheley and Wright 1995.
155. Resnick et al. 1997.
156. Blumstein 1995; Fox 1996; Kennedy 1997; Sickmund, Snyder, and Poe-Yamagata 1997.
157. Snyder and Sickmund 1995.
158. Blumstein 1995, 1996; see also Kennedy 1997.
159. See, e.g., Elliott, Huizinga, and Menard 1989; Johnston, O'Malley, and Bachman 1993; Office of National Drug Control Policy 1995; Osgood 1995.
160. Bureau of Justice Statistics 1992; Osgood 1995; National Criminal Justice Reference Service 1997.
161. "Drug Use Up, Study Shows" 1997.
162. Office of National Drug Control Policy 1995.

163. Ibid.
164. Osgood 1995, 32.
165. See, e.g., Osgood et al. 1988; Elliott et al. 1989; Gottfredson and Hirschi 1990; Dembo et al. 1992; Resnick et al. 1997.
166. Ewing 1990; Stephens 1997.
167. Garfinkel and McLanahan 1986; Wright and Wright 1995.
168. Stephens 1997.
169. See Merton 1938; Cohen 1955; Cloward and Ohlin 1960.
170. Reckless 1961; Magid and McKelvey 1987.
171. Wilson and Daly 1985, 69.
172. Hirschi 1969. See also Sutherland and Cressey 1943; Sykes and Matza 1957.
173. Heide 1984; Cheatwood and Block 1990.
174. My clinical observations about the relationship among multiple offenders engaged in concurrent felonies and homicide are consistent with empirical findings reported by Cheatwood 1996.
175. Friedman 1993, 509.
176. Friedman 1992.
177. See, e.g., Wynne and Hess 1986; Lerner 1994.
178. Roth 1994a, 1994b, 8.
179. Reiss and Roth 1993; Moffitt, Lynam, and Silva 1994; Coccaro 1995.
180. Reiss and Roth 1993, 115.
181. See, e.g., Glueck and Glueck 1950; Eysenck 1977; Mednick and Christiansen 1977; Jeffrey 1979; Wilson and Herrnstein 1985; Fishbein 1990; Widom 1991; Lewis 1992; Pincus 1993; Reiss and Roth 1993; Moffitt et al. 1994; Roth 1994b; Goleman 1995.
182. Eysenck 1977.
183. Benjamin et al. 1996; Ebstein et al. 1996.
184. Reiss and Roth 1993; Coccaro 1995.
185. Goleman 1995.
186. Jeffrey 1979.
187. Wilson 1975.
188. Reiss and Roth 1993, 123. See also Moffitt et al. 1994.
189. Sarason and Sarason 1996.
190. Lewis et al. 1989, 1991; Lewis 1992.
191. Lewis, Lovely et al. 1988, 587.
192. Hughes et al. 1991.
193. Bailey 1996a.
194. Myers and Scott 1998.
195. Santtila and Haapasalo 1997.

■ Chapter 3

1. Eigen 1981; Bonnie 1989; Cornell, Staresina, and Benedek 1989.
2. "Young Suspect to Be Tried as Adult" 1997.
3. "Malcolm Shabazz Sentenced" 1997.
4. "2 Boys Convicted" 1995; "12- and 13-Year-Old Killers" 1996.
5. "18-Year-Old Gets Life" 1997.
6. Kaczor 1995a, 1995b, 1995c.
7. Brawning 1995.
8. Harper 1997.
9. Fagan 1995.
10. Dix 1988; Heide 1992; Territo, Halsted, and Bromley 1995.
11. Dix 1988; Heide 1992.
12. Dix 1988.
13. Dix 1988; Heide 1992.
14. Bonnie, 1989, 193-194.
15. Ellison 1987; Sickmund 1994; Coordinating Council on Juvenile Justice and Delinquency Prevention 1996.
16. DeFrances and Strom 1997.
17. Heide and Pardue 1986; Howell, Krisberg, and Jones 1995; Torbet et al. 1996; Dighton 1997.
18. Wilson and Howell 1993, cited in Howell, Krisberg, and Jones 1995.
19. Butts et al. 1996.
20. Sickmund 1994, 3; DeFrances and Strom 1997.
21. DeFrances and Strom 1997.
22. Ibid.
23. Ibid.
24. Gilliard and Beck 1996.
25. Howell, Krisberg, and Jones 1995.
26. Ogloff 1987.
27. Sanders 1989; Skovron, Scott, and Cullen 1989; Finkel et al. 1994; Crosby et al. 1995.
28. Gewerth & Dorne 1991; Streib 1994.
29. *Eddings v. Oklahoma* 1982.
30. *Thompson v. Oklahoma* 1988.
31. *Stanford v. Kentucky* 1989.
32. *Furman v. Georgia* 1972.
33. Streib 1997.
34. Ibid., 9.
35. Snell 1996, 8.
36. *Gregg v. Georgia* 1976.
37. Streib 1997, 4.
38. Ibid., 8.
39. Much of the material presented under mental status defenses appeared previously in Heide 1992.
40. Cornell, Benedek, and Staresina 1989.
41. Petrila and Otto 1996.
42. Rule 702 of the Federal Rules of Evidence.
43. Cornell, Benedek, and Staresina 1989; Fitch 1989; Melton et al. 1997.
44. Melton et al. 1997.
45. Ibid.
46. Heide 1992, 108.
47. Melton et al. 1997.
48. *Ford v. Wainwright* 1986.
49. Melton et al. 1997.
50. Fitch 1989; Melton et al. 1997.

51. For a more expansive discussion of mental status defenses, see Dix 1988; Melton et al. 1997.
52. Melton et al. 1997.
53. Stone 1975, 1978; Schopp 1991.
54. Wettstein, Mulvey, and Rogers 1991.
55. Melton et al. 1997.
56. Ibid.
57. Ibid.
58. Morris 1986; Schopp 1991; Heide 1992; Melton et al. 1997.
59. Morris 1986; Heide 1992; Melton et al. 1997.
60. See, e.g., Simon 1967; Wettstein et al. 1991.
61. Morris 1986.
62. See, e.g., Cornell, Staresina, and Benedek 1989, 172-174.
63. See, e.g., Pasewark 1981; Morris 1986; Cornell, Staresina, and Benedek 1989; Steadman 1993; Melton et al. 1997.
64. "Commitment Following an Insanity Acquittal" 1981; Morris 1986; Melton et al. 1997.
65. Dix 1988; Melton et al. 1997.
66. Cornell, Staresina, and Benedek 1989; Melton et al. 1997.

67. Rogers 1986, 223.
68. Schopp 1991, 71.
69. American Psychiatric Association 1994.
70. Rogers 1986.
71. Rogers 1986; Schopp 1991; Melton et al. 1997.
72. Schopp 1991.
73. Ibid., 71.
74. Shapiro 1984; Rogers 1986.
75. Shapiro 1984.
76. Ibid.
77. *Cirack v. State* 1967 (no longer law in Florida).
78. Dix 1988.
79. Melton et al. 1997.
80. Gillespie 1988.
81. Ewing 1987.
82. Browne 1987.
83. Gillespie 1988.
84. Heide 1992; Mones 1993.
85. Ewing 1987.
86. Heide 1992.
87. Ibid., 74-91.

■ Chapter 4

1. Leong 1989; Fitch 1989.
2. Heide 1992.
3. Leong 1989.
4. Heide 1992; Florida Statutes §921.142(7) 1995.
5. *Eddings v. Oklahoma* 1982; Greenwald 1983; Ellison 1987; Gewerth and Dorne 1991.
6. See, e.g., Florida Statutes §921.142(6) 1995.
7. See, e.g., Rogers 1988.
8. Pincus 1993; Moffitt, Lynam, and Silva 1994.
9. Pope, Butcher, and Seelen 1993.
10. Butcher 1990.
11. Heide and Solomon 1997.
12. Brandt 1988. See, e.g., Marten 1965; Herman 1986; Rogers 1986; Schacter 1986.
13. See, e.g., Rogers 1988.
14. Brandt 1988.
15. Leong 1989.
16. Grinder and Bandler 1981; professional training taken with international neurolinguistic programming trainers Edward and Maryann Reese, Southern Institute for NLP, Largo, Florida.
17. Bagley and Reese 1988; O'Hanlon and Martin 1992; Solomon and Heide 1995.
18. Harris 1988; Reitsma-Street and Leschied 1988; Heide 1992.
19. Warren 1971; Posey 1988; Van Voorhis 1988, 1994.
20. Sullivan, Grant, and Grant 1957; Van Voorhis 1994.
21. Warren 1983.

22. Warren 1969, 1971, 1978; Harris 1979, 1983, 1988; Heide 1982, 1983b, 1992; Posey 1988; Van Voorhis 1994.
23. Harris 1983.
24. Van Voorhis 1988, 1994.
25. Harris 1983. See, e.g., Werner 1975.
26. Palmer 1974, 1978; Heide 1982, 1983b; Van Voorhis 1988, 1994.
27. Harris 1983, 1988; Warren 1983; Van Voorhis 1994.
28. See, e.g., Harris, 1983, 1988; Van Voorhis 1988.
29. Harris 1988.
30. Sullivan et al. 1957; Warren 1983.
31. Warren 1983; Van Voorhis 1994.
32. Warren 1983.
33. Heide, 1983a, 1984, 1992.
34. Harris 1983.
35. Ibid.
36. Warren 1969, 1971, 1983; Harris 1988; Van Voorhis 1994.
37. Ibid.
38. Ibid.
39. Sullivan et al. 1957; Heide 1992.
40. Heide 1982, 1983b.
41. Roth 1994a.
42. Osgood 1995, 34.
43. Fromm 1973; Heide 1986, 1992.
44. Morgan 1975; "The Youth Crime Plague" 1977; Taft 1983; Press et al. 1986; Heide 1986; Annin 1996.
45. Heide 1986.
46. Fromm 1973.

PART II

1. Warren 1983; Harris 1983, 1988; Van Voorhis 1994.
2. Ibid.
3. Harris 1983.
4. Warren 1966, 1983; Harris 1983, 1988; Van Voorhis 1994.
5. Heide 1992.
6. Rosenhan and Seligman 1989.
7. Ibid.
8. Ibid.
9. Ibid.
10. See, e.g., Wertham 1941; Reinhardt 1970; Gardiner 1985; Leyton 1990; Mones 1991; Heide 1992.

Chapter 5

1. Harris 1983.
2. Heide 1992.
3. Grinder and Bandler 1981; professional training taken with international NLP trainers Edward and Maryann Reese, Southern Institute for NLP, Largo, Florida.

Chapter 6

1. Harris 1983.
2. Samenow 1984.
3. MacDonald 1980.

Chapter 7

1. Florida Statutes §782 1997.
2. Zimbardo 1975.

Chapter 8

1. Harris 1983.
2. Ibid.
3. Heide 1984.
4. Florida Statutes §782 1997.
5. Blumstein and Heinz 1995.

Chapter 9

1. Harris 1983.
2. Blumstein 1995, 1996; Blumstein and Heinz 1995.

Chapter 10

1. American Psychiatric Association 1994.

Chapter 11

1. Eth 1989.

PART III

Chapter 12

1. Boyer 1996a, 1996b.
2. Annin 1996.
3. See, e.g., Barr 1992; Biskup and Cozic 1992; Cowan, Myerscough, and Smith 1992; Kramer 1992; Weaver 1992; Myers et al. 1995; Streib 1995.
4. Streib 1983, 1987, 1992, 1994, 1995, 1997; Streib & Sametz 1989.
5. See, e.g., Cornell, Staresina, and Benedek 1989; Bonnie 1989; Ewing 1990; Myers et al. 1995.
6. Heide 1984.
7. See, e.g., Sykes 1958; Toch 1977; Silverman 1996.
8. Ibid.
9. Krisberg et al. 1995. See, e.g., Andrews et al. 1990; Lipsey 1992; Palmer 1992.
10. Howell 1995c, 20.
11. Wilson and Howell 1993.
12. Wilson and Howell 1993; Howell 1995b; Howell and Krisberg 1995.
13. Howell 1995c, 14.
14. Bailey 1994, 1995, 1996a.
15. Bailey 1995, 7.
16. Benedek, Cornell, and Staresina 1989; Myers 1992.
17. Tate, Reppucci, and Mulvey 1995.

18. See, e.g., Agee 1979; Washbrook 1979; Petti and Wells 1980; Myers and Kemph 1988.
19. Cornell 1989; Ewing 1990.
20. Benedek et al. 1989; Tate et al. 1995.
21. Myers 1992. See, e.g., Rosner et al. 1978.
22. Myers 1992.
23. Myers 1992; Tate et al. 1995.
24. Keith 1984.
25. Smith 1965; Scherl and Mack 1966; McCarthy 1978; Myers and Kemph 1988; Bailey 1996a.
26. Myers and Kemph 1988.
27. Bailey 1996a, 1996b.
28. Myers 1992; Bailey 1996b.
29. Carek and Watson 1964; Pfeffer 1980; Mouridsen and Tolstrup 1988.
30. See, e.g., Haizlip, Corder, and Ball 1984.
31. Myers 1992.
32. Myers 1992. See, e.g., Russell 1965; Gardiner 1985.
33. Myers 1992, 53.
34. Gardiner 1985; Myers 1992.
35. Fiddes 1981; Sorrells 1981; Myers 1992.
36. Cornell, Benedek, and Benedek 1989; Myers 1992.
37. Myers 1992, 55.
38. Myers 1992.
39. Myers 1992; Tate et al. 1995.
40. Reiss and Roth 1993; Roth 1994b.
41. Myers 1992.
42. Myers 1992. See also Puig-Antich 1982; Campbell et al. 1984; Post, Rubinow, and Uhde 1984; Kaplan et al. 1990; Kafantaris et al. 1992. For descriptions of the types of drugs, see Preston and Johnson 1990; Medical Economics Data Production Company 1998.
43. Coccaro 1995. For a description of this type of drug, see Medical Economics Data Production Company 1998.
44. Benedek et al. 1989, 234. See, e.g., Tupin 1987.
45. Myers 1992, 56.
46. Medlicott 1955; Foster 1964; Hellsten and Katila 1965; Duncan and Duncan 1971; Corder et al. 1976; Tanay 1976; Cormier and Markus 1980; Gardiner 1985.
47. Benedek et al. 1989, 239.
48. Benedek et al. 1989.
49. Heide 1992.
50. Toupin 1993.
51. See also Heide in press.
52. Warren 1966, 1969, 1971, 1978, 1983; Agee 1979; Heide 1992; Van Voorhis 1994.
53. Agee 1979, 1.
54. Agee 1979.
55. Gendreau and Ross 1979; Gendreau 1981, 1996; Greenwood and Zimring 1985; Ross and Fabiano 1985; Greenwood 1986; Andrews et al. 1990.
56. Bailey 1996a, 1996b.
57. Tate et al. 1995.
58. Benedek et al. 1989.
59. Goldstein and Huff 1993; Branch 1997.
60. Heide 1992; Finkelhor and Dziuba-Leatherman 1994; Widom 1989c.
61. Solomon and Heide 1997.
62. Briere 1992; Sanford 1990; Herman 1992.
63. American Psychiatric Association 1994. Diagnoses not clarified here were presented in Table 4.4.
64. Osofsky and Scheeringa 1997.
65. Jenkins 1995.
66. Crimmins et al. 1997; Steiner, Garcia, and Zakee 1997.
67. Solomon and Heide 1994.
68. Warren 1969, 1971; Palmer 1975; Harris 1988; Reitsma-Street and Leschied 1988; Andrews et al. 1990; Heide 1992.
69. Ellis 1986; Meichenbaum 1977, 1985; Gibbs 1993; Hollin 1993.
70. DeJong n.d.
71. Goldstein and Glick, 1987; Goldstein 1988, 114-122; Goldstein 1993.
72. See, e.g., Empey and Rabow 1961; Greenwood and Zimring 1985; Gibbs 1993.
73. Goldstein 1988.
74. Heide, McCann, and Solomon 1992.
75. Azar 1997.
76. Goldstein 1988; Agee 1995.
77. Agee 1995, 181, emphasis in original.
78. Heide 1992.
79. Altschuler and Armstrong 1994.
80. Bailey 1994, 1996a.
81. Altschuler and Armstrong 1984; Armstrong and Altschuler 1994; Bailey 1996a.
82. Altschuler and Armstrong 1984, 1994; Armstrong and Altschuler 1994.
83. Agee 1995, 184.
84. Roth 1994a, 1994b.
85. See, e.g., Hirschi 1969.
86. Coordinating Council on Juvenile Justice and Delinquency Prevention 1996, 11.
87. Ibid.
88. Coordinating Council on Juvenile Justice and Delinquency Prevention 1996.
89. Ibid., 112.
90. Bailey 1995, 7.
91. Howell 1995b.
92. Wiebush et al. 1995; Gendreau and Goggin 1997; Van Voorhis 1997.

▪ Chapter 13

1. Reiss and Roth 1993, 101-129, 297; Roth 1994a.
2. American Psychological Association 1993a, 1993b.
3. American Psychological Association 1993a, 14.
4. Satcher et al. 1996, v.
5. President's Crime Prevention Council 1995.
6. Rosenberg 1995.
7. American Psychological Association 1993a, 1993b; Howell 1995b; Foote 1997; Loeber and Farrington 1998.
8. Tremblay et al. 1991, 1992; Tolan and Guerra 1994; Howell 1995b; Thornberry, Huizinga, and Loeber 1995; Coordinating Council on Juvenile Justice and Delinquency Prevention 1996; Foote 1997; Loeber and Farrington 1998.
9. Hawkins and Catalano 1992; Hawkins, Catalano, and Miller 1992; Institute of Medicine 1994; Olds and Kitzman 1993; Yoshikawa 1994, as cited in Howell 1995b; Powell and Hawkins 1996.
10. American Psychological Association 1993a; Kelley et al. 1997; Loeber and Farrington 1998.
11. DeJong 1994, chap. 4; Howell 1995b; Howell, Krisberg, Hawkins, and Wilson 1995; Wilson and Howell 1995.
12. Hawkins, Catalano, and Brewer 1995; Howell 1995b.
13. Brewer et al. 1995; Howell 1995b.
14. Howell 1995b.
15. Coordinating Council on Juvenile Justice and Delinquency Prevention 1996.
16. Powell et al. 1996; Powell and Hawkins 1996.
17. Streib 1995; Heide 1996.
18. Attorney General Daniel E. Lungren's Policy Council on Violence Prevention 1995.
19. Ibid., 7.
20. Ibid., 13.
21. Gottfredson and Hirschi 1990.
22. Hirschi 1969; Gottfredson and Hirschi 1990.
23. Resnick et al. 1997.
24. See, e.g., Tremblay et al. 1991, 1992.
25. Heide 1992.
26. Straus 1994, 148-161.
27. Haugaard et al. 1995; Murray 1995b.
28. American Psychological Association 1993a; Murray 1995c.
29. Heide 1992; Haugaard et al., 1995.
30. Heide 1992; Rivara et al. 1997.
31. Heide 1992.
32. See, e.g., DeJong n.d.; Tremblay et al. 1991, 1992; Bannister 1996; Embry et al. 1996; Farrell, Meyer, and Dahlberg 1996.
33. See, e.g., American Psychological Association 1993a; Attorney General Daniel E. Lungren's

Policy Council on Violence Prevention 1995, 193-194, 209-213.
34. Goldstein and Glick 1987; Goldstein 1988; Tremblay et al. 1991, 1992; DeJong 1994, 19-33; Coordinating Council on Juvenile Justice and Delinquency Prevention 1996, 57. See, e.g., Prothrow-Stith 1987; Kelder et al. 1996.
35. Sloan 1997.
36. Heide 1992.
37. Resnick et al. 1997.
38. National Criminal Justice Reference Service 1994; Ansari and Kress 1996; Stephens 1997.
39. Clinton 1995.
40. DeAngelis 1995.
41. Becker 1994; Straus 1994, 168-169; Murray 1995a; Coordinating Council on Juvenile Justice and Delinquency Prevention 1996, 56. See, e.g., Ringwalt et al. 1996.
42. May and Martin 1993; May, Christoffel, and Sprang 1994; Holmes et al. 1995.
43. See, e.g., DeJong 1994, 35-47; "Help Member Focus" 1995.
44. See, e.g., Ringwalt et al. 1996.
45. Straus 1994, 169-171; Stephens 1997.
46. Marans and Berkman 1997.
47. National Crime Prevention Council 1994a, 1.
48. National Crime Prevention Council 1994b; Cronin 1995.
49. Straus 1994, 171-172.
50. Straus 1994.
51. Coordinating Council on Juvenile Justice and Delinquency Prevention 1996, 58; see, e.g., McGillis 1996.
52. Straus 1994, 163-165.
53. Ibid., 162-163.
54. Straus 1994, 165-167; Coordinating Council on Juvenile Justice and Delinquency Prevention 1996, 58.
55. Straus 1994, 167.
56. Costello 1995.
57. Sampson, Raudenbush, and Earls 1997.
58. Hsia 1997.
59. Ibid., 2.
60. Ibid., 4.
61. Reiss and Roth 1993.
62. Ibid.
63. Family and Medical Leave Act of 1993; Stockfisch 1997.
64. Magid and McKelvey 1987.
65. Myers and Scott 1998.
66. Straus 1994, 190.
67. Coordinating Council on Juvenile Justice and Delinquency Prevention 1996, 56.
68. Straus 1994, 172-174.

69. Magid and McKelvey 1987; Schorr 1988; American Psychological Association 1993a; Gilliard and Beck 1996; Bonczar and Beck 1997, 5-6.
70. American Psychological Association 1993a; U.S. Department of Justice 1996a, 1996b.
71. Roth 1995b.
72. Jacobs and Potter 1995; O'Donnell 1995; U.S. Department of Justice 1996a, 1996b.
73. Blumstein 1995; Fox 1996; Snyder, Sickmund, and Poe-Yamagata 1996; Kennedy 1997.
74. Kennedy 1997.
75. Sheley and Wright 1993; U.S. Department of Justice 1996a.
76. Straus 1994.
77. Congressional Budget Office, U.S. Congress 1992.
78. "S&L Bailout" 1996.
79. American Psychological Association 1993a; National Criminal Justice Reference Service 1994; Straus 1994, 195-200; Osofsky 1995.
80. DeJong 1994, 49-57.
81. Ibid., 42-43, 49-57.
82. An example is Rise High Projects Inc. in Chicago.
83. Attorney General Daniel E. Lungren's Policy Council on Violence Prevention 1995, 212-213.
84. Donnelly 1991.
85. Egeland, Jacobvitz, and Sroufe 1988.

References

Abrahamse, A. F. (1996). The coming wave of violence in California. In P. K. Lattimore & C. A. Nahabedian (Eds.), *The nature of homicide: Trends and changes—Proceedings of the 1996 meeting of the Homicide Research Working Group* (pp. 40-52). Washington, DC: National Institute of Justice.

Adams, K. A. (1974). The child who murders: A review of theory and research. *Criminal Justice and Behavior, 1,* 51-61.

Adelson, L. (1972). The battering child. *Journal of the American Medical Association, 222,* 159-161.

Agee, V. L. (1979). *Treatment of the violent incorrigible adolescent.* Lexington, MA: Lexington Books.

Agee, V. L. (1995). Managing clinical programs for juvenile delinquents. In B. Glick & A. Goldstein (Eds.), *Managing delinquency programs that work* (pp. 173-186). Laurel, MD: American Correctional Association.

Altschuler, D. M. (1995, November). *Juveniles and violence: Is there an epidemic and what can be done?* Paper presented at the annual meeting of the American Society of Criminology, Boston.

Altschuler, D., & Armstrong, T. (1984). Intervening with serious juvenile offenders. In R. Mathias, P. DeMuro, & R. Allinson (Eds.), *Violent juvenile offenders* (pp. 187-206). San Francisco: National Council on Crime and Delinquency.

Altschuler, D., & Armstrong, T. (1994). *Intensive aftercare for high-risk juveniles: A community care model.* Washington, DC: U.S. Department of Justice, Office of Juvenile Justice and Delinquency Prevention.

American Psychiatric Association. (1994). *Diagnostic and statistical manual of mental disorders* (4th ed.). Washington, DC: Author.

American Psychological Association. (1993a). *Violence and youth: Psychology's response,* Vol. 1: *Summary report of the American Psychological Commission on Violence and Youth.* Washington, DC: Author.

American Psychological Association. (1993b). *Violence and youth: Psychology's response,* Vol. 2: *Reason to hope: A psychosocial perspective on violence and youth.* Washington, DC: Author.

Andrews, D. A., Zinger, I., Hoge, R. D., Bonta, J., Gendreau, P., & Cullen, F. T. (1990). Does correctional treatment work? A clinically relevant and psychologically informed meta-analysis. *Criminology, 28,* 369-404.

Annin, P. (1996, January 22). "Superpredators" arrive: Should we cage the new breed of vicious kids? *Newsweek,* p. 57.

Ansari, B., & Kress, D. (1996). Minneapolis youth homicide study. In P. K. Lattimore & C. A. Nahabedian (Eds.), *The nature of homicide: Trends and changes—Proceedings of the 1996 meeting of the Homicide Research Working Group* (pp. 64-65). Washington, DC: National Institute of Justice.

Anthony, E. J., & Rizzo, A. (1973). Adolescent girls who kill or try to kill their fathers. In E. J. Anthony & C. Koupernik (Eds.), *The impact of disease and death* (pp. 330-350). New York: Wiley Interscience.

Anti-Defamation League. (1995a, June 27). ADL survey documents and analyzes growing menace of Neo-Nazi Skinheads and their international connections. *U.S. Newswire.* (Available on-line)

Anti-Defamation League. (1995b, June 28). Text of ADL report, "The Skinhead International: A Worldwide Survey of Neo-Nazi Skinheads." *U.S. Newswire.* (Available on-line)

Armstrong, T. L., & Altschuler, D. M. (1994). Recent developments in programming for high-risk juvenile parolees: Assessment findings and program prototype development. In R. A. Roberts (Ed.), *Critical issues in crime and justice* (pp. 189-213). Thousand Oaks, CA: Sage.

Attorney General Daniel E. Lungren's Policy Council on Violence Prevention. (1995, August). *Violence prevention: A vision of hope* (pamphlet). Sacramento: California Attorney General's Office, Crime and Violence Prevention Center.

Azar, B. (1997, November). Defining the trait that makes us human. *The APA Monitor,* pp. 1, 15.

Bagley, D. S., & Reese, E. J. (1988). *Beyond selling.* Cupertino, CA: Meta.

Bagnall, J. (1994a, May 14). Boy, 16, guilty in depanneur slaying. *The Gazette* (Montreal), p. A1.

Bagnall, J. (1994b, June 18). New face of fear: Impassive teenage killers. *The Gazette* (Montreal), p. A1.

Bailey, S. (1994). Critical pathways of child and adolescent murderers. *Chronicle, International Association of Juvenile and Family Court Magistrates, 1*(3), 5-12.

Bailey, S. (1995). Young offenders, serious crimes. *British Journal of Psychiatry, 167,* 5-7.

Bailey, S. (1996a). Adolescents who murder. *Journal of Adolescence, 19,* 19-39.

Bailey, S. (1996b). Current perspectives on young offenders: Aliens or alienated? *Journal of Clinical Forensic Medicine, 3,* 1-7.

Bannister, T. (1996). *Evaluation of violence prevention programs in middle schools* (National Institute of Justice research in brief). Washington, DC: U.S. Department of Justice, Office of Justice Programs.

Barkley, R. A. (1990). *Attention deficit hyperactivity disorder: A handbook for diagnosis and treatment.* New York: Guilford.

Barkley, R. A. (1997). *Defiant children: A clinician's manual for assessment and parent training* (2nd ed.). New York: Guilford.

Barongan, C., & Hall, G. C. N. (1995). The influence of misogynous rap music on sexual aggression against women. *Psychology of Women Quarterly, 19*(2), 195-207.

Barr, W. B. (1992). Violent youths should be punished as adults. In D. Biskup & C. Cozic (Eds.), *Youth violence* (pp. 216-220). San Diego: Greenhaven.

Baxter, N. (1994, October 5). Is juvenile crime scare reality or hype? *Phoenix Gazette* (Northwest Community), p. 5.

Becker, J. (1994). *Mentoring high-risk kids.* Minneapolis, MN: Johnson Institute-QVS, Inc.

Bell, C. C., & Jenkins, E. (1994, November 29). *Statement before the Subcommittee on Juvenile Justice of the Senate Committee on Juvenile Crime: Breaking the cycles of violence,* presented by C. C. Bell, Community Mental Health Council.

Bender, L. (1959). Children and adolescents who have killed. *American Journal of Psychiatry, 116,* 510-513.

Bender, L., & Curran, F. J. (1940). Children and adolescents who kill. *Criminal Psychopathology, 1,* 297-321.

Benedek, E. P., & Cornell, D. G. (1989). Clinical presentations of homicidal adolescents. In E. P. Benedek & D. G. Cornell (Eds.), *Juvenile homicide* (pp. 37-57). Washington, DC: American Psychiatric Press.

Benedek, E. P., Cornell, D. G., & Staresina, L. (1989). Treatment of the homicidal adolescent. In E. P. Benedek & D. G. Cornell (Eds.), *Juvenile*

homicide (pp. 221-247). Washington, DC: American Psychiatric Press.

Benjamin, J., Li, L., Patterson, C., Greenberg, B. D., Murphy, D. L., & Hamer, D. H. (1996). Population and familial association between the D4 and dopamine receptor gene and measures of novelty seeking. *Nature Genetics, 12,* 81-84.

Bergman, B. (1995, August 14). Wild in the streets. *Maclean's,* p. 18.

Bergman, L. (1992). Dating violence among high school students. *Social Work, 37*(1), 21-27.

Bernstein, J. I. (1978). Premeditated murder by an eight year old boy. *International Journal of Offender Therapy and Comparative Criminology, 22,* 47-56.

Biskup, D., & Cozic, C. (Eds.). (1992). *Youth violence.* San Diego: Greenhaven.

Bjerregaard, B., & Smith, C. (1995). Gender differences in gang participation, delinquency, and substance abuse. In M. W. Klein, C. L. Maxson, & J. Miller (Eds.), *The modern gang reader* (pp. 93-105). Los Angeles: Roxbury.

Blanchfield, M. (1995, August 15). Battersby's father calls prison term "very light." *Ottawa Citizen,* p. A1.

Blassnig, R. (1994, June 5). Canada may get tough with juvenile offenders. *Buffalo News* (News), p. 4.

Block, C. R., & Block, R. (1995). Street gang crime in Chicago. In M. W. Klein, C. L. Maxson, & J. Miller (Eds.), *The modern gang reader* (pp. 202-211). Los Angeles: Roxbury.

Block, C. R., & Christakos, A. (1995). Chicago homicides from the sixties to the nineties: Major trends in lethal violence. In C. R. Block & R. Block (Eds.), *Trends, risks, and interventions in lethal violence: Proceedings of the third annual symposium of the Homicide Research Working Group* (pp. 17-50). Washington, DC: National Institute of Justice.

Block, R. L. (1977). *Violent crime: Environment, interaction, and death.* Lexington, MA: Lexington Books.

Blumstein, A. (1995, August). Violence by young people: Why the deadly nexus? *National Institute of Justice Journal,* pp. 2-9.

Blumstein, A. (1996, June). Youth violence, guns, and illicit markets. *National Institute of Justice Research Review,* pp. 1-3.

Blumstein, A., & Heinz, H. J. (1995). Youth violence, guns, and the illicit-drug industry. In C. R. Block & R. Block (Eds.), *Trends, risks, and interventions in lethal violence: Proceedings of the third annual symposium of the Homicide Research Working Group* (pp. 3-15). Washington, DC: National Institute of Justice.

Bonczar, T. P., & Beck, A. J. (1997, March). *Lifetime likelihood of going to state or federal prison.*

Washington, DC: U.S. Department of Justice, Office of Justice Programs, Bureau of Justice Statistics.

Bonnie, R. J. (1989). Juvenile homicide: A study in legal ambivalence. In E. P. Benedek & D. G. Cornell (Eds.), *Juvenile homicide* (pp. 183-217). Washington, DC: American Psychiatric Press.

Bortner, M. A. (1988). *Delinquency and justice.* New York: McGraw-Hill.

Bowles, S. (1997, December 3). Even those closest to teen cannot answer why. *USA Today*, pp. A1-A2.

Boy allows burning for soda and a quarter. (1995, October 13). *Tampa Tribune* (Nation/World), p. 10.

Boy held in deaths. (1996, February 5). *Tampa Tribune* (Nation/World), p. 4.

Boy murdered mother with bow, arrows. (1995, October 2). *Tampa Tribune* (Nation/World), p. 2.

Boyer, B. (1996a, November 9). Judge: "Too late" for teen. *Tampa Tribune* (Nation/World), pp. 1, 11.

Boyer, B. (1996b, December 8). Prison adds teen to juvenile roll. *Tampa Tribune* (Florida/Metro), p. 1.

Branch, C. (1997). *Clinical interventions with gang adolescents and their families.* Boulder, CO: Westview.

Brandt, J. (1988). Malingered amnesia. In R. Rogers (Ed.), *Clinical assessment of malingering and deception* (pp. 65-83). New York: Guilford.

Brawning, M. (1995, September 18). Relocating Crumitie proved a failure. *The Ledger* (Lakeland, FL), p. B4.

Brewer, D. D., Hawkins, J. D., Catalano, R. F., & Neckerman, H. J. (1995). Preventing serious, violent, and chronic juvenile offending: A review of evaluations of selected strategies in childhood, adolescence, and the community. In J. C. Howell, B. Krisberg, J. D. Hawkins, & J. J. Wilson (Eds.), *A sourcebook: Serious, violent, and chronic juvenile offenders* (pp. 61-141). Thousand Oaks, CA: Sage.

Brewer, V. E., Damphousse, K. R., & Edison, W. G. (1996). *Murder in Space City* re-examined: Houston homicide twenty years later. In P. K. Lattimore & C. A. Nahabedian (Eds.), *The nature of homicide: Trends and changes—Proceedings of the 1996 meeting of the Homicide Research Working Group* (pp. 100-105). Washington, DC: National Institute of Justice.

Briere, J. N. (1992). *Child abuse trauma.* Newbury Park, CA: Sage.

Browne, A. (1987). *When battered women kill.* New York: Free Press.

Bureau of Justice Statistics. (1992, December). *Drugs, crime, and the justice system: A national report from the Bureau of Justice Statistics.* Washington, DC: U.S. Department of Justice, Office of Justice Programs, Bureau of Justice Statistics.

Burgess, A. W., Groth, A. N., Holmstrom, L. L., & Sgroi, S. M. (1978). *Sexual assault of children and adolescents.* Lexington, MA: Lexington Books.

Busch, K. G., Zagar, R., Hughes, J. R., Arbit, J., & Bussell, R. E. (1990). Adolescents who kill. *Journal of Clinical Psychology, 46,* 472-485.

Butcher, J. N. (1990). *MMPI-2 in psychological treatment.* New York: Oxford University Press.

Butts, J. A., & Snyder, H. N. (1997, September). *The youngest delinquents: Offenders under age 15* (OJJDP bulletin). Washington, DC: U.S. Department of Justice, Office of Juvenile Justice and Delinquency Prevention.

Butts, J. A., Snyder, H. N., Finnegan, T. A., Aughenbaugh, A. L., & Poole, R. S. (1996). *Juvenile court statistics 1994.* Washington, DC: U.S. Department of Justice, Office of Juvenile Justice and Delinquency Prevention.

Bynum, J. E., & Thompson, W. E. (1995). *Juvenile delinquency: A sociological approach* (3rd ed.). Boston: Allyn & Bacon.

Campbell, M., Small, A. M., Green, W. H., Jennings, S. J., Perry, R., Bennett, W. G., & Anderson, L. (1984). Behavioral efficacy of haloperidol and lithium carbonate: A comparison in hospitalized aggressive children with conduct disorder children. *Archives of General Psychiatry, 41,* 650-656.

Candisky, C. (1995, March 5). Juvenile crime legislation is taking form. *Columbus Dispatch*, p. D1.

Carek, D. J., & Watson, A. S. (1964). Treatment of a family involved in fratricide. *Archives of General Psychiatry, 11,* 533-542.

Carnegie Council on Adolescent Development. (1995, October). *Great transitions: Preparing adolescents for a new century.* New York: Carnegie Corporation of New York.

Chachere, V. (1995, September 30). Student shot dead at school. *Tampa Tribune* (Nation/World), p. 1.

Chard, J. (1995, June). Factfinder on crime and the administration of justice in Canada. *Juristat, 15*(10), 1-25. (Canadian Centre for Justice Statistics)

Cheatwood, D. (1996). Interactional patterns in multiple-offender homicides. *Justice Quarterly, 13*(1), 107-128.

Cheatwood, D., & Block, K. J. (1990). Youth and homicide: An investigation of the age factor in criminal homicide. *Justice Quarterly, 7*(2), 265-292.

Chen, J. (1996). Firearms in the homicides and suicides of youths. In P. K. Lattimore & C. A. Nahabedian (Eds.), *The nature of homicide: Trends and changes—Proceedings of the 1996 meeting of the Homicide Research Working Group* (pp. 52-57). Washington, DC: National Institute of Justice.

Chin, K.-L. (1995). Chinese gangs and extortion. In M. W. Klein, C. L. Maxson, & J. Miller (Eds.), *The modern gang reader* (pp. 46-52). Los Angeles: Roxbury.

Chiricos, T. (1994, March 29). Media hysteria over crime, violence creates moral panic: Sudden firestorm ignores facts—Crime has not become worse. *Arizona Republic*, p. B5.

Cirack v. State, 201 So. 2d 706 (File 1967); no longer law.

Clary, M. (1994, February 23). Who's to blame? *Los Angeles Times*, p. E1.

Clinton, H. R. (1995). *It takes a village and other lessons children teach us.* New York: Simon & Schuster.

Cloward, R. A., & Ohlin, L. E. (1960). *Delinquency and opportunity.* New York: Free Press.

Coccaro, E. F. (1995, January-February). The biology of aggression. *Scientific American*, pp. 38-47.

Cohen, A. (1955). *Delinquent boys: The culture of the gang.* New York: Free Press.

Commitment following an insanity acquittal. (1981). *Harvard Law Review, 94*, 605-607.

Congressional Budget Office, U.S. Congress. (1992, January). *A CBO study: The economic effects of the savings and loan crisis.* Washington, DC: Government Printing Office.

Contenta, S. (1995, April 8). Mourners grapple with "senseless act." *Toronto Star*, p. A2.

Coordinating Council on Juvenile Justice and Delinquency Prevention. (1996, March). *Combating violence and delinquency: The National Juvenile Justice Action Plan.* Washington, DC: U.S. Department of Justice, Office of Juvenile Justice and Delinquency Prevention.

Corder, B. F., Ball, B. C., Haizlip, T. M., Rollins, R., & Beaumont, R. (1976). Adolescent parricide: A comparison with other adolescent murder. *American Journal of Psychiatry, 133*, 957-961.

Cormier, B. M., Angliker, C. C. J., Gagne, P. W., & Markus, B. (1978). Adolescents who kill a member of the family. In J. M. Eekelaar & S. N. Katz (Eds.), *Family violence: An international and interdisciplinary study* (pp. 466-478). Toronto: Butterworth.

Cormier, B. M., & Markus, B. (1980). A longitudinal study of adolescent murderers. *Bulletin of the American Academy of Psychiatry and Law, 8*, 240-260.

Cornell, D. G. (1989). Causes of juvenile homicide: A review of the literature. In E. P. Benedek & D. G. Cornell (Eds.), Juvenile homicide (pp. 3-36). Washington, DC: American Psychiatric Press.

Cornell, D. G. (1990). Prior adjustment of violent juvenile offenders. *Law and Human Behavior, 14*, 569-577.

Cornell, D. G. (1993). Juvenile homicide: A growing national problem. *Behavioral Sciences and the Law, 11*, 389-396.

Cornell, D. G., Benedek, E. P., & Benedek, D. M. (1987a). Characteristics of adolescents charged with homicide. *Behavioral Sciences and the Law, 5*, 11-23.

Cornell, D. G., Benedek, E. P., & Benedek, D. M. (1987b). Juvenile homicide: Prior adjustment and a proposed typology. *American Journal of Orthopsychiatry, 57*, 383-393.

Cornell, D. G., Benedek, E. P., & Benedek, D. M. (1989). A typology of juvenile homicide offenders. In E. P. Benedek & D. G. Cornell (Eds.), *Juvenile homicide* (pp. 59-84). Washington, DC: American Psychiatric Press.

Cornell, D. G., Miller, C., & Benedek, E. P. (1988). MMPI profiles of adolescents charged with homicide. *Behavioral Sciences and the Law, 6*, 401-407.

Cornell, D. G., Staresina, L., & Benedek, E. P. (1989). Legal outcome of juveniles charged with homicide. In E. P. Benedek & D. G. Cornell (Eds.), *Juvenile homicide* (pp. 163-182). Washington, DC: American Psychiatric Press.

Costello, L. (Ed.). (1995). *Part of the solution: Creative alternatives for youth.* Washington, DC: National Assembly of State Arts Agencies.

Cowan, F. J., Myerscough, E. A., & Smith, D. A. (1992). The death penalty should be imposed on juvenile murderers. In D. Biskup & C. Cozic (Eds.), *Youth violence* (pp. 221-226). San Diego: Greenhaven.

Crawford, S. (1995a, February 26). A crime that shocks; Spate of parent killings leaves experts baffled by frequent lack of remorse. *Dallas Morning News*, p. A35.

Crawford, S. (1995b, August 3). Lawsuit is settled in '91 hate slaying. *Dallas Morning News*, p. A28.

Creechan, J. (1994, May 29). Facts and fallacies about young offenders and the YOA. *Ottawa Citizen*, p. A11.

Crime may be down, but fear is going up. (1993, December 8). *The Record* (Hackensack, NJ), p. B8.

Crime may be down, but not on TV news. (1997, August 13). *Tampa Tribune* (Nation/World), p. 2.

Crimmins, S., Langley, J. M., Ryder, J. M., & Brownstein, H. (1997, November). *Posttraumatic stress disorder (PTSD) in adult male offenders.* Paper presented at the annual meeting of the American Society of Criminology, San Diego.

The crisis at juvenile hall [editorial]. (1994, February 11). *Sacramento Bee*, p. B6.

Cronin, R. C. (1995, July). *Innovative community partnerships: Working together for change.* Washington, DC: U.S. Department of Justice, Office of Juvenile Justice and Delinquency Prevention.

Crosby, C. A., Britner, P. A., Jodl, K. M., & Portwood, S. G. (1995). The juvenile death penalty and the Eighth Amendment: An empirical investigation of societal consensus and proportionality. *Law and Human Behavior, 19,* 245-261.

Davey, C. (1994, April 17). AG candidate gets tough for campaign. *Dayton Daily News,* p. B3.

DeAngelis, T. (1995, September). A nation of hermits: The loss of community. *The APA Monitor,* pp. 1, 46.

Death wears a boy's face. (1995, September 25). *Tampa Tribune* (Metro), p. 4.

DeFrances, C. J., & Strom, K. (1997, March). *Juveniles prosecuted in state courts.* Washington, DC: U.S. Department of Justice, Office of Justice Programs, Bureau of Justice Statistics.

DeJong, W. (1994, November). *Preventing interpersonal violence among youth: An introduction to school, community, and mass media strategies.* Washington, DC: U.S. Department of Justice, Office of Justice Programs, National Institute of Justice Issues and Practices.

DeJong, W. (n.d.). *Building the peace: The Resolving Conflict Creatively Program (RCCP).* Washington, DC: U.S. Department of Justice, Office of Justice Programs, National Institute of Justice.

Dembo, R., Williams, L., Wothke, W., Schmeidler, J., Getreu, A., Berry, E., & Wish, E. D. (1992). The generality of deviance: Replication of a structural model among high-risk youths. *Journal of Research in Crime and Delinquency, 29,* 200-216.

Dexter, B. (1995, August 17). Family's petition is gaining support. *Toronto Star,* p. NY2.

Diaz, K. (1993, September 15). Slaying in Lino Lakes apparently capped a night of gunplay for boy, woman. *Star Tribune* (Minneapolis), p. A1.

Dighton, D. (1997). Criminal court: States broaden scope of transfer laws. *The Compiler* (Illinois Criminal Justice Information Agency), pp. 11-14.

Dix, G. E. (1988). *Gilbert law summaries: Criminal law* (14th ed.). Chicago: Harcourt Brace Jovanovich Legal and Professional Publications.

Dolik, H. (1993, July 20). "Short" jail term causes anger. *Calgary Herald,* p. B1.

Donnelly, A. H. C. (1991). What have we learned about prevention? What should we do about it? *Child Abuse & Neglect, 15*(1), 99-106.

Donnerstein, E. (1984). Pornography: Its effect on violence against women. In N. M. Malamuth & E. Donnerstein (Eds.), *Pornography and sexual aggression* (pp. 53-81). Orlando, FL: Academic Press.

Donnerstein, E., Linz, D., & Penrod, S. (1987). *The question of pornography: Research findings and policy implications.* New York: Free Press.

Dranoff, L. S. (1997, March). How the law treats youth crime; Canada's Young Offenders Act. *Chatelaine,* p. 20.

Drug use up, study shows. (1997, August 14). *Tampa Tribune* (Nation/World), p. 4.

Duncan, J. W., & Duncan, G. M. (1971). Murder in the family. *American Journal of Psychiatry, 127,* 74-78.

Dunn, M. (1996, February 21). No ordinary trial for no ordinary rapper. *Tampa Tribune* (Florida/Metro), p. 4.

Easson, W. M., & Steinhilber, R. M. (1961). Murderous aggression by children and adolescents. *Archives of General Psychiatry, 4,* 27-35.

Ebstein, R. P., Novick, O., Umansky, R., Priel, B., Osher, Y., Blaine, D., Bennett, E. R., Nemanov, L., Katz, M., & Belmaker, R. H. (1996). Dopamine D4 receptor (D4DR) exon III polymorphism associated with the human personality trait of novelty seeking. *Nature Genetics, 12,* 78-80.

Eddings v. Oklahoma, 102 S.Ct. 869 (1982).

Eftimiades, M., Goulding, S. C., Duignan-Cabrera, A., Campbell, D., & Posesta, J. S. (1997, June 23). Kids without a conscience? *People Weekly,* pp. 46-53.

Egeland, B., Jacobvitz, D., & Sroufe, L. A. (1988). Breaking the cycle of abuse. *Child Development, 59,* 1080-1088.

Eigen, J. P. (1981). Punishing youth homicide in Philadelphia. *Journal of Criminal Law and Criminology, 72,* 1072-1093.

18-year-old gets life in slaying of tourist. (1997, September 23). *Miami Herald,* p. B5.

Eitzen, D. S. (1995, May 15). *Violent crime: Myths, facts and solutions—The conservative and progressive answers.* Paper presented at the symposium, "The Shadow of Violence: Unconsidered Perspectives," Hastings College, Hastings, NE. (Available on-line: http://www.lexis-nexis.com/universe)

Elders, M. J. (1993, November 1). *Violence as a public health issue.* Hearing of the Human Resources and Intergovernmental Relations Subcommittee of the House Government OPS Committee. Washington, DC: Government Printing Office.

Elliott, D. S., Huizinga, D., & Menard, S. (1989). *Multiple problem youth: Delinquency, substance use, and mental health problems.* New York: Springer-Verlag.

Ellis, A. (1986). Rational-emotive therapy and cognitive behavior therapy: Similarities and differences. In A. Ellis & R. Geiger (Eds.), *Handbook of rational-emotive therapy* (Vol. 2, pp. 31-45). New York: Springer.

Ellison, W. J. (1987). State execution of juveniles: Defining "youth" as a mitigating factor for imposing a sentence of less than death. *Cumberland School of Law, 11*(1), 1-38.

Ember, C. R., & Ember, M. (1993). Issues in cross-cultural studies of interpersonal violence. *Violence and Victims, 8,* 217-233.

Embry, D. D., Flannery, D. J., Vazsonyi, A. T., Powell, K. E., & Atha, H. (1996). PeaceBuilders: A theoretically-driven, school-based model for early violence prevention. *American Journal of Preventive Medicine, 12*(5), 91-100.

Empey, L. T., & Rabow, J. (1961). The Provo experiment in delinquency rehabilitation. *American Sociological Review, 26,* 679-695.

Eth, S. (1989). The adolescent witness to homicide. In E. P. Benedek & D. G. Cornell (Eds.), *Juvenile homicide* (pp. 87-113). Washington, DC: American Psychiatric Press.

Ewing, C. P. (1987). *Battered women who kill.* Lexington, MA: Lexington Books.

Ewing, C. P. (1990). *When children kill.* Lexington, MA: Lexington Books.

Expulsion isn't a vacation. (1994, January 17). *Denver Post,* p. B7.

Eysenck, H. J. (1977). *Crime and personality* (3rd ed.). London: Routledge & Kegan Paul.

Fagan, J. (1995). Separating the men from the boys: The comparative advantage of juvenile versus criminal court sanctions on recidivism among adolescent family offenders. In J. C. Howell, B. Krisberg, J. D. Hawkins, & J. J. Wilson (Eds.), *A sourcebook: Serious, violent, and chronic juvenile offenders* (pp. 238-260). Thousand Oaks, CA: Sage.

Fallstrom, J. (1993, July 18). More kids committing felonies in Lake. *Orlando Sentinel* (Lake Sentinel), p. 1.

Family and Medical Leave Act of 1993, 29 U.S.C., §§2611-2615 (1995).

Farnsworth, C. H. (1995, August 24). Killings by teen-agers up sharply in Canada. *The New York Times,* p. A10.

Farrell, A. D., Meyer, A. L., & Dahlberg, L. L. (1996). Richmond youth against violence: A school-based program for urban adolescents. *American Journal of Preventive Medicine, 12*(5), 13-21.

Federal Bureau of Investigation. (1985-1997). *Crime in the United States* (1984-1996). Washington, DC: Government Printing Office.

Fendrich, M., Mackesy-Amiti, M. E., Goldstein, P., Spunt, B., & Brownstein, H. (1995). Substance involvement among juvenile murderers: Comparisons with older offenders based on interviews with prison inmates. *International Journal of the Addictions, 30,* 1363-1382.

Fiagome, C. (1995, February 13). Jacksonville's tough answer to problems of youth crimes. *Christian Science Monitor* (The U.S.), p. 1.

Fiddes, D. O. (1981). Scotland in the seventies: Adolescents in care and custody—A survey of adolescent murder in Scotland. *Journal of Adolescence, 4,* 47-58.

Finch, S. (1994, June 24). Juvenile crime bill approved by both houses. *The Times-Picayune* (New Orleans), p. B1.

Finkel, N. J., Hughes, K. C., Smith, S. F., & Hurabiell, M. L. (1994). Killing kids: The juvenile death penalty and community sentiment. *Behavioral Sciences and the Law, 12,* 5-20.

Finkelhor, D., & Dziuba-Leatherman, J. (1994). Victimization of children. *American Psychologist, 49,* 173-183.

Fishbein, D. H. (1990). Biological perspectives in criminology. *Criminology, 28,* 27-72.

Fitch, W. L. (1989). Competency to stand trial and criminal responsibility in the juvenile court. In E. P. Benedek & D. G. Cornell (Eds.), *Juvenile homicide* (pp. 143-162). Washington, DC: American Psychiatric Press.

Flewelling, R. L. (1996). Exploring the recent surge in youth homicide rates: Geographic variations. In P. K. Lattimore & C. A. Nahabedian (Eds.), *The nature of homicide: Trends and changes—Proceedings of the 1996 meeting of the Homicide Research Working Group* (pp. 58-63). Washington, DC: National Institute of Justice.

Florida Center for Children and Youth. (1993). *Key facts about the children: A report on the status of Florida's children,* Vol 4: *The 1993 Florida kids count data book.* Tallahassee: Author.

Florida Statutes §921.142(7) (1995).

Florida Statutes §782 (1997).

Folks, M. (1994, March 6). Girl's guilt sheds light on killing; officials release tapes in cabdriver's slaying. *Sun Sentinel* (Fort Lauderdale), p. B1.

Foote, J. (1997, October). *Expert panel issues report on serious and violent juvenile offenders* (OJJDP Fact Sheet No. 68). Washington, DC: U.S. Department of Justice, Office of Juvenile Justice and Delinquency Prevention.

Ford v. Wainwright, 106 S.Ct. 2595 (1986).

Foster, H. H. (1964). Closed files on juvenile homicides: A case report. *Journal of Offender Therapy, 8,* 56-60.

Fox, J. A. (1995, April 11). The dean of death. *USA Today,* p. A1.

Fox, J. A. (1996). *Trends in juvenile violence.* Washington, DC: U.S. Department of Justice, Bureau of Justice Statistics.

Fox, J. A., & Levin, J. (1994). *Overkill: Mass murder and serial killing exposed.* New York: Plenum.

Friedman, H. L. (1992). Changing patterns of adolescent sexual behavior: Consequences for health and development. *Journal of Adolescent Health, 13,* 345-350.

Friedman, H. L. (1993). Promoting the health of adolescents in the United States of America: A global perspective. *Journal of Adolescent Health, 14,* 509-519.

Fromm, E. (1973). *The anatomy of human destructiveness.* Greenwich, CT: Fawcett.

Furman v. Georgia, 408 U.S. 238 (1972).

Gamache, D. (1991). Domination and control: The social context of dating violence. In B. Levy (Ed.), *Dating violence* (pp. 69-83). Seattle, WA: Seal.

Ganey, T. (1995, May 7). Legislature in 1995: All talk and no action? *St. Louis Post-Dispatch,* p. C1.

Gardiner, M. (1985). *The deadly innocents: Portraits of children who kill.* New Haven, CT: Yale University Press.

Garfinkel, I., & McLanahan, S. S. (1986). *Single mothers and their children: A new American dilemma.* Washington, DC: Urban Institute Press.

Gelles, R. J., & Conte, J. R. (1990). Domestic violence and sexual abuse of children: A review of research in the eighties. *Journal of Marriage and the Family, 52,* 1045-1058.

Gendreau, P. (1981). Treatment in corrections: Martinson was wrong. *Canadian Psychology, 22,* 332-338.

Gendreau, P. (1996). The principles of effective intervention with offenders. In A. T. Harland (Ed.), *Choosing correctional options that work: Defining the demand and evaluating the supply* (pp. 117-130). Thousand Oaks, CA: Sage.

Gendreau, P., & Goggin, C. (1997). Correctional treatment: Accomplishments and realities. In P. Van Voorhis, M. Braswell, & D. Lester (Eds.), *Correctional counseling and rehabilitation* (pp. 271-280). Cincinnati, OH: Anderson.

Gendreau, P., & Ross, R. R. (1979). Effective correctional treatment: Bibliography and cynics. *Crime & Delinquency, 25,* 463-489.

Gersham, R. (1994, June 30). Girl who killed mom to get 3-year sentence. *St. Petersburg Times* (Hernando Times), p. 11.

Gest, T., & Friedman, D. (1994, August 29). The new crime wave. *U.S. News & World Report,* p. 26.

Gewerth, K. E., & Dorne, C. K. (1991). Imposing the death penalty on juvenile murderers: A constitutional assessment. *Judicature, 75*(1), 6-15.

Gibbs, J. C. (1993). Moral-cognitive interventions. In A. P. Goldstein & R. C. Huff (Eds.), *The gang intervention handbook* (pp. 159-185). Champaign, IL: Research Press.

Gillespie, C. K. (1988). *Justifiable homicide: Battered women, self-defense, and the law.* Columbus: Ohio State University Press.

Gilliard, D. K., & Beck, A. J. (1996, August). *Prison and jail inmates, 1995* (Bureau of Justice Statistics bulletin). Washington, DC: U.S. Department of Justice, Office of Justice Programs.

Girl "scared" over shooting. (1995, August 22). *Tampa Tribune* (Florida/Metro), p. 3.

Glovin, D. (1994, April 17). Reclaiming lost youth: States try many routes to reach delinquents. *The Record* (Hackensack, NJ) (Review & Outlook), p. 1.

Glueck, S., & Glueck, E. (1950). *Unraveling juvenile delinquency.* Cambridge, MA: Harvard University Press.

Goetting, A. (1989). Patterns of homicide among children. *Criminal Justice and Behavior, 16*(1), 63-80.

Goetting, A. (1995). *Homicide in families and other special populations.* New York: Springer.

Goldberg, L. (1994a, February 27). Juvenile justice "fails massively." *San Francisco Examiner,* p. A1.

Goldberg, L. (1994b, March 2). Search for solutions to juvenile crime. *San Francisco Examiner,* p. A1.

Goldstein, A. P. (1988). *The Prepare curriculum.* Champaign, IL: Research Press.

Goldstein, A. P. (1993). Interpersonal skills training interventions. In A. P. Goldstein & R. C. Huff (Eds.), *The gang intervention handbook* (pp. 87-157). Champaign, IL: Research Press.

Goldstein, A. P., & Glick, B. (1987). *Aggression replacement training: A comprehensive intervention for aggressive youth.* Champaign, IL: Research Press.

Goldstein, A. P., & Huff, R. C. (Eds.). (1993). *The gang intervention handbook.* Champaign, IL: Research Press.

Goldstein, P. J. (1985). The drugs/violence nexus: A tripartite conceptual framework. *Journal of Drug Issues, 4,* 493-506.

Goldstein, P. J., Brownstein, H. H., & Ryan, P. J. (1992). Drug-related homicide in New York: 1984 and 1988. *Crime & Delinquency, 38,* 459-476.

Goldstein, P. J., Brownstein, H. H., Ryan, P. J., & Bellucci, P. A. (1990, Winter). Crack and homicide in New York City, 1988: A conceptually based event analysis. *Contemporary Drug Problems,* pp. 651-687.

Goldstein, P. J., Hunt, D., Des Jarlais, D. C., & Deren, S. (1987). Drug dependence and abuse. In R. W. Amler & H. B. Dull (Eds.), *Closing the gap: The burden of unnecessary illness* (pp. 89-101). New York: Oxford University Press.

Goleman, D. (1995, October 3). Early violence leaves its mark on the brain. *The New York Times,* p. C1.

Goode, E. (1993). *Drugs in American society* (4th ed.). New York: McGraw-Hill.

Gottfredson, M. R., & Hirschi, T. (1990). *A general theory of crime.* Stanford, CA: Stanford University Press.

Gray, J. (1997, May 9). Congress votes $1.5 billion to cut back youth crime. *The New York Times* (Themes of the Time, Spring 1998), p. 10.

Greco, C. M., & Cornell, D. G. (1992). Rorschach object relations of adolescents who committed homicide. *Journal of Personality Assessment, 59,* 574-583.

Greenwald, H. B. (1983). Eighth Amendment: Minors and the death penalty—Decision and avoidance. *Journal of Criminal Law and Criminology, 73,* 1525-1552.

Greenwood, P. W. (1986). *Correctional supervision of juvenile offenders: Where do we go from here?* Santa Monica, CA: RAND.

Greenwood, P. W., & Zimring, F. E. (1985). *One more chance: The pursuit of promising intervention strategies for chronic juvenile offenders.* Santa Monica, CA: RAND.

Gregg v. Georgia, 428 U.S. 153 (1976).

Grinder, J., & Bandler, R. (1981). *Trance-formations.* Moab, UT: Real People Press.

Grylls, J. (1994, December 23). Vandals get 15 years for death train crash. *Daily Mail* (London), p. 4.

Hackett, G. (1988, January 11). Kids: Deadly force. *Newsweek,* pp. 18-19.

Haizlip, T., Corder, B. F., & Ball, B. C. (1984). Adolescent murderer. In C. R. Keith (Ed.), *Aggressive adolescent* (pp. 126-148). New York: Free Press.

Hamm, M. S. (1993). *American Skinheads: The criminology and control of hate crime.* Westport, CT: Praeger.

Hamm, M. S. (1995). The differences between street gangs and neo-Nazi Skinheads. In M. W. Klein, C. L. Maxson, & J. Miller (Eds.), *The modern gang reader* (pp. 62-64). Los Angeles, CA: Roxbury.

Harker, V. (1994, January 30). Armed, young and dangerous. *Arizona Republic,* p. A19.

Harper, J. (1997, September 13). City Lites killer gets 2nd death sentence. *St. Petersburg Times* (Seminole), p. 1.

Harper, T. (1995, September 27). Victims to rally for vote on crime bill. *Toronto Star,* p. A10.

Harris, P. W. (1979). *The interpersonal maturity of delinquents and nondelinquents.* Ph.D. dissertation, State University of New York at Albany.

Harris, P. W. (1983). The interpersonal maturity of delinquents and nondelinquents. In W. S. Laufer & J. M. Day (Eds.), *Personality theory, moral development and criminal behavior* (pp. 145-64). Lexington, MA: D. C. Heath.

Harris, P. W. (1988). The interpersonal maturity level classification system: I-level. *Criminal Justice and Behavior, 15,* 58-77.

Harris, R. (1993, August 22). A nation's children in lock-up. *Los Angeles Times,* p. A1.

Harris, R. (1994, August 3). Brazil bemoans its homeless children. *Los Angeles Times,* p. A4.

Haugaard, J. J., Bonner, B. L., Linares, O., Tharinger, D., Weisz, V., & Wolfe, D. A. (1995). Recommendations for education and training in child abuse and neglect: Issues from high school through postdoctoral levels. *Journal of Clinical Child Psychology, 24*(Suppl.), 78-83.

Hawkins, J. D., & Catalano, R. F. (1992). *Communities that care.* San Francisco: Jossey-Bass.

Hawkins, J. D., Catalano, R. F., & Brewer, D. D. (1995). Preventing serious, violent, and chronic juvenile offending: Effective strategies from conception to age 6. In J. C. Howell, B. Krisberg, J. D. Hawkins, & J. J. Wilson (Eds.), *A sourcebook: Serious, violent, and chronic juvenile offenders* (pp. 47-60). Thousand Oaks, CA: Sage.

Hawkins, J. D., Catalano, R. F., & Miller, J. Y. (1992). Risk and protective factors for alcohol and other drug problems in adolescence and early adulthood: Implications for substance abuse prevention. *Psychological Bulletin, 112,* 64-105.

Hays, J. R., Solway, K. S., & Schreiner, D. (1978). Intellectual characteristics of juvenile murderers versus status offenders. *Psychological Reports, 43,* 80-82.

Heide, K. M. (1982). *Classification of offenders ordered to make restitution by I-level and by specific personality dimensions.* Ph.D. dissertation, State University of New York at Albany.

Heide, K. M. (1983a). An assessment of personality development among a sample of adolescent murderers. In T. Palmer (Ed.), *The differential view: The IDTA seventh annual conference proceedings* (pp. 10-26). Montreal: International Differential Treatment Association.

Heide, K. M. (1983b). An empirical assessment of the value of using personality data in restitution outcome prediction. In W. S. Laufer & J. M. Day (Eds.), *Personality theory, moral development and criminal behavior* (pp. 251-277). Lexington, MA: D. C. Heath.

Heide, K. M. (1984, November). *A preliminary identification of types of adolescent murderers.* Paper presented at the annual meeting of the American Society of Criminology, Cincinnati, OH.

Heide, K. M. (1986). A taxonomy of murder: Motivational dynamics behind the homicidal acts of adolescents. *Journal of Justice Issues, 1*(1), 4-19.

Heide, K. M. (1988). Dreams, delusions, disappointments, dollars, and dilemmas: The juvenile justice system in the late 1980s. *Judicature, 72*(3), 190-194.

Heide, K. M. (1992). *Why kids kill parents: Child abuse and adolescent homicide.* Columbus, OH: Ohio State University Press. (cloth)

Heide, K. M. (1993a). Juvenile involvement in multiple offender and multiple victim parricides. *Journal of Police and Criminal Psychology, 9*(2), 53-64.

Heide, K. M. (1993b). Weapons used by juveniles and adults to kill parents. *Behavioral Sciences and the Law, 11*, 397-405.

Heide, K. M. (1994a). Evidence of child maltreatment among adolescent parricide offenders. *International Journal of Offender Therapy and Comparative Criminology, 38*, 151-162.

Heide, K. M. (1994b). Homicide: 25 years later. In M. Moore (Ed.), *Economic and social issues in the New South: Perspectives on race and ethnicity conference proceedings* (pp. 64-84). Tampa: University of South Florida, Institute on Black Life.

Heide, K. M. (1995). *Why kids kill parents: Child abuse and adolescent homicide.* Thousand Oaks, CA: Sage. (paperback)

Heide, K. M. (1996). Why kids keep killing: The correlates, causes, and challenge of juvenile homicide. *Stanford Law and Policy Review, 7*(1), 43-49.

Heide, K. M. (1997a). Associate editor's editorial: Killing words. *International Journal of Offender Therapy and Comparative Criminology, 41*, 3-8.

Heide, K. M. (1997b). Juvenile homicide in America: How can we stop the killing? *Behavioral Sciences and the Law, 15*, 203-220.

Heide, K. M. (in press). Youths who kill. In M. D. Smith & M. Zahn (Eds.), *Homicide studies: A sourcebook of social research.* Thousand Oaks, CA: Sage.

Heide, K. M., McCann, D., & Solomon, E. P. (1992). Intervention after the tragedy. In K. M. Heide, *Why kids kill parents: Child abuse and adolescent homicide* (pp. 139-150). Columbus: Ohio State University Press.

Heide, K. M., & Pardue, B. W. (1986). Juvenile justice in Florida: A legal and empirical analysis. *Law and Policy, 8*, 437-462.

Heide, K. M., & Solomon, E. P. (1997). Mental health professionals in forensic arenas. *Journal of Police and Criminal Psychology, 12*(2), 35-41.

Hellsten, P., & Katila, O. (1965). Murder and other homicide, by children under 15 in Finland. *Psychiatric Quarterly Supplement, 39*(1), 54-74.

Help member focus (pediatrician Marilyn Bull). (1995, Spring). *Help Network News* (Children's Memorial Medical Center, Chicago), pp. 10-11.

Herman, D. H. J. (1986). Criminal defenses and pleas in mitigation based on amnesia. *Behavioral Sciences and the Law, 4*, 5-26.

Herman, J. L. (1992). *Trauma and recovery.* New York: Basic Books.

Hewitt, B., Alexander, B., Norman, P., Day, N., Francis, E., Duignan-Cabrera, A., & Dampier, C.

(1997, November 24). Reversal of fortune. *People Weekly*, pp. 116-118, 122.

Hewitt, B., Harmes, J., & Stewart, B. (1997, November 3). The avenger. *People Weekly*, pp. 116-120, 122.

Hirschi, T. (1969). *Causes of delinquency.* Berkeley: University of California Press.

Hirth, D. (1994, March 9). Juvenile crime bills up for vote: Some judges oppose tough tactics. *Orlando Sentinel*, p. D1.

Hollin, C. R. (1993). Cognitive-behavioral interventions. In A. P. Goldstein & R. C. Huff (Eds.), *The gang intervention handbook* (pp. 55-85). Champaign, IL: Research Press.

Holmes, L. J., Ziskin, L. Z., O'Dowd, K. J., & Martin, R. M. (1995). Medical partnerships with community-based organizations in violence prevention. *New Jersey Medicine, 92*(2), 96-98.

Holmes, R. M., & Holmes, S. (1994). *Murder in America.* Thousand Oaks, CA: Sage.

Hotaling, G. T., & Sugarman, D. B. (1986). An analysis of risk markers in husband to wife violence: The current state of knowledge. *Violence and Victims, 1*, 101-124.

Howell, J. C. (1994, April). *Gangs* (OJJDP Fact Sheet No. 12). Washington, DC: U.S. Department of Justice, Office of Juvenile Justice and Delinquency Prevention.

Howell, J. C. (1995a). Gangs and youth violence. In J. C. Howell, B. Krisberg, J. D. Hawkins, & J. J. Wilson (Eds.), *A sourcebook: Serious, violent, and chronic juvenile offenders* (pp. 261-274). Thousand Oaks, CA: Sage.

Howell, J. C. (Ed.). (1995b, June). *Guide for implementing the comprehensive strategy for serious, violent, and chronic juvenile offenders.* Washington, DC: U.S. Department of Justice, Office of Juvenile Justice and Delinquency Prevention.

Howell, J. C. (1995c). A national perspective. In B. Glick & A. P. Goldstein (Eds.), *Managing delinquency programs that work* (pp. 11-23). Laurel, MD: American Correctional Association.

Howell, J. C., & Krisberg, B. (1995). Conclusion. In J. C. Howell, B. Krisberg, J. D. Hawkins, & J. J. Wilson (Eds.), *A sourcebook: Serious, violent, and chronic juvenile offenders* (pp. 275-277). Thousand Oaks, CA: Sage.

Howell, J. C., Krisberg, B., Hawkins, J. D., & Wilson, J. J. (Eds.). (1995). *A sourcebook: Serious, violent, and chronic juvenile offenders.* Thousand Oaks, CA: Sage.

Howell, J. C., Krisberg, B., & Jones, M. (1995). Trends in juvenile crime and youth violence. In J. C. Howell, B. Krisberg, J. D. Hawkins, & J. J. Wilson (Eds.), *A sourcebook: Serious, violent, and chronic juvenile offenders* (pp. 1-35). Thousand Oaks, CA: Sage.

Hsia, H. (1997, June). *Allegheny County, PA: Mobilizing to reduce juvenile crime.* Washington, DC: U.S. Department of Justice, Office of Juvenile Justice and Delinquency Prevention.

Hughes, J. R., Zagar, R., Arbit, J., & Busch, K. G. (1991). Medical, family, and scholastic conditions in urban delinquents. *Journal of Clinical Psychology, 47,* 448-464.

Hum, P., & Bohuslawsky, M. (1994, March 31). Stats show no trend in crime by youths. *Ottawa Citizen,* p. A1.

Humphries, E. A. (1995, September 12). Young criminals just need direction. *Calgary Herald,* p. A12.

Hustak, A. (1995, April 8). Children who kill. *The Gazette* (Montreal), p. B1.

Incompetency standards in death penalty and juvenile cases. (1984). *Mental and Physical Disability Law Reporter, 8*(2), 92-93.

Institute of Medicine. (1994). *Reducing risk factors for mental disorders: Frontiers for preventive intervention research.* Washington, DC: National Academy Press.

Jacobs, J. B., & Potter, K. A. (1995). Keeping guns out of the "wrong" hands: The Brady Law and the limits of regulation. *Northwestern University School of Law, 86*(1), 93-119.

Jaeger, R. W. (1995, April 29). Third teen convicted in hired-murder plot. *Wisconsin State Journal,* p. A1.

Jeffrey, C. R. (1979). *Biology and crime.* Beverly Hills, CA: Sage.

Jenkins, E. (1995). Violence exposure, psychological distress and risk behaviors in a sample of inner-city youth. In C. R. Block & R. Block (Eds.), *Trends, risks, and interventions in lethal violence: Proceedings of the third annual symposium of the Homicide Research Working Group* (pp. 287-298). Washington, DC: National Institute of Justice.

Jenkins, E., & Bell, C. (1994). Violence among inner city high school students and post-traumatic stress disorder. In S. Friedman (Ed.), *Anxiety disorders in African Americans* (pp. 76-88). New York: Springer.

Jimenez, M. (1994, March 18). Relatives seek answers for boy's massacre of family. *Ottawa Citizen,* p. A3.

Johnson, C., Webster, B., & Connors, E. (1995, February). *Prosecuting gangs: A national assessment* (National Institute of Justice research in brief). Washington, DC: U.S. Department of Justice, Office of Justice Programs.

Johnston, L. D., O'Malley, P. M., & Bachman, J. G. (1993). *National survey results on drug use from the Monitoring the Future Study, 1975-1992, Vol. 1: Secondary school students.* Rockville, MD: National Institute on Drug Abuse.

Kaczor, B. (1995a, August 28). Appeal of plea sends killing suspect to trial. *Tampa Tribune* (Florida/Metro), p. 4.

Kaczor, B. (1995b, August 29). British tourist testifies again in rest stop slaying. *Tampa Tribune* (Florida/Metro), p. 7.

Kaczor, B. (1995c, August 30). Teen convicted of attempt to murder British tourist. *Tampa Tribune* (Florida/Metro), p. 7.

Kafantaris, V., Campbell, M., Padron-Gayol, M. V., Small, A. M., Locascio, J. J., & Rosenberg, C. R. (1992). Carbamazepine in hospitalized aggressive conduct-disordered children: An open pilot study. *Psychopharmacology Bulletin, 28*(2), 193-199.

Kaihla, P. (1994, August 15). Kids who kill. *Maclean's,* pp. 32, 38-39.

Kalogerakis, M. G. (1971). Homicide in adolescents: Fantasy and deed. In J. Fawcett (Ed.), *Dynamics of violence* (pp. 93-103). Chicago: American Medical Association.

Kantrowitz, B. (1993, August 2). Teen violence: Wild in the streets. *Newsweek,* pp. 40-46.

Kaplan, S. L., Busner, J., Kupietz, S., Wassermann, E., & Segal, B. (1990). Effects of methylphenidate on adolescents with aggressive conduct disorder and ADDH: A preliminary report. *Journal of the American Academy of Child and Adolescent Psychiatry, 29,* 719-723.

Keith, C. R. (1984). Individual psychotherapy and psychoanalysis with the aggressive adolescent: A historical review. In C. R. Keith (Ed.), *The aggressive adolescent* (pp. 191-208). New York: Free Press.

Kelder, S. H., Orpinas, P., McAlister, A., Frankowski, R., Parcel, G. S., & Friday, J. (1996). The Students for Peace project: A comprehensive violence-prevention program for middle school students. *American Journal of Preventive Medicine, 12*(5), 22-31.

Kelley, B. T., Huizinga, D., Thornberry, T., & Loeber, R. (1997, June). *Epidemiology of serious violence* (OJJDP bulletin). Washington, DC: U.S. Department of Justice, Office of Juvenile Justice and Delinquency Prevention.

Kennedy, D. M. (1997). *Juvenile gun violence and gun markets in Boston* (NIJ research review). Washington, DC: U.S. Department of Justice, National Institute of Justice.

Kids who kill their parents and the reason why. (1997, November 5). *Geraldo Rivera* (television program). (Available on-line: Syndicated News Transcripts)

King, C. H. (1975). The ego and the integration of violence in homicidal youth. *American Journal of Orthopsychiatry, 45,* 134-145.

Kirschner, D. (1992). Understanding adoptees who kill: Dissociation, patricide, and the psychodynamics of adoption. *International Journal of Offender Therapy and Comparative Criminology*, *36*, 323-334.

Kramer, R. (1992). The juvenile justice system is too lenient. In D. Biskup & C. Cozic (Eds.), *Youth violence* (pp. 212-215). San Diego: Greenhaven.

Krisberg, B., Currie, E., Onek, D., & Wiebush, R. G. (1995). Graduated sanctions for serious, violent, and chronic juvenile offenders. In J. C. Howell, B. Krisberg, J. D. Hawkins, & J. J. Wilson (Eds.), *A sourcebook: Serious, violent, and chronic juvenile offenders* (pp. 142-170). Thousand Oaks, CA: Sage.

Kuhns, J. B. (1995, November). *Characterizing drug using violent offenders: A foundation for theoretical development.* Paper presented at the annual meeting of the American Society of Criminology, Boston.

Lacayo, R. (1995, June 12). Violent reaction. *Time*, pp. 24-30.

Landau, E. (1993). *The White power movement.* Brookfield, CT: Millbrook.

Lawrence, R. (1998). *School crime and juvenile justice.* New York: Oxford University Press.

LeBlanc, A. N. (1995, April). Falling murder of five-year-old Eric Morse by two other children in Chicago, Illinois. *Esquire*, pp. 84-100.

LeDuc, D., & St. George, D. (1995, November 5). Man burned to death after cops leave him. *Tampa Tribune* (Nation/World), p. 10.

Lee, A. S., Lee, E. S., & Chen, J. (1995). Young killers. In M. Reidel & J. Boulahanis (Eds.), *Proceedings of the 1995 meeting of the Homicide Research Working Group* (pp. 15-20). Washington, DC: National Institute of Justice.

Lee, E. F. (1993, December 19). Putting kids in adult prisons turns out criminals. *Houston Chronicle* (Outlook), p. 1.

Leong, G. B. (1989). Clinical issues for the forensic examiner. In E. P. Benedek & D. G. Cornell (Eds.), *Juvenile homicide* (pp. 115-141). Washington, DC: American Psychiatric Press.

Lerner, R. M. (1994). *America's youth in crisis.* Thousand Oaks, CA: Sage.

Leslie, C. (1988, December 5). Pencils, papers and guns. *Newsweek*, p. 92.

Levin, J., & Fox, J. (1985). *Mass murder: America's growing menace.* New York: Plenum.

Levy, B. (Ed.). (1981). *Dating violence.* Seattle, WA: Seal Press.

Levy, B., & Lobel, K. (1991). Lesbian teens in abusive relationships. In B. Levy (Ed.), *Dating violence* (pp. 203-208). Seattle, WA: Seal Press.

Lewis, D. O. (1992). From abuse to violence: Psychophysiological consequences of maltreatment. *Journal of the American Academy of Child and Adolescent Psychiatry, 31*, 383-391.

Lewis, D. O., Lovely, R., Yeager, C., & Femina, D. D. (1989). Toward a theory of the genesis of violence: A follow-up study of delinquents. *Journal of the American Academy of Child and Adolescent Psychiatry, 28*, 431-436.

Lewis, D. O., Lovely, R., Yeager, C., Ferguson, G., Friedman, M., Sloane, G., Friedman, H., & Pincus, J. H. (1988). Intrinsic and environmental characteristics of juvenile murderers. *Journal of the American Academy of Child and Adolescent Psychiatry, 27*, 582-587.

Lewis, D. O., Moy, E., Jackson, L. D., Aaronson, R., Restifo, N., Serra, S., & Simos, A. (1985). Biopsychosocial characteristics of children who later murder: A prospective study. *American Journal of Psychiatry, 142*, 1161-1167.

Lewis, D. O., Pincus, J. H., Bard, B., Richardson, E., Feldman, M., Prichep, L. S., & Yeager, C. (1988). Neuropsychiatric, psychoeducational, and family characteristics of 14 juveniles condemned to death in the United States. *American Journal of Psychiatry, 145*, 584-589.

Lewis, D. O., Shanok, S. S., Grant, M., & Ritvo, E. (1983). Homicidally aggressive young children: Neuropsychiatric and experimental correlates. *American Journal of Psychiatry, 140*, 148-153.

Lewis, D. O., Shanok, S. S., Pincus, J. H., & Glaser, G. H. (1979). Violent juvenile delinquents: Psychiatric, neurological, psychological, and abuse factors. *Journal of the American Academy of Child Psychiatry, 18*, 307-319.

Lewis, D. O., Yeager, C. A., Cobham-Portorreal, C. S., Klein, N., Showalter, C., & Anthony, A. (1991). A follow-up of female delinquents: Maternal contributions to the perpetuation of deviance. *Journal of the American Academy of Child Psychiatry, 30*, 197-201.

Leyton, E. (1990). *Sole survivor: Children who murder their parents.* New York: Pocket Books.

Lincoln teen shoots grandparents, kills 1. (1995, April 28). *State Journal-Register* (Springfield, IL) (Local), p. 1.

Lipsey, M. W. (1992). Juvenile delinquency treatment: A meta-analytic inquiry into the variability of effects. In T. D. Cook (Ed.), *Meta-analysis for explanation: A casebook* (pp. 83-127). New York: Russell Sage.

Loeber, R., & Farrington, D. P. (Eds.). (1998). *Serious and violent juvenile offenders: Risk factors and successful interventions.* Thousand Oaks, CA: Sage.

Lopez, R. J. (1994, January 23). Should young criminals grow old in prison? *Los Angeles Times* (City Times), p. 14.

Lorente, R., & Bustos, S. R. (1995, August 21). Cops accuse girl, 10, of shooting brother, 3. *Tampa Tribune* (Metro), p. 6.

Los Angeles Sheriff's Department, Operation Safe Streets Street Gang Detail. (1995). L.A. style: A street gang manual of the Los Angeles Sheriff's Department. In M. W. Klein, C. L. Maxson, & J. Miller (Eds.), *The modern gang reader* (pp. 34-45). Los Angeles: Roxbury.

Lotto win helps fund son's trial. (1995, September 25). *Tampa Tribune* (Metro), p. 4.

Luntz, B. K., & Widom, C. S. (1994). Antisocial personality disorder in abused and neglected children grown up. *American Journal of Psychiatry, 151*, 670-674.

MacDonald, A. (1980). *The Turner diaries.* New York: Barricade Books.

Mack, J., Scherl, D., & Macht, L. (1973). Children who kill their mothers. In A. J. Anthony & C. Koupernik (Eds.), *The child in his family: The impact of disease and death* (pp. 319-332). New York: Wiley Interscience.

Magid, K., & McKelvey, C. A. (1987). *High risk: Children without a conscience.* New York: Bantam Books.

Mahoney, A. R. (1987). *Juvenile justice in context.* Boston: Northeastern University Press.

Malcolm Shabazz sentenced to juvenile center. (1997, September 1). *Jet*, p. 23.

Malmquist, C. P. (1971). Premonitory signs of homicidal aggression in juveniles. *American Journal of Psychiatry, 128*, 461-465.

Malmquist, C. P. (1990). Depression in homicidal adolescents. *Bulletin of the American Academy of Psychiatry and the Law, 18*(1), 23-36.

Mannies, J. (1994, December 30). Missouri Democrats raising profile: Juvenile-crime bill is priority, party says. *St. Louis Post-Dispatch*, p. B1.

Marans, S., & Berkman, M. (1997). Child development: Community policing—Partnership in a climate of violence (OJJDP bulletin). Washington, DC: U.S. Department of Justice, Office of Juvenile Justice and Delinquency Prevention.

Marten, G. W. (1965). Adolescent murderers. *Southern Medical Journal, 58*, 1217-1218.

Martinson, R. (1974). What works? Questions and answers about prison reform. *The Public Interest, 36*, 22-45.

May, J. P., Christoffel, K. K., & Sprang, M. L. (1994). Counseling patients about guns. *Chicago Medicine, 97*(7), 13-16.

May, J. P., & Martin, K. L. (1993). A role for the primary care physician in counseling young African-American men about homicide prevention. *Journal of General Internal Medicine, 8*, 380-382.

Mayers, J. (1995, March 24). Capitol report. *Wisconsin State Journal*, p. B3.

Maynard, M. (1994, March 17). Firearms at school won't be tolerated [letter to editor]. *Atlanta Constitution*, p. A6.

McCarthy, J. (1995, January 24). "Get tough" juvenile measures presented at statehouse forum. *Charleston Gazette* (West Virginia), p. A5.

McCarthy, J. B. (1978). Narcissism and the self in homicidal adolescents. *American Journal of Psychoanalysis, 38*, 19-29.

McCully, R. S. (1978). The laugh of Satan: A study of a familial murderer. *Journal of Personality Assessment, 42*(1), 81-91.

McGillis, D. (1996, January). *Beacons of hope: New York City's school-based community centers.* Washington, DC: U.S. Department of Justice, Office of Justice Programs, National Institute of Justice.

McGinniss, J. (1991). *Cruel doubt.* New York: Simon & Schuster.

Medical Economics Data Production Company. (1998). *Physicians' desk reference* (52nd ed.). Montvale, NJ: Author.

Medlicott, R. W. (1955). Paranoia of the exalted type in a setting of folie à deux: A study of two adolescent homicides. *British Journal of Medical Psychology, 28*, 205-223.

Mednick, S. A., & Christiansen, K. O. (Eds.). (1977). *Biosocial bases of criminal behavior.* New York: Gardner.

Meehan, P. J., & O'Carroll, P. W. (1995). Gangs, drugs, and homicide in Los Angeles. In M. W. Klein, C. L. Maxson, & J. Miller (Eds.), *The modern gang reader* (pp. 236-241). Los Angeles: Roxbury.

Meichenbaum, D. (1977). *Cognitive behavior modification: An integrative approach.* New York: Plenum.

Meichenbaum, D. (1985). *Stress inoculation training.* New York: Pergamon.

Meloff, W., & Silverman, R. A. (1992). Canadian kids who kill. *Canadian Journal of Criminology, 34*(1), 15-34.

Melton, G. B., Petrila, J., Poythress, N. G., & Slobogin, C. (1997). *Psychological evaluations for the courts* (2nd ed.). New York: Guilford.

Menninger, K., & Mayman, M. (1956). Episodic dyscontrol: A third order of stress adaptation. *Bulletin of the Menninger Clinic, 20*, 153-165.

Merton, R. (1938). Social structure and anomie. *American Sociological Review, 3*, 672-682.

Messerschmidt, J. W. (1993). *Masculinities and crime: Critique and reconceptualization.* Lanham, MD: Rowman & Littlefield.

Michaels, J. J. (1961). Enuresis in murderous aggressive children and adolescents. *Archives of General Psychiatry, 5*, 94-97.

Miller, D., & Looney, J. (1974). The prediction of adolescent homicide: Episodic dyscontrol and dehumanization. *American Journal of Psychoanalysis, 34*, 187-198.

Miller, T. C. (1995, April 6). Youth crimes not up, just worse. *St. Petersburg Times* (Pasco Times), p. 1.

Moehringer, J. R. (1997, October 10). Tale of rampage. *Tampa Tribune* (Nation/World), p. 4.

Moffitt, T. E., Lynam, D. R., & Silva, P. A. (1994). Neuropsychological tests predicting persistent male delinquency. *Criminology, 32,* 277-300.

Mohr, J. W., & McKnight, C. K. (1971). Violence as a function of age and relationship with special reference to matricide. *Canadian Psychiatric Association Journal, 16,* 29-32.

Mones, P. (1985). The relationship between child abuse and parricide. In E. H. Newberg & R. Bourne (Eds.), *Unhappy families: Clinical and research perspectives on family violence* (pp. 31-38). Littleton, MA: PSG Publishing.

Mones, P. (1991). *When a child kills: Abused children who kill their parents.* New York: Pocket Books.

Mones, P. (1993). When the innocent strike back: Abused children who kill their parents. *Journal of Interpersonal Violence, 8,* 297-299.

Moore, J. B. (1993). *Skinheads shaved for battle: A cultural history of American Skinheads.* Bowling Green, OH: Bowling Green University Popular Press.

Morgan, T. (1975, January 19). They think I can kill because I'm 14. *New York Times Magazine,* pp. 9-11, 16, 21-22, 24, 26, 28, 30, 32, 34.

Morris, N. (1986). Insanity defense. In *National Institute of Justice Crime File Study Guide.* Rockville, MD: U.S. Department of Justice, National Institute of Justice, National Criminal Justice Reference Service.

Mouridsen, S. E., & Tolstrup, K. (1988). Children who kill: A case study of matricide. *Journal of Child Psychology and Psychiatry, 29,* 511-515.

Murray, B. (1995a, September). Good mentoring keeps at-risk youth in school. *The APA Monitor,* p. 49.

Murray, B. (1995b, September). Key skill for teen parents: Having realistic expectations. *The APA Monitor,* p. 51.

Murray, B. (1995c, September). Kids learn keys to healthy relationships. *The APA Monitor,* p. 48.

Myers, W. C. (1992). What treatments do we have for children and adolescents who have killed? *Bulletin of the American Academy of Psychiatry and the Law, 20*(1), 47-58.

Myers, W. C. (1994). Sexual homicide by adolescents. *Journal of American Academy of Adolescent Psychiatry, 33,* 962-969.

Myers, W. C., & Kemph, J. P. (1988). Characteristics and treatment of four homicidal adolescents. *Journal of the American Academy of Child and Adolescent Psychiatry, 27,* 595-599.

Myers, W. C., & Kemph, J. P. (1990). DSM-III-R classification of homicidal youth: Help or hindrance. *Journal of Clinical Psychiatry, 51,* 239-242.

Myers, W. C., & Mutch, P. A. (1992). Language disorders in disruptive behavior disordered homicidal youth. *Journal of Forensic Sciences, 37,* 919-922.

Myers, W. C., & Scott, K. (1998). Psychotic and conduct disorder symptoms in juvenile murderers. *Journal of Homicide Studies, 2*(2), 160-175.

Myers, W. C., Scott, K., Burgess, A. W., & Burgess, A. G. (1995). Psychopathology, biopsychosocial factors, crime characteristics, and classification of 25 homicidal youths. *Journal of the American Academy of Child and Adolescent Psychiatry, 34,* 1483-1489.

National Crime Prevention Council. (1994a, August). *Partnerships to prevent youth violence* (BJA bulletin). Washington, DC: U.S. Department of Justice, Office of Justice Programs, Bureau of Justice Assistance.

National Crime Prevention Council. (1994b, September). *Working as partners with community groups* (BJA bulletin). Washington, DC: U.S. Department of Justice, Office of Justice Programs, Bureau of Justice Assistance.

National Criminal Justice Reference Service. (1994). *Preventing interpersonal violence among youth: An introduction to school, community, and mass media.* Rockville, MD: Author.

National Criminal Justice Reference Service. (1997, April). *Fact sheet: Drug use trends.* Rockville, MD: National Criminal Justice Reference Service, White House Office of National Drug Control Policy, Drug Policy Information Clearinghouse.

Nicholson, D. (1996, February 4). Murder suspects were "good kids," neighbors say. *Tampa Tribune* (Florida/Metro), pp. 1, 3.

19-year-old murderer of 3 boys sentenced to death. (1994, March 20). *Los Angeles Times,* p. A4.

Nordland, R. (1992, March 9). Deadly lessons. *Newsweek,* pp. 22-24.

Nunziata, J. (1994, May 29). MP's views: Changes would restore confidence by boosting protection of public. *Ottawa Citizen,* p. A11.

O'Donnell, C. R. (1995). Firearm deaths among children and youth. *American Psychologist, 50,* 771-776.

Office of National Drug Control Policy. (1995, April). *National drug control strategy: Executive summary.* Washington, DC: Office of National Drug Control Policy, Executive Office of the President.

Ogloff, J. R. (1987). The juvenile death penalty: A frustrated society's attempt for control. *Behavioral Sciences and the Law, 5,* 447-455.

O'Halloran, C. M., & Altmaier, E. M. (1996). Awareness of death among children: Does a life-threatening illness alter the process of discovery? *Journal of Counseling and Development, 74,* 259-262.

O'Hanlon, W. H., & Martin, M. (1992). *Solution-oriented hypnosis.* New York: Norton.

O'Keeffe, N. K., Brockopp, K., & Chew, E. (1986). Teen dating violence. *Social Work, 31,* 465-468.

Olds, D. L., & Kitzman, H. (1993). Review of research on home visiting for pregnant women and parents of young children. *The Future of Children, 3*(3), 53-92.

Olson, D. (1997, Fall). Juvenile crime. *The Compiler* (Illinois Criminal Justice Information Agency), pp. 7-8.

Ommachen, E. (1995, February 14). Ontario girl charged in baby's death. *Idaho Statesman,* p. A1.

Onstad, K. (1997, March). What are we afraid of: The myth of youth crime. *Saturday Night, 2*(112), 46.

Orwen, P. (1993, December 5). The downside of zero tolerance: Ontario locks up more kids than any other province—It doesn't seem to be helping. *Toronto Star,* p. E1.

Osgood, D. W. (1995, January). *Drugs, alcohol, and violence.* Boulder, CO: Regents of the University of Colorado, Institute of Behavioral Science.

Osgood, D. W., Johnston, L. D., O'Malley, P. M., & Bachman, J. G. (1988). The generality of deviance in late adolescence and early adulthood. *American Sociological Review, 53,* 81-93.

Osofsky, J. D. (1995). The effects of exposure to violence on young children. *American Psychologist, 50,* 782-788.

Osofsky, J. D., & Scheeringa, M. S. (1997). Community and domestic violence exposure: Effects on development and psychopathology. In D. Cicchetti & S. L. Toth (Eds.), *Rochester Symposium on Developmental Psychology* (Vol. 8, pp. 155-180). Rochester, NY: University of Rochester Press.

Ovenden, N. (1995, September 14). Return of death penalty urged. *Vancouver Sun,* p. A4.

Palmer, T. (1974). The Youth Authority's Community Treatment Project. *Federal Probation, 38*(1), 3-13.

Palmer, T. (1975). Martinson revisited. *Journal of Research in Crime and Delinquency, 12,* 133-152.

Palmer, T. (1978). *Correctional intervention and research.* Lexington, MA: Lexington Books.

Palmer, T. (1992). *The re-emergence of correctional interventions.* Newbury Park, CA: Sage.

Paluszny, M., & McNabb, M. (1975). Therapy of a six-year-old who committed fratricide. *Journal of the American Academy of Child Psychiatry, 14,* 319-336.

Pasewark, R. A. (1981). Insanity plea: A review of the research literature. *Journal of Psychiatry and Law, 9,* 357-401.

Patterson, R. M. (1943). Psychiatric study of juveniles involved in homicide. *American Journal of Orthopsychiatry, 13,* 125-130.

Pazniokas, M. (1995, April 9). Confronting the end of innocence: Treatment or punishment best for young offenders? *Hartford Courant,* p. A1.

Pennsylvania State Sen. Fisher, Rep. Piccola introduce legislation to deal with violent juvenile offenders. (1995, May 10). *PR Newswire.* (Available on-line)

Petrila, J., & Otto, R. K. (1996). *Law and mental health professionals: Florida.* Washington, DC: American Psychological Association.

Petti, T. A., & Davidman, L. (1981). Homicidal school-age children: Cognitive style and demographic features. *Child Psychiatry and Human Development, 12,* 82-89.

Petti, T., & Wells, K. (1980). Crisis treatment of an adolescent who accidentally killed his twin. *American Journal of Psychiatry, 3,* 434-443.

Pfeffer, C. R. (1980). Psychiatric hospital treatment of assaultive homicidal children. *American Journal of Psychotherapy, 34*(2), 197-207.

Pincus, J. H. (1993). Neurologist's role in understanding violence. *Archives of Neurology, 8,* 867-869.

Podolsky, E. (1965). Children who kill. *General Practitioner, 31,* 98.

Pommer, M. (1995, January 23). Panel offers plan to get tough on kids. *Capital Times* (Madison, WI), p. A1.

Pope, H. S., Butcher, J. N., & Seelen, J. (1993). *The MMPI, MMPI-2 and MMPI-A in court: A practical guide for expert witnesses and attorneys.* Washington, DC: American Psychological Association.

Posey, C. D. (Ed.). (1988). Special issue: Correctional classification based upon psychological characteristics. *Criminal Justice and Behavior, 15*(1).

Post, R. M., Rubinow, D. R., & Uhde, T. W. (1984). Biochemical mechanisms of action of carbamazepine in affective illness and epilepsy. *Psychopharmacological Bulletin, 20,* 585-590.

Post, S. (1982). Adolescent parricide in abusive families. *Child Welfare, 61,* 445-455.

Powell, K. E., Dahlberg, L. L., Friday, J., Mercy, J. A., Thornton, T., & Crawford, S. (1996). Prevention of youth violence: Rationale and characteristics of 15 evaluation projects. *American Journal of Preventive Medicine, 12*(5), 3-12.

Powell, K. E., & Hawkins, D. F. (Eds.). (1996). Youth violence prevention: Descriptions and baseline data from 13 evaluation projects. *Ameri-*

can Journal of Preventive Medicine, 12(5) [entire issue].

Prashaw, R. (1994, May 29). Church council's view: Don't get tough, get serious. *Ottawa News*, p. A11.

President's Crime Prevention Council. (1995). *Preventing crime and promoting responsibility: 50 programs that help communities help their youth.* Washington, DC: Government Printing Office.

Press, A., Carroll, G., McCormick, J., & Brown, K. A. (1986, November 24). Children who kill. *Newsweek*, pp. 93-94.

Preston, J., & Johnson, J. (1990). *Clinical psychopharmacology made ridiculously simple.* Miami, FL: MedMaster, Inc.

Pre-teen charged with double murder. (1995, April 23). *The Sunday Gazette Mail* (Charleston, WV), p. A4.

Price, H. B. (1995, June 11). Guns taking terrible toll on young. *The State Journal-Register* (Springfield, IL) (Editorial), p. 13.

Prothrow-Stith, D. (1987). *The violence prevention curriculum for adolescents.* Newton, MA: Education Development Center.

Prothrow-Stith, D., & Weissman, M. (1991). *Deadly consequences.* New York: HarperCollins.

Puig-Antich, J. (1982). Major depression and conduct disorder in prepuberty. *Journal of the American Academy of Child Psychiatry, 21,* 118-128.

Ray, O., & Ksir, C. (1993). *Drugs, society, and human behavior.* St. Louis, MO: C. V. Mosby.

Reckless, W. (1961, December). A new theory of delinquency and crime. *Federal Probation, 25,* 42-46.

Reinhardt, J. M. (1970). *Nothing left but murder.* Lincoln, NE: Johnsen.

Reiss, A. J., & Roth, J. A. (Eds.). (1993). *Understanding and preventing violence.* Washington, DC: National Academy Press.

Reitsma-Street, M., & Leschied, A. W. (1988). The conceptual level matching model in corrections. *Criminal Justice and Behavior, 15,* 92-108.

Resnick, M. D., Bearman, P. S., Blum, R. W., Bauman, K. F., Harris, K. M., Jones, J., Tabor, J., Beuhring, T., Sieving, R. E., Shew, M., Ireland, M., Bearinger, L., & Udry, J. R. (1997). Protecting adolescents from harm: Findings from the National Longitudinal Study on Adolescent Health. *Journal of the American Medical Association, 278,* 823-832.

Restifo, N., & Lewis, D. O. (1985). Three case reports of a single homicidal adolescent. *American Journal of Psychiatry, 142,* 388.

Riga, A. (1995, July 23). Kids who kill. *Ottawa Citizen,* p. A1.

Rimbach, J. (1994, June 9). Teen may face trial as adult in homicide: Why was suspect on street? *The Record* (Hackensack, NJ), p. A1.

Ringwalt, C. L., Graham, L. A., Paschall, M. J., Flewelling, R. L., & Browne, D. C. (1996). Supporting adolescents with guidance and employment (SAGE). *American Journal of Preventive Medicine, 12*(5), 31-38.

Rivara, F. P., Mueller, B. A., Somes, G., Mendoza, C. T., Rushforth, N. B., & Kellermann, A. L. (1997). Alcohol and illicit drug abuse and the risk of violent death in the home. *Journal of the American Medical Association, 278,* 569-575.

Robinson, M. (1995, April 25). Love triangle may have led to murder: Spurned teen allegedly behind slayings. *Denver Post,* p. B1.

Rogers, R. (1986). *Conducting insanity evaluations.* New York: Van Nostrand Reinhold.

Rogers, R. (1988). *Clinical assessment of malingering and deception.* New York: Guilford.

Rojek, D. G. (1996). Changing homicide rates. In P. K. Lattimore & C. A. Nahabedian (Eds.), *The nature of homicide: Trends and changes—Proceedings of the 1996 meeting of the Homicide Research Working Group* (pp. 106-125). Washington, DC: National Institute of Justice.

Romero, D. (1995, March 21). Target: Parents. *Los Angeles Times,* pp. E1, E5.

Rosenberg, M. L. (Chairman). (1995, October). "Bridging Science and Program" (National Violence Prevention Conference program), Des Moines, IA.

Rosenhan, D. L., & Seligman, M. E. P. (1989). *Abnormal psychology* (2nd ed.). New York: Norton.

Rosner, R., Weiderlight, M., Rosner, M. B. H., & Wieczorek, R. R. (1978). Adolescents accused of murder and manslaughter: A five year descriptive study. *Bulletin of the American Academy of Psychiatry and Law, 7,* 342-351.

Ross, R. R., & Fabiano, E. (1985). *Time to think: A cognitive model of delinquency prevention and offender rehabilitation.* Johnson City, TN: Institute of Social Sciences and Arts.

Roth, J. A. (1994a). *Psychoactive substances and violence* (National Institute of Justice research in brief). Washington, DC: U.S. Department of Justice, Office of Justice Programs.

Roth, J. A. (1994b). *Understanding and preventing violence* (National Institute of Justice research in brief). Washington, DC: U.S. Department of Justice, Office of Justice Programs.

Roth, S. F. (1995a). American and Canadian firearms laws: Comparisons and contrasts in cultures and policy. In M. Reidel & J. Boulahanis (Eds.), *Proceedings of the 1995 meeting of the Homicide Research Working Group* (pp. 51-66). Washington, DC: National Institute of Justice.

Roth, S. F. (1995b). Gun-related violence. In C. R. Block & R. Block (Eds.), *Trends, risks, and interventions in lethal violence: Proceedings of the third annual symposium of the Homicide Re-*

search Working Group (pp. 265-278). Washington, DC: National Institute of Justice.

Rowley, J. C., Ewing, C. P., & Singer, S. I. (1987). Juvenile homicide: The need for an interdisciplinary approach. Behavioral Sciences and the Law, 5, 3-10.

Rusnell, C. (1995, August 23). Grits to examine changes to act. Calgary Herald (Alberta), p. A1.

Russell, D. H. (1965). A study of juvenile murderers. Journal of Offender Therapy, 9(3), 55-86.

Russell, D. H. (1979). Ingredients of juvenile murder. International Journal of Offender Therapy and Comparative Criminology, 23, 65-72.

Russell, D. H. (1984). A study of juvenile murderers of family members. International Journal of Offender Therapy and Comparative Criminology, 28, 177-192.

Russell, D. H. (1986). Girls who kill. International Journal of Offender Therapy and Comparative Criminology, 30, 171-176.

S&L bailout may cost more. (1996, July 13). Tampa Tribune (Business and Finance), p. 8.

Sadoff, R. L. (1971). Clinical observations on parricide. Psychiatric Quarterly, 45(1), 65-69.

Samenow, S. (1984). Inside the criminal mind. New York: Times Books.

Sampson, R. J., Raudenbush, S. W., & Earls, F. (1997). Neighborhoods and violent crime: A multilevel study of collective efficacy. Science, 277, 918-924.

Sanders, A. L. (1989, July 11). Bad news for death row. Time, pp. 48-49.

Sanders, W. B. (1994). Gangbangs and drive-bys: Grounded culture and juvenile gang violence. Hawthorne, NY: Aldine de Gruyter.

Sanford, L. T. (1990). Strong at the broken places: Overcoming the trauma of childhood abuse. New York: Random House.

Santtila, P., & Haapasalo, J. (1997). Neurological and psychological risk factors among young homicidal, violent, and nonviolent offenders in Finland. Homicide Studies, 1, 234-253.

Sarason, I. G., & Sarason, B. R. (1996). Abnormal psychology: The problem of maladaptive behavior. Upper Saddle River, NJ: Prentice Hall.

Sargent, D. (1962). Children who kill: A family conspiracy? Social Work, 7, 35-42.

Satcher, D., Powell, K. E., Mercy, J. A., & Rosenberg, M. L. (1996). Opening commentary: Violence prevention is as American as apple pie. American Journal of Preventive Medicine, 12(5), 1-2.

Sautter, R. C. (1995, January). Standing up to violence. Phi Delta Kappan, 76(5), K1-K12.

Save youths worth saving [editorial]. (1993, August 20). Atlanta Constitution, p. A12.

Schacter, D. L. (1986). Amnesia and crime: How much do we really know? American Psychologist, 41, 286-295.

Scherl, D. J., & Mack, J. E. (1966). A study of adolescent matricide. Journal of the American Academy of Child Psychiatry, 5, 569-593.

Schiraldi, V. (1995, October 1). Arresting juvenile crime. Tampa Tribune (Commentary), p. 1.

Schmideberg, M. (1973). Juvenile murderers. International Journal of Offender Therapy and Comparative Criminology, 17, 240-245.

Schopp, R. F. (1991). Automatism, insanity, and the psychology of criminal responsibility. New York: Cambridge University Press.

Schorr, L. B. (1988). Within our reach: Breaking the cycle of disadvantage. New York: Doubleday.

Scott, S. (1994, February 5). For widow, killing raises questions, too: Juvenile justice system on trial. The Gazette (Montreal), p. A1.

Scudder, R. G., Blount, W. R., Heide, K. M., & Silverman, I. J. (1993). Important links between child abuse, neglect, and delinquency. International Journal of Offender Therapy and Comparative Criminology, 37, 315-323.

Sendi, I. B., & Blomgren, P. G. (1975). A comparative study of predictive criteria in the predisposition of homicidal adolescents. American Journal of Psychiatry, 132, 423-427.

Shapiro, D. (1984). Psychological evaluation and expert testimony. New York: Van Nostrand Reinhold.

Sharp, D. (1997, December 3). Student gun violence creeps into small-community schools. USA Today, p. A2.

Sheley, J. F., & Wright, J. D. (1993). Gun acquisition and possession in selected juvenile samples. Washington, DC: U.S. Department of Justice, Office of Justice Programs, National Institute of Justice.

Sheley, J. F., & Wright, J. D. (1995). In the line of fire: Youth, guns, and violence in America. Hawthorne, NY: Aldine de Gruyter.

Shirk, M. (1994, March 5). Policy-makers study trail of crime. St. Louis Post-Dispatch, p. B13.

Shooting accident kills girl, 13: Boy, 15, cited. (1995, September 26). Chicago Sun-Times (News), p. 17.

Sickmund, M. (1994, October). How juveniles get to criminal court (OJJDP update and statistics). Washington, DC: U.S. Department of Justice, Office of Juvenile Justice and Delinquency Prevention.

Sickmund, M., Snyder, H. N., & Poe-Yamagata, E. (1997, August). Juvenile offenders and victims: 1997 update on violence. Washington, DC: U.S. Department of Justice, Office of Juvenile Justice and Delinquency Prevention.

Silverman, I. J. (1996). Corrections: A comprehensive view. St. Paul, MN: West.

Silverman, I. J., & Dinitz, S. (1974). Compulsive masculinity and delinquency. *Criminology, 11,* 498-515.

Silverman, R. A. (1990). Trends in Canadian youth homicide: Some unanticipated consequences of a change in the law. *Canadian Journal of Criminology, 32,* 651-656.

Silverman, R. A., & Kennedy, L. (1993). *Deadly deeds: Murder in Canada.* Toronto: Nelson Canada.

Silvern, L., Waelde, L. C., Karyl, J., Hodges, W. F., Starke, J., Heidt, E., & Min, K. (1994). Relationships of parental abuse to college students' depression, trauma symptoms, and self-esteem. *Child, Youth, and Family Services Quarterly, 17*(1), 7-9.

Silverstein, K. (1994, February 11). Laying down the law: Punishing juvenile delinquents. *Scholastic Update, 126*(9), 14.

Simon, R. J. (1967). *The jury and the insanity defense.* Boston: Little, Brown.

Skovron, S. E., Scott, J. E., & Cullen, F. T. (1989). The death penalty for juveniles: An assessment of public support. *Crime & Delinquency, 35,* 546-561.

Slayings by teenagers increase as communities seek answers. (1995, September 3). *Tampa Tribune* (Nation/World), p. 10.

Sleek, S. (1994, January). APA works to reduce violence in media. *The APA Monitor,* pp. 6-7.

Sloan, J. (1997, May 4). Students prefer school of hard knocks. *Tampa Tribune* (Nation/World), pp. 1, 10.

Smith, C., & Thornberry, T. P. (1995). The relationship between childhood maltreatment and adolescent involvement in delinquency. *Criminology, 33,* 451-481.

Smith, M. D., & Feiler, S. M. (1995). Absolute and relative involvement in homicide offending: Contemporary youth and the baby boom cohorts. *Violence and Victims, 10,* 327-333.

Smith, S. (1965). The adolescent murderer: A psychodynamic interpretation. *Archives of General Psychiatry, 13,* 310-319.

Snell, T. L. (1996, December). *Capital punishment 1995* (Bureau of Justice Statistics bulletin). Washington, DC: U.S. Department of Justice, Office of Justice Programs.

Snyder, H. N. (1994, May). *Juvenile violent crime arrest rates, 1972-1992* (OJJDP Fact Sheet No. 14). Washington, DC: U.S. Department of Justice, Office of Juvenile Justice and Delinquency Prevention.

Snyder, H. N. (1997, November). *Juvenile arrests, 1996* (Juvenile Justice bulletin). Washington, DC: U.S. Department of Justice, Office of Juvenile Justice and Delinquency Prevention.

Snyder, H. N., & Sickmund, M. (1995). *Juvenile offenders and victims: A focus on violence.* Washington, DC: U.S. Department of Justice, Office of Juvenile Justice and Delinquency Prevention.

Snyder, H. N., Sickmund, M., & Poe-Yamagata, E. (1996). *Juvenile offenders and victims: 1996 update on violence.* Washington, DC: U.S. Department of Justice, Office of Juvenile Justice and Delinquency Prevention.

Solomon, E. P., Berg, L. R., Martin, D. W., & Villee, C. (1996). *Biology.* Philadelphia: W. B. Saunders.

Solomon, E. P., & Heide, K. M. (1994, November). *Intervention strategies for victims of trauma: A brief therapy model.* Paper presented at the annual meeting of the American Society of Criminology, Miami, FL.

Solomon, E. P., & Heide, K. M. (1995, November). *A solution-focused model for treating victims and offenders: Strategies for rapid rapport building.* Paper presented at the annual meeting of the American Society of Criminology, Boston.

Solomon, E. P., & Heide, K. M. (1997, November). *Type III trauma: Toward a more effective conceptualization of psychological trauma.* Paper presented at the annual meeting of the American Society of Criminology, San Diego.

Solomon, E., Schmidt, R., & Ardragna, P. (1990). *Human anatomy and physiology.* Philadelphia: W. B. Saunders.

Solway, I. S., Richardson, L., Hays, J. R., & Elion, V. H. (1981). Adolescent murderers: Literature review and preliminary research findings. In J. R. Hays, T. K. Roberts, & K. Solway (Eds.), *Violence and the violent individual* (pp. 193-210). Jamaica, NY: Spectrum.

Sorrells, J. M. (1977). Kids who kill. *Crime & Delinquency, 23,* 313-320.

Sorrells, J. M., Jr. (1981). What can be done about juvenile homicide? *Crime & Delinquency, 16,* 152-161.

Spitz, J. J. (1995, January 8). "The party's over" for young offenders, but critics are wary. *Orlando Sentinel,* p. A1.

Stanford v. Kentucky, 492 U.S. 361 (1989).

Steadman, H. (1993). *Before and after Hinckley: Evaluating insanity defense reform.* New York: Guilford.

Stearns, A. (1957). Murder by adolescents with obscure motivation. *American Journal of Psychiatry, 114,* 303-305.

Steiner, H., Garcia, I. G., & Zakee, M. (1997). Posttraumatic stress disorder in incarcerated juvenile delinquents. *Journal of the American Academy of Child and Adolescent Psychiatry, 36,* 357-365.

Stephens, G. (1997). *Youth at risk: Saving the world's most valuable resource.* Bethesda, MD: World Future Society.

Stephens, S. (1994, February 1). Boys get life terms in girl's fire death. *The Plain Dealer* (Cleveland, OH), p. A1.

Still, L. (1994, March 30). Jury ignores "alter ego," finds teen guilty: Family calls for registry. *Vancouver Sun*, p. A3.

Still, T. W. (1994, March 20). Tough juvenile stance a smart bet [editorial]. *Wisconsin State Journal*, p. A15.

Stockfisch, J. R. (1997, February 5). Congress eyes family leave expansion. *Tampa Tribune* (Business/Finance), pp. 1, 8.

Stone, A. A. (1975). *Mental health and law: A system in transition*. Rockville, MD: National Institute of Mental Health, Center for Studies of Crime and Delinquency.

Stone, A. A. (1978). The insanity defense. In R. W. Rieber & H. J. Vetter (Eds.), *The psychological foundations of criminal justice* (Vol. 2, pp. 162-176). New York: John Jay.

Straus, M. (1994). *Violence in the lives of adolescents*. New York: Norton.

Streib, V. L. (1983). Death penalty for children: The American experience with capital punishment for crimes committed while under age eighteen. *Oklahoma Law Review, 36*, 613-641.

Streib, V. L. (1987). *Death penalty for juveniles*. Bloomington: Indiana State University Press.

Streib, V. L. (1992). The death penalty should not be imposed on violent youths. In D. Biskup & C. Cozic (Eds.), *Youth violence* (pp. 243-250). San Diego: Greenhaven.

Streib, V. L. (1994). Perspectives on the juvenile death penalty in the 1990s. In S. R. Humm, B. A. Ort, M. M. Anbari, W. S. Lader, & W. S. Biel (Eds.), *Child, parent and state: Law and policy reader* (pp. 646-656). Philadelphia: Temple University Press.

Streib, V. L. (1995). Sentencing juvenile murderers: Punish the last offender or save the next victim? *University of Toledo Law Review, 26*, 765-786.

Streib, V. L. (1997, August). *The juvenile death penalty today: Present death row inmates under juvenile death sentences and death sentences and executions for juvenile crimes, Jan. 1, 1973, to June 1997*. Unpublished manuscript, Ohio Northern University.

Streib, V. L., & Sametz, L. (1989). Executing female juveniles. *Connecticut Law Review, 22*(1), 3-59.

Substitute teacher dies after attack by 4th-grader. (1995, October 12). *Tampa Tribune* (Nation/World), p. 10.

Sullivan, C. L., Grant, M. Q., & Grant, J. D. (1957). The development of interpersonal maturity: Application to delinquency. *Psychiatry, 20*, 373-385.

Suspended S.C. student returns, shoots teacher, kills himself. (1995, October 13). *Tampa Tribune* (Nation/World), p. 2.

Sutherland, E. H., & Cressey, D. R. (1943). *Principles of criminology*. Philadelphia: J. B. Lippincott.

Sykes, G. M. (1958). *The society of captives: A study of a maximum security prison*. Princeton, NJ: Princeton University Press.

Sykes, G. M., & Matza, D. (1957). Techniques of neutralization: A theory of delinquency. *American Sociological Review, 22*, 664-670.

Taft, P. B., Jr. (1983, July 11). Juvenile criminals. *Family Circle*, pp. 18-20, 25-28.

Tanay, E. (1973). Adolescents who kill parents: Reactive parricide. *Australian and New Zealand Journal of Psychiatry, 7*, 263-277.

Tanay, E. (1976). Reactive parricide. *Journal of Forensic Sciences, 21*(1), 76-82.

Tate, D. C., Reppucci, N. D., & Mulvey, E. P. (1995). Violent juvenile delinquents: Treatment effectiveness and implications for future action. *American Psychologist, 50*, 777-781.

Taub, J. (1994, April 5). Drive-by slaying raises questions about Young Offenders Act. *Ottawa Citizen*, p. A8.

Teacher hailed for subduing gunman. (1996, February 5). *Tampa Tribune* (Nation/World), p. 2.

Teen charged in triple slaying at flea market. (1995, April 6). *Tampa Tribune* (Nation/World), p. 7.

Teen murder suspects denied bail. (1995, May 3). *United Press International*. (Available on-line)

Territo, L., Halsted, J., & Bromley, M. (1995). *Crime and justice in America* (3rd ed.). St. Paul, MN: West.

Texas Youth Commission. (1996, December). *Review of treatment programs*. Austin, TX: Author.

Texas Youth Commission. (1997, February). *Specialized treatment recidivism effectiveness summary*. Austin, TX: Author.

Thom, D. (1949). Juvenile delinquency and criminal homicide. *Journal of the Maine Medical Association, 40*, 176.

Thompson v. Oklahoma, 487 U.S. 815 (1988).

Thornberry, T. P. (1994). *Violent families and youth violence* (Fact Sheet No. 21). Washington, DC: U.S. Department of Justice, Office of Juvenile Justice and Delinquency Prevention.

Thornberry, T. P., & Burch, J. H. (1997, June). *Gang members and delinquent behavior* (Juvenile Justice bulletin). Washington, DC: U.S. Department of Justice, Office of Juvenile Justice and Delinquency Prevention.

Thornberry, T. P., Huizinga, D., & Loeber, R. (1995). The prevention of serious delinquency and violence: Implications from the program of research on the causes and correlates of delinquency. In J. C. Howell, B. Krisberg, J. D. Hawkins, & J. J. Wilson (Eds.), *A sourcebook: Serious, violent, and chronic juvenile offenders* (pp. 213-237). Thousand Oaks, CA: Sage.

Toch, H. (1977). *Living in prison: The ecology of survival.* New York: Free Press.

Toch, T., Gest, T., & Guttman, M. (1993, November 8). Violence in schools. *U.S. News & World Report,* p. 30.

Tolan, P., & Guerra, N. (1994). *What works in reducing adolescent violence: An empirical review in the field.* Boulder, CO: University of Colorado, Center for the Study and Prevention of Violence.

Tooley, K. (1975). The small assassins. *Journal of the American Academy of Child Psychiatry, 14,* 306-318.

Torbet, P., Gable, R., Hurst, H., Montgomery, I., Szymansky, L., & Thomas, D. (1996). *State responses to serious and violent juvenile crime.* Washington, DC: U.S. Department of Justice, Office of Juvenile Justice and Delinquency Prevention.

Toupin, J. (1993). Adolescent murderers: Validation of a typology and study of their recidivism. In A. V. Wilson (Ed.), *Homicide: The victim/offender connection* (pp. 135-156). Cincinnati, OH: Anderson.

Tremblay, R. E., McCord, J., Boileau, H., Charlebois, P., Gagnon, C., LeBlanc, M., & Larivee, S. (1991). Can disruptive boys be helped to become competent? *Psychiatry, 54,* 148-161.

Tremblay, R. E., Vitaro, F., Bertrand, L., LeBlanc, M., Beauchesne, H., Bioleau, H., & David, L. (1992). Parent and child training to prevent early onset of delinquency: The Montreal Longitudinal-Experimental Study. In J. McCord & R. E. Tremblay (Eds.), *Preventing antisocial behavior: Interventions from birth through adolescence* (pp. 117-138). New York: Guilford.

Troyer, K. (1995, September 9). Girl, 11, wounded in accidental shooting. *St. Petersburg Times,* p. B1.

Tucker, L. S., & Cornwall, T. P. (1977). Mother-son "folie à deux": A case of attempted patricide. *American Journal of Psychiatry, 134,* 1146-1147.

Tupin, J. (1987). Psychopharmacology and aggression. In L. Roth (Ed.), *Clinical treatment of the violent person* (pp. 79-94). New York: Guilford.

Turner, C. (1994, April 9). Canadians troubled by outbreak of violence. *Los Angeles Times,* p. A17.

Tustin, L. (1995, March 13). Real culprit in youth crime isn't the law. *Toronto Star,* p. A17.

12- and 13-year-old killers incarcerated in Illinois. (1996, February 1). *Criminal Justice Newsletter,* p. 3.

2 boys convicted for dropping child from 14th floor. (1995, November 29). *Tampa Tribune* (Nation/World), p. 10.

2 teens charged with man's murder. (1995, April 30). *Chicago Tribune,* p. C3.

Upton, S., & Buchanan, C. (1994, May 3). Grieving students protest stabbing of teen in Hull. *Ottawa Citizen,* p. A1.

U.S. Advisory Board on Child Abuse and Neglect. (1993). *Neighbors helping neighbors: A new national strategy for the protection of children.* Washington, DC: National Clearinghouse on Child Abuse and Neglect.

U.S. Department of Commerce, Economics and Statistics Administration, Bureau of the Census. (1994). *Statistical abstract of the United States.* Washington, DC: Government Printing Office.

U.S. Department of Health and Human Services, Centers for Disease Control and Prevention, National Center for Health Statistics. (1990). *Vital statistics of the United States,* Vol. 1: *Natality.* Washington, DC: Government Printing Office.

U.S. Department of Justice. (1987). *Bureau of Justice Statistics special report: Survey of youth in custody.* Washington, DC: Government Printing Office.

U.S. Department of Justice. (1996a). *Reducing youth gun violence: An overview of programs and initiatives.* Washington, DC: U.S. Department of Justice, Office of Juvenile Justice and Delinquency Prevention.

U.S. Department of Justice. (1996b). *Reducing youth gun violence: A summary of programs and initiatives.* Washington, DC: U.S. Department of Justice, Office of Juvenile Justice and Delinquency Prevention.

U.S. Department of Justice. (1997, August). *1995 National Youth Gang Survey.* Washington, DC: U.S. Department of Justice, Office of Juvenile Justice and Delinquency Prevention.

VandeWater, J. (1995, January 3). Violent crime brings changing view of juvenile codes. *St. Louis Post-Dispatch* (St. Charles), p. 1.

Vansun. (1995, August 2). Young offenders need programs, not just prison sentences [editorial]. *Vancouver Sun,* p. A14.

Van Voorhis, P. (1988). A cross classification of five offender typologies: Issues of construct and predictive validity. *Criminal Justice and Behavior, 15,* 109-124.

Van Voorhis, P. (1994). *Psychological classification of the adult prison male.* Albany: State University of New York Press.

Van Voorhis, P. (1997). An overview of offender classification systems. In P. Van Voorhis, M. Braswell, & D. Lester (Eds.), *Correctional counseling and rehabilitation* (pp. 81-105). Cincinnati, OH: Anderson.

Vienneau, D. (1994, June 9). Judge's aim is to catch "bad" kids at an early age. *Toronto Star,* p. A3.

Vienneau, D. (1995, September 8). Parents may face legal bills for young offenders. *Toronto Star,* p. A3.

Violent youths . . . The cloak of anonymity is being lifted. (1994, July 27). *San Diego Union-Tribune*, p. B6.

Virginia governor and lawmakers agree on juvenile justice plan. (1996, February 1). *Criminal Justice Newsletter*, pp. 2-3.

Walker, S., Spohn, C., & DeLone, M. (1996). *The color of justice: Race, ethnicity, and crime in America*. Belmont, CA: Wadsworth.

Walsh, B. (1993, July 28). Tougher justice advocated. *The Times-Picayune* (New Orleans), p. A8.

Walshe-Brennan, K. S. (1974). Psychopathology of homicidal children. *Royal Society of Health, 94,* 274-276.

Walshe-Brennan, K. S. (1977). A socio-psychological investigation of young murderers. *British Journal of Criminology, 17*(1), 53-63.

Warren, M. Q. (1966). *Interpersonal maturity level classification: Juvenile diagnosis and treatment of low, middle, and high maturity delinquents.* Unpublished manuscript, California Youth Authority, Sacramento.

Warren, M. Q. (1969). The case for differential treatment of delinquents. *Annals of the American Academy of Political and Social Science, 381,* 47-59.

Warren, M. Q. (1971). Classification of offenders as an aid to effective management and effective treatment. *Journal of Criminal Law, Criminology and Police Science, 62,* 239-258.

Warren, M. Q. (1978). The "impossible child," the difficult child, and other assorted delinquents: Etiology, characteristics and incidence. *Canadian Psychiatric Association Journal, 23*(Suppl.), SS41-SS60.

Warren, M. Q. (1983). Applications of interpersonal maturity level theory to offender populations. In W. S. Laufer & J. M. Day (Eds.), *Personality theory, moral development and criminal behavior* (pp. 23-50). Lexington, MA: D. C. Heath.

Washbrook, R. A. H. (1979). Bereavement leading to murder. *International Journal of Offender Therapy and Comparative Criminology, 23*(1), 57-64.

Weaver, R. S. (1992). Violent youths need rehabilitation, not harsh punishment. In D. Biskup & C. Cozic (Eds.), *Youth violence* (pp. 227-233). San Diego: Greenhaven.

Werner, E. (1975). Relationships among interpersonal maturity, personality configurations, intelligence and ethnic study. *British Journal of Criminology, 15,* 51-68.

Wertham, F. (1941). *Dark legend: A study in murder.* New York: Duell, Sloan, & Pearce.

Weston, B. (1994, July 14). Brutal boyfriends, battered girlfriends. *San Francisco Examiner*, p. B1.

West Publishing. (1995). *West's Florida criminal laws and rules 1995.* St. Paul, MN: Author.

Wettstein, R. M., Mulvey, E. P., & Rogers, R. (1991). A prospective comparison of four insanity defense standards. *American Journal of Psychiatry, 148,* 21-27.

What can be done about the scourge of violence among juveniles? (1994, December 30). *The New York Times*, p. A24.

"What's going on?" Calgary stunned as two young girls face charges in robbery, death of man. (1995, July 14). *Tampa Tribune* (Nation/World), p. 4.

Wheeler, J. L. (1993). *Remote controlled: How TV affects you and your family.* Hagerstown, MD: Review and Herald Publishing Association.

Whitely, P., Tizon, A., Birkland, D., & Norton, D. (1994, March 25). "It was one gang against another": Police have talked with parents of youth suspected of killing girl at Ballard High. *Seattle Times*, p. A1.

Widom, C. S. (1989a). Child abuse, neglect, and adult behavior: Research design and findings on criminality, violence, and child abuse. *American Journal of Orthopsychiatry, 59,* 355-366.

Widom, C. S. (1989b). Child abuse, neglect, and violent criminal behavior. *Criminology, 27,* 251-271.

Widom, C. S. (1989c, April 14). The cycle of violence. *Science, 244,* 160-166.

Widom, C. S. (1989d). Does violence beget violence? A critical examination of the literature. *Psychological Bulletin, 106,* 3-28.

Widom, C. S. (1991). A tail on an untold tale: Response to "Biological and Genetic Contributors to Violence"—Widom's untold tale. *Psychological Bulletin, 109,* 130-132.

Wiebush, R. G., Baird, C., Krisberg, B., & Onek, D. (1995). Risk assessment and classification for serious, violent, and chronic juvenile offenders. In J. C. Howell, B. Krisberg, J. D. Hawkins, & J. J. Wilson (Eds.), *A sourcebook: Serious, violent, and chronic juvenile offenders* (pp. 171-212). Thousand Oaks, CA: Sage.

Wilkerson, I. (1994, May 22). The most dangerous criminals in America are also its youngest. *News Tribune* (Tacoma, WA), p. E1.

Willis, D. J. (1995). Psychological impact of child abuse and neglect. *Journal of Clinical Child Psychology, 24*(Suppl.), 2-4.

Wilson, E. O. (1975). *Sociobiology: The new synthesis.* Cambridge, MA: Harvard University Press.

Wilson, J. J., & Howell, J. C. (1993). *A comprehensive strategy for serious, violent, and chronic offenders.* Washington, DC: U.S. Department of Justice, Office of Juvenile Justice and Delinquency Prevention.

Wilson, J. J., & Howell, J. C. (1995). Comprehensive strategy for serious, violent, and chronic juvenile offenders. In J. C. Howell, B. Krisberg,

J. D. Hawkins, & J. J. Wilson (Eds.), *A source-book: Serious, violent, and chronic juvenile offenders* (pp. 36-46). Thousand Oaks, CA: Sage.

Wilson, J. Q. (1994). What to do about crime. *Commentary, 98*(3), 25-34. (American Jewish Committee)

Wilson, J. Q., & Herrnstein, R. J. (1985). *Crime and human nature.* New York: Simon & Schuster.

Wilson, M., & Daly, M. (1985). Competitiveness, risk taking, and violence: The young male syndrome. *Ethology and Sociobiology, 6*(1), 59-73.

Woods, S. M. (1961). Adolescent violence and homicide: Ego disruption and the 6 and 14 dysrhythmia. *Archives of General Psychiatry, 5*, 528-534.

Wright, K. N., & Wright, K. E. (1995). *Family life, delinquency, and crime: A policymaker's guide* (research summary). Washington, DC: U.S. Department of Justice, Office of Juvenile Justice and Delinquency Prevention.

Wyatt, N. (1993, July 5). Adolescent arrested in Montreal rampage. *Calgary Herald*, p. A6.

Wynne, E., & Hess, M. (1986). Long-term trends in youth conduct and the revival of traditional value patterns. *Educational Evaluation and Policy Analysis, 8*, 294-308.

Yates, A., Beutler, L. E., & Crago, M. (1983). Characteristics of young, violent offenders. *Journal of Psychiatry and Law, 11*(2), 137-149.

Yeomans, A. (1995, September 11). Teen on trial again in Briton's death. *Tampa Tribune* (Florida/Metro), p. 6.

Yoshikawa, H. (1994). Prevention as cumulative protection: Effects of early family support and education on chronic delinquency and its risks. *Psychological Bulletin, 115*, 28-54.

Young suspect to be tried as adult. (1997, November 15). *Tampa Tribune* (Nation/World), p. 10.

Youth accused of murder. (1994, June 4). *The Herald* (London), p. 3.

The youth crime plague. (1977, July 11). *Time*, pp. 18-20.

Youthful killers given 2nd chance. (1995, September 26). *Tampa Tribune* (Nation/World), p. 14.

Youth remanded in murder case. (1995, May 4). *Irish Times* (Home News), p. 9.

Youths accused of murder. (1993, December 31). *The Herald* (London), p. 8.

Zagar, R., Arbit, J., Sylvies, R., Busch, K., & Hughes, J. R. (1990). Homicidal adolescents: A replication. *Psychological Reports, 67*, 1235-1242.

Zellner, W. W. (1995). *Countercultures: A sociological analysis.* New York: St. Martin's.

Zenoff, E. H., & Zients, A. B. (1979). Juvenile murderers: Should the punishment fit the crime? *International Journal of Law and Psychiatry, 2*(4), 533-553.

Zimbardo, P. G. (1975). Transforming experimental research into advocacy for social change. In M. Deutsch & H. Hornstein (Eds.), *Applying social psychology: Implications for research, practice, and training* (pp. 33-66). Hillsdale, NJ: Lawrence Erlbaum.

Zimring, F. E. (1984). Youth homicide in New York: A preliminary analysis. *Journal of Legal Studies, 13*, 81-99.

Index

ABA. *See* American Bar Association
Accidental death, 19-20
ADHD. *See* Attention-deficit hyperactivity
    disorder
ADL. *See* Anti-Defamation League
Adolescent defined, 5-6
Adolescent parricide offenders, 10, 31-32, 35-36,
    88
Adopted child syndrome, 32
African Americans:
    as offenders, 12, 13, 14
    as victims, 14-15
Aftercare, treatment and, 230, 235-236
Age, 5-6, 17
Agee, V., 229-232
Alabama, 10
Alcohol abuse:
    and prosecution, 63
    and psychological assessment, 76-77, 78-79t,
        81, 83t
    and treatment, 230, 235
    as homicide causation, 20, 32-33, 34, 37t, 45-46
    drunk driving, 20, 53
ALI. *See* American Law Institute
AMA. *See* American Medical Association
American Bar Association (ABA), 61
American Law Institute (ALI), 61, 84-85
American Medical Association, 242
APA. *See* American Psychological Association
American Psychological Association, 42, 239-240
American Psychological Association's Commission
    on Youth and Violence, 239-240
Amnesia, 35, 68
Amnesty International, 56
Anger Expression Scale, 68
Anger management, 230, 233-234
Anti-Defamation League (ADL), 11
Antisocial personality disorder, 83t, 232
Arkansas, xx, 12, 18
ATEs. *See* Aversive treatment evaders
Attempted murder, 19
Attention-deficit/hyperactivity disorder (ADHD),
    31, 83t, 239, 252
Automatism defense, 62-63
Aversive treatment evaders (ATEs), 229-230

Bailey, S., 32, 224-225, 230, 237
Behavioral observation, 71-72
Behavioral restructuring, 230, 232-233
Bell, C, 42-43
Bell, C., and Jenkins, E., 42-43
Benedek, E. P., 32-33, 35-36, 226, 227-228
Benedek, D. M., 32-33, 35-36, 226
Benedek, E. P., Cornell, D. G., and Staresina, L.,
    227-228
Biological causation factors, 37t, 49-51, 239
Bipolar disorder, 232
Block, C., 10-11
Block, R., 10-11, 19
Blumstein, A., 44, 159, 178-179
Borderline personality disorder, 232
Boredom, 37t, 47-48
Boyd, N., 22
Brazil, 26

California, 16, 28
Canada, 22-25, 27, 62
Capital Offender Program (Texas), 237, 238
Capital punishment. *See* Death penalty
Case study:
    advantages of, 89
    homicide causation profile, 33
    homicide causation research, 30-33
    limitations of, 29, 88-89
    of death penalty, 1, 56-58, 60-61, 69
Case study, Brian Clark:
    activities, 205
    behavioral observation, 202-203
    case commentary, 216-217
    clinical evaluation, 202
    conviction/sentencing, 214-215
    diagnostic and treatment considerations, 214
    emotional control, 206-207
    family constellation, 203-204
    follow-up data, 215-216
    friends, 205
    future orientation, 208
    girlfriends, 205
    homicide motivation, 208-211, 216-217
    jail, adjustment in, 208

making sense of murder, 216-217
mental health history, 206
mitigating sentencing factors, 211-214
personality development, 203
physical health history, 206
prior delinquency, 207-208
prognosis, 214, 217
religious affiliation, 207
school history, 204-205
sexual history, 205
social history, 203-208
substance abuse, 206
work history, 205
Case study, Calvin Thomas:
  activities, 134
  behavioral observation, 131-132
  case commentary, 146-147
  clinical evaluation, 131
  conviction/sentencing, 142-143
  diagnostic and treatment considerations,
    141-142
  emotional control, 135
  family constellation, 132-133
  family consultation, 138-140
  follow-up data, 143-146
  friends, 134
  future orientation, 136
  girlfriends, 134
  homicide motivation, 136-138, 146-147
  jail, adjustment in, 136
  making sense of murder, 146-147
  mental health history, 135
  mitigating sentencing factors, 141
  personality development, 132
  physical health history, 135
  prior delinquency, 136
  prognosis, 142, 147
  religious affiliation, 135
  school history, 133, 140-141
  sexual history, 134
  social history, 132-136
  substance abuse, 135
  work history, 133-134
Case study, David Collins:
  activities, 150
  behavioral observation, 148-149
  case commentary, 159-160
  clinical evaluation, 148
  conviction/sentencing, 156
  diagnostic and treatment considerations,
    155-156
  emotional control, 151
  family constellation, 149
  follow-up data, 156-158
  friends, 150
  future orientation, 152
  girlfriends, 150

homicide motivation, 153-155
jail, adjustment in, 152, 158
making sense of murder, 155
mental health history, 151
personality development, 149
physical health history, 151
prior delinquency, 152
prognosis, 156, 159-160
religious affiliation, 151
school history, 150
sexual history, 150
social history, 149-152
substance abuse, 150-151
work history, 150
Case study, Jerry Johnson:
  activities, 114-115
  behavioral observation, 112-113
  case commentary, 129-130
  clinical evaluation, 112
  competency issues, 122-123
  conviction/sentencing, 124
  diagnostic and treatment considerations, 124
  family constellation, 113-114
  family consultation, 117-119
  follow-up data, 124-129
  friends, 115, 119
  future orientation, 116
  girlfriends, 115
  homicide motivation, 120-122, 123
  jail, adjustment in, 116, 118
  making sense of murder, 123
  mental health history, 118
  military interest, 114-115, 119
  personality development, 113
  physical health history, 118
  prior delinquency, 116
  prognosis, 124, 129-130
  sanity issues, 123
  school history, 114, 119
  social history, 113-116
  substance abuse, 115-116
  work history, 114, 119
Case study, Joel Westerlund:
  activities, 185-186
  behavioral observation, 181-182
  case commentary, 200-201
  clinical evaluation, 181
  conviction/sentencing, 180, 196-197
  diagnostic and treatment considerations,
    195-196
  family constellation, 183-185
  family consultation, 188-189
  follow-up data, 197-200
  friends, 186
  future orientation, 188
  girlfriends, 186
  homicide motivation, 189-194

jail, adjustment in, 188
making sense of murder, 194
mental health history, 186-187
personality development, 182-183
physical health history, 186
prior delinquency, 187
prognosis, 195-196, 200-201
sanity issues, 195
school history, 185
sexual history, 186
social history, 183-188
substance abuse, 186
work history, 185
Case study, Malcolm Farrell:
activities, 164
behavioral observation, 161-162
case commentary, 178-179
clinical evaluation, 161
conviction/sentencing, 167-171, 173
diagnostic and treatment considerations, 172
emotional control, 165
family constellation, 163
follow-up data, 173-178
friends, 164
future orientation, 166
gang involvement, 177-178
girlfriends, 164
homicide motivation, 167-171, 179
jail, adjustment in, 166, 176
making sense of murder, 179
mental health history, 165
mitigating sentencing factors, 172
personality development, 162-163
physical health history, 165
prior delinquency, 166
prognosis, 172, 179
religious affiliation, 165-166
sanity issues, 172
school history, 163-164, 167
sexual history, 164
social history, 163-166
social services history, 166-167
substance abuse, 164-165
work history, 164
Case study, Mark sentenced to death, 1, 56-58, 60-61, 69
Case study, Peter Daniels:
activities, 96
behavioral observation, 92
case commentary, 110-111
clinical evaluation, 91-92
conviction/sentencing, 107
delinquency history, 97
diagnostic and treatment considerations, 106-107
emotional control, 97
family constellation, 93-94, 99-100

family consultation, 98-100
follow-up data, 107-110
friends, 95
future orientation, 97
girlfriends, 95-96
homicide motivation, 100-104, 105
jail, adjustment in, 97-98
making sense of murder, 105
mental health history, 97
mitigating sentencing factors, 105-106
personality development, 92-93
prognosis, 107, 111
religious affiliation, 97
sanity issues, 104-105
school history, 94-95, 98
social history, 93-98
substance abuse, 96, 98, 104
work history, 95
Causation. *See* Causation/correlation
Causation/correlation:
adopted child syndrome, 32
alcohol abuse, 20, 32-33, 34, 37t, 45-46
and females, 29
and "little kids," 29-30
biological factors, 37t, 49-51, 227
boredom, 37t, 47-48
case study limitations on, 29, 88-89
case study profile of, 33
case study research on, 29, 30-33
child (physical) abuse, 31-32, 34, 35, 37-40
child neglect, 37-40
conflict situations, 35-36
crime situations, 35-36
cumulative factors, 37t, 49-51, 229, 239
diathesis-stress theory, 51
drug abuse, 11, 32-33, 34, 37t, 45-46
drug-related violence, model of, 76
educational difficulties, 31, 34
empirical research on, 34-36
episodic dyscontrol syndrome, 31
fantasy, 12
gang participation, 32
government leadership crisis, 37t, 41-42
gun access, 37t, 44-45
home environment, 31-32
intelligence level, 31
involvement in other antisocial behavior, 32
learning disabilities, 31, 252
low emotional control, 37t, 47
low self-esteem, 37t, 46-47
male role model absence, 37t, 40-41
mental retardation, 31
neurological impairment, 31, 34, 49-51, 239
parental psychopathology, 32, 34
personality characteristics, 37t, 46-48, 229
poor judgment, 37t, 48
poverty, 37t, 46

prejudice/hatred, 37t, 48
prior delinquency, 32
psychological disorder, 30-31
psychotic situations, 35-36
research literature on, 28-36
resource availability, 37t, 44-46, 229
Satanic involvement, 12-13
sexual abuse, 31-32, 39-40
situational factors, 37-41, 229
social difficulties, 33
societal influences, 37t, 41-44, 229
spouse abuse, 32, 35
substance abuse, 32-33
violence exposure, 37t, 38, 42-44, 253
Centers for Disease Control and Prevention, 13,
    240
Chen, J., 15
Child abuse:
    and psychological assessment, 82
    and relationship to delinquency, 38
    as homicide causation, 31-32, 34, 35, 37-40
    increase in, 37-38
Child maltreatment, types defined, 39t
Child neglect, 37-40
Children defined, 6
Clinical evaluation, 70-71
Clinton, B., 240
Clinton, H., 246
Cognitive behavioral restructuring, 230, 232-233
Colorado, 16, 19
Community-based treatment facilities, 236-237
Community involvement, homicide prevention
        and, 241-242, 243t, 246-249
Community reentry counseling, 230, 235, 237
Competency issues, 59-60
Conduct disorder, 31, 83t, 232
Conflict situations, 35-36
Consistent discipline, 230, 234-235
Coopersmith Inventory, 68
Corder, B., and colleagues, 35
Cornell, D., 29, 32-33, 35-36, 226
Cornell, D., Benedek, E. P., and Benedek, D. M.,
    32-33, 35-36, 226
Correlation. See Causation/correlation
Counteractive to power subtype, 87-88, 162-163
Crime Classification Manual (CCM), 36
Crime situations, 35-36
Criminal justice system. See Prosecution
Cult groups, 12-13
Cultural conformist, 87-88, 113, 132, 149
Cumulative causation factors:
    and treatment, 229
    and solutions, 241-242
    biological factors, 37t, 49-51
    nothing left to lose concept, 37t, 49

Daly, M., 47
Death penalty:
    aggravating factors, 66
    and prosecution, 52, 55-58
    case study of Mark, 1, 56-58, 60-61, 69
    mitigating factors, 66
    foreign countries, 56
Defenses. See Mental status defenses
Delinquency history, 32, 77
DeLone, M., 14-15
Depression, 83t, 232
Diagnoses, 31
Diathesis-stress theory, 51
Differential treatment, 229-230, 236
Diminished capacity, 63
Diminished responsibility, 63
Discipline, 230, 234-235, 245
Dissociative Experiences Scale, 68
Donnell, case of, 65, 71-72, 82, 84-85
Double homicide, 9-10
Driving under the influence (DUI), 20
Driving while intoxicated (DWI), 20
Drug abuse:
    and prosecution, 63
    and psychological assessment, 76-77, 78-79t,
        81, 83t
    and treatment, 230, 235
    as homicide causation, 11, 32-33, 34, 37t, 45-46
Drunk driving, 20, 53
DUI. See Driving under the influence
DWI. See Driving while intoxicated

Eddings v. Oklahoma (1982), 55
Education:
    and homicide prevention, 241-242, 243t,
        245-246
    and treatment, 230, 235, 236
    for substance abuse, 230, 235
Elders, J., 14-15
Emotional control, 37t, 47
    and homicide prevention, 245
    and treatment, 234
    anger management, 230, 233-234
    Emotional incest defined, 39t
    Emotional neglect defined, 39t
Empathy training, 230, 234
Empirical research, 34-36
England, 25
Episodic dyscontrol syndrome, 31
Ewing, C.P., 21, 28
Eysenck, H., 50

Family:
    as homicide victims, 9-10, 13, 16, 88
    assessment consultation, 82

changes in family structure, 40-41
Federal Bureau of Investigation (FBI), 9, 36
Females:
    and homicide causation, 29
    and homicide characteristics, 13-16
    Fendrich, M., 33
First-degree murder, 53
Florida, 5, 8, 16, 18, 19, 20, 28, 52-53
Forcible rape, 40
Fox, J. A., 6, 9-10
Fox, J. A., and Levin, J., 9-10
Foreign countries:
    and homicide characteristics, 22-26
    death penalty, 56
Forensic evaluation, 68-83
France, 25, 26
Furman v. Georgia (1972), 55

Gabor, T., 23
Gangs, 10-11, 32, 177-178
Gardiner, M., 226
GBMI. *See* Guilty but mentally Ill
Georgia, 10, 55, 56
Germany, 22, 25
Goldstein's model of drug-related violence, 76
Government leadership:
    and homicide causation, 37t, 41-42
    and homicide prevention, 241-242, 243t, 249,
        251-252
Great Britain, 22, 25, 26, 62
Gregg v. Georgia (1976), 56
Group membership:
    cult groups, 12-13
    gangs, 10-11
    hate groups, 11
Guilty but mentally ill, 62
Gun control, 252

Hate groups, 11, 48
Home environment, 31-32
Homicide arrest rates, 6-7, 14-15, 22, 255n11
    urban, 7
Homicide motivation, 8-9, 10, 77, 80-82. *See also*
    Causation/correlation
Homicide syndromes, 10-11
Hospitalization, psychiatric, 226

Identity Church, 11
Illinois, 9, 10, 11, 17, 52
Incarceration:
    adjustment in jail, 77. *See specific case studies*
        (jail, adjustment to)
    adjustment in prison. *See specific case studies*
        (follow-up data)

    and rehabilitation in prison, 224-225
    conditions of, 222-223
    life in prison, 222-225
    population in prison, 252
India, 25
Insanity defense, 60-62
    ABA truncation of the ALI test, 61
    Irresistible Impulse Test, 61
    M'Naghten, 60, 61, 84-85
    Model Penal Code Test, 61
Institutional placement, treatment and, 226
Intelligence level, 31
Interpersonal maturity level (I-level), 72-75
    and treatment, 229-230
    counteractive to power, 87-88, 162-163
    cultural conformist, 87-88, 113, 132, 149
    manipulator, 87-88, 162-163
    neurotic acting out, 88, 182, 203
    passive conformist, 87-88, 92-93
    undifferentiated subtype, 149
Involuntary manslaughter, 53
Irresistible Impulse Test, 61

Jail, adjustment to, 77. *See specific case studies*
Jeffrey, C. R., 50
    Jenkins, E., 42-43
Jonesboro, Arkansas, massacre at, xx, 18
Judgment, 37t, 48
Juvenile defined, 5-6
Juvenile homicide characteristics:
    accidental death, 19-20
    acquaintance victims, 9-10, 13
    adolescent defined, 5-6
    African American offenders, 12, 13, 14
    African American victims, 14-15
    age, 5-6, 17
    alcohol abuse, 20, 32-33, 34, 37t, 45-46
    attempted murder, 19
    children defined, 6
    cult groups, 12-13
    double homicide, 9-10
    drug abuse, 11, 32-33, 34, 37t, 45-46
    drunk driving, 20, 53
    family member victims, 9-10, 12-13
    females, 13-16
    forecasts of juvenile homicide, 6-7, 21, 239
    gangs, 10-11, 34
    guns, 8, 15, 18, 22, 37t, 44-45, 252
    group membership, 10-13
    hate groups, 11
    homicide arrest rates, 6-7, 14-15, 22, 255n11
    homicide syndromes, 10-11
    increase in juvenile homicide, 5-7, 219
    juvenile defined, 5-6
    juvenile population, 6-7
    jurisdictional differences, 3

legislation, 21-22, 24-25, 240
"little kids," 17, 25
mass murder, xx, 9-10, 18, 26
media depiction, 20-21
motivation, 8-9, 10, 77, 80-82
public perception, 21
race, 12, 13, 14-15
racism, 9, 11
relationship violence, 16
same-sex relationship violence, 16
school homicide, xx, 12-13, 18-19
societal response, 21-22
unknown victims, 9-10, 13
urban homicide arrest rates, 7
U.S. vs. Canada, 22-25
U.S. vs. other countries, 22-26
weapons, 8, 15, 18, 22, 37t, 44-45, 252
White offenders, 12, 13
White victims, 14-15
youth defined, 5

Kemph, J. P., 32
Kentucky, 55
Ku Klux Klan, 11

Law Enforcement Agency Directors (LEAD), 249
Le Blanc, M., 22
Legal system. See Prosecution
Legislation:
    Canada, 24-25
    United States, 21-22, 240
Levin, J., 9-10
Lewis, D.O., 34, 51
"Little kids":
    and homicide causation/correlation, 29-30
    and homicide characteristics, 17

Males, role model absence of, 37t, 40-41
Malingering, 67
Martinow, R., 224
Manipulator, 87-88, 162-163
Mass murder, 9-10, 26
Material review, assessment and, 69-70
Media:
    and homicide prevention, 241-242, 244t,
        252-253
    and violence prevention, 241-242, 244t,
        252-253
    juvenile homicide depiction, 20-21
    violence exposure in, 10, 42, 253
Medical neglect defined, 39t
Menninger, K., 31
Mental health professionals, 58, 65-67
Mental retardation, 31, 66-67

Mental status, psychological assessment and, 82-83
Mental status issues and defenses, 58-64
    automatism defense, 62-63
    competency issues, 59-60
    diminished capacity, 63
    diminished responsibility, 63
    insanity defense, 60-62
    provocation, 54
    self-defense, 63-64
    voluntary intoxication, 63
    See also Psychological assessment
Michigan, 52
Minnesota, 8
Minnesota Multiphasic Personality Inventory
    (MMPI), 35, 67-68
Mississippi, 12-13
Missouri, 18
MMPI. See Minnesota Multiphasic Personality
    Inventory
M'Naghten Test, 60, 61, 84
Model Penal Code, 54, 61
Murder, degrees and types of homicide, 53
Music, violence and, 43, 76, 84
Myers, W., 32, 36, 225-227
Myers, W., and Kemph, J. P., 32

National Endowment for the Arts, 248
National Longitudinal Study on Adolescent
    Health, 242, 246
National Violence Prevention Conference, 13, 240
Netherlands, 22
Neurological impairment, 31, 49-51
Neurotic acting out, 88, 182, 203
New Jersey, 8
NGRI. See Not guilty by reason of insanity
Nihilistic killers, 81-82
North Carolina, 12
Norway, 22
Not guilty by reason of insanity (NGRI), 60-62

Office of Juvenile Justice and Delinquency
    Prevention (OJJDP), 224, 240
Ohio, 8, 9
Oklahoma, 55
Oppositional defiant disorder, 83t
Oregon, 16
Ouimet, M., 23
Overt sexual abuse defined, 40

Panel on the Understanding and Control of
    Violent Behavior, 50
Parental Stress Services, 244
Parent Resource Institute for Drug Education, 45
Parents, homicide prevention and, 241-244

Parents, violence prevention and, 241-244
Parents Anonymous, 244
Parents United International Inc., 244
Passive conformist, 87-88, 92-93
Peer communities, treatment and, 230, 233
Pennsylvania, 10, 250
Personality characteristics:
   and treatment, 229
   boredom, 37t, 47-48
   low emotional control, 37t, 47
   low self-esteem, 37t, 46-47
   poor judgment, 37t, 48
   prejudice/hatred, 37t, 48
Personality development:
   counteractive to power, 87-88, 162-163
   cultural conformist, 87-88, 113, 132, 149
   interpersonal maturity level (I-level), 72-75,
     87-88, 92, 229-230
   manipulator, 87-88, 162-163
   neurotic acting out, 88, 182, 203
   passive conformist, 87-88, 92-93
   undifferentiated subtype, 149
Posttraumatic stress disorder (PTSD), 83t, 232
Poverty, 37t, 46, 251-252
Personality disorders, 31. *See also* Antisocial
     personality disorder; Borderline personality
     disorder; Conduct disorder
Physical abuse defined, 39 t. *See also* Child abuse;
     Sexual abuse
Physical neglect defined, 39 t. *See also* Neglect
Prevention:
   Allegheny County, Pennyslvania, 249-250
   and the need for partnerships, 241-242
   and risk factors, 240-241
   as a public health issue, 240-241
   community involvement, 241-242, 243t, 246-249
   educational system involvement, 241-242,
     243t, 245-246
   government leadership involvement, 241-242,
     243t, 249, 251-252
   individual involvement, 241-242, 243t, 253-254
   media involvement, 241-242, 244t, 252-253
   parental involvement, 241-244
   societal strategies for, 239-241, 243-244t
Prison. *See* Incarceration
Prosecution:
   adult criminal court transfer, 54-55
   adult criminal justice system, 52, 53
   competency issues, 59-60
   death penalty, 52, 55-58
   first-degree murder, 53
   involuntary manslaughter, 53
   juvenile justice system, 52
   life imprisonment, 52
   mental status defenses, 58-64
   second-degree murder, 53
   voluntary manslaughter, 53

Prosocial skills training, 230, 233
Provocation, 54
Psychiatric hospitalization, 226
Psychological abuse, 39 t
Psychological assessment:
   amnesia, 68
   and treatment, 230-232
   attention-deficit/hyperactivity disorder, 83t
   behavioral observation, 71-72
   child maltreatment, 82
   clinical evaluation, 70-71
   conduct disorder, 83t
   corroboration, need for, 69-70
   current mental health, 82-83
   delinquency history, 77
   depression, 83t
   family consultation, 82
   homicide motivation, 77, 80-82
   implications of, 65-68
   incarceration adjustment, 77
   interpersonal maturity level (I-level), 72-75,
     87-88, 92, 229-230
   nihilistic killers, 81-82
   personality development, 72-75
   pertinent material review, 69-70
   posttraumatic stress disorder, 83t, 232
   referral reasons, 69
   social history, 75-77
   substance abuse/dependence 76-77, 78-79t,
     81, 83t
   testing for, 36, 60, 61, 67-68
   See also specific case studies
Psychological disorder, 30-31
Psychological testing, 67-68
Psychopharmacological treatment, 227-228, 230,
    236
Psychotherapy, 225
Psychotic youth situations, 35-36
PTSD. *See* Posttraumatic stress disorder
Public perception, 21
Public safety, 221-222

Race, 12, 13, 14-15
Racism, 11, 37t, 48
Recidivism, 222
Referral, assessment and, 69
Rehabilitation, 222, 237
   and incarceration, 224-225
   community reentry counseling, 230, 235, 237
Reiss, A. J., 50-51
Reiss, A. J., and Roth, J. A., 50-51
Relationship violence, 16
Religious groups, 247
Reno, J., 5
Research literature:
   case studies, 29, 30-33

empirical studies, 34-36
    on homicide causation, 28-36
    on treatment, 225-228
Resource availability:
    and poverty, 37t, 46
    and substance abuse, 11, 20, 32-33, 34, 37t,
        45-46
    and treatment, 229
    gun access, 37t, 44-45
Rorschach Psychodiagnostic Test, 36, 68
Roth, J. A., 50-51
Rwanda, 26

Same-sex relationship violence, 16
Savings and Loan Crisis of the 1980s, cost of, 250
Schizophrenia, 232
School homicide, xx, 12-13, 18-19
Schopp, R.F., 62
SCID-D. See Structured Clinical Interview for
    DSM-IV Dissociative Disorders
Scotland, 26
Second-degree murder, 53
Self-defense, 63-64
Self-esteem, 37t, 46-47
Sentence Completion Test, 68
Sexual abuse, 31-32, 39-40
Sickmund, M., 14-15
Silverman, R., 22
Situational factors:
    and treatment, 229
    child abuse, 31-32, 34, 35, 37-40
    child neglect, 37-40
    male role model absence, 37t, 40-41
Skinheads, 10, 11, 48
Snyder, H., 14-15
Snyder, H., and Sickmund, M., 14-15
Social difficulties, 33
Social history, 75-77
Socialization of children, 220, 241-242
Societal influences:
    and treatment, 229
    government leadership crisis, 37t, 41-42
    violence exposure, 37t, 38, 42-44, 253
Societal response, 21-22, 24-25
Societal problem, 219-220
Sorrells, J.M., 33
South Carolina, 18-19
Spohn, C., 14-15
Stanford v. Kentucky (1989), 55
Staresina, L., 227-228
Streib, V., 55-56
Structured Clinical Interview for DSM-IV
    Dissociative Disorders (SCID-D), 68
Substance abuse defined, 83t
Substance dependence defined, 83t
Survivors' Coping Strategies Survey, 82

Television, violence and, 42, 75
Texas, 11, 17, 238
Thompson v. Oklahoma (1988), 55
Tough Love, 244
Toupin, J., 228
Treatment:
    aftercare, 230, 235-236
    and aversive treatment evaders (ATEs), 229-230
    and incarceration conditions, 222-223
    and public safety, 221-222, 237
    and recidivism, 222
    and rehabilitation, 222, 224-225, 237
    anger management, 230, 233-234
    assessment, 230-232
    Capital Offender Program, 237, 238
    cognitive behavioral restructuring, 230, 232-233
    community-based facilities, 236-237
    community reentry counseling, 230, 235, 237
    consistent discipline, 230, 234-235
    differential treatment, need for, 229-230, 236
    education, 230, 236
    effective intervention components, 230-236
    emotional control, 234
    empathy training, 230, 234
    graduated sanctions, 236-237
    institutional placement, 226
    positive peer communities, 230, 233
    prosocial skills training, 230, 233
    psychiatric hospitalization, 226
    psychopharmacological, 227-228, 230, 236
    psychotherapy, 225
    research literature on, 225-228
    substance abuse education, 230, 235
    victimization and trauma history, 231-232
    vocational programs, 230, 236
Typologies of juvenile homicide offenders, 35-36,
    226, 228

University of Iowa, 13
Urban homicide arrest rates, 7

Verbal abuse defined, 39t
Victims:
    acquaintance, 9-10, 13
    African American, 14-15
    family member, 9-10, 13, 88
    unknown, 9-10, 13
    White, 14-15
    Videogames, violence and, 43
Violence exposure, 37t, 38, 42-44, 253
Vocational programs, 230, 236
Violent Crime and Law Enforcement Act (1994),
    240
Voluntary intoxication, 63
Voluntary manslaughter, 53

WAIS-R. *See* Wechsler Adult Intelligence Scale-Revised
Waller, I., 22
Walker, S., 14-15
Walker, S., Spohn, C., and DeLone, M., 14-15
Washington, 11, 28
Weapons, 8, 15, 18, 22, 37t, 44-45, 252
Wechsler Adult Intelligence Scale-Revised (WAIS-R), 68
Whites:
    as offenders, 12, 13
    as victims, 14-15
White supremacy groups, 11

Wilson, E. O., 50
Wilson, J. Q., 21
Wilson, M., 47
Wilson, M., and Daly, M., 47
Wisconsin, 9

Young Offenders Act (Canada), 24
Youth Crime Prevention Council (YCPC), 249, 250
Youth defined, 5

Zagar, R., and colleagues, 32

About the Author

KATHLEEN M. HEIDE, Ph.D., is Professor of Criminology at the University of South Florida, Tampa. She received her bachelor of arts degree in psychology from Vassar College and her master's and doctoral degrees in criminal justice from the State University of New York at Albany. She is a licensed mental health counselor and serves as the Director of Education at the Center for Mental Health Education, Assessment, and Therapy in Tampa. She is a court-appointed expert in matters relating to homicide, sexual battery, children, and families. Dr. Heide's publications include the widely acclaimed book, *Why Kids Kill Parents: Child Abuse and Adolescent Homicide* (Sage, 1995), as well as numerous articles and presentations in the areas of homicide, family violence, and youth violence. She has been the recipient of several research grants and six teaching awards and has been honored by many professional and community agencies. She has served as a member of several boards of directors of community agencies mandated to provide services to sexual abuse and assault victims, psychiatric patients, individuals in crisis, and women offenders. She is President of the Tampa Bay Association for Women Therapists and currently serves on the executive boards of the Hillsborough Constituency for Children and the Vassar Club of Tampa Bay. Dr. Heide has appeared as an expert on many nationally broadcasted talk shows, including *Geraldo, Larry King Live, Maury Povich,* and *Sally Jesse Raphaël.* Her research has been featured in popular magazines such as *Newsweek, Psychology Today,* and *U.S. News & World Report,* as well as in professional journals and scholarly presses.